W9-BKK-789

U·X·L

HISPANIC AMERICAN

BIOGRAPHY 2ND EDITION

# U·X·L
# HISPANIC AMERICAN
# BIOGRAPHY 2ND EDITION

**Sonia G. Benson, Rob Nagel, and Sharon Rose, Editors**

Haverstraw King's Daughters
Public Library
10 W. Ramapo Road
Garnerville, NY 10923

U·X·L®

THOMSON
GALE

Detroit • New York • San Diego • San Francisco • Cleveland • New Haven, Conn. • Waterville, Maine • London • Munich

## U•X•L Hispanic American Biography, 2nd Edition

Sonia G. Benson, Rob Nagel, and Sharon Rose, Editors

**Project Editor**
Carol DeKane Nagel

**Permissions**
Kim Davis

**Imaging and Multimedia**
Robyn Young

**Product Design**
Mary Claire Krzewinski, Michael Logusz

**Composition**
Evi Seoud

**Manufacturing**
Rita Wimberley

©2003 by U•X•L. U•X•L is an imprint of The Gale Group, Inc., a division of Thomson Learning, Inc.

U•X•L® is a registered trademark used herein under license. Thomson Learning™ is a trademark used herein under license.

*For more information, contact:*
The Gale Group, Inc.
27500 Drake Rd.
Farmington Hills, MI 48331-3535
Or you can visit our Internet site at http://www.gale.com

**ALL RIGHTS RESERVED**
No part of this work covered by the copyright hereon may be reproduced or used in any form or by any means—graphic, electronic, or mechanical, including photocopying, recording, taping, Web distribution, or information storage retrieval systems—without the written permission of the publisher.

For permission to use material from this product, submit your request via Web at http://www.gale-edit.com/permissions, or you may download our Permissions Request form and submit your request by fax or mail to:

Permissions Department
The Gale Group, Inc.
27500 Drake Rd.
Farmington Hills, MI 48331-3535
Permissions Hotline:
248-699-8006 or 800-877-4253, ext. 8006
Fax: 248-699-8074 or 800-762-4058

Cover photographs reproduced by permission of AP/Wide World Photos (Sandra Cisneros); The Granger Collection, New York (Emiliano Zapata; top right); and Arte Público Press (Luis Valdez).

While every effort has been made to ensure the reliability of the information presented in this publication, The Gale Group, Inc. does not guarantee the accuracy of the data contained herein. The Gale Group, Inc. accepts no payment for listing; and inclusion in the publication of any organization, agency, institution, publication, service, or individual does not imply endorsement of the editors or publisher. Errors brought to the attention of the publisher and verified to the satisfaction of the publisher will be corrected in future editions.

**LIBRARY OF CONGRESS CATALOGING-IN-PUBLICATION DATA**

UXL Hispanic American biography / Sonia G. Benson, Rob Nagel, and Sharon Rose, editors.— 2nd ed.

    p. cm. — (UXL Hispanic American reference library) Rev. ed. of: Hispanic American biography / Rob Nagel and Sharon Rose, editors. ©1995.

   Includes bibliographical references and index.

    ISBN 0-7876-6599-1 (hardcover : alk. paper)

    1. Hispanic Americans—Biography—Juvenile literature. I. Benson, Sonia. II. Nagel, Rob. III. Rose, Sharon (Sharon A.). IV. Hispanic American biography. V. Series.

E184.S75 U94 2002                               20'.009268–dc19
2002010347

Printed in the United States of America
10 9 8 7 6 5 4 3 2 1

# CONTENTS

# READER'S GUIDE

*U•X•L Hispanic American Biography,* 2nd Edition, profiles one hundred Hispanic Americans, both living and deceased, prominent in fields ranging from civil rights to athletics, politics to literature, entertainment to science, religion to the military. Spanish founders as well as figures central to contemporary Hispanic cultural movements in the United States and Latin America are featured, and a black-and-white portrait accompanies each entry. A list of sources for further reading is provided at the end of each entry, and cross-references to others profiled in the volume are noted in bold letters within the text. *U•X•L Hispanic American Biography* concludes with a subject index.

## Related reference sources:

*U•X•L Hispanic American Almanac,* 2nd Edition, features a comprehensive range of historical and current information on the life and culture of Hispanic America, the community of people in the United States whose ancestors—or they themselves—came from Spain or from the Spanish-speaking countries of South and Central America, Mexico, Puerto Rico, or Cuba. The *Almanac* is organized into fourteen subject chapters including immigration, family and religion, jobs and education, literature, and sports. The volume contains 120 black-and-white photographs and maps, a glossary, and a cumulative subject index.

*U•X•L Hispanic American Chronology,* 2nd Edition, explores significant social, political, economic, cultural, and educational milestones in Hispanic American history. Arranged by year and then by month and day, the chronology spans from 25,000 B.C. to 2002 and contains more than one hundred black-and-white illustrations, extensive cross references, a glossary, and a subject index.

*U•X•L Hispanic American Voices,* 2nd Edition, presents twenty-one full or excerpted articles, memoirs, essays, speeches, letters, and other notable works of Hispanic Americans. Each entry is accompanied by an introduction, boxes explaining events discussed in the text, and a glossary of terms used in the document. The volume also contains one hundred black-and-white illustrations and a subject index.

## Advisors

Special thanks are due for the invaluable comments and suggestions provided by U•X•L's Hispanic American Reference Library advisors:

Margarita Reichounia
Librarian, Bowen Branch
Detroit Public Library
Detroit, Michigan

Linda Garcia
Librarian, Southern Hills Middle School
Boulder, Colorado

## Comments and Suggestions

We welcome your comments on *U•X•L Hispanic American Biography* as well as your suggestions for people to be featured in future editions. Please write: Editors, *U•X•L Hispanic American Biography,* U•X•L, 27500 Drake Rd., Farmington Hills, MI 48331-3535; call toll-free: 1-800-877-4253; fax: 248-414-5043; or send e-mail via www.gale.com.

# Linda Alvarado

Business owner
Born in 1951, Albuquerque, New Mexico

*"Baseball has been a sport in which Hispanics have achieved tremendous success. And in that regard, many role models and outstanding individuals have emerged as players."*

Linda Alvarado. *Reproduced courtesy of Linda Alvarado.*

L inda Alvarado has never let tradition influence her career path. As the only girl in a family of six children, she grew up competing with boys. Years later, she is still doing so as a female executive of a business usually run by males. She is president of her own building company, Alvarado Construction, Inc., and a limited partner in the ownership group of the Colorado Rockies, a major league baseball team that played its first season in 1993. "As the first Hispanic woman to enter the dugout," Milton Jamail pointed out in *Hispanic,* "some Hispanics see her as someone who can make a difference for the fans and players of this all-American sport."

Born Linda B. Martinez in 1951, she grew up in Albuquerque, New Mexico. Her father worked for the Atomic Energy Commission, and her mother was a homemaker. "It was a very positive environment," she told Carol Hopkins in *Notable Hispanic American Women.* "Even though I was the only girl, the expectation for me was no different." She credits her parents with giving her confidence and self-esteem and encouraging her to excel in the classroom and in athletics. Active in both high school and college sports, she played basketball, volleyball, and softball, and also ran track.

## Launches Construction Career

After Alvarado graduated from California's Pomona College, she continued to work as a lab assistant in the college's botany department. Her stay there was brief, however, as she "overwatered and drowned all the plants," she told Hopkins. She then took a job with a California development company and learned all about the construction business, from preparing bids for a building project to writing a contract for the actual work. Much to her surprise, Alvarado found she liked the work. She returned to school and took classes in estimating, blueprint reading, and scheduling to expand her knowledge of the construction business.

In 1974 Alvarado and a partner started the Martinez Alvarado Construction Management Corporation in Denver, Colorado. She borrowed $2,500 from her parents to get going. Within two years, she bought out her partner and soon became a general contractor (the person or company in charge of hiring and organizing all the carpenters, electricians, plumbers, and other tradespeople on a building project). Since that time, her company—now known as Alvarado Construction, Inc.—has completed dozens of large-scale building projects, including office buildings, bus stations, airport hangers, and a convention center. These accomplishments fill Alvarado with a sense of pride. "There is enormous satisfaction," she told Hopkins, "knowing that one started from ground zero and has a terrific final project, something of great permanence and beauty."

In the early 2000s, Alvarado Construction, Inc., is a multimillion dollar enterprise that employs 450 workers and has offices in Denver and San Francisco. It specializes in commercial, industrial, environmental, and heavy engineering projects throughout the western United States. Some of the company's projects include the Colorado Convention Center, the Denver Bronco stadium, the Navy/Marine Training Facility in Aurora, and the High Energy Research Laboratory. Alvarado remains at the helm as chief executive officer and president.

## Invests in Major League Baseball

In the early 1990s, Alvarado was able to turn her life-long interest in sports into a business opportunity. She became a partner in the Colorado Rockies baseball team because she wanted to show that women can get involved in nontraditional fields. She also believed it was important to give something back to the city of Denver. "I really felt it was in the best interest of my company to support the community in a more substantial way," she explained to Jamail.

Perhaps the main reason Alvarado chose to invest in baseball is its record of providing Hispanics with a road to accomplishment. "Baseball has been a sport in which Hispanics have achieved tremendous success," she pointed out to Jamail. "And in that regard, many role models and outstanding individuals have emerged as players." As a Hispanic owner, Alvarado believes she has now brought that sense of accomplishment full circle.

## Serving on Corporate Boards

Alvarado is a member of the board of directors of several other large companies. Boards of directors are groups of businesspeople who help a company make decisions and choose leaders. Hispanics have for many years been neglected when corporations choose directors, and although the percentage of Hispanics on boards has risen in the 2000s, they are greatly underrepresented. Alvarado was, in 2001, the only Hispanic serving on the boards of four Fortune 1000 companies. In the 2000s Alvarado served as corporate director for Pepsi Bottling Company, Qwest, Pitney Bowes, and Lennox International. She served as the chairman of the board of the Denver Hispanic Chamber of Commerce and as commissioner of the White House Initiative for Hispanic Excellence in Education. Recognizing the inroads she has made as a Hispanic and as a woman, Alvarado is mindful of those who helped pave the way before her and those who will follow afterward. Whenever she has had to resign from a board, Alvarado recommends another Hispanic or woman to replace her. "I'm not there because I'm good," she told Hopkins. "I'm there because someone ahead of me was great."

In 1995 President Bill Clinton appointed Alvarado to the President's Advisory Commission on Educational Excellence for Hispanic Americans. *Hispanic Business* magazine named Alvarado one of the "100 Most Influential Hispanics in America." She was named the 1996 United States Hispanic Chamber of Commerce Business Woman of the Year (for the second time), the 1996 Revlon Business Woman of the Year, and a Sara Lee Front Runner for shaping our country in government, arts, humanities, and business, among her many awards.

An outstanding example of Latina entrepreneurship with a solid commitment to the Hispanic community, Alvarado is a highly sought-after speaker throughout the nation and serves as a role model to women, girls, Hispanic Americans, and anyone else pursuing the American Dream.

## For More Information

*Hispanic,* April 1993, pp. 18–22.
*Notable Hispanic American Women,* Gale, 1993, p. 11–12.
Prussell, Deborah, "Linda Alvarado: Women in Construction," IMDiversity.com, Women's Village. Available at http://www.imdiversity.com/villages/woman/Article_Detail.asp?Article_ID=4825 (accessed June 21, 2002).
Riley, Jennifer, "America's Big Companies Are Bringing More Latinos into Their Boardrooms," *Hispanic,* November 2000.

# Julia Alvarez

Writer, educator
Born March 27, 1950, New York, New York

*"I am a Dominican, hyphen, American. As a fiction writer, I find that the most exciting things happen in the realm of that hyphen—the place where two worlds collide or blend together."*

**A**s Julia Alvarez stepped up to give a talk about her first novel, based on her Dominican family's immigration to the United States, a Dominican girl in the audience turned to her friend and said, "What she got to say to us? She's a white girl." Nevertheless, by the time Alvarez finished her speech, the girls were laughing along with her. Alvarez, who related this story in *Essence,* may not appear to be a Dominican. She writes in English, not Spanish. She is an American citizen by birth. Yet, in her work, Alvarez has pulled together her Dominican roots and her experiences as a young woman growing up in the United States. Considered to be one of the most important contributors to Hispanic American literature and among the most talented writers in the United States today, Alvarez is increasingly known for her novels, which place immigration, alienation, heritage, and identity all in the context of family relations.

## Early Years in the Dominican Republic

Alvarez's parents met in the United States, where her father, a doctor, ran a hospital and her mother was a student. Alvarez was born in the United States and was encouraged to identify herself as an American, but the family soon moved back to the Dominican Republic. There she spent her early years on her mother's family compound, a walled-in area containing several houses and other buildings. Her father's once wealthy family had supported the wrong side during the revolution in the Dominican Republic while her mother's parents benefited from their support of the people in power. Alvarez and her sisters were brought up along with their cousins and supervised by her mother, maids, and many aunts. Although her own family was not as well off as their relatives, Alvarez did not feel inferior. None of her cousins were allowed to forget that she was born in America.

Alvarez's family was highly influenced by American attitudes and goods. The children ate American food, attended the American school, and for a special treat, ate ice cream from the American ice cream parlor. American cars were bought at the American dealership, shopping was done at the Americans' store, and American appliances were flaunted in the compound. The entire extended family was obsessed with America; to the children, it was a fantasy land. In an article in *American Scholar,* Alvarez remarked: "Although I was raised in the Dominican Republic by Dominican parents in an extended Dominican family, mine was an American childhood."

The members of Alvarez's mother's family were respected because of their ties with America. Alvarez's uncles had attended Ivy League colleges, and her grandfather was a cultural attaché to the United Nations. The Dominican Republic was at the time ruled by a dictator, Rafael Leonidas Trujillo Molina, and for a time the Alvarezes felt safe because it seemed he could not victimize a family with such strong American ties. But when Alvarez's father secretly joined the forces attempting to oust Trujillo, the police set up surveillance (close watch) of the compound. It was rumored that, respected family or not, her father was soon to be arrested. Just before the police were to capture him in 1960, a U.S. agent, known to Alvarez as Tio Vic, tipped him off; he ushered the family into an airplane and out of the country.

The flight to the United States was a big moment for Julia Alvarez, as she explained in *American Scholar:* "All my childhood I had dressed like an American, eaten American foods, and befriended American children. I had gone to an American school and spent most of the day speaking and reading English. At night, my prayers were full of blond hair and blue eyes and snow.... All my childhood I had longed for this moment of arrival. And here I was, an American girl, coming home at last." Life in New York was not as sweet as the ten-year-old had imagined it would be, however. Instead of feeling like home, the Bronx alienated Alvarez.

## Moving to the United States

Alvarez found solace in books and writing in her new home, as she told *Contemporary Authors:* "I found myself turning more and more to writing as the one place where I felt I belonged and could make sense of myself, my life, all that was happening to me. I realized that I had lost the island we had come from, but with the words and encouragement of my teacher, I had discovered an even better world: the one words can create in a story or poem."

Alvarez left home at the age of thirteen to attend boarding school and never lived at home again. She attended Connecticut College in New England, where she won a poetry prize. In 1971, she received a bachelor's degree with highest honors from Middlebury College. She won a poetry prize from the Academy of American Poetry in 1974 and a creative writing fellowship from Syracuse University, where she graduated with an M.F.A. in 1975. Alvarez then worked as a poet-in-residence in Kentucky, Delaware, and North Carolina. Later, she taught English at Phillips Andover Academy in Andover, Massachusetts. "I was a migrant poet," she remarked in an interview with Jonathan Bing in *Publisher's Weekly.* "I would go anywhere."

Alvarez then worked at the University of Vermont, where she taught as a visiting assistant professor of creative writing in 1981, and then at the George Washington University, as the Jenny McKean Moore Visiting Writer, in 1984. It was during these years that Alvarez put together her first poetry collection, called *Homecomings,* which was published by Grove in 1984. According to Fred Muratori, writing in the

Julia Alvarez. *Reproduced by permission of Jerry Bauer.*

*New England Review and Bread Loaf Quarterly,* "33," a sequence of sonnets that "fills half the volume" is a "diary-like assemblage of meditations, stories, and confessions." While Alvarez's reputation as a writer grew, she continued her career in academia. Alvarez taught at the University of Illinois at Urbana as assistant professor of English from 1985 to 1988, and then moved to Middlebury College as an associate professor of English. By the end of the decade, she had received several awards for her poetry.

## From Poetry to Fiction

During her early years as a writer, Alvarez revealed to Bing, she had not enthusiastically considered the prospect of "writing something bigger than a poem." Yet "Homecoming," according to Alvarez, is "a narrative poem, longer than the others. It's almost as if it's the beginning of a story." As she told Catherine Wiley in an interview published in the *Bloomsbury Review,* she "started writing stories, thinking that [she] would just write a few." She was approached by an agent after accepting the 1986 G. E. Foundation Award for Younger Writers, and was placed with editor Shannon Ravenal of Algonquin books. Ravenal promoted Alvarez's work, encouraged her, and guided her in the organization of various stories. In 1991, Algonquin published the resulting work, Alvarez's first novel, *How the García Girls Lost Their Accents.*

*How the García Girls Lost Their Accents* is a series of fifteen interrelated stories about a Dominican family that has moved to the United States. Like Alvarez and her siblings, the four sisters in the family, Carla, Sandra, Yolanda, and Sofia, must work hard to make a place in their new home. The book begins with stories from "1989–1972," and includes tales of Yolanda's return to the Dominican Republic; Sofia's unwillingness to obey her father; and Mamita's troubles with her daughters. The second part of the novel, titled "1960–1970," returns to a time when the girls were newcomers to the United States. Stories reveal Carla's exposure to a pervert; Yolanda seeing snow for the first time and worrying she is witnessing the fall-out from an atom bomb; and Sandi's shock when the American wife of another man kisses her father. The final section, "1960–1956," portrays the García family's life in the Dominican Republic in reverse order—from their dramatic getaway from the country to Yolanda's earlier theft of

a kitten from its mother. *How the García Girls Lost Their Accents* won praise from critics, many of whom echoed reviewer Ilan Stavans in *Commonweal* when he wrote that, while the book is "imperfect and at times unbalanced, this is a brilliant debut—an important addition to the canon of Hispanic letters in the U.S."

Alvarez's family also reacted to the novel. Alvarez explained in her interview with Wiley that "the person I thought would give me the hardest time—my father—not at all. He called up after he read it, weeping, saying that he was so proud of me. My sisters were a little taken aback.... Each one reacted differently, and they all have come around. One of them said that it was really hard for her, but she really felt that it was for her to deal with. But they're also very proud of me and feeling kind of mixed." Alvarez's mother was less enthusiastic about the publication of a work so similar to the Alvarez family's story.

## More Novels

Alvarez published her second novel, *In the Time of the Butterflies,* in 1994. As the author explained in her conversations with Bing, the book contains a story that she had wanted to tell for some time, "but I didn't know how to do it." The resulting work is historical fiction, a recreation of the lives of three Dominican sisters—Patria, Minerva, and Maria Teresa Mirabal—who were murdered for their attempts to overthrow Trujillo the same year Alvarez's family fled to the United States. Known as "Las Mariposas," or "The Butterflies," the women's political struggle is celebrated in parts of Latin America. The book is also about the fourth sister,

Dedé, who survived because she stayed home the night her sisters were killed, and to whom Alvarez dedicated her work.

The novel concludes with what Susan Miller of *Newsweek* described as a "gut-wrenching climax." "The novel's 300-plus pages are full of pathos and passion, with beautifully crafted anecdotes interstitched to create a patchwork quilt of memory and ideology," asserted Stavans in the *Nation*. Other critics, though for the most part positive about the book, were not as convinced by the characters and the story and their link to history.

*¡Yo!,* the 1997 sequel to *How the García Girls Lost Their Accents,* finds the four adult García sisters arguing about Yo's portrayal of them in her books. The novel begins with what a *Publishers Weekly* critic called an "exuberant and funny" first chapter. The book, divided in three parts, focuses on the life of Yo through the perspectives of various narrators, people who have known Yo at different times in her life, from her childhood and college years to her early thirties. The daughter of the family maid, a farmer, an abused wife, Yo's college professor, and a boyfriend all make appearances. Reviews of *¡Yo!* were mixed.

Alvarez's fourth novel, *In the Name of Salomé,* came out in 2000. It is a historical novel, based in the Dominican Republic, Cuba, and the United States, that spans from the late nineteenth century to the 1960s. The two protagonists are a mother and daughter, both poets, and the novel shifts back and forth between their perspectives. The mother, Salomé Ureña Henríquez, is a powerful Dominican poet and political activist, married to the president of the country. She is able to incite a revolution in her country with the sheer force of her poetry. Salomé dies when her daughter, Camilla, is only three. Camilla then spends her childhood in exile, away from her country, first in Cuba and then in the United States, under the tremendous shadow of her mother. Camilla becomes a quiet poet and a professor. Through the views of these two women, Alvarez examines the human experience in relation to the history of the three countries. The novel is based on historic figures, but in her acknowledgment, Alvarez states that it is not biography or history "but a work of the imagination" attempting to capture and express "history and poetry and presences of the past." The novel received widespread acclaim, with many critics calling it Alvarez's best work to date.

## Poetry, Essays, and Children's Books

With the publication of *The Other Side/El Otro Lado* in 1995, Alvarez brought her talents as a poet to the attention of those who knew only her fiction. Some critics, including Rochelle Ratner of *Library Journal,* were charmed by Alvarez's poems. "Alvarez … writes poems as impressive as her fiction." The poems, declared a *Publishers Weekly* critic, are "direct, reflective, and often sensuous." In 1996, Alvarez's first poetry collection was republished in *Homecoming: New and Collected Poems*. This volume contains forty-six sonnets and a number of separate poems. Christine Stenstrom of *Library Journal* found the collection "vivid and engaging," and most appreciated the poems in the "Housekeeping" series.

Alvarez published her first book of non-fiction in 1998, the essay collection *Some-*

*thing to Declare.* The twenty-four essays are divided into two parts, both autobiographical. Essays in the first section are devoted to Alvarez's childhood, family, immigration, and the cultural divide she experienced. The second section focuses on her writing. Critics loved the voice and humor of the author, especially her gossipy revelations about herself. Laura Jamison observed in *People Weekly:* "Reading Julia Alvarez's new collection is like curling up with a glass of wine in one hand and the phone in the other, listening to a big-hearted, wisecracking friend share her hard-earned wisdom about family, identity, and the art of writing."

Alvarez began to publish children's books in 2000, with *The Secret Footprints,* based on a Dominican legend about a tribe of underwater beings with their feet turned backwards so that when someone finds their footprints they will assume they were walking in the opposite direction. She followed this in 2001 with *How Tia Lola Came to Stay,* the story of a colorful and vivacious aunt from the Dominican Republic arriving to help out her newly divorced sister with her niece and nephew in Vermont. Reviews for both books were mixed. In 2002, Alvarez's novel for young readers, *Before We Were Free,* was released. It is the highly autobiographical story of a twelve-year-old girl in 1960 who is forced to flee from her home in the Domincan Republic because of the political situation there under Trujillo's dictatorship. Alvarez also created a film for PBS's *American Voices* series called *The Suitor,* which features Yolanda García from her earlier novels. Actress Salma Hayek produced and starred in a film version of *In the Time of the But-*terflies, which aired on the Showtime television network in the fall of 2002. Starring with Hayek were **Edward James Olmos** and **Marc Anthony** (see entries).

Alvarez continued her writing and her teaching at Middlebury College into the 2000s. In promotional material for the New England Library Association she describes herself as a writer in terms of a hybrid, someone who, within themselves, weaves together two different worlds and is a true mixture of both: "More and more, the kind of writer I am reflects the kind of population we have on this planet—people who are mixtures, hybrids who have families who have come from somewhere else and have families that are mixtures or weaves of very different traditions. That's who I am."

## For More Information

Alvarez, Julia, *American Scholar,* Winter 1987, pp. 71–85.

Alvarez, Julia, "Black Behind the Ears," *Essence,* February 1993, pp. 42, 129, 132.

"Alvarez, Julia," *Contemporary Authors,* Volume 147, Gale, 1995, pp. 15–17.

Alvarez, Julia, Interview with Catherine Wiley, *Bloomsbury Review,* March, 1992, pp. 9–10.

Bing, Jonathan, "Julia Alvarez: Books That Cross Borders," *Publishers Weekly,* December 16, 1996, pp. 38–39.

Jamison, Laura, "Something to Declare," review, *People Weekly,* September 21, 1998.

"Julia Alvarez," New England Library Association (NELA). Available at http://www.nelib.org/conf_archOpen.asp?ID=175&subCat=2 (accessed June 21, 2002).

*Library Journal,* August, 1994, p. 123.

McHugh, Clare, review of *¡Yo!, People,* January 20, 1997, p. 33.

Miller, Susan, "Family Spats, Urgent Prayers," *Newsweek,* October 17, 1994, p. 77.

Muratori, Fred, review of *Homecoming, New England Review and Breadloaf Quarterly,* Winter 1986, pp. 231–32.

*Publishers Weekly,* October 14, 1996, p. 62; August 14, 2000, p. 354; February 26, 2001, p. 87.

Ratner, Rochelle, review of *The Other Side/El Otro Lado, Library Journal,* April 15, 1995, p. 80.

Rifkind, Donna, "Speaking American," *New York Times Book Review,* October 6, 1991, p. 14.

Siciliano, Jano, "Julia Alvarez," Bookreporter interview, September 22, 2000. Available at http://www.bookreporter.com/brc/author.asp?author=751 (accessed June 21, 2002).

Stavans, Ilan, "Daughters of Invention," *Commonweal,* April 10, 1992, pp. 23–25.

Stavans, Ilan, review of *In the Time of the Butterflies, Nation,* November 7, 1994, p. 552.

Stenstrom, Christine, review of *Homecoming: New and Collected Poems, Library Journal,* April 1, 1996, p. 84.

Rudolfo Anaya. *Reproduced by permission of Cynthia Farah.*

# Rudolfo Anaya

Writer, educator
Born October 30, 1937, Pastura, New Mexico

*"Each community has art to offer, and now we've come to a place in American history where we celebrate that."*

Rudolfo Alfonso Anaya is hailed as one of the founding fathers of Chicano (Mexican American) literature. He is a prolific writer, publishing novels, short stories, plays, poetry, and screenplays. Anaya draws on the memories of his childhood in New Mexico, as well as on Mexican folklore, to portray the experiences of Hispanics in the American Southwest. Many critics believe his first novel, *Bless Me, Ultima,* most successfully presents those experiences. A prize-winning bestseller when it was published in 1972, the novel is now required reading for many high school and college students.

Anaya was born in 1937 in the small rural village of Pastura, New Mexico. His mother, Rafaelita Mares, came from a family of farmers. His father, Martin Anaya, was a *vaquero,* an expert horseman who enjoyed working with cattle. Carrying on their strong Mexican heritage, the family spoke only Spanish at home. "As far as I knew," Anaya wrote in *Contemporary Authors Autobiography Series,* "all of the world spoke Spanish."

When Anaya was still a young boy, his family moved to the nearby town of Santa

Rosa. Going to public school, where only English was spoken, was at first a frightening experience for him, but he quickly became a good student. Throughout grade school, he enjoyed the company of a group of close friends. By the eighth grade, however, he began to notice changes in the group. "Prejudices I had not known before appeared," he wrote in his autobiography. "We who had always been brothers now separated into Anglos [whites] and Mexicans. I did not understand the process."

## Diving Accident Causes Temporary Paralysis

When Anaya was fifteen, his family moved to a barrio (a Spanish-speaking neighborhood) in Albuquerque, New Mexico. Shortly thereafter, he experienced an event that changed his life: in a frightening diving accident, he fractured two neck vertebrae and was paralyzed. He described the experience in his autobiography: "I floated to the top of the water, opened my eyes, saw the light of the sun shining in the water. I tried to move, I couldn't. Face down, my shouts for help were only bubbles of water." Anaya was pulled from the water by a friend and spent months in therapy to regain the use of his legs. He recovered from the accident with a greater appreciation for life, determined to do more than his healthy friends had ever done.

In 1956 Anaya graduated from Albuquerque High School. He attended Browning Business School for two years, but dropped out because he did not find the study of business fulfilling. He then enrolled in the University of New Mexico to study

English. While there, he began to question why he never had any Mexican teachers and why he never read any Mexican literature. He felt the education he received did not reflect the long history of Hispanics in the southwestern United States.

Another question that plagued Anaya at this time was one of faith. He had been raised a devout Catholic, but his readings at the university caused him to question his religious beliefs. In turn, this loss of faith led him to write poetry and prose. "I lost my faith in God," he wrote in his autobiography, "and if there was no God there was no meaning, no secure road to salvation.... That may be why I write. It is easier to ascribe those times and their bittersweet emotions to my characters."

## Love of Art Fostered in Childhood

Anaya believes he was further drawn to writing because his warm, tradition-filled childhood filled him with a love for art. He cited examples of art that surrounded him in the homes of his youth: detailed carvings in door frames, brightly painted walls, decorative altars, lively music, and melodic language. "There is something in the Mexican character which, even under the most oppressive circumstances, struggles to keep art and its humanizing effect alive.... The Mexican possesses a very artistic soul," he wrote in *Contemporary Authors Autobiography Series*.

After he graduated from college in 1963, Anaya became a public school teacher in Albuquerque. Three years later he married Patricia Lawless. In 1971, after having earned master's degrees in English and in guidance and counseling, Anaya became the director of counseling at the University of New Mexico in Albuquerque. A few years later he began teaching creative writing and Chicano literature in the university's English department. He maintained a position in this department for the next nineteen years, until his retirement in 1993.

During the 1960s, Anaya began work on his novel *Bless Me, Ultima*. Haunted by the Mexican American stories and tales of his childhood, he tried to capture the memory of those times and people. He worked on the story for seven years, then endured rejection by dozens of publishers. In 1972 Anaya finally found a Chicano publishing house in California that wanted to publish the book. *Bless Me, Ultima* was an instant success. The novel was honored with the prestigious Premio Quinto Sol Award, given annually to the best novel written by a Chicano author. Anaya became a celebrity.

## Novel Explores Young Boy's Struggles

*Bless Me, Ultima* follows the life of Antonio, a young boy growing up in a small village in New Mexico around the time of World War II. As he matures, Antonio struggles to understand the roles of good and evil in life. He also has to choose between the nomadic (wandering) lifestyle of his father's family and the farming lifestyle of his mother's family. Throughout the novel, a folk healer named Ultima tries to bring harmony and well-being to Antonio and his family.

Anaya continued to use Mexican American myth and folklore in his next two novels, *Heart of Aztlán* (1976) and *Tortuga* (1979). *Heart of Aztlán* describes a Mexican American family's move from a rural area to a barrio in Albuquerque—and the problems, both social and religious, they face adjusting to city life. (Aztlán is the mythological land of origin of the Aztec. Many Mexican Americans believe it occupied the geographic region now known as the American Southwest.) *Tortuga* tells the story of a sixteen-year-old boy who is paralyzed. Because he has to wear a shell-like body cast, his friends call him Tortuga (Spanish for "turtle"). While recovering in a hospital for a year, Tortuga becomes more spiritually and psychologically mature.

In 1994 Anaya finally received major recognition when he signed a contract with Warner Books to publish six books. As part of the deal, Warner agreed to publish both mass market paperback and color-illustrated hardcover editions of *Bless Me, Ultima*. Warner also decided to publish a Spanish edition of the novel, the first time this major company has ever released a Spanish-language book. Anaya was pleased to have the chance to present his culture to a mainstream audience. "Each community has art to offer," he explained in *Publishers Weekly,* "and now we've come to a place in American history where we can celebrate that."

## Mystery Novels and Beyond

During the 1990s, Anaya wrote three mystery novels set in New Mexico and centering around some of the same characters: *Alburquerque* (the original spelling of the New Mexico city; 1992); *Zia Summer*

(1995); and *Rio Grande Fall* (1996). The novels encompass the traditions of the Native American and Hispanic culture of the Southwest as well as pop culture and modern life. In the first, a young boxer does battle with powerful real estate development that threatens traditional New Mexican culture. In *Zia Summer,* private detective Sonny Baca is up against a terrorist cult and nuclear waste plans that threaten his home. The leader of the cult remains at large at the end of the novel, providing the material for Baca's return in *Rio Grande Fall,* in which he is hired by Albuquerque's balloon festival to find the bloodthirsty terrorist.

William Clark, in a *Publisher's Weekly* article on these later novels by Anaya, summarizes: "Underpinning Anaya's most recent novels—with their new emphasis on contemporary social issues and the more accessible style he says he's consciously adopted—are the themes he has consistently probed since his first book, the seminal [original] Chicano coming-of-age novel, *Bless Me, Ultima,* appeared in 1972: spirituality and healing; Chicano tradition and myth; the sacredness of the land; the role of shaman-like [priest or healer-like] figures as mentors and guides; and the quest for personal, communal and cultural identity."

Along with the mystery novels, Anaya has been writing children's books, including *Farolitos of Christmas* and *Farolitos for Abuelo* (both 1995), picture books centered on the festive candles hidden in paper bags that light up the holidays, and, in the latter book, honor the life of a grandfather who has just died. He published *My Land Sings:* *Stories from the Rio Grande* in 1999, a retelling of five folk tales from the Pueblo Indians, the Spanish, and the Mexicans from the sixteenth century to the present. Along with the traditional folk tales, Anaya has added five of his own folk-like tales to the book, treating themes of culture and spirituality. In 2000 he published the long poem/picture book *Elegy on the Death of César Chávez.*

Anaya retired from his professorship at the University of New Mexico in 1993. In 2001, he won the presidential National Medal of Arts Award. For many, Anaya will always be remembered for his groundbreaking novel *Bless Me Ultima.* The effect of the book has not diminished in the decades since it was written. In the city of Austin, Texas, a campaign by the mayor called "What If All Austin Reads the Same Book" was initiated in 2002 in an attempt to get people talking about issues together. The mayor chose, for the campaign's first book, *Bless Me Ultima.*

## For More Information

Clark, William, "Rudolfo Anaya: 'The Chicano Worldview,'" *Publishers Weekly,* June 5, 1995, p. 41.

*Contemporary Authors Autobiography Series,* Volume 4, Gale, 1986, pp. 15–28.

*English Journal,* September 1992, pp. 20+.

*Hispanic Writers,* 2nd Edition, Gale, 2000.

"National Library Week, April 14–20, 2002: Getting on the Same Page: 'What If All of Austin Reads the Same Book' Gets Austin Residents Reading and Talking Together," Austin City Connection, April 15, 2002. Available at http://www.ci.austin.tx.us/library/news/nr20020415.htm (accessed June 21, 2002).

*Publishers Weekly,* March 21, 1994, p. 24; July 29, 1996, p. 73; November 20, 2000, p. 68.

# Marc Anthony

Latin and pop singer
Born September 16, 1968, New York, New York

*"When I first started ... I would have rather jumped off a bridge than sing for an audience. [But] from the first salsa show I ever did, I knew I found something special."*

He may not have as much name recognition as fellow Latin stars Ricky Martin, Enrique Iglesias, and **Jennifer Lopez** (see entry), but even in such company, Marc Anthony is a standout. Latin singers are known for the passion in their music and lyrics, and in this regard neither Martin's "Livin' La Vida Loca" nor Iglesias's "Bailamos" can hold a candle to Anthony's "I Need to Know." As for sheer sex-symbol appeal, it may be hard to compete with Jennifer Lopez, but Anthony certainly gives his male counterparts a run for their money.

And whereas critics have sometimes—unfairly—questioned whether some others are "really" Latin singers, Anthony's cultural credentials are fully in order. Rather than singing pop, he established himself with salsa, a music that blends Latin styles with rock, jazz, and R&B. Raised poor in New York City, Anthony went on to become the world's biggest-selling salsa singer.

## Puerto Rico, New York

Marc Anthony Ruiz was the eighth child of Felipe, a hospital lunchroom worker, and Guillermina Muniz, both natives of Puerto

Marc Anthony. *Reproduced by permission of Jack Vartoogian.*

Rico. He grew up poor in Spanish Harlem, which is a part of New York, but it took him a little while to figure that out: "I thought I lived in Puerto Rico for the first seven years of my life," he told *People*. "My father had a rule: for two days a week, we had to speak Spanish in the house."

Music kept the family tied to its Latin roots, and at family sing-alongs as a small child, Anthony began to discover his powers as a singer. "I made my sister-in-law cry," he recalled. "I thought, 'Hmm, there's something going on here.'" His father, who had once hoped to make a living as a musician, encouraged the boy's interest and began teaching him how to compose songs. Anthony, however, was not immediately drawn to salsa or the music of his parents. "I was raised in New York during the Seventies and Eighties," he told the *Daily Telegraph.* "So I was exposed to everything. Jimi Hendrix. Motown. Disco. Salsa. You name it."

By the time he was in his teens, Anthony began getting work singing on TV commercials. At fifteen he held the job of water boy for Panamanian American singer **Rubén Blades** (see entry). He worked with a voice coach, and soon took a coveted slot as back-up singer for the boy band Menudo, one of whose members happened to be Ricky Martin. As for Anthony, he continued to remain in the background, going on to sing backup for a group called the Latin Rascals.

## Taking Center Stage

He would not remain in the background for long, however. In 1991 producer/musician Little Louis Vega, who had just signed a contract with Atlantic Records, invited Anthony to be his singer, and they went on to score a hit in urban nightclubs with "Rebel." Soon "Ride on the Rhythm" topped the *Billboard* dance charts, and in 1992 Anthony and Vega played as openers for one of Latin music's great heroes, **Tito Puente** (see entry).

In 1993 Anthony released his first solo album, *Otra Nota,* which he followed two years later with *Todo a Su Tiempo.* As his music career got underway, he was also working on getting an acting career going as well. His film debut was in the 1995 *Hackers.* His first important film performances came in 1996, with *Big Night* and *The Substitute,* and in 1999 he had a much bigger role alongside Academy Award-winner Nicholas Cage in *Bringing Out the Dead.*

## Breakthrough in the English-Speaking Market

When Anthony performed at New York's Madison Square Garden in October 1997 to promote the recently released *Contra la Corriente,* he became the first salsa performer to play a sold-out show at that prestigious (and large) concert venue. A year later, the album won him a Grammy, but much greater success would follow in 1999.

As *Contra la Corriente* was hitting the market, musician Paul Simon cast Anthony in the lead role in his Broadway musical *Capeman,* which opened in early 1998. Anthony played a Puerto Rican youth who killed two other teens in New York in 1959. Rubén Blades was in the play as well. The play did not do well and closed after two months, but Anthony was praised for his musical contribution. In fact, Paul Simon compared him to a young Frank Sinatra.

Up to that point, Anthony had been singing in Spanish, but with the success of *Contra la Corriente* he and his management decided it was time to break into the mainstream English market. Therefore *Marc Anthony,* his fourth album, consisted almost entirely of songs in English. Its first single, "I Need to Know" hit the Top 10 in October 1999, and in February 2000, Anthony performed alongside Ricky Martin and Cuban singer Ibrahim Ferrer at the Grammy Awards. *Marc Anthony* would go on to become triple platinum.

"You Sang to Me" gave Anthony his second Top-10 hit in April 2000, and in September he reached the Top 40 with "My Baby You." The latter was dedicated to Arianna, his five-year-old daughter by a former girlfriend, New York City policewoman Debbie Rosado. Of the song Anthony said, "It's a daddy professing his love."

## Showered With Underwear

As of May 2000, Arianna had a new step-mother: former Miss Universe Dayanara Torres. Anthony and Torres had a son, Cristian Anthony Muniz, on February 5, 2001.

The fact that he is married to a beauty queen says a great deal about Anthony's appeal to the opposite sex.

At the end of 1999, Anthony signed a set of contracts, collectively worth $50 million, with Columbia Records and Latin sister label Sony Discos. The latter in 1999 released *Desde un Principio/From the Beginning,* a CD of selections from Anthony's first three albums, exposing new legions of fans to his Spanish music. And Anthony remained close to his cultural roots: after purchasing Ochoa Studio in Puerto Rico, he began work in fall 2000 for a new album, a Spanish-language CD, released by Sony Discos. *Libre* was released by Columbia/Sony Discos in 2001 to the great relief of Anthony's many fans who love his salsa. Those who feared he had sold out to pop music raved about the new album. But lest the millions of fans who loved *Marc Anthony* be concerned, in May 2002 Anthony came out with another English-language album, *Mended.* In 2002 he was also working on a film produced by Salma Hayek, based on **Julia Alvarez**'s novel *In the Time of the Butterflies* (see entry). The film was shot in Vera Cruz, Mexico, with an all-Latin cast.

Among Anthony's many awards are the *Billboard* Award, for new artist of the year, 1994; the Grammy Award, for best tropical Latin performance, for *Contra la Corriente,* 1998; the Grammy Award nomination, for best male pop vocal performance, for "I Need to Know," 2000; the Latin Grammy Award, song of the year, for "Dimelo (I Need to Know)," 2000; Latin Grammy Award nominations, for record of the year and best male pop vocal performance, both for "Dimelo (I Need to Know)," 2000; Latin Grammy Award nomination, for best tropical song, "Da La Vuelta," 2000; (with Jennifer Lopez) Latin Grammy Award nominations for best pop performance by a duo or group with vocal and best music video, both for "No Me Ames," 2000; American Music Award nominations, favorite pop/rock male artist, favorite adult contemporary artist, and favorite Latin artist, 2000; multi-platinum certification (2 million sales), *Marc Anthony,* 2000; and the Grammy Award nomination, for best male pop vocal performance, for "You Sang to Me," 2001.

## For More Information

"Best of Both Worlds: Don't Say Crossover to Marc Anthony," *Time,* September 15, 2001, p. 9+.

Cobo, Leila, "Anthony Rides Success of Dual Marketing Plan," *Billboard,* August 5, 2000, p. 100.

Collis, Clark, "Marc Anthony," *Daily Telegraph,* January 6, 2000, p. 25.

Dougherty, Steve and Natasha Stoynoff, "Fine Tuning," *People,* December 13, 1999, p. 185.

Johns, Michael-Anne, *Marc Anthony,* Andrews McMeel, 2000.

Marc Anthony Online (official Web site). Available at http://www.marcanthonyonline.com (accessed June 21, 2002).

Márquez, Herón, *Latin Sensations,* Lerner, 2001.

Udovitch, Mim, "Q&A: Marc Anthony," *Rolling Stone,* April 27, 2000, p. 33.

*Nobody Like Marc Anthony/nadie como marc.* Available at http://www.angelfire.com/nj2/marcanthony/ (accessed June 21, 2002).

# Desi Arnaz

Bandleader, actor, producer
Born March 2, 1917, Santiago, Cuba
Died December 2, 1986, Del Mar, California

*"[Arnaz was] a man who lived the immigrant dream. It's such a great dream, and an absolutely true story."—Laurence Luckinbill, Back Stage*

**D**esi Arnaz achieved fame and fortune playing the hassled husband to his real-life wife on the long-running television series *I Love Lucy.* His character, Ricky Ricardo, was loosely based on his real role as a Cuban bandleader married to a zany American beauty. Behind the scenes, he was a talented producer, director, musician, and businessman.

He was born Desiderio Alberto Arnaz y De Acha III on March 2, 1917, in Santiago, Cuba. His father was mayor of the city and was quite wealthy. The elder Arnaz had plans for his son to study law at the University of Notre Dame in South Bend, Indiana, then return to Cuba to practice. Those plans drastically changed on August 12, 1933. Fulgencio Batista y Zaldívar, a sergeant in the Cuban army, led a revolt that overthrew the president of Cuba, Gerardo Machado. During the takeover, Arnaz's father was jailed, and all of his money and property was seized.

Arnaz, sixteen years old at the time, fled with his mother to Miami, Florida. His father joined them after he was released six months later. Arnaz spoke hardly any English and had to struggle through classes at St. Patrick's High School in Miami. At night, he helped support his family through a variety of jobs: cleaning birdcages, working in a railyard, bookkeeping, and driving taxis.

Since his dream of attending law school was lost, Arnaz tried for a career in music. In 1937 he auditioned and was hired as a singer at the Roney Plaza Hotel in Miami Beach. While touring through Miami with his orchestra, famed bandleader Xavier Cugat saw Arnaz perform. Impressed, Cugat asked the young singer to join his group.

## Feels Greatest Pleasure Playing Music

After a year with Cugat, Arnaz left to form his own Latin dance band. The group quickly became successful and played at some of the best night clubs in the United States, including New York City's famed Copacabana. Laurence Luckinbill, Arnaz's future son-in-law, told Amy Hersh of *Back Stage* years later that Arnaz "was a man who was not alive unless he was playing music. It was a way out for him, the way he conquered fear and gave the most pleasure to those who knew him."

Director George Abbot saw Arnaz perform at the Copacabana one evening in 1939 and offered the singer the leading role in his Broadway musical *Too Many Girls.* The following year, a studio in Hollywood made a film version of the play with Arnaz recreating his role. The female lead was played by an actress named Lucille Ball.

Despite having careers that often put them at opposite ends of the United States, Arnaz and Ball fell in love. On November 30, 1940, after Arnaz's band finished its last set in a New York nightclub, Arnaz and Ball drove to Greenwich, Connecticut, and were married by a justice of the peace. Over the next ten years, the couple was hardly together. Arnaz made a few movies, including *Father Takes a Wife* and *Holiday in Havana,* but mostly he toured the country with his orchestra. Meanwhile, Ball worked on her successful radio program, *My Favorite Husband.*

## The Beginning of Television History

In 1950 the couple had the idea of turning *My Favorite Husband* into a television show. Ball wanted Arnaz to play her husband in the series, but CBS network producers did not accept the idea. They thought Americans would not watch a show about an all-American woman married to a Cuban man who led an orchestra. To prove CBS wrong, Arnaz and Ball went on tour across the country as a husband-and-wife comedy team. Each successive performance drew a larger and larger audience. Finally convinced, CBS let Arnaz and Ball have their television show. *I Love Lucy* went on the air in the fall of 1951.

The show was an instant success. During its first six years, *I Love Lucy* always ranked in the top three television shows. In the series, Arnaz played the straight-man to his

Desi Arnaz. *Reproduced by permission of AP/Wide World Photos.*

wife's hilarious character, and often performed a Latin musical number as part of the show. In addition to acting in front of the camera, Arnaz worked behind it as head of Desilu Productions, the couple's production team. Among the other popular television shows he helped produce were *The Danny Thomas Show, Our Miss Brooks,* and *The Untouchables.* Arnaz is credited with the idea of using three cameras to record each episode, which allowed for fine editing afterward. This technique is still used to film situation comedies on television.

## Fortune Follows

Desilu Productions became an entertainment empire. It owned a record company, a music-publishing firm, motion picture and television studios, real estate in California, and the Desi Arnaz Western Hills Hotel in Palm Springs, California. In 1958 Arnaz and Ball sold 190 episodes of *I Love Lucy* to CBS for six million dollars. Because Arnaz insisted on filming the show rather than on performing it live, high-quality copies of each episode existed for endless reruns. The show is still televised daily around the world.

Arnaz and Ball had two children, Lucie and Desi, Jr., both of whom went on to work in the entertainment business. Unlike their television marriage, Arnaz and Ball's real-life one was not happy. In 1960 the couple divorced. Two years later Arnaz sold his share of Desilu to Ball for three million dollars and went into semiretirement on his horse farm in Del Mar, California. The following year he married Edith Mack Hirsch.

Over the next twenty years, Arnaz occasionally worked on television productions. He helped create several series pilots and the comedy series *The Mothers-in-Law,* which ran from 1967 to 1969. In 1982 he played a dramatic role in *The Escape Artist,* a film by Francis Ford Coppola. Poor health marked his later years, and he died from lung cancer at his home in 1986. Luckinbill told Hersh he would always remember Arnaz as "a man who lived the immigrant dream. It's such a great dream, and an absolutely true story."

## For More Information

Andrews, Bart, *The "I Love Lucy" Book,* Doubleday, 1985.
Arnaz, Desi, *A Book,* William Morrow, 1976.
*Back Stage,* February 8, 1991, pp. 33, 43.
*New York Times,* December 3, 1986, p. D26.
*People,* February 18, 1991, pp. 84–95.

# Judith Baca

Artist, educator
Born September 20, 1946, Los Angeles, California

*"If we cannot imagine peace as an active concept, how can we ever hope for it to happen?"*

J udith Francisca Baca started her career as an artist by creating colorful murals (large wall paintings) to decorate the city of Los Angeles, California. Her work reflects her deep interest in social problems (particularly those dealing with race) and has earned her international attention. Her best-known work is *The Great Wall of Los Angeles,* a 13-foot high, half-mile long outdoor mural thought to be the longest mural in the world. In addition to her work as a muralist and painter, Baca helped found the Social and Public Art Resource Center (SPARC) in Venice, California, an organization that fosters the development of Hispanic artists.

Baca was born September 20, 1946, in south-central Los Angeles. A second-generation Chicana (Mexican American woman), she was raised in a strong female household with her mother, grandmother, and two aunts, one of whom was mentally retarded. She did not know her musician father well, but enjoyed a happy childhood. "It was a very strong, wonderful, matriarchal (mother as leader) household," she related to Yleana Martinez in *Notable Hispanic American Women*. "I was everybody's child. I had a wonderful playmate in my grown-up aunt who wasn't grown up in her head. It was like she was five, my age, only she was big."

When Baca was six, she moved with her mother to Pacoima, California. Since she had spent most of her childhood in a Spanish-speaking household, she had a difficult time adjusting to school, where only English was spoken. She often felt alone in the classroom. During this time, however, her interest in art developed when one of her teachers allowed her to sit in a corner and paint while the rest of the class carried on.

After graduating from a Catholic high school in 1964, Baca enrolled in California State University in Northridge. She earned a bachelor's degree in art in 1969, then returned to her high school to teach. She tried out her first cooperative art project that year when she rounded up a group of ethnically diverse students to paint a mural at the school. It was "a method to force the group into cooperation," she told Martinez. It was a method she would use again many times in future projects.

## Fired for War Protests

At this same time Baca became active in the peace movement against the war in Vietnam. She and many nuns who taught at the high school participated in marches. Her school's administration, however, did not approve of these antiwar activities and fired all of those teachers involved. Left with no job, Baca feared her teaching career was over.

Baca soon found a position in a special program for artists with the City of Los Angeles Cultural Affairs Division. Her new job required her to travel to schools and parks to teach art. In those areas, she

Judith Baca. *Reproduced by permission of the Social and Public Art Resource Center (SPARC).*

noticed the art the teenagers had already created. "As she observed the graffiti, the tattoos, and the decorated cars," Anne Estrada noted in *Hispanic,* "she recognized a visual language used by these teenagers to express who they were and how they feel about their lives." Hoping to bring these teenagers together, she formed her own painting group, "Las Vistas Nuevas." The group—made up of twenty kids from different gangs and neighborhood groups—soon worked together to paint Baca's first mural, in Hollenbeck Park.

## Inspired by Mexican Muralists

Around this time, Baca began to study the Mexican tradition of mural painting and some of its great artists, including **Diego Rivera** (see entry) and José Clemente Orozco. She traveled to Mexico to take classes in mural materials and techniques and to look at the mural works of Mexico's masters. She told Martinez that, like those Mexican artists who came before her, "I believe taking art to the people is a political act. I am a Mexican mural painter in the true sense, but I took it to the next level. To keep an art form living it has to grow and change."

Baca returned to Los Angeles and expanded her program into the Citywide Mural Project. Under her supervision, almost 250 murals were painted. Baca was the first in the city to work with a multicultural group of youth to produce murals. Her most ambitious project during the 1970s was the *Great Wall,* painted on the walls of a San Fernando Valley drainage canal. The half-mile-long mural depicts the city's multiethnic history with a series of pictures showing important events from the Stone Age to the 1950s. Baca developed the concept, hired the workers, and helped raise the money for the project. Some of the teenagers who worked on the project did so to fulfill court sentences. The *Great Wall* took five summers, spread out over a period of nine years, to complete.

In 1976 Baca cofounded the Social and Public Art Resource Center (SPARC) in Venice, California, along with filmmaker Donna Deitch, and artist Christina Schlesinger. The nonprofit, multicultural art center brings together artists, community groups, and youth groups to create murals and preserve other public art. SPARC is an internationally recognized center that also keeps a library of sixteen thousand slides of public art from around the world.

## Begins Work on World Wall and Other Projects

In 1987 Baca began an even grander project, *World Wall: A Vision of the Future Without Fear.* The work addresses issues of war, peace, cooperation, interdependence, and spiritual growth. Its images depict the changes—both spiritual and material—that must occur on the planet before world harmony can be achieved. The portable mural is made up of 10-by-30-foot panels. Four panels were painted by teams under Baca's supervision in Los Angeles. The mural was first displayed in Finland, where selected Finnish artists added a work called "Alternative Dialogues." The mural then traveled to Russia during the fall of the Communist Party in the then-Soviet Union. There a Moscow artist added his artistic vision called "Waiting for the End of the 20th Century." In 1999, an Israeli artist collaborated with a Palestinian artist to produce a new panel: "Inheritance Compromise." In 2001 two Mexican women artists added "Tlazolteotl: The Creative Force of the UnWoven." The painting represents the changes in Mexican women's life due to relocation from rural areas into the cities and the influence of the Mexican-United States border. As the mural continues to travel throughout the world, more and more panels will be added: coming up are additions from the First Nation people (Native Canadians, or Indians) of Canada, the Australian Bushwomen, and prisoners of Brazil.

In 2000 Baca created a mural in the Denver International Airport called "La Memoria de Nuestra Tierra," (Our Land's Memory). The 10-by-50 foot layered mural depicts immigrants walking the long journey from Mexico to the United States

Southwest during the huge migration that took place in the early twentieth century, when a bloody revolution was terrorizing the Mexican people. The *Denver Rocky Mountain News* quoted Baca describing her intentions with this work: "[I] wanted to create an artwork that would give dignity to the Mestizo's [someone whose origins are a mixture of Native American and Spanish or Mexican] story and the stories of the countless others who toiled in the mines, fields and railroads of Colorado. Not only to tell the forgotten stories of people who, like birds or water, traveled back and forth across the land freely, before there was a line that distinguished which side you were from, but to speak to our shared human condition as temporary residents of the earth."

Among many other projects, Baca initiated work on a 524-foot mural in Durango, Colorado, with local sculptor Shan Wells and sixteen area high school students in 2001. It is called "The Land Has Memory." She also continues to be active in SPARC, which established the "Neighborhood Pride: Great Walls Unlimited Program" in the late 1980s that has been responsible for more than a hundred new murals in the city of Los Angeles. SPARC is also experimenting with digital mural-making techniques in the SPARC/César Chávez Digital Mural Lab, which was created as a collaboration between SPARC and the University of California in 1996.

Among muralists in the 2000s, Judith Baca remains a star and a leader. Howard Fox, the curator of modern and contemporary art at the Los Angeles County Museum of Art is quoted in a May 29, 2002, *New York Times* article: "To the extent that people outside of Southern California know about the mural tradition here, they have to know about Judith Baca's *Great Wall of Los Angeles*. It is the largest, most ambitious and articulated of all the projects. It was conceived and produced in the spirit of public service and community celebration. It has an exalted status, and it has earned it."

Baca, who is a professor of art at the University of California, Los Angeles, César Chávez Center of Interdisciplinary Studies of Chicano/a Studies and World Arts and Cultures Department, believes her art reflects her commitment to help solve social problems. Whether on a local or a global level, she tries to inspire people to act on the positive possibilities in life. In her artist's statement for *World Wall,* she wrote that people have an easier time imagining a world caught in nuclear war than one that exists in perfect peace. She believes we must be able to imagine and picture peace in order to achieve it. "If we cannot imagine peace as an active concept," she wrote, "how can we ever hope for it to happen?"

## For More Information

Baca, Judith, "The Art of the Mural," PBS American Family Web site. Available at http://www.pbs.org/americanfamily/mural.html (accessed June 21, 2002).

*Hispanic,* May 1991, pp. 16–18.

Lippard, Lucy, *Mixed Blessings: Art for a Multicultural America,* Penguin Books, 1988.

*Notable Hispanic American Women,* Gale, 1993, pp. 35–38.

Tannenbaum, Barbara, "Where Miles of Murals Preach a People's Gospel, *New York Times,* May 26, 2002.

Veolz Chandler, Mary, "Mud and Blood: DIA Mural Captures Flight of Emigrants from Mexican Revolution," *Denver Rocky Mountain News,* February 2, 2000. Available online at http://www.sscnet.ucla.edu/chavez/Baca-denver.html (accessed June 21, 2002).

# Joan Baez

Singer, songwriter, activist
Born January 9, 1941, Staten Island, New York

*"I have been true to the principles of nonviolence, developing a stronger and stronger aversion to the ideologies of both the far right and the far left and ... [to] the suffering they continue to produce all over the world."*

O ften called the "Queen of the Folksingers," Joan Baez has earned fame as much for her political activism as for her singing. During the 1960s, she often made headlines by using her musical talent to campaign against America's involvement in the Vietnam War and against social injustice. Through her music, writings, and travels, she has continued her fight against social ills—not only in America but around the world—to the present day.

Joan Chandos Baez was born in 1941 on Staten Island, New York. From her Scottish mother, Joan Bridge, and her Mexican father, Albert Baez, she inherited a rich multiethnic tradition. She also inherited their nonviolent Quaker religious beliefs, which would eventually inspire her own interests in peace and justice. Baez's father was a physicist who once turned down a high-paying job developing war weapons because of his moral concerns. In her 1987 autobiography, *And a Voice to Sing With,* Baez wrote that her father's decision left an imprint on his children. She and her sisters "would never have all the fine things little girls want when

they are growing up. Instead we would have a father with a clear conscience. Decency would be his legacy to us."

## Exposed to Racism Early in Life

While growing up, Baez was often taunted by other children because of her Hispanic roots and dark skin. In junior high school she felt isolated from her classmates. "So there I was," she wrote in her autobiography, "with a Mexican name, skin, and hair: the Anglos couldn't accept me because of all three, and the Mexicans couldn't accept me because I didn't speak Spanish." Her pacifist (antiwar) views further distanced her from her classmates.

In large part, loneliness led Baez to begin singing. Believing music to be a path to popularity, she spent a summer developing her voice and learning to play the ukulele. She soon gained a reputation as an entertainer and made her first stage appearance in a school talent show. She also became known to her peers as a talented artist who could draw Disney characters and paint school election posters with ease.

In 1958 Baez graduated from high school, then moved with her family to Boston, Massachusetts, after her father had accepted a teaching position at the Massachusetts Institute of Technology. Although she enrolled in Boston University, Baez's interest in her music kept her away from her classes. Due to such singers and groups as Pete Seeger and the Kingston Trio, folk music was undergoing a revival during the late 1950s. Coffee houses that featured local singers became gathering spots for college students throughout the country. When Baez began singing in Boston-area coffee houses, she quickly attracted a large following of fans.

## Makes Professional Debut Before Thousands

While singing at a Chicago nightclub in 1959, Baez caught the attention of Bob Gibson, a popular folk singer. Impressed, he asked her to appear with him at the first Newport (California) Folk/Jazz Festival being held in August of the year. Baez's three-octave soprano voice and down-to-earth stage presence captivated the festival crowd of thirteen thousand. She became a celebrity overnight. Many large record companies offered her recording contracts, but she chose to sign her first contract with Vanguard, a small label known for its quality classical music recordings. Her first solo album, simply titled *Joan Baez,* was released in 1960. Composed of traditional folk songs, the album also featured a Scottish ballad and a song sung in Spanish—a nod to her parents.

Around the time the album was released, Baez moved to California's Pacific coast. During the next three years, she toured the country performing concerts. As she grew increasingly popular, Baez began to think more about the world and her place in it. "I was in a position now to do something more with my life than just sing," she wrote in *And a Voice to Sing With.* "I had the capacity to make lots and lots of money. I could reach lots and lots of people."

Baez used her celebrity status to publicize her views on equal rights and pacificism. When she discovered that African Americans were not admitted to her concerts at white

Joan Baez. *Reproduced by permission of AP/Wide World Photos.*

colleges in the South, she organized her own tour of performances at black colleges. To protest the Vietnam War, Baez refused to pay the portion of her federal income taxes she believed went to support the war effort. A rising national leader in the growing protest movements of the 1960s, Baez soon considered her work for social change more important than her performing career.

## Jailed for Political Demonstrations

While Baez's pacifist activities drew praise from some, they also drew anger from others. U.S. Army bases all over the world banned her albums. In 1967 she was jailed for her part in antiwar demonstrations. The following year she married David Harris, another leader in the war resistance movement. Despite the criticism she received for her political activities, she maintained her enormous popularity as a singer because of the power of her voice and the sincerity of the message in her songs.

In one of the highlights of her career, Baez performed at the famous Woodstock Music Festival, held near Bethel, New York, during the summer of 1969. The five-day event brought together some of the most important popular musicians of the decade. The concert, with its theme of "five days of peace, love, and music," drew more than 500,000 people from all over America.

Through the 1970s, despite having a son (she divorced her husband in 1971), Baez continued her musical career and her social and political activities. "The Night They Drove Old Dixie Down," a cut off her album *Blessed Are ...,* became one of the most popular songs of 1972 and Baez's biggest commercial hit. That same year she organized a gathering of women and children who joined hands around the Congress building in Washington, D.C., to protest the continued U.S. involvement in Vietnam. Baez also joined and began working for Amnesty International, a worldwide organization that helps to free people who have been imprisoned for their religious or political beliefs. In 1979 Baez founded Humanitas International, an organization that promotes human rights and nonviolence through eduction.

## Social Cause Revives Career

Baez's popularity began to decline in the early 1980s. However, her career received a boost in 1985 when she opened the U.S. portion of Live Aid, the multi-act rock concert that raised money for famine victims in Ethiopia. In 1987 Baez released *Recently,* her first album in eight years, and published *And a Voice to Sing With.* In her autobiography she wrote about her disappointment in a new generation of young people who seemed more interested in obtaining materials things than in helping others.

Hoping to set an example for younger generations, Baez has continued her activism, something of which she is proud. "I have been true to the principles of nonviolence," she wrote in her autobiography, "developing a stronger and stronger aversion to the ideologies of both the far right and the far left and ... [to] the suffering they continue to produce all over the world." In 1988 she toured the Middle East, hoping to find solutions to the conflicts between the area's warring countries. In 1991 she announced plans to develop low-income housing in California. Two years later she toured the city of Sarajevo in war-torn Bosnia and Hercegovina.

Baez's voice is what first brought her fame, and it has lasted throughout the years. In an early review in the *New York Times,* Bob Shelton wrote that her voice was "as lustrous and rich as old gold." In an article for the *New York Times* twenty-eight years later, Stephen Holden wrote that Baez's voice, "though quite different in texture from the ethereal folk soprano of her first albums, remains a powerful instrument." Baez's 1993 release, *Play Me Backwards,* was nominated for a Grammy Award for best contemporary folk album. Many critics considered it the best album of her long career. In 1995 she came out with a live album called *Ring Them Bells,* and was joined by Mary Chapin Carpenter, the Indigo Girls, and other singers of later generations who have been inspired by her remarkable music career. In 1997 she released *Gone From Danger,* her first studio album recording since 1992, on which she sang music composed by such notables as Dar Williams, Richard Shindell, and Sinead Lohan. Baez continued to do concert tours throughout the world in to the twenty-first century and produced more live albums. Two reissued and expanded volumes, released in 2001, of her groundbreaking early folk music were well received by critics and devoted audiences from all generations.

## For More Information

Baez, Joan, *And a Voice to Sing With,* Summit Books, 1987.

Baez, Joan, *Daybreak,* Dial Press, 1968.

Garza, Hedda, *Joan Baez,* Chelsea House, 1991.

"Joan Baez," All Music Guide. Available at http://www.allmusic.com/cg/amg.dll?p=amg&sql=Bx9 5f8qbtbt04~C (accessed June 21, 2002).

Joan Baez Web Pages. Available at http://baez.woz. org/ (accessed June 21, 2002).

*New York Times,* November 13, 1961; December 12, 1989, p. C24.

# Lourdes G. Baird

Federal judge, attorney
Born May 12, 1935, Quito, Ecuador

*As a U.S. attorney in California, Baird presided over the largest federal judicial district in the nation.*

Lourdes G. Baird. *Reproduced by permission of AP/Wide World Photos.*

**A**fter having married and raised three children, Lourdes G. Baird decided to change her life. She went go back to school to prepare for a new career as a lawyer. She soon rose through the legal ranks to became one of the handful of women in the United States who serve as federal prosecutors (lawyers representing the U.S. government in cases involving federal crimes). As a U.S. attorney in California, Baird presided over the largest federal judicial district in the nation. Even though she began her work as a lawyer and a judge late in life, she made her mark quickly and has been widely praised for her abilities.

Baird was born in Ecuador in 1935, the seventh child of James Gillespie and Josefina Delgado. Her family moved from South America to Los Angeles when she was just one year old. Because her mother was a devout Catholic, Baird was educated in Catholic, all-girl schools. She has said that her all-girls high school was a great experience. The nuns in charge were positive role models who passed on their independent spirit to the students in the classroom and on the athletic field. To this day, Baird remains physically active in such activities as hiking, jogging, and cross-country skiing.

After graduating high school, Baird briefly attended secretarial school. In 1956 she married businessman William Baird. Together they had three children: William, Jr., Maria, and John. Baird stayed home to take care of the children for eleven years. When her youngest child entered school, she decided it was time to resume her education as well.

## Goes Back to School

Much older than her fellow students, Baird was nervous about attending Los Angeles City College. As she went along, however, she gained confidence. After attending the college for five years as a part-time student, Baird earned her associate of arts degree in 1971. She then transferred to the University of California at Los Angeles and began work on a bachelor's degree in sociology. By 1973 she had earned her degree and had been accepted to law school at the same university. Her marriage came to an end in 1975, but Baird continued with her legal studies. After she graduated in 1976, she took the bar exam (an examination that allows lawyers to practice) and passed it on her first attempt.

Over the next twelve years, Baird moved up steadily through various city, county, and state court levels. She was hired right out of law school to work as an assistant prosecutor in the United States Attorney's Office in California. In 1983 she worked as a private lawyer in a prestigious Los Angeles law firm. Three years later California Governor George Deukmejian appointed Baird to a Los Angeles Municipal Court judgeship. In 1988 the governor promoted Baird to the position of Los Angeles County Superior Court judge.

During this period Baird was heavily involved in social and civic organizations. She worked for the California Women Lawyers Association, was president of her college alumni group, served on legal advisory committees, and was active in several Hispanic legal organizations.

## Nominated for U.S. Attorney Position

In 1989 California Senator Pete Wilson nominated Baird to fill the position of U.S. attorney for the Central District of California. Some twelve million people live in the district, making the position one of the most powerful in the country. What was unusual about her nomination was that she was a Democrat and Wilson was a Republican. But Baird's legal work had made her well known throughout the state, and members of both political parties praised her nomination.

In order for Baird to be placed in the position, she had to win the consent of President George Bush, the U.S. Senate, and the Federal Bureau of Investigation. Her qualifications, career, judicial decisions, and reputation were carefully investigated and evaluated. Eight months passed before she was cleared and approved for the position in 1990.

## Focuses on Drugs

During her two years as U.S. attorney for the Central District of California, Baird was responsible for a staff of more than 140 lawyers. Her department handled the federal legal problems of the largest district in the nation, one that is filled with crime. Baird's immediate focus was on drug abuse. She once observed that illegal drugs were the reason behind the majority of crimes brought before her. "Crime is rampant," she told Henry Weinstein of the *Los Angeles Times*. "My experience on the bench has indicated to me the horror of drugs—the main problem in the United States." Baird's stand on crime is a tough one—she firmly believes in the death penalty in certain situations. But she also believes more treatment facilities are needed in the country to help those who have a drug problem.

In April 1992 Baird's office was thrust into one of the biggest legal cases in the United States in the 1990s—the Rodney King trial. A year before, a black motorist named Rodney King had been chased and stopped by several white Los Angeles police officers. An eighty-one-second videotape showed that the police officers savagely beat King after he had been stopped. Four officers were brought to trial for the beating, but a jury found them not guilty. The verdict in the case set off a riot in Los Angeles, one of the worst ever recorded in the United States. Sixty people died and property damage totaled more than $800 million.

After the riot, Baird headed up a new prosecution of the officers, this time for having violated King's civil rights—a federal offense. Although Baird did not personally handle the prosecution in court, her administrative skills figured prominently in the case. In April 1993 two of the officers—Laurence Powell and Stacy Koon—were found guilty and sentenced to jail.

## Federal Justice

On April 2, 1992, President George Bush nominated Baird to a new seat as a federal judge on the U.S. District Court for the Central District of California. The Senate confirmed her nomination in August 1992, and she served in that capacity into the 2000s. She was appointed in 2000 by Chief Justice William H. Rehnquist as chair of the Committee on the Administrative Office. Baird was named the University of California, Los Angeles, School of Law "Alumnus of the Year," and the Hispanic Women's Council "Woman of Promise," both in 1991.

## For More Information

"Baird, Lourdes G.," Judges of the United States Courts. Available at http://air.fjc.gov/servlet/uGetInfo?jid=77 (accessed June 21, 2002).
*Detroit Free Press,* August 6, 1992, p. 3A.
*Los Angeles Times,* November 30, 1989, p. B1; December 4, 1989, p. B6; July 19, 1990, p. B1.
*Wall Street Journal,* April 19, 1993, p. A1.

# Rubén Blades

Singer, actor, lawyer, politician
Born July 16, 1948, Panama City, Panama

*"A country is not abandoned because we are far from its territory, a country is abandoned when we remove it from our heart."*

Rubén Blades is a multitalented celebrity whose interests range from music to film to politics. He grew up in Panama City, Panama, but emigrated to New York in 1974 with only $100 in his pocket. During the next twenty years, he became an international entertainer and earned a law degree from Harvard University. Although Blades has often been separated from his native Panama, his interests have remained with its government and its people. In May 1994 he made a strong run for the presidency of his homeland and his active interest in Panamanian politics resurfaced in the early 2000s.

Blades's parents met in the 1940s while both were performers in Panama City nightclubs. His mother, Anoland Benita, was a cabaret singer while his father, Rubén Dario Blades, was a conga player in a band. Born in 1948 in a poor neighborhood in Panama City, Blades grew up listening not only to his parents' music but also to that of Elvis Presley and the Beatles. He wanted to become a musician, but his father—who was also a policeman—insisted that the young Blades attend college to study law. Blades kept up with his music by singing with local Latin bands while studying for law classes at the University of Panama. After he graduated and passed the bar (an exam allowing lawyers to practice), he became a lawyer for the Bank of Panama. He then headed to the United States for a visit.

The visit turned out to be longer than Blades had expected. While in New York City, he hovered between careers for a time, still weighing his love for music against his interest in law. The growing popularity of salsa finally won him over. *Salsa* (Spanish for "sauce") is a musical blend of various Afro-Caribbean folk styles. In the 1970s, Latin record producers in New York City began to promote the spicy dance music. After working for a while in the mailroom of Fania Records, a leading salsa label, Blades signed a contract with the company. In 1978 he and trombonist Willie Colón recorded *Siembra,* one of the best-selling salsa albums of all time.

## Protest Songs Bring Danger and Success

Blades began to experiment with salsa music. He added elements of jazz and rock to the Latin beat, replacing the sound of the standard horns with that of a synthesizer. In writing his own songs, he moved away from love themes to tales of life in the barrios (Spanish neighborhoods) of New York. He borrowed ideas from his friend, Colombian novelist **Gabriel García Márquez** (see entry), and explored political issues in song. As Anthony DePalma noted in the *New York Times Magazine,* "The words [Blades] sings are not of partying, but of protest, of indignance against greed, corruption, and spiritual sloth."

Blades's resulting work stirred up controversy. In 1980 he wrote "Tiburon," a song that condemned superpowers for interfering with the political affairs of smaller countries. Many people were outraged, interpreting the song as a direct criticism of U.S. involvement in the problems of Panama. The song was banned on Miami's Latin-music radio stations, and Blades had to wear a bulletproof vest while performing there.

Despite these negative reactions, Blades's musical popularity grew. He became a leader of the *Nueva Cancion* ("New Song") movement that blended poetry and protest politics with a Latin rhythm. In an attempt to reach a larger audience, Blades signed with mainstream record company Elektra/Asylum in 1984, becoming the first Latin artist to do so. With each successive album, Blades has stretched the limits of Latin music. In the process, he has won three Grammy Awards. On his albums, he has recorded duets in Spanish with such artists as **Linda Ronstadt** (see entry) and Joe Jackson. In 1988 he surprised the Latin-music world by releasing a record in English, *Nothing but the Truth,* which featured singers Sting, Elvis Costello, and Lou Reed. Blades's song "Pedro Navaja" was the best-selling salsa single recorded to date.

## Doesn't Recognize Barriers

Some Hispanics criticized Blades for abandoning his roots, but he told Guy D. Garcia of *Time* that he was open to exploring everything before him: "I refuse to acknowledge a barrier. I think the barriers are in the mind and in the heart." His desire not to remain still had become evident in 1984. That year he had put his rising musical career on hold while he studied for a master's degree in international law from Harvard University. After having completed his year-long studies, Blades changed course again and delved into acting.

In 1985 he had starred in the film *Crossover Dreams,* the story of a Latin singer who leaves his family and friends behind as he switches to mainstream music.

Rubén Blades. *Reproduced by permission of AP/Wide World Photos.*

When his efforts fail, he is left with nothing. Since that beginning, Blades has acted in several major films, including Robert Redford's *The Milagro Beanfield War* (1986), *Fatal Beauty* (1987) with Whoopi Goldberg, and *A Million to Juan* (1994) a slapstick comedy with **Paul Rodriguez** and **Edward James Olmos** about a hard-working Mexican immigrant trying to obtain a green card and somehow getting a million dollars, and the action/drama *Scorpion Spring* (1996) with Matthew McConaughey and Esai Morales, about a desperate drug runner. He played the part of the artist **Diego Rivera** (see entries) in the historical film *Cradle Will Rock* (1999), and co-starred in actor/director Robert Duvall's 2002 movie *Assassination Tango*. He has also appeared on stage. In 1998, musician Paul Simon cast Blades in a major role in his Broadway musical *Capeman*. The musical, however, did not do well.

Blades's celebrity status did not kept him from keeping a close eye on the politics in Panama. He was disturbed by the corruption in its government and the poor living conditions of its people. In 1989 he was critical of the United States when it invaded Panama and ousted corrupt President Manuel Noriega. With hopes of bringing democracy back to a country long ruled by dictators, Blades helped found a political party in Panama in 1991 called *Papá Egoró* ("Mother Earth" in one of Panama's native languages).

## Makes a Bid for Presidency

At first, Blades did not say whether he would run for the Panamanian presidency. He told Garcia he simply hoped to create "what up to this point has been a mythical place: a Latin America that respects and loves itself, is incorruptible, romantic, nationalistic, and has a human perception of the needs of the world at large." Some Panamanian politicians, however, said Blades had no business returning to interfere in their government. In a speech reported by the Associated Press in 1993, Blades responded to his critics: "A country is not abandoned because we are far from its territory," he said, "a country is abandoned when we remove it from our heart." Later that year, he officially announced his run for the presidency.

In the months before the May 1994 election, Blades led the presidential campaign polls. But the election showed different results as Ernesto Pérez Balladeras became

Panama's new president. Blades came in second, receiving almost one-quarter of the vote.

After the election, Blades returned to the United States to resume his music and film career, with a healthy stream of albums and films to his credit. His 1999 album *Tiempos,* was called the best Latin music album of the year by *Rolling Stone* magazine. In 2002 he released an album called *Mundo,* in which he calls for an end to racism in the world. *Mundo* is a fusion of Irish, Arabic, and Afro-Cuban rhythms combined with salsa to reflect the shared roots of humankind.

At a press conference in Panama in April 2002, Blades told reporters he was thinking about running in the Panama presidential elections again in 2004. "I realize now that my biggest error [in the presidential race] was not to have spent enough time in Panama. I failed to understand that going into politics means big responsibilities, and that you have got to give yourself completely or not at all," he explained, as quoted in a Reuters article.

## For More Information

Marton, Betty A., *Rubén Blades,* Chelsea House, 1992.

*New Republic,* November 1, 1993, pp. 10–11.

*New York Times,* March 17, 1994, p. A14; May 9, 1994, p. A4.

*New York Times Magazine,* June 21, 1987, pp. 24–31.

"Rubén Blades," All Music Guide. Available at http://www.allmusic.com/cg/amg.dll?p=amg&sql=Bwijxlfde5cqw~C (accessed June 21, 2002).

"Salsa Star Blades' New Album Is Call Against Racism," Reuters, April 30, 2002. Available at http://english.planetarabia.com/content/article.cfm/102845/112382/ (accessed June 21, 2002).

*Time,* January 29, 1990, pp. 70–72.

# Bobby Bonilla

Professional baseball player, businessperson
Born February 23, 1963, New York, New York

*"There is no pressure in baseball. Pressure is growing up in the South Bronx. We're talking about houses burning and people starving."*

Bobby Bonilla. *Reproduced by permission of AP/Wide World Photos.*

**W**hen he was very young, Roberto Martin Antonio "Bobby" Bonilla knew that he wanted to escape his rough New York Bronx neighborhood. He wanted to avoid the crime, violence, and drug addiction that he saw all around him. With a little luck, the help of his family and friends, and a lot of talent, Bonilla escaped from his neighborhood into major league baseball.

Born in 1963, Bonilla is one of four children of Roberto and Regina Bonilla. While raising the family, his mother worked on a college degree in social work. His father was an electrician who sometimes took his young son with him on jobs. "My father would go up into these old buildings where the wires all look the same, so you couldn't tell negative from positive," Bonilla told Bruce Newman of *Sports Illustrated*. "Sometimes he'd get knocked off the ladder by the shocks, but he always got right back up there."

Even though Bonilla's parents divorced when he was eight, his father kept worrying about his children's welfare. By nine o'clock each night, the elder Bonilla would drive by their house and honk his horn. The Bonilla children had to wave from the windows to reassure him that they were all at home. His mother kept close tabs on the children, too. Bonilla wanted to go to a vocational school, but his mother wanted him to receive a better education. She enrolled him in a mostly white, middle-class school that took two city bus rides and nearly half-an-hour to reach.

## Night-Time Batting Practice

Bonilla loved baseball and took his bat along everywhere. Batting practice could occur at any time. Much to the dismay of the younger brother who shared his bedroom, Bonilla actually slept with the bat. If something woke him up during the night, he'd hop up and take a couple of swings before settling back to sleep.

Although Bonilla excelled in baseball in high school, no major league team had sent scouts to see him play before he graduated in 1981. "There are a lot of kids with talent in the cities," he explained to Newman, "and major league teams should be taking advantage of that. Maybe they're scared to go into the neighborhoods."

One person who had seen Bonilla play and knew what he could do was his high school coach, Joe Levine. When Levine learned that a national high school all-star team was going to tour Scandinavia during the summer of 1981, he filled out an application for the future baseball star. Bonilla was quickly accepted.

## Performance in Europe Gains Attention

While playing for the all-star team, Bonilla caught the attention of a team member's father who was connected with the Pittsburgh Pirates. When he returned from Europe, the Pirates offered him a minor league contract. After he batted only .217 his first season, Bonilla started taking classes at a technical college to learn to become a repairman in case his baseball career didn't work out. Because he was a switch hitter (batted either left- or right-handed) who showed promise, however, the Pirates gave him several seasons in the minors to work on his skills.

In 1985, during spring training, Bonilla broke his right leg in a collision with another player. Even though he recovered after four months, he was sent to the Pirates' lowest minor league team. When the Pirates failed to place him on their protected roster that winter, the Chicago White Sox picked

him up. Four months later Pittsburgh gained him back in a trade.

Bonilla spent four seasons as a Pirate, racking up impressive statistics, collecting awards and honors, and helping the team win two divisional titles. He was named to the National League All-Star Team in 1988 and 1989. Bonilla also led National League third basemen in double plays for 1989. He finished the 1991 season among the top five hitters in eight offensive categories and was seventh in RBIs (runs-batted-in) with 100.

## Signs Richest Baseball Contract

In 1992, after having become a free agent, Bonilla returned to his hometown of New York as the highest paid professional baseball player. He signed a five-year, $29 million contract with the New York Mets. "New York City was in my heart," Bonilla told a reporter for *Jet*. "I was born and raised there. The Mets showed an interest and I said this could be a lot of fun. It'll be hard to knock the smile off my face."

However, Bonilla's first season with the Mets was disappointing. The team finished fifth in the National League East and the players were criticized by sportswriters for collecting high salaries and delivering poor performances. Bonilla improved his record in 1993 with 87 RBIs and a career-best 34 home runs, but sat out the end of the season with a shoulder injury.

In 1994 the New York Mets started a rebuilding program, trading many older players and bringing up younger ones. Bonilla became one of the leaders on the team. Bouncing back from his shoulder injury, he put together a solid season. Before the players' strike ended the baseball season early in August, Bonilla was hitting almost .300. Although he started the 1995 season in very good form, he was traded to the Baltimore Orioles in July. In 1996, Bonilla helped Baltimore win 88 games and make the playoffs. As designated hitter in 44 of 159 games, he had his best season in years, finishing with 28 homers and 116 RBI.

Bonilla was a free agent in the 1996 season and was picked up by the Florida Marlins. He was the team's oldest player and was suffering from bad hamstrings and Achilles tendons—his injuries were beginning to show on the field. Nevertheless his team won the 1997 World Series. In 1998 he was again traded to the New York Mets and did some rehabilitation work. The Mets released him in 2000 and the Atlanta Braves signed him in 2000. He finished the 2001 season with the St. Louis Cardinals. Apparently coming upon the end of his baseball playing career, he held the record for the most home runs, 237, by a switch-hitter and he shared the major league record for most doubles in one inning and the most sacrifice flies of a single season (1996).

In 1998, Bonilla joined forces with a business partner, Mark Risi, in a home theater business, and looked forward to working with technology in his post-baseball career. Throughout his career, Bonilla has received numerous awards for his charitable work, including the Thurmon Munson Award and the Gary Carter Award for his excellence of character and love of humanity.

## For More Information

*Jet,* December 23, 1991, p. 46.

Knapp, Ron, *Sports Great Bobby Bonilla,* Enslow, 1993.

Rappoport, Ken, *Bobby Bonilla,* Walker and Co., 1993.

Shouler, Ken, "Swinging for the Fences: With a World Series Championship Under His Belt, Bobby Bonilla Sets His Sights on His Place in Baseball History," *Cigar Aficionado,* July/August 1998.

*Sports Illustrated,* October 14, 1991, pp. 34–41.

# Alvar Núñez Cabeza de Vaca

Spanish explorer, writer
Born c. 1490, Jerez de la Frontera, Spain
Died c. 1560, Seville, Spain

*"Cabeza de Vaca was one of the few Spanish explorers who managed to befriend American Indians and live among them in peace."*

T he remarkable life of Alvar Núñez Cabeza de Vaca was filled with action, excitement, fame, danger, courage, and hardship. He survived shipwrecks, attacks by hostile Native Americans, and grave illness in the New World. He then wrote an account of his adventures so future generations would understand the origins of the Spanish in the New World. Cabeza de Vaca was one of the few Spanish explorers who managed to befriend American Indians and live among them in peace.

Cabeza de Vaca was born around 1490 into a noble Spanish family whose name means "head of a cow" in English. In the early thirteenth century, one of his ancestors helped King Sancho of Navarre (ancient kingdom in northern Spain) win a battle by finding a secret route through enemy lines. The ancestor, who was a shepherd, marked the road for the king's soldiers with the skull of a cow. In gratitude, the king made him a nobleman and gave him the name Cabeza de Vaca.

Little is known about Cabeza de Vaca's early life. The oldest of four children, he was raised by his grandfather in the Canary Islands (off the northwest coast of Africa). In 1511 he became a soldier and fought with the Spanish army in Spain and in Italy. He was a big, strong man with a red beard. It is believed that he married, but there is no record of his wife's name or of any children.

## Sails to the New World

In 1527 Cabeza de Vaca was named royal treasurer of an expedition sent to settle and seek gold in Florida. Commanded by Pánfilo de Narváez, the expedition set out across the Atlantic Ocean with an army of six hundred men in five small ships. The ships stopped in Santo Domingo, where about 140 men deserted to live on the island. Narváez and the remaining men then spent the winter in Cuba. In April 1528 Narváez finally landed on the shores of what is now Tampa Bay, Florida. There he took possession of the land originally claimed by Spanish explorer **Juan Ponce de León** (see entry).

Native Americans in the area were not pleased to see the Spanish. Earlier gold-hungry explorers had already made a poor impression through their cruelty and greed. The Native Americans directed Narváez to travel north to a place called Apalachen (present-day site of Tallahassee) to find gold.

Narváez decided to march inland toward Apalachen, taking some three hundred soldiers with him, including Cabeza de Vaca. He directed the remaining soldiers to sail north along the unknown coastline and meet him in about a year. The ships were never seen again. It was later learned that they had searched in vain for Narváez before finally giving up and sailing to Mexico.

In the meantime, Narváez and his men trudged through swamps and forests for two months until they reached Apalachen. There they discovered no gold—only a small, poor village of unfriendly Native Americans who pelted them with arrows. Discouraged and hungry, the Spaniards moved on into the Florida panhandle to find food, to escape the Native Americans, and to await their ships.

## Undertakes Desperate Voyage

When the Spanish ships never appeared, Narváez became desperate. He had lost many soldiers to starvation, Native American attacks, and illness. He decided to build boats to take his men back to the safety of Cuba or Mexico. None of the men were shipbuilders and no proper materials were available, but the explorers improvised to construct five seaworthy barges. Cabeza de Vaca described the process in his later account: "From the tails and manes of the horses, we made ropes and rigging; from our shirts, sails; and from the junipers growing there we made the oars."

While they were building the ships, forty men died of hunger and illness. When they hunted inland for food, Native Americans attacked. Desperate, the Spaniards were forced to kill and eat their horses, one at a

Alvar Núñez Cabeza de Vaca.

time. After the last horse was slaughtered, 242 men set out to sea in their crude boats in 1528. They sailed west, trying to keep close to shore. They suffered terribly from a lack of fresh water.

After six weeks, winds and a strong current separated the boats. Cabeza de Vaca's barge was cast ashore on present-day Galveston Island, off the southeast coast of Texas. One more boat joined his group a few days later. The others were lost at sea. Only eighty explorers now remained—the first Europeans to set foot in Texas. The Native Americans who greeted them were friendly, but had little food to share with the ragged Spaniards. After a difficult winter on the island, only fifteen Spanish explorers survived. The Spanish named the island *La Isla de Mal Hado* ("The Island of Bad Luck"). In the spring, fourteen Spaniards left for the Texas mainland. Cabeza de Vaca, who was ill, stayed behind.

## Treated as a Medicine Man by Native Americans

Cabeza de Vaca later traveled to the mainland. For several years he lived among the Native Americans. At first he was their captive. He then became a trader who traveled among several tribes along the coast. Luckily, the Native Americans considered him to be a medicine man (healer), so he was respected and allowed to travel freely. During his travels, he became the first European to see the North American bison, or buffalo.

In 1533 Cabeza de Vaca came upon three other Spanish survivors—Alonso de Castillo, Andres Dorantes, and their Muslim slave, Estevanico. They had been living as slaves with another tribe of Native Americans. The four men realized they were the only survivors out of Narváez's original group of hundreds. They agreed to attempt an escape the following summer when the tribes gathered to harvest prickly pears (fruit from the cactus of the same name).

In 1534 the four men managed to meet and break away, traveling north and west. Using diplomacy and their reputations as medicine men, the Spaniards traveled from one tribe of Native Americans to the next. They maintained the good will of all. The men moved on through Texas, into present-day New Mexico, and possibly into present-day Arizona before heading south into Mexico.

## Eight-Year Journey Ends

In 1536 the four weary travelers finally came out of the wilderness and encountered a band of surprised Spanish soldiers in western Mexico. The soldiers guided them to civilization in Mexico City, where the four men were greeted as heroes and warmly welcomed by the Spanish inhabitants. The men's tales of Indian customs, enslavement, shipwreck, and survival excited the city. The explorers calculated that their eight-year journey had taken them across six thousand miles of land and water since their arrival in Florida in 1528. Cabeza de Vaca found it was difficult to adjust to city life after so much time in the wilderness. "I could not wear any [clothes] for some time," he later wrote, "nor could we sleep anywhere but on the ground."

The explorers submitted a report on their travels, which led to further expeditions headed by Franciscan friar Marcos de Niza and explorer **Francisco Vásquez de Coronado** (see entry). Cabeza de Vaca left for Spain in 1537 to write his own account of the adventure. The finished book was titled *Relacion de los Naufragios* ("The Story of the Ship-Wrecked Ones").

However, this was not the end of Cabeza de Vaca's travels. In 1540 he was named governor of Spanish settlements on the Río de la Plata in the present-day South American country of Paraguay. Once again he sailed across the ocean, this time landing in Brazil, South America. He marched overland with 280 men to his post at Asunción, bartering with native people along the way for survival.

Cabeza de Vaca made a good name for himself through his honest dealings with the native people of the region. However, he angered some Spanish for neglecting what they considered to be his duty as a conqueror. In 1544 he was thrown out of his office as governor. He was then sent to Spain to be tried on a variety of charges, including the claim that he tried to subvert the authority of the king. The trial dragged on for years. Although he was found guilty, his punishment was lightened by the king. In spite of his many accomplishments and the wealth of information that he passed along to Europeans, Cabeza de Vaca spent his final years in poverty.

## For More Information

Syme, Ronald, *First Man to Cross America: The Story of Cabeza de Vaca,* Morrow, 1961.

Terrell, John Upton, *Journey Into Darkness,* Morrow, 1962.

Wojciechowska, Maia, *Odyssey of Courage,* Athenium, 1965.

# José Canseco

Professional baseball player
Born July 2, 1964, Havana, Cuba

*"Maybe I've learned how to handle failure. God knows, I've had my failures. But it's getting better every day. I never thought it could."*

José Canseco. *Reproduced by permission of AP/Wide World Photos.*

José Canseco, outfielder for the Texas Rangers and home run-hitting star, has been a dominating force in baseball since his debut with the Oakland Athletics in 1986. He helped the A's earn back-to-back pennants and was a guiding force in the team's World Series victory in 1989. Unfortunately, Canseco's battles off the field have been equally famous. He has had run-ins with the media and the law. He has been troubled by rumors of steroid drug use—which were never proven—and some of his teammates have accused him of being distant and cold. Wherever he goes, however, fans rush to his side to meet a man many consider to be one of the best players the game of baseball has ever seen.

Canseco and his identical twin brother Osvaldo (Ozzie) were born in Cuba in 1964 to Barbara Capaz and José Canseco, Sr. The elder Canseco had been an oil company executive, but lost his job, house, and car when the communist government of Fidel Castro seized control of Cuba in 1959. Finally given permission to leave the island nation in late 1965, the Canseco family settled in Opa-Locka, Florida, northwest of Miami. To support the family, Canseco's father worked as a gas station attendant during the day and as a security guard at night.

The young Canseco did not begin to play baseball until he was ten years old, preferring instead to play soccer and basketball. In school he took his studies seriously and was an straight-A honor student through junior high school (to this day, his favorite magazine is *National Geographic* and his favorite television programs are PBS documentaries on wildlife).

## Accused of Steroid Abuse

In high school Canseco was a good, but not great, baseball player. At five-feet-eleven-inches and 165 pounds, he was considered too small to make the majors, and most team scouts thought he had reached his growth peak at seventeen. However, his powerful hitting caught the eye of a scout for the Oakland Athletics, and the team offered him a minor league contract in 1982. Over the next three years, due to rigorous weight training, Canseco grew four inches and put on forty pounds. Some say this phenomenal growth was from steroid drug use, but Canseco, who doesn't drink alcohol or smoke, has denied the drug charges.

After having played in the minor leagues for several years, Canseco was brought up to the Athletics' major league club in 1986. He impressed the fans almost immediately with his good looks and exciting plays. After a great season with 33 home runs, 117 runs-batted-in, and 15 stolen bases, Canseco was named the American League's Rookie of the Year. He was not a favorite with sports reporters, however. Despite the prodding of his coaches, Canseco continued to respond to reporters' questions with answers that were barely civil.

## Sets Major League 40–40 Record

In 1988 the media played up Canseco's boast to hit forty home runs and steal forty bases in a single season. That feat had never been accomplished before in major league baseball, and few thought Canseco likely to set the record. Much to everyone's surprise, however, Canseco's boast proved prophetic. He finished the 1988 season with 42 home runs (including a World Series grand slam), 124 runs-batted-in, and 40 stolen bases. For his record-breaking performance, he was given the American League's Most Valuable Player award. Then his troubles began.

During the off-season between 1988 and 1989, Canseco's personal life began to make the news. He was arrested in Miami for driving 120 miles per hour. He was arrested on the campus of the University of California at San Francisco for carrying a loaded semiautomatic pistol. He cut short, or even failed to show up at, appearances at several baseball card shows and award banquets. In October 1988 he married Esther Haddad (a Miss Miami beauty queen). Over the next four-and-a-half years, the couple had a stormy relationship. Canseco filed for divorce in 1991. Even though the divorce was granted in 1992, the couple had an on-again, off-again relationship until early 1993.

A bad wrist injury at the start of the 1989 season sidelined Canseco for several months. When he recovered, his 16 home runs and 52 runs-batted-in helped the Athletics advance to their second World Series appearance in two years. This time the A's won, beating the San Francisco Giants in a series that began with an unforgettable, frightening earthquake that rumbled the stadium.

## Trade Surprises Everyone

Near the end of the 1992 season, the Oakland A's surprised the sports world by trading Canseco to the Texas Rangers in exchange for three players. Canseco, who had hit 44 home runs and had driven in 122 runs during the 1991 season, was surprised as well. "I still can't believe all of this happened," he told Leigh Montville in *Sports Illustrated*. "I can't believe it happened this way." Even though he had been plagued by back and shoulder injuries all season and had barely hit .250, he did not believe his career was over. He vowed to work hard during the off-season to regain his strength.

Although Canseco did come back, his 1993 season was marked by two embarrassing events. In May, while playing the outfield, he let a fly ball bounce off the top of his head and over the fence for a home run. That same month, he convinced his manager to let him pitch an inning against the Boston Red Sox. After throwing 33 pitches, he tore a ligament in his right elbow. He had surgery on the elbow in July and sat out the remainder of the season. Many believed his career had indeed come to an end.

At the beginning of the 1994 season, however, Canseco was healthy and optimistic. "Maybe I've learned how to handle failure," he told Richard Hoffer of *Sports Illustrated*. "God knows, I've had my failures. But it's getting better every day. I never thought it could." As the Rangers DH (designated hitter) that season, Canseco proved he was getting better. Before the season came to an early end in August because of the players' strike, Canseco had hit 31 home runs and had batted in 90 runs. Rangers manager Kevin Kennedy believed Canseco's change in attitude helped his performance. "He wants to be the one of the best players in the game again," he told Jack

Curry of the *New York Times*. "He wants to be the old José again."

Canseco did eventually recover from his injuries and had a few years of top playing. In 1998 he signed for one year with the Toronto Blue Jays. The salary was considerably less than he was used to at $750,000, and the Blue Jays had no interest in re-signing Canseco to a long-term deal. Nonetheless, he had a great season and hit 46 homers for the Blue Jays in 1998. Canseco's success was somewhat overshadowed by Mark McGwire's record-breaking 70 homers that year with **Sammy Sosa** (see entry) close behind him. The season's success was also overshadowed by charges brought against him for striking his wife Jessica, to which he entered a no-contest plea.

In 1999 Canseco was an outfielder and designated hitter for the New York Yankees, and that year he became the fifteenth player in major league history to hit 30 or more home runs in eight or more seasons.

In February 2002 Canseco signed with the Montreal Expos, but just a few months later, on May 13, 2002, he announced his retirement, explaining that his injuries were beginning to affect his game. He left baseball only 38 home runs short of 500 and with many records. Canseco, who enjoys investments, had already started his own company called Canseco Financial Group, an investment vehicle for wealthy athletes.

## For More Information

*Hispanic*, April 1989, p. 28–31.
*New York Times*, June 7, 1994, p. B11.
Price, S. L., "Life Is Beautiful: Coming Off His Best Season in Years, the Once Larger-Than-Life José Canseco Has Downsized His World but Still

Hopes to Make a Big Impact with the Devil Rays," *Sports Illustrated,* March 22, 1999, p. 64.

*Sports Illustrated,* August 20, 1990, pp. 42–50; September 14, 1992, pp. 36–37; March 14, 1994, pp. 38–40.

# Luisa Capetillo

Labor leader, author
Born October 28, 1879, Arecibo, Puerto Rico
Died April 10, 1922, Río Piedras, Puerto Rico

*"Capetillo was a tireless feminist who battled a culture that denied women educational opportunities, career choices, and economic advancement."*

L uisa Capetillo was a leader in the political and labor struggles in Puerto Rico at the beginning of the twentieth century. She was also a tireless feminist who battled a culture that denied women educational opportunities, career choices, and economic advancement. Capetillo criticized a society that forced girls into marriages based not on love but on a financial agreement between parents. Many of her ideas were far ahead of her time, and she was overlooked as an important historical figure until recently.

Capetillo was born on October 28, 1879, in Arecibo, Puerto Rico. Her mother, Margarita Peron, was French, and her father, Luis Capetillo, was Spanish. She might have had some formal schooling, but she was mostly self-taught. Because she had learned French from her mother, she was able to study the works of French writers by herself.

Achieving knowledge on her own probably led to the growth of Capetillo's independent spirit in adulthood. History remembers her as the first woman to wear pants—instead of skirts or dresses—in public. Dressing in pants, like the men of the times, was a symbolic statement of Capetillo's personal freedom.

## Fights for Workers' Rights

Capetillo lived in the period when industry was just beginning to develop in Puerto Rico. Although wages for men were extremely low, those for women were even lower. Capetillo believed that fair pay was a worker's right, regardless of gender. She felt that better wages for everyone would result in happier families, less domestic violence, and more educational opportunities for children.

Capetillo's main concern lay with the plight of working women. In 1911 she wrote a book called *Mi opinión sobre las libertades, derechos y deberes de la mujer como compañera, madre y ser independiente* ("My Opinion on the Freedom, Rights, and Duties of the Woman as Companion, Mother, and as an Independent Woman"). In this book she highlights the vast differences between the lives of wealthy women and the lives of working women in the early twentieth century. Wealthy women were not obligated to take jobs outside the home to help support their families; in addition, they had the financial resources to hire other women to look after their children. Capetillo's book makes clear that working women in the early 1900s did not have these luxuries but, rather, were victims of substandard economic and social conditions.

## Arrested for Union Activities

Capetillo first became involved in the labor movement in 1907, when she took part in a strike in her city's tobacco factories. She was active in the local union, the Federation of Free Workers, and served as a reporter for the union's newspaper. Three years later she founded her own newspaper, *La Mujer* ("The Woman"), to bring attention to women's issues.

During the next few years Capetillo traveled quite a bit, promoting workers' rights. She journeyed to New York to write articles for a newspaper called *Cultura obrera* ("Workers' Culture"). She also met with union leaders in Florida. From 1914 to 1916 she lived in Cuba, teaching workers how to start cooperatives. (A cooperative is a group that combines its members' money or talents to buy things or to accomplish specific goals).

In 1918 Capetillo returned to Puerto Rico and immediately helped organize strikes by farm workers. That same year she was arrested for violence, disobedience, and being disrespectful to a police officer. At the time, activist-type agitation by a woman was considered shocking.

## Writings Reveal Forward-Looking Beliefs

Capetillo left behind many written works that are just now being rediscovered and studied. Dedicated to all workers, her essays and books reveal her dreams of a better world in the future. In *La humanidad en el futuro* ("Humanity in the Future"), published in 1910, she writes about a utopian society (a perfect society governed by ideal laws), the power of the church and the state, private and

public property, and marriage. Her 1911 book about women and economics analyzes gender roles in society and suggests that, through education, women can overcome the restrictions society places on them. But Capetillo did not limit her ideas to political or social essays. She also wrote several dramas. The theater gave her a chance to creatively and publicly express her radical opinions about the social oppression of women.

Capetillo died of tuberculosis on April 10, 1922, at the age of forty-two. She was survived by her three children, her feminist writings, and her hopes for a better world.

## For More Information

Capetillo, Luisa, *Mi opinión sobre las libertades, derechos y deberes de la mujer como compañera, madre y ser independiente* (title means "My Opinion on the Freedom, Rights, and Duties of the Woman as Companion, Mother, and as an Independent Woman"), Tomes Publishing Company, 1911.

López Antonetty, Evelina, *Luisa Capetillo,* Centro de Estudios Puertorriqueños (Hunter College), 1986.

Valle Ferrer, Norma, *Luisa Capetillo: Historia de una mujer proscrita* (title means "Luisa Capetillo: History of an Exiled Woman"), Editorial Cultural, 1990.

# Lynda Cordoba Carter

Actress, singer, dancer
Born c. July 24, 1951, Phoenix, Arizona

*"[My mother] taught me more than anything to survive in a dignified, honorable, gracious way."*

Lynda Carter became famous by portraying Wonder Woman on television during the 1970s. The role of a superhero was appropriate for a girl from humble beginnings whose hard work and many talents led her to success in the entertainment world and in life. During her varied career she has been a beauty queen, television star, cosmetics model, wife, and mother.

Lynda Jean Cordoba Carter was born sometime in the early 1950s in Phoenix, Arizona. Her mother, Jean Carter, was of Mexican descent; her father was of English descent. When she was ten years old, her parents divorced and her father left the family. Carter's mother raised her three children alone and supported them by working nights in a factory. Carter admired and appreciated her mother's determination and honor. "She taught me more than anything to survive in a dignified, honorable, gracious way," Carter explained to a reporter from *People*.

Carter made her acting and singing debut in a pizza parlor when she was fifteen. By the time she was seventeen, she was singing and dancing in nightclubs in Reno and Las Vegas, Nevada. After she graduated from high school, she attended Arizona State University. Her academic career came to an end when she won the Miss World-U.S.A. title in 1973. After her reign as beauty queen, she studied acting. In 1975 she won the role that would make her famous: Diana Prince/Wonder Woman in the television series *Wonder Woman*.

## Portrays Feminist Superhero

The strikingly beautiful twenty-five-year-old won thousands of fans when she first appeared as the superpowered Wonder Woman. Costumed in shiny red boots, a red-white-and-blue body suit, and a gold headband and bracelet, Carter portrayed the feminist superhero for four years. During this time, she also appeared in television movies and specials, and portrayed the character of Bobbie Jo James in the 1976 motion picture *Bobbie Jo and the Outlaw*.

After her *Wonder Woman* series ended in 1979, Carter continued to act in made-for-television movies. One movie role that received a great deal of attention was her 1983 portrayal of acting legend Rita Hayworth in *Rita Hayworth: The Love Goddess*. While some friends of Hayworth did not want details of her life televised, others thought Carter was the wrong actress to play the part of the screen legend. She disagreed. "I really wanted the challenge," Carter explained to a reporter from *People*. "We both had Hispanic backgrounds. We were both in show business at an early age. We both sing and dance."

## Earns Awards for Television Work

During the early 1980s Carter also appeared in her own highly rated television specials. For her 1984 special, *Lynda Carter: Body and Soul,* she was nominated for an Emmy Award. In 1986 Carter was presented with the Golden Eagle Award for Consistent Performance in Television and Film.

A versatile performer, Carter also managed a career as a singer/dancer. She developed a nightclub act that originally played in Reno and Las Vegas. She then took her act around the world, performing in cities such as London, England; Monte Carlo, Monaco; and Mexico City, Mexico.

Carter has also been seen in fashion magazines as a model for Maybelline cosmetics. In addition, she served as a beauty and fashion director for Maybelline. Within two years after she signed on with the company, sales of its products tripled. A sharp businesswoman, Carter also founded her own company, Lynda Carter Productions, which continues to produce television programs.

## Faces Controversy in Personal Life

Not all Carter's ventures have been successful. Her first marriage to her talent agent ended in divorce in 1982. She blamed the failure of the marriage on the fact that it was based on business. In 1984 she married Robert Altman, a banker. They have two children, a son, Jamie, and a daughter, Jessica. In 1991 Altman was accused of being involved in a financial scandal surrounding the vast Bank of Credit and Commerce International. While Altman had to resign from his job and defend himself, Carter insisted he was innocent. The bad publicity generated by the case often made life difficult for the couple, but Carter remained optimistic. "This is just another challenge in my life," she told Paula Chin of *People,* "and nothing is going to derail us." In 1993 a New York jury found Altman innocent of all charges in the case.

Despite her busy personal and professional life, Carter finds time to help others. She served as the American Cancer Society's national crusade chairperson in 1985 and 1986, and was the honorary chairperson

Lynda Cordoba Carter. *Reproduced by permission of Arte Público Press.*

for Exceptional Children's Foundation in 1987 and 1988. She worked on a national "Stay Drug Free" campaign and has appeared on talk shows, hosted fund-raisers, and awards ceremonies. She was also an active member of the National Committee for Arts for the Handicapped, Feed the Hungry, and the Committee for Creative Nonviolence. She has been active with Democratic campaigns, including the Al Gore presidential campaign of 2000. In 2000, *Wonder Woman: The Complete History* was published with a forward by Lynda Carter.

## For More Information

*Contemporary Theater, Film, and Television,* Volume 5, Gale, 1988, pp. 49–50.

"Lynda Carter Biography," Wonderland: The Ultimate Wonderwoman Site. Available at http://lacosa.sion.com/ww/html/miscel/bios/bios1.htm (accessed June 21, 2002).

*People,* November 7, 1983, p. 109; March 19, 1984, p. 9; October 15, 1984, p. 11; February 9, 1987, p. 7; September 2, 1991, pp. 58–59.

# Pablo Casals

Cellist, conductor, composer
Born December 29, 1876, Vendrell, Catalonia, Spain
Died October 22, 1973, San Juan, Puerto Rico

*"The pursuit of music and the love for my neighbors have been inseparable with me, and if the first has brought me the purest and most exalted joys, the second has brought me peace of mind, even in the saddest moments."*

Pablo Casals was a master musician with three loves: God, the wonders of nature, and the music of Johann Sebastian Bach. He believed the beauty found in these three could reach beyond the different languages and borders of countries, and he tried to use his music to draw humanity together in peace. When injustice and conflict among people continued, Casals responded by silencing his music.

Casals was born in 1876 in the Spanish seaside town of Vendrell. He was the son of Pilar Ursula Defilló and Carlos Casals, the local church organist and choirmaster. From the very beginning of his life, Casals was surrounded by music. As his father practiced the piano, the young Casals would rest his head against the instrument and sing along to the music he felt. By the age of four, Casals was playing the piano. The following year he joined the church choir. At age six he was composing songs with his father, and at nine he could play the violin and organ.

Casals was thoughtful and sensitive even as a child. From the age of ten, he began each day with a walk outdoors to find inspiration from nature. Upon returning home he would always play some of the music of Bach on his piano. He claimed this routine filled him "with an awareness of the wonder of life, with the incredible marvel of being a human being," he related to Albert E. Kahn in the book *Joys and Sorrows: Reflections by Pablo Casals as Told to Albert E. Kahn.*

## Develops Unusual Cello Technique

When he was eleven, Casals decided to study the cello after hearing the instrument in a chamber music recital. Although his father wanted him to apprentice to a carpenter, his mother insisted he follow his interest in music. She enrolled him in the Municipal School of Music in Barcelona, Spain.

Learning the cello quickly, Casals soon disagreed with his instructors about cello technique. He preferred to bow and finger the instrument in his own style. His experiments produced a range of sound that was considered unusually expressive. Many thought his style was revolutionary and credited Casals with elevating the cello to a higher position as a solo instrument.

Casals's reputation spread quickly. In 1894, at age eighteen, he was invited to perform informal concerts for the Queen Regent of Spain, Maria Cristine. During the next few years he played with orchestras in Paris and Madrid. In 1899 he made his formal debut as a concert soloist with the prestigious orchestra of French conductor Charles Lamoureux. What audiences heard in his playing was a reverence for the world around him. This was especially evident in his interpretation of the music of Bach.

## Brings New Light to the Music of Bach

Sometime in 1890, while browsing through a Barcelona bookstore, Casals had found a volume of Bach's Six Suites for solo cello. The discovery was enlightening. While these suites had always been considered mere musical exercises, Casals saw something deeper and richer in them. He practiced the suites every day for twelve years before playing them in public. He continued to play at least one suite every day for the rest of his life. Casals's performance of Bach's suites astounded listeners and made the music world take a new look at these compositions. While many thought Bach's solo music for strings had no warmth or artistic value, Casals showed that Bach was "a fully human creator whose art had poetry and passion, accessible to all people," H. L. Kirk wrote in *Pablo Casals: A Biography.*

While Casals had been in school, he came to understand the suffering and inequality of man as he walked among the poor on the streets of Barcelona. He vowed to use his gift from God—his music—for the welfare of others. "The pursuit of music and the love for my neighbors have been

Pablo Casals. *Reproduced by permission of AP/Wide World Photos.*

inseparable with me," he related to José Maria Corredor in the book *Conversations With Casals,* "and if the first has brought me the purest and most exalted joys, the second has brought me peace of mind, even in the saddest moments." Throughout his career Casals helped the disadvantaged by writing letters and organizing concerts. He also refused to perform in countries whose governments he considered unjust.

During the Spanish Civil War in the 1930s, Casals supported the Republican cause. When Nationalist General Francisco Franco seized control of the government in 1939, Casals left Spain, announcing he would never return until Franco was removed. He settled in Prades, France, giving occasional concerts until 1946. That year, as a further protest against military dictatorships around the world, Casals vowed never to perform again. A peaceful man, he believed his silence was the loudest, strongest protest he could make.

## Four Years of Silence

Casals did not play his cello in public again until 1950, when friends persuaded him to participate in a musical festival celebrating the two hundredth anniversary of Bach's death. Even though he performed, Casals did not abandon his cause. At the end of every concert he gave, Casals played his arrangement of a Spanish folk ballad, "Song of the Birds," to protest the oppressive government in Spain.

Casals never returned to Spain. In 1956 he settled in Puerto Rico, his mother's native homeland. He started the world-famous Casals Festival to spur artistic and cultural activities on the island. With his help, a symphony orchestra and a conservatory of music were also organized there.

Although Casals resumed performing, he refused to play in any country that officially recognized the Franco government in Spain. The United States was one of these countries. He wavered from that decision only once, in 1961. U.S. President John F. Kennedy, a man Casals greatly admired, asked him to perform at the White House and Casals agreed.

Throughout his life, Casals was inspired by the beauty he found in nature and in music. Through both his cello and his silence, he sought to promote harmony among people. At Casals's funeral in 1973, his recording of "The Song of the Birds" was played as his last poignant plea for peace in the world.

## For More Information

Casals, Pablo, *Song of the Birds: Sayings, Stories, and Impressions of Pablo Casals,* Robsons Books, 1985.

Casals, Pablo, and Albert E. Kahn, *Joys and Sorrows: Reflections by Pablo Casals as Told to Albert E. Kahn,* Simon and Schuster, 1970.

Corredor, José Maria, *Conversations With Casals,* Hutchinson, 1956.

Garza, Hedda, *Pablo Casals,* Chelsea House, 1993.

Kirk, H. L., *Pablo Casals: A Biography,* Holt, Rinehart, Winston, 1974.

# Rosemary Casals

Professional tennis player
Born September 16, 1948, San Francisco, California

*"The other kids had nice tennis clothes, nice rackets, nice white shoes, and came in Cadillacs. I felt stigmatized because we were poor."*

Rosemary Casals earned her reputation as a rebel in the staid tennis world when she began competing in the early 1960s. During a tennis career that spanned more than two decades, she won more than 90 tournaments and worked for the betterment of women's tennis. She was a motivating force behind many of the changes that shook the tennis world during the 1960s and 1970s. Many of these changes helped make tennis the popular sport that it is today.

Casals was born in 1948 in San Francisco, California, to poor parents who had immigrated to the United States from the Central

American country of El Salvador. Less than a year after Casals was born, her parents decided they could not care for her and her older sister Victoria. Casals's great-uncle and great-aunt, Manuel and Maria Casals, then took the young girls in and raised them as their own. When the children grew older, Manuel Casals took them to the public tennis courts of San Francisco and taught them how to play the game. He became the only coach Casals would ever have.

While still just a teenager, Casals began to rebel on the court. She hated the tradition of younger players competing only against each other on the junior circuit. Gutsy and determined right from the start, Casals wanted to work as hard as possible to better her game. For an added challenge, she often entered tournaments to play against girls who were two or three years older.

## Set Apart by Height and Class

Junior tennis was the first of several obstacles Casals faced during her tennis career. At five-feet-two-inches tall, she was one of the shortest players on the court. Another disadvantage for her was class distinction. Traditionally, tennis was a sport practiced in expensive country clubs by the white upper class. Casals's ethnic heritage and poor background immediately set her apart from most of the other players. "The other kids had nice tennis clothes, nice rackets, nice white shoes, and came in Cadillacs," Casals related to a reporter from *People*. "I felt stigmatized because we were poor."

Unfamiliarity with country club manners also made Casals feel different from the other players. Traditionally, audiences applauded

Rosemary Casals. *Reproduced by permission of Archive Photos, Inc.*

only politely during matches and players wore only white clothes on the court. Both of these practices seemed foolish to Casals. She believed in working hard to perfect her game and expected the crowd to show its appreciation for her extra efforts. In one of her first appearances at the tradition-filled courts at Wimbledon, England—site of the British tennis championships—she was nearly excluded from competition for not wearing white. Later in her career, she became known for her brightly colored outfits.

## Wins With Aggressive Style

The frustrations Casals endured due to her size and background affected her playing style. Despite her sweet-sounding nicknames,

"Rosie" and "Rosebud," she was known as a determined player who used any shot available to her to score a point—even one between her legs. "I wanted to *be* someone," Casals was quoted as saying in Alida M. Thacher's *Raising a Racket: Rosie Casals*. "I knew I was good, and winning tournaments—it's a kind of way of being accepted." By age sixteen Casals was the top junior and women's level player in northern California. At seventeen she was ranked eleventh in the country and was earning standing ovations for her aggressive playing style.

More experience on the national and international levels of play helped Casals improve her game. In 1966 she and Billie Jean King, her doubles partner, won the U.S. hard-court and indoor tournaments. That same year they reached the quarter-finals in the women's doubles at Wimbledon. In 1967 Casals and King took the doubles crown at Wimbledon and at the United States and South African championships. The two dominated women's doubles play for years, becoming one of the most successful duos in tennis history. (They are the only doubles team to have won U.S. titles on grass, clay, indoor, and hard surfaces.) Casals was also a successful individual player, ranking third among U.S. women during this period.

## Fights for Rights of Professional and Women Players

Despite her victories on the courts, Casals continued to fight tennis traditions on several fronts. Amateur tennis players (those who are unpaid) had always been favored over professionals (those who were paid). Because many tennis players came from non-wealthy back-grounds, they were forced to accept money in order to continue playing. This, in turn, made them professionals and prevented them from entering major tournaments that allowed only amateurs to play, such as Wimbledon. Fighting against this discrimination, Casals worked for an arrangement that allowed both amateur and professional tennis players to compete in the same tournaments.

Casals's next challenge was to overcome the vast difference in prize monies awarded to male and female players. Even though they worked just as hard and played just as often as men, women earned much smaller prizes. In 1970 Casals and other women threatened to boycott traditional tournaments if they were not paid higher prize money and not given more media attention. The ruling body of U.S. tennis, the United States Lawn Tennis Association (USLTA), refused to listen to their demands. In response, the women established their own tournament, the Virginia Slims Invitational. The attention generated by this successful tournament quickly brought about the formation of other women's tournaments and greater prize monies for women.

Casals soon became involved in another innovation: World Team Tennis (WTT). WTT involved tennis teams, each made up of two women and four men, from cities throughout the United States. Matches included both singles and doubles games. During her years with WTT, Casals played with the Detroit Loves and the Oakland Breakers and coached the Los Angeles Strings.

The strain of almost constantly playing took a physical toll on Casals. She underwent knee surgery in 1978 and was forced to change career directions. Since 1981 she has been president of Sportswomen, Inc., a California company she formed to promote a Women's Classic tour for older female players. She also began Midnight Productions television company and has broadened her own sporting activities to include golf. Casals continues to search for new chances to improve the game of tennis. In 1990, she again teamed with Billie Jean King to win the U.S. Open Seniors' women's doubles championship. She was inducted into the International Tennis Hall of Fame in 1996.

## For More Information

Jacobs, Linda, *Rosemary Casals: The Rebel Rosebud,* EMC Corporation, 1975.
*People,* May 31, 1982, p. 85.
Thacher, Alida M., *Raising a Racket: Rosie Casals,* Children's Press, 1976.

# Sylvia L. Castillo

Founder, National Network of Hispanic Women
Born September 2, 1951, Los Angeles, California

*"The more isolated we stay as women, the less opportunity we have."*

Sylvia L. Castillo is a clinical social worker who has led the call for greater communication and support among Hispanic professional women across the country. In the 1980s she cofounded the National Network of Hispanic Women and its English-language magazine, *Intercambios,* to inspire young Hispanic women to pursue higher education and challenging careers. For her work she has been honored by the United Nations Council on Women and the California State Assembly.

Castillo was born in 1951 in Los Angeles, California. Her grandparents had immigrated to the United States from Mexico. Her parents were Henry Castillo, a truck driver, and Lucille Miramontes Castillo, a pharmacy clerk who eventually worked her way up to become a medical representative for a home health care agency. Castillo's mother was an influential presence in her life, passing on the idea that opportunities arose through hard work.

## Interested in Women's Mental Health

Castillo attended an all-girls parochial school (a private school run by a church or other religious organization) where she was student body president in her senior year. After she graduated in 1969, she hoped for a career in psychology (the science of human behavior). She was especially interested in women's mental health issues. "If a mother feels good, then her daughters feel good," she related to Ann Malaspina in *Notable Hispanic American Women.* "If a mother has good self-esteem, her children will have good self-esteem."

Sylvia earned a bachelor's degree in social psychology from the University of California at Santa Barbara in 1973. Three years later she completed work on a master's degree in social welfare administration from the University of California at Berkeley. For nine years she worked as a career and mental health counselor and academic advisor at different colleges.

## Newsletter Reaches out to Professional Hispanic Women

During her years of research, Castillo began wondering what it took for a Hispanic student to succeed. To find an answer, she interviewed dozens of successful Hispanic women who worked in higher education. What she discovered, instead, was that they all shared a problem—they felt isolated. This led Castillo to focus on the difficulties faced by Hispanic professional women. To help these Hispanic women share their experiences and offer each other practical information on careers, Castillo started a newsletter, *Intercambios* ("Interchange").

Each issue of the newsletter had a theme, such as careers in science and technology or health and the Hispanic woman. *Intercambios* profiled successful Hispanic women and printed the latest studies done on Hispanics and their culture. Controversial topics such as affirmative action were also explored.

*Intercambios* proved popular and led to the development of the National Network of Hispanic Women (NNHW), an organization of Hispanic women dedicated to educational, career, and leadership development. Castillo worked without pay to recruit a board of advisors to help launch the group. She asked a wide range of Hispanic teachers, bankers, scientists, businesspeople, and community activists for support and advice. NNHW quickly began its work of drawing Hispanic women together to improve their professional opportunities. By the mid-1980s the Network had some five hundred members and *Intercambios* had sixty-five hundred subscribers.

## Sidelined by Illness

In 1986, because of illness, Castillo was forced to resign her leadership roles in the NNHW and at *Intercambios*. During that year she married Steven Castillo Long and moved to Maui, Hawaii. Before long she was actively involved with the Puerto Rican community and with women's groups there. All the while, she kept in touch with the NNHW.

In the early 1990s the NNHW faced trouble raising enough money to continue, and Castillo returned to Los Angeles. She felt it was necessary for Hispanic women to change in order to handle the economic uncertainties of the 1990s. "As we're affected by down-sizing, mergers, job loss, we're going to have to redefine success," Castillo observed, "otherwise it will be easy for the Hispanic woman to internalize that she's failed."

## For More Information

*Hispanic Business,* July 1988, pp. 25–26.
*Hispanic USA,* May 1985, pp. 14–15.
*Notable Hispanic American Women,* Gale, 1993, pp. 85–87.

# Lauro Cavazos

Former U.S. secretary of education, educator
Born January 4, 1927, King Ranch, Texas

*"Education is perhaps our most serious deficit."*

auro Cavazos's career in education has been full of ups and downs. He rose through the ranks as a teacher, principal, professor, and college president to become the U.S. secretary of education in 1988. This appointment made him the first Hispanic member of a president's cabinet (the group of advisors who are also heads of the federal government's executive departments). Shortly after his appointment by President Ronald Reagan, Cavazos told Robert Marquand of the *Christian Science Monitor,* "Education is perhaps our most serious deficit." His vision of the problems of education in America, however, did not match his actions on them. Highly criticized for being ineffective, Cavazos was forced to resign his position in December 1990.

Lauro Fred Cavazos, Jr., was born in 1927 at Texas's legendary King Ranch to the ranch's cattle foreman, Lauro Fred Cavazos, and his wife, Tomasa Quintanilla. Bilingualism (speaking two languages) was an issue early in Cavazos's life: while growing up he spoke Spanish to his mother and English to his father. Through the second grade he attended the ranch's two-room Hispanic elementary school. When his family left the ranch and moved to the nearby city of Kingsville, the young Cavazos attended a public school, where he became its first Hispanic student.

## Education Wins out Over Fishing

After high school, Cavazos enlisted in the U.S. Army. Upon his return home, he planned to become a commercial fisherman. His father, who had always stressed education, made it clear that college would come first. Cavazos turned out to have a talent for

Lauro Cavazos. *Reproduced by permission of AP/Wide World Photos.*

education. After first attending Texas A & I University, he transferred to Texas Tech University where he earned a bachelor's degree in zoology (the study of animals and animal life) in 1949 and a master's degree in cytology (the study of cells) in 1951. He continued his education at Iowa State University, earning a doctorate in physiology (the study of how living organisms function) in 1954.

That same year Cavazos married Peggy Ann Murdock, a registered nurse. They eventually went on to raise a family of ten children. Cavazos began teaching classes at the Medical College of Virginia and, later, at Tufts University School of Medicine in Massachusetts. In 1975 he was appointed dean of the medical school at Tufts. In 1980 he left Tufts to became the first Hispanic president of Texas Tech University.

## Texas-Sized Controversies

While at Texas Tech, Cavazos helped improve fundraising, increased the number of minority students, and enhanced the university's research programs. He headed a committee to study the reasons for dropouts in area schools. He also visited local schools regularly, helping to increase Hispanic enrollment through his personal appearances.

Despite these achievements, Cavazos also earned his share of negative publicity while at Texas Tech. In 1984 he attempted to limit the number of professors that were granted tenure (status granted to long-serving teachers that prevents them from being fired without a proper hearing). Outraged, the faculty at the college fought his proposal. The controversy came to the attention of then-President Ronald Reagan. Approving of Cavazos's stance, the president honored him with an Outstanding Leadership Award. The argument between the Texas Tech faculty and Cavazos continued for two years until he compromised with a modified policy regarding tenure.

Another controversy marked Cavazos's term as Texas Tech's president. The school's football team was charged with violating national college rules regarding the recruitment of high school players. As a result, the team was put on a one-year probation by the National Collegiate Athletic Association.

## Becomes First Hispanic in the Presidential Cabinet

In spite of the bad publicity, President Reagan nominated Cavazos for the prestigious post of U.S. secretary of education in late 1988. When fellow Republican George Bush succeeded Reagan as president the following January, he reappointed Cavazos to the post. Many people applauded the move. Cavazos had a reputation as someone who was willing to listen to and work things out with his opponents.

As the country's education leader, Cavazos promoted the same policies that concerned him in Texas. He worked to make education more easily available to the poor and to minorities. He supported bilingualism in schools. He spoke in favor of school "choice"—the idea that parents should be allowed to choose the best local school for their children. This was Cavazos's major theme, as he explained to Thomas H. Sharpe in *Hispanic:* "The key to the primary issues of education has to be the parent.... I feel that teachers and parents should be given more responsibility for decisions they make at the school level."

## Focuses Attention on Hispanic Education

Cavazos was sensitive to the educational needs of Hispanics in the United States. He brought this issue to the attention of the Congress and the president. In 1989 he helped persuade President Bush to sign an executive order creating the President's Council on Educational Excellence for Hispanic Americans. Concerned with the high drop-out rate of Hispanics, Cavazos traveled extensively to encourage students to stay in school.

Many education leaders, however, were not happy with Cavazos's tenure as secretary.

They believed he simply liked making appearances that did not do enough to solve more serious educational problems. Many shared the view of *Time*'s Susan Tifft, who wrote that Cavazos "comes across as a man with no clear-cut agenda who prefers speech-making to policymaking." Cavazos also came under fire when he was accused of breaking government travel rules by allowing his wife to accompany him on business trips and by scheduling expensive flights on an airline for which one of his children worked.

President Bush, who had made the 1988 campaign pledge to be the "education President," was also attacked for not bringing about quicker solutions to the problems in education. The controversy surrounding the secretary continued until December 1990, when Cavazos resigned his position at the Department of Education. He was replaced by Lamar Alexander, a former governor of Tennessee.

Cavazos took a position as a professor at Tufts University in 1991. He also worked with the Association of American Medical Colleges on the Health Professions Partnership Initiative to increase the participation of minorities in the health professions. In February 2002 a panel of five former secretaries of education, Cavazos among them, convened to address the current problems in education. Cavazos expressed his concern with the quality of teachers in today's schools, stressing the need for better teacher training, better resources available to schools, and more minority teachers.

## For More Information

*Christian Science Monitor,* October 21, 1988.

"Commencement Speaker Sets Trail of Firsts," *Walden Ponder,* Walden University, summer 2001. Available at http://www.waldenu.edu/ponder/0601/text.html (accessed June 21, 2002).

"Education Summit Draws 500," *Daily Dialogue,* Duke University, February 22, 2002.

*Hispanic,* May 1989, p. 32.

*Time,* May 29, 1989, p. 76; December 24, 1990, p. 64.

*U.S. News and World Report,* May 21, 1990, pp. 14–16.

# César Chávez

Labor leader, founder of the United Farm Workers
Born March 31, 1927, Yuma, Arizona
Died April 23, 1993, San Luis, Arizona

*For most of his life, César Chávez chose to live penniless and without property, devoting everything he had, including his frail health, to the UFW.*

R enowned labor leader César Estrada Chávez was raised in a poor family of migrant farm workers. He had little time for school or leisure activities in his youth, and he experienced racial prejudice because of his Mexican American heritage. Despite these obstacles, Chávez rose to become a gifted leader and organizer who inspired thousands of people to better their lives. During the 1960s he founded the United Farm Workers, an organization that led its members in the fight for improved working conditions.

Chávez was born to Librado Chávez and Juana Estrada in 1927 on the family's farm in Arizona. He was a child during the Great Depression, a period in the late 1920s and 1930s when the United States suffered from an extremely slow economy and widespread unemployment. During this time many people lost their jobs and homes, and some were forced to wander the country in search of work. In the American Southwest, farmers were further devastated by the effects of a severe drought on their crops. They could hardly sell what they could grow, and eventually they were not able to grow anything at all.

The Chávez family fell victim to the drought. With no money coming in, Librado Chávez could not pay the taxes on their land, and the farm was lost in 1937. The Chávezes were forced to become migrant farm workers, wandering throughout Arizona and California following the harvest of other landowners' crops. Since his family never stayed in one place for very long, Chávez attended over thirty different schools and achieved only a seventh grade education.

## The Plight of Migrant Farm Workers

Life for migrant farm workers was incredibly difficult. They toiled in the hot sun for hours picking beans, peas, grapes, beets, cucumbers, tomatoes, cotton, and other crops. Sometimes they were paid fifty cents for every basket they picked. Other times they were paid only twenty cents. At the end of the day, some farm owners subtracted money from the laborers' pay for any water they drank while in the fields. At night, farm workers slept in run-down shacks or in their cars if they could not afford a room. And, since many of the migrant laborers were of Mexican or Mexican American descent and knew little English, unscrupulous farm owners often took advantage of the language bar-

rier and swindled them out of the money they had rightfully earned for their work.

Throughout the 1930s and 1940s, Chávez and his family faced prejudice everywhere— in the schools, in the fields, in the towns. Restaurants refused to serve Mexican Americans and theaters allowed them to sit only in certain sections. In 1944, when he was seventeen years old, Chávez joined the U.S. Navy to fight in World War II. Even while fighting for his country, he experienced discrimination. After two years of service, Chávez returned to California to work on the farms. In 1948 he married Helen Fabela, settled down in a one-room shack in the town of Delano (where he picked grapes and cotton), and began to raise a family. Over the years, the couple had eight children.

The prejudices and poor working conditions facing migrant farm workers before the war did not change when it ended. Because of the experiences of his childhood, Chávez was greatly concerned with solving the problems of the nation's farm laborers. In 1952 he met Fred Ross, founder of the Community Service Organization (CSO), a group that sought better living conditions for migrant workers. Impressed with Ross and his ideas, Chavez began working for the CSO as a community organizer. Going from door to door at night, he helped some workers with their day-to-day problems, instructed others on how to become U.S. citizens, and encouraged all to register to vote. By 1958 Chávez had become director of the CSO in California and Arizona.

## Struggles to Form a Union

Chávez heard many complaints from migrant workers as he traveled between the

César Chávez. *Reproduced by permission of AP/Wide World Photos.*

two states. He was especially concerned about claims that landowners often used Mexican farmhands—who were illegally bused across the U.S. border—to work in the fields for the lowest of wages. This prevented migrant workers already living in the United States from getting jobs on American farms. Since the workers were not organized as a group, however, they could not effectively protest the situation. Over the next few years, Chávez tried to convince CSO leaders to develop a special farm labor union that would work to improve the rights of migrant workers. When the CSO refused to do so, Chávez resigned from the organization in 1962.

Chávez and his family then settled again in Delano, California, where he began to organize the National Farm Workers Association. For several years, Chávez worked eighteen-hour days for very little or no money at all. He drove to the fields and talked to the workers, urging them to join the National Farm Workers Association. The uneducated migrant workers were a difficult group to organize, and at times Chávez felt discouraged and defeated. But by continually pressing ahead with his efforts, he began to meet with success and the union slowly increased its ranks.

## Huelga!

In 1965 the National Farm Workers Association was catapulted to national attention. Migrant grape pickers in Delano, who worked under harsh conditions for a dollar an hour, went on strike. They wanted the association to back them, but Chávez thought the union was still too young and weak. National

Farm Workers Association members disagreed and voted to join the strike. Once the *Huelga* (Spanish for "strike") was on, Chávez worked tirelessly for the cause. The picket lines grew as more and more workers left the fields. Nonetheless, the landowners refused to give in to the workers' demands for better wages and working conditions. Some even threatened the workers with violence.

Chávez believed in nonviolent methods of social change. He had studied the life and teachings of Mohandas Gandhi, who had helped India gain its independence from England in 1947 through nonviolent means. Chávez responded to the landowners' threats by calling for a countrywide boycott of grapes. By discouraging the American people from buying grapes until working conditions for grape pickers improved, he attracted national attention to the plight of the farm workers. Many large labor unions supported Chávez and the strikers, including the AFL-CIO and the United Auto Workers. Robert F. Kennedy, an influential senator from New York, also gave his support to the cause.

In March 1966 the strikers marched 250 miles from Delano to the California capital of Sacramento to take their demands to state officials. By the time they arrived in Sacramento, one of several large grape companies had agreed to sign a contract with the workers. But the fight was not yet over. Soon the Teamsters Union, the powerful truckers' alliance led by Jimmy Hoffa, began to compete with the National Farm Workers Association for its members. To strengthen the association, Chávez merged his organization with part of the AFL-CIO, America's oldest and strongest group of unions. The new union was called the United Farm Workers Organizing Committee (UFWOC). After 1972 it was known simply as the United Farm Workers (UFW).

## Fast Gains National Attention

The struggle against the grape growers continued throughout the late 1960s. In February 1968, to draw more attention to the strike, Chávez began a twenty-five-day fast, during which he ate no solid food. People across the nation sympathized with Chávez's commitment to the cause and his nonviolent means to achieve justice. The grape boycott spread and the grape companies lost money. Finally, in June 1970, vineyard owners agreed to a contract with the UFWOC that gave workers health insurance benefits and a raise in pay.

But the celebration did not last long. Chávez quickly turned his attention to the problems of America's lettuce workers. The Teamsters Union had signed contracts with lettuce growers that hurt rather than helped migrant workers. Chávez again organized strikes and rallies, and he called for a national boycott of lettuce. The struggle against the growers and the Teamsters, which at times had turned violent, finally came to an end in 1975 when California governor Jerry Brown passed the Agricultural Labor Relations Act. This was the first bill of rights for farm workers ever enacted in the United States, and it allowed them to vote on which union would best represent their needs. In elections held in August of that year, the UFW clearly beat the Teamsters.

In the 1980s Chávez protested against grape growers who used pesticides (chemicals used to kill insects) on their crops. He believed the pesticides were dangerous not only to the farm workers who picked the grapes but also to the general public who consumed the grapes. He called for another boycott, and in 1988 he fasted for thirty-six days. Although his fast again gained national attention, the boycott did not take hold as earlier ones had. The fight for farm workers' rights continued.

"For most of his life," Peter Matthiessen wrote in the *New Yorker,* "César Estrada Chávez chose to live penniless and without property, devoting everything he had, including his frail health, to the UFW." While in Arizona on union business in April 1993, Chávez died in his sleep. Messages of sympathy came from leaders of churches and government, including Pope John Paul II and U.S. president Bill Clinton. More than thirty-thousand mourners formed a three-mile-long funeral procession to carry Chávez's body to its final resting place. A year after Chávez died, famed playwright and director **Luis Valdez** (see entry) began writing a script for a film biography about the late labor leader.

## "Si Se Puede": The Legacy

In August 1994, President Clinton presented Helen Chávez with the Medal of Freedom, America's highest civilian honor, for her late husband. In the presentation ceremony the president praised Chávez for having "faced formidable, often violent opposition with dignity and nonviolence.... César Chávez left our world better than he found it, and his legacy inspires us still.... The farm workers who labored in the fields and yearned for respect and self —sufficiency pinned their hopes on this remarkable man who, with faith and discipline, soft spoken humility and amazing inner strength, led a very courageous life."

On August 18, 2000, the governor of California signed legislation making March 31

César Chávez Day—a full, paid holiday for state employees—in honor of the labor leader. Texas had the holiday on a "volunteer" status, and Arizona was working on adding the holiday in the upcoming elections.

Chávez is remembered by his motto, "Si Se Puede!" (Yes We Can!), which is still found on the United Farm Workers banners as well as on projects to improve conditions for underprivileged or minority communities.

## For More Information

Cedeño, Maria E., *César Chávez,* Millbrook, 1993.

Chávez, César, Richard J. Jensen, and John C. Hammerback, *The Words of César Chávez,* College Station: Texas A & M University Press, 2002.

Franchere, Ruth, *César Chávez,* HarperCollins Children's Books, 1986.

Matthiesson, Peter, and Ilan Stavans, *Sal Si Puedes (Escape If You Can): César Chávez and the New American Revolution,* Berkeley: University of California Press, 2000.

*New Yorker,* May 7, 1993, p. 82.

Roberts, Maurice, *César Chávez and La Causa,* Children's Press, 1986.

Rodriguez, Consuelo, *César Chávez,* Chelsea House, 1991.

"The Story of César Chávez," United Farm Workers Web site. Available at http://www.ufw.org/cecstory.htm (accessed June 21, 2002).

# Evelyn Cisneros

Ballerina, educator
Born 1955, Long Beach, California

*"I'm proud to be able to represent my people, although I've never been through what many of them have."*

As principal dancer with the San Francisco Ballet Company, Evelyn Cisneros has achieved national fame. She has danced such classic ballets as *Swan Lake, Sleeping Beauty,* and *Romeo and Juliet,* as well as many modern works. Her grace, talent, and hard work have made her a role model for dancers and for other Hispanic Americans as well. In 1992 she was listed in *Hispanic Business*'s "100 Influentials."

Cisneros was born in 1955 in Long Beach, California. While growing up, she was extremely shy. To help her overcome her fears, her mother enrolled her in a ballet class. One of her teachers immediately recognized Cisneros's dancing abilities and encouraged her to study tap, jazz, and flamenco dancing as well.

Cisneros was an enthusiastic pupil who took her lessons very seriously. By the time she reached high school, she was making three-hour round-trip drives every day to her dance classes in Los Angeles. Despite the difficult and tiring schedule, she still managed to keep up with her school work.

## Enters the World of Ballet

Cisneros's years of training were rewarded in 1977 when, at the age of twenty-two, she was invited to join the San Francisco Ballet. She was such an outstanding dancer that the company's artistic director created a ballet for her just two years later. It was a tribute to Native Americans entitled *A Song for Dead Warriors.* The ballet and her performance in it were later honored by being broadcast on the *Great Performances—Dance in America* series on public television.

*A Song for Dead Warriors* is a personal favorite of the ballerina for whom it was created. "I feel very special about being able to make a statement about the Indian situation in the country," Cisneros told a reporter for *Nuestro.* "I dated an Indian guy for five years. I met his family and went to pow-wows with him. I saw how deep the sadness goes."

During the 1980s Cisneros's fame grew. She made headlines in newspapers and was featured on the covers of *Dance Magazine* twice and *Ballet News.* Despite this fact, she has been content to remain with the small, regional San Francisco Ballet rather than switch to a national company. She has cited the many opportunities presented to her over the years in San Francisco as the main reason.

## Performs for Her Community

In San Francisco, Cisneros has been able to reach out and help not only the area's artistic community but also its Hispanic community. In September 1991 she was selected as a godparent for the new School of Creative Arts for San Francisco State University. In 1988 she participated as a spokesperson in the Fifth Annual Chicano/Latino Youth Leadership Conference held at California State University in Hayward. "I'm proud to be able to represent my people," she told a reporter for *Nuestro,* "although I've never been through what many of them have." Cisneros has also lent her talents to many benefits, including the Children's Hospital National Telethon in June 1991.

Cisneros has made guest appearances in ballets around the world. In America she has danced behind the symphony orchestras

Evelyn Cisneros performing. *Reproduced by permission of Archive Photos, Inc.*

from Detroit and Los Angeles. In Tucson, Arizona, she danced at the Heard Museum to celebrate the opening of the new American Indian Wing of the museum. In 1982 she performed *Stravinsky Piano Pieces* in a live television broadcast from the White House. Cisneros has danced with the Royal New Zealand Ballet and has performed in Mexico City, Mexico, and in Madrid, Spain. In 1984 and again in 1988 she was asked by the famed Cuban ballerina Alicia Alonso to perform at the International Ballet Festival held in Havana, Cuba.

## Retirement From Dance

In 1999 Cisneros retired as a dancer. She then served as the host of public television station KQED's monthly current events program *Bay Windows* for a year. She also stepped into a new position as artistic consultant with the San Francisco Ballet, in which she hosted and created workshops, pre-performance talks, and community matinees. In November 2001 Cisneros was appointed ballet education coordinator of the San Francisco Ballet. In this capacity, she continued to host workshops and took on a variety of other projects to educate students and teachers about the ballet.

## For More Information

*Ballet News,* February 1985.

*Dance Magazine,* December 1983; August 1988; January 1992, pp. 100–03.

*Hispanic,* July 1989, p. 36+.

*Nuestro,* August 1985.

San Francisco Ballet Web site. Available at http://www.sfballet.org/community/staff/ (accessed June 21, 2002).

Simon, Charnan, *Evelyn Cisneros: Prima Ballerina,* Childrens Press, 1990.

# Henry G. Cisneros

Former secretary of U.S. Department of Housing and Urban Development, former mayor of San Antonio, Texas, businessperson
Born June 11, 1947, San Antonio, Texas

*"We can go four whole years wallowing in examples of absolute despair, but it's time to say to people: You can do it. We can do it. I have seen it done."*

Henry G. Cisneros was the first Hispanic mayor of a prominent American city and, beginning in 1992, served as a key member of President Bill Clinton's cabinet (a body of consultants on government policy). Well-educated, charismatic, and fluent in both Spanish and English, for years Cisneros was the first Hispanic spokesperson called by the media to comment on current social and political issues. While he was mayor of San Antonio, Texas, he helped forge closer ties between his city's Hispanic and Anglo (white) communities. As secretary of the U.S. Department of Housing and Urban Development (HUD), Cisneros tried to overcome the great economic problems in the country that have left millions of people of all ethnic backgrounds in a state of poverty.

Cisneros was one of five children born in a middle-class Hispanic section of San Antonio to Elvira and George Cisneros. His family has a long history in the American Southwest. His father's ancestors were given land grants in New Mexico by the Spanish almost three hundred years ago. His mother's father took part in the Mexican Revolution in the early 1900s, barely escaping to Texas with his life.

Cisneros's family was very close-knit and hardworking. No weekday television was allowed, except for the news or *National Geographic* specials. During the summers, the Cisneros children were given chores, reading assignments, and creative projects by their mother. Weekend trips to the museum, opera, and symphony were common.

## Changes Career Path From Flying to Politics

Cisneros attended San Antonio's Catholic schools and was such an excellent student he was allowed to skip the third grade. After he graduated from high school at the age of 16, he wanted to enter the U.S. Air Force Academy in Colorado to become a pilot. Because he was too young and too small to be accepted, he enrolled at Texas A&M University. He originally studied aeronautical engineering but switched to city management during his sophomore year. By the time he graduated from college in 1968, he had made up his mind that he would one day be mayor of San Antonio. The next year, he married Mary Alice Perez, whom he had met in high school.

In 1970, after earning a master's degree in urban planning from Texas A&M, Cisneros moved to Washington, D.C. to work at various government jobs. The following year, he became the youngest person ever to be named a White House fellow (a graduate student who serves as an assistant to a member of the president's cabinet or White House staff). He served under Eliot L. Richardson, then secretary of Health, Education, and Welfare. After his fellowship ended, Cisneros attended the John F. Kennedy School of Government at Harvard University, where he earned a master's degree in public administration. In 1975 he received a doctoral degree in that field from George Washington University in Washington, D.C. He then returned to his hometown.

That same year Cisneros won a seat on San Antonio's city council, becoming the youngest councilperson in the city's history. He subsequently won two more elections, serving on the council for a total of six years. Cisneros gained a reputation as a sharp politician. He worked to strengthen the city in many ways and gained federal funds to improve living conditions in San Antonio's Hispanic sections.

Henry G. Cisneros. *Reproduced by permission of AP/Wide World Photos.*

## Becomes Mayor of San Antonio

In 1981 Cisneros ran for mayor of the city and won. San Antonio is the ninth-largest city in the United States, and Cisneros became the first Mexican American to head a major American city. He was well-liked by his constituency and was reelected to three additional two-year terms. His popularity did not rest with San Antonio's Hispanic community alone, but with all ethnic groups in the area. Instead of asking for federal funds to improve his city, he worked to attract high-tech companies to San Antonio to provide more jobs and a better economy for everyone.

The improvements Cisneros brought to San Antonio gained national attention. In

1984 Democratic presidential candidate Walter F. Mondale seriously considered Cisneros as his possible running mate. The following year, Cisneros was elected to a one-year term as president of the National League of Cities.

Citizens urged Cisneros to run for governor of Texas in 1990, but a family crisis forced him to change his goals. His son, John Paul, had been born in 1987 with a heart defect. At the time, doctors did not know if surgery could correct his problem. (He finally underwent successful surgery in late 1993). His son's health became his biggest priority, and Cisneros wished to stay close to home to spend as much time as possible with his family. He also turned down an appointment as a U.S. senator from Texas in 1992.

## A National Government Official

Cisneros could not, however, remain out of public service for long. Racial tensions exploded and riots erupted in Los Angeles in April 1992 following the emotionally charged trial of white police officers accused of beating African American motorist Rodney King. In response, Cisneros immediately flew to the city and tried to calm its angry residents. That same year he worked hard on Bill Clinton's Democratic presidential campaign. After Clinton was elected president, he asked Cisneros to join his administration as the secretary of Housing and Urban Development. Since directing HUD would still allow Cisneros time to spend with his family, he accepted.

From the beginning, however, Cisneros's job at HUD was not easy. For nearly ten years prior to his appointment, HUD had

been severely mismanaged. In addition, the 1980s saw a dramatic rise in the number of homeless people in the United States. Cisneros made the elimination of homelessness HUD's top priority. In addition to walking the streets of Washington, D.C.'s poorest neighborhoods at night—talking to homeless men, women, and children about their plight—he opened his agency's building on cold nights as a temporary shelter for people with no place else to go.

Cisneros remained frustrated that government often moves too slowly, that people continue to sleep in cardboard boxes in Washington, D.C. But within eighteen months of his appointment, his tactics actually began to make a noticeable difference. Old and dangerous housing projects were torn down in cities in Washington and across the nation, and tenants were moved to better housing in better neighborhoods. Cisneros remains optimistic about the future. "We can go four whole years wallowing in examples of absolute despair," he told Lori Montgomery of the *Detroit Free Press,* "but it's time to say to people: You can do it. We can do it. I have seen it done."

## Scandal Ends His HUD Career

In July 1994, Cisneros's former girlfriend, Linda Medlar, filed suit against him, claiming he had gone back on a promise to pay her $4,000 a month in support money. Cisneros's affair with Medlar was not news. He had publicly admitted to it in 1988 and acknowledged the problems it had caused in his marriage.

In late 1994 FBI agents who had conducted background interviews with Cisneros after he was nominated to be HUD secretary indicated that he had misled them about the payments to Medlar. It had not been a secret that he had agreed to support her. At issue was the amount of money he reportedly gave her. The FBI accusation led to a full Justice Department investigation.

In November 1996, as the investigation into the charges dragged on, Cisneros resigned from his post heading HUD and in January 1997 took a position as president and chief operating officer of Univisión, a huge television network with nineteen stations, thirty broadcast affiliates, and a presence on more than nine hundred cable systems. In December 1997, a grand jury charged Cisneros with eighteen counts of conspiracy, false statements, and obstruction of justice, all in regard to the payments he made to Medlar. In 1999 Cisneros pleaded guilty to a charge of lying to FBI investigators about the payments. He paid a $10,000 fine and was later pardoned by President Bill Clinton.

Cisneros successfully led Univisión from January 1997 to August 2000. He left that position to found and become chairman and chief executive officer of American City Vista, a joint venture with KB Homes, southern California's largest home builder. Going back to his roots in urban planning, he formed a company dedicated to building large-scale communities in city areas where there hadn't been any real development in recent years. These "villages within cities," as his company called them, provided new residential options for buyers of various backgrounds and incomes. In the spring of 2001 American City Vista opened its first subdivision, the largest development to be constructed in the San Fernando valley of southern California in many years. In order to plan the communities, Cisneros held town hall meetings with residents and included local employers and school districts in planning discussions.

At around the same time that he founded American City Vista, Cisneros teamed up with the longtime president of the National Council of La Raza, Raul Yzaguirre, to create the New American Alliance, a nonprofit organization that seeks to raise charitable funds from the growing population of wealthy Hispanics and use the funds on worthy Hispanic causes. Within its first two years the New American Alliance had raised over $1 million, most of which provided scholarships for young Hispanic students seeking business degrees.

## For More Information

"Cisneros Says New Venture Gives Him Freedom to Perform True Public Service," *Politico: The Magazine for Latino Politics and Culture,* August 25, 2000. Available at http://www.politicomagazine. com/hcisnerosqa082500.html (accessed June 21, 2002).

*Detroit Free Press,* August 3, 1994, pp. 1A, 7A.

Diehl, Kemper, and Jan Jarboe, *Cisneros: Portrait of a New American,* Corona, 1985.

Gillies, John, *Señor Alcalde: A Biography of Henry Cisneros,* Dillon, 1988.

Martinez, Elizabeth Coonrod, *Henry Cisneros: Mexican-American Leader,* Millbrook, 1993.

"Newsmaker: Henry Cisneros: Interview with Charlayne Hunter-Gault," Online Newshour, PBS Online, August 26, 1996. Available at http://www. pbs.org/newshour/bb/election/august96/cisneros_ 8-26.html (accessed June 21, 2002).

*U.S. News & World Report,* February 21, 1994, pp. 30–31.

# Sandra Cisneros

Poet, author
Born 1954, Chicago, Illinois

*"It was not until this moment when I separated myself, when I considered myself truly distinct, that my writing acquired a voice."*

In her poetry and stories, Mexican American author Sandra Cisneros writes about Mexican and Mexican American women who find strength to rise above the poor conditions of their lives. These types of characters have not been presented so clearly in writing before. Cisneros is determined to introduce them to American readers, and so far her efforts have been successful. A reviewer for the *Washington Post Book World* described Cisneros as "a writer of power and eloquence and great lyrical beauty."

Cisneros's ability to write about these strong characters comes from her childhood experiences. Born in Chicago, Illinois, in 1954, she grew up in poverty. As the only girl in a family of seven children, Cisneros spent a lot of time by herself. Because her family moved often, she was not able to form lasting friendships. "The moving back and forth, the new school, were very upsetting to me as a child," she explained to Jim Sagel in *Publishers Weekly*. "They caused me to be very introverted and shy. I do not remember making friends easily." Instead, Cisneros became a quiet, careful observer of the people and events around her, and recorded her feelings through secret writings at home.

Because she was too shy to volunteer or speak up in class, Cisneros often received poor grades while attending Catholic schools in Chicago. Her Mexican American mother and her Mexican father, however, both knew the importance of education. Her mother made sure all the children in the family had library cards, and her father made sure they all studied so they wouldn't have to work as hard for a living as he did. "My father's hands are thick and yellow," Cisneros wrote in *Glamour* magazine, "stubbed by a history of hammer and nails and twine and coils and springs. 'Use this' my father said, tapping his head, 'not this' showing us those hands."

## Shyness Masks Her Talent

Although Cisneros learned to study hard, she was still too shy to share her creative writings at school. She felt many of her early teachers were not interested in her experiences. Finally, in the tenth grade, Cisneros was encouraged by one of her teachers to read her works to the class. She was also encouraged to work on the school's literary magazine, and eventually became its editor.

After high school, Cisneros attended Loyola University in Chicago to study English. Her father thought she might find a good husband if she went to college. What Cisneros discovered instead was the desire to be a writer. After graduating from college, encouraged by another teacher who recognized her writing talent, Cisneros enrolled in the poetry section of the Iowa Writer's Workshop, a highly respected graduate school for aspiring writers.

Cisneros's old fears about sharing her writings with others soon came back. Many of Cisneros's classmates had come from more privileged backgrounds than she had, and she felt she could not compete with them. As she explained in an interview in *Authors and Artists for Young Adults,* "It didn't take me long to learn—after a few days of being there—that nobody cared to hear what I had to say and no one listened to me even when I did speak. I became very frightened and terrified that first year."

## Realizes the Importance of Her Heritage

She soon realized, however, that her experiences as a Mexican American and as a woman were very different, but just as important as anything her classmates wrote about. "It was not until this moment when I separated myself, when I considered myself truly distinct, that my writing acquired a voice," she explained to Sagel. Out of this insight came her first book, *The House on Mango Street.*

Published in 1984, the book is composed of a series of connected short passages or stories told by Esperanza Cordero, a Mexican American girl growing up in a Chicago barrio (Spanish-speaking neighborhood). Much like Cisneros when she was young, Esperanza wants to leave her poor neighborhood to seek a better life for herself. As Esperanza tells her stories, readers come to understand how people live in the barrio. Although Esperanza gains enough strength by the end of the book to leave her house on Mango Street, she is reminded by one of the other characters that she must never forget who she is and where she came from: "You will always be Esperanza. You will always

Sandra Cisneros. *Reproduced by permission of AP/Wide World Photos.*

be Mango Street. You can't erase what you know. You can't forget who you are."

*The House on Mango Street* was a successful book. Many schools, from junior high schools through colleges, have used it in their classes. The book's success, however, didn't provide an easy life for Cisneros. After graduating from Iowa with a masters degree in creative writing, she worked as a part-time teacher. In 1986 she moved to Texas after receiving a fellowship (a financial award) to help her finish writing *My Wicked, Wicked Ways,* a book of poetry. After this volume was published in 1987, Cisneros's money ran out, and she could not find a job. She wanted to stay in Texas and even tried to start a private writing program. She passed out fliers in supermarkets to get interested people to join, but the program failed. Sad and broke, Cisneros had to leave Texas to take a teaching job at California State University in Chico, California.

## Signs Major Publishing Contract

While in California, Cisneros received another grant of money to help her write a book of fiction. This new award from the National Endowment for the Arts revitalized Cisneros and inspired her to write *Women Hollering Creek and Other Stories*. Random House offered to publish the book in 1991, making Cisneros the first Chicana (Mexican American woman) to receive a major publishing contract for a work about Chicanas. The book, a series of short stories about strong Mexican American women living along the Texas-Mexico border, received praise from critics across the nation.

In 1994 another large publishing company issued *Loose Woman,* Cisneros's second collection of poetry. The main theme behind many of the poems in the book was love and its powerful forms. A reviewer for *Publishers Weekly* wrote that the book again presents "a powerful, fiercely independent woman of Mexican heritage, though this time the innocence has long been lost. "And at the beginning of 1995, Random House issued a Spanish-language translation of *The House on Mango Street, La casa en Mango Street.* In addition, Cisneros published a children's picture book in 1994, *Hairs/Pelitos,* which presents diversity, individuality, and family bonds to readers ages four to eight. Her 1997 collection of folk stories, *El arroyo de la llorona y otros cuentos,* (The Creek of the Weeping Woman and Other Stories) received very good reviews. Her 2002 book, *Caramelo,* is the story of Mexican migrants who move back and forth between Chicago and Mexico, as told by a very wise little girl.

The writer was making news headlines in Texas for two years—not about her literary works, but over the color of her house. Cisneros lives in a historic district of San Antonio, so when she painted her house a very brilliant purple in 1997, the city board objected. For two years the dispute went on, until the paint faded to a shade of lavender, which the city deemed "historically appropriate."

Cisneros feels it is important for people of all races in America to understand the lives of Mexican Americans, especially Mexican American women. And she feels it is her duty to write about them. As she stated in *Authors and Artists for Young Adults,* "I feel very honored to give them a form in my writings and to be able to have this material to write about is a blessing."

## For More Information

*Authors and Artists for Young Adults,* Volume 9, Gale, 1992.

Ganz, Robin, "Sandra Cisneros: Border Crossings and Beyond," *Melus,* spring 1994, p. 11.

*Glamour,* November 1990, pp. 256–57.

*Publishers Weekly,* March 29, 1991, pp. 74–75; April 25, 1994, p. 61–62.

"Sandra Cisneros," Voices From the Gap: Women Writers of Color. Available at http://voices.cla. umn.edu/authors/SandraCisneros.html (accessed June 21, 2002).

*Washington Post Book World,* June 9, 1991, p. 3.

# Roberto Clemente

Professional baseball player, philanthropist
Born August 18, 1934, Carolina, Puerto Rico
Died December 31, 1972, near San Juan, Puerto
Rico

*"I like people that suffer because these people have a different approach to life from the people that have everything and don't know what suffering is."*

Roberto Clemente. *Reproduced by permission of Transcendental Graphics.*

R oberto Clemente was a baseball star well-loved by Puerto Ricans. As a right-fielder for the Pittsburgh Pirates from 1955 to 1972, he won four National League batting titles, twelve Golden Glove awards, and was named the National League's Most Valuable Player in 1966. He was a proud man who demanded more respect for Hispanic players. His lifelong dream was to build a youth sports facility in Puerto Rico for poor children. In 1972, while flying relief supplies to earthquake victims in Nicaragua, his plane went down off the coast of Puerto Rico.

Clemente was born in 1934 in Puerto Rico, the youngest of the seven children of Melchor and Luisa Clemente. His father was a foreman on a sugarcane plantation, and his mother ran a grocery store for plantation workers. The young Clemente was raised to respect honesty, generosity, and his elders. "When I was a boy," he was quoted in *Smithsonian,* "I realized what lovely persons my father and mother were. I learned the right way to live. I never heard any hate in my house. Not for anybody."

Another lesson Clemente learned from his parents was the value of working hard. When he was nine years old, he wanted to buy a bicycle. In order to earn money, he began delivering milk to his neighbors. He earned a penny a day. After three years, he had saved enough money for the bicycle. The experience of having to work hard for what he wanted stayed with Clemente all his life. "I am from the poor people," he said. "I represent the poor people. I like workers. I like people that suffer because these people have a different approach to life from the people that have everything and don't know what suffering is."

## Signs First Baseball Contract

Clemente excelled at baseball as a child. He worked constantly and intensely at perfecting his skills. Even though his father told him he was too old to keep playing ball, he played amateur softball on the sandlots of his hometown of Carolina until he was 18 years old. At that time he was spotted by a scout from the professional hardball team in the Puerto Rican town of Santurce. He signed with the club for $40 per month, plus a $500 bonus.

Clemente was a star with the Santurce team for two seasons before he caught the attention of major league scouts. In 1954 the Los Angeles Dodgers signed him up and sent him to their minor league team in Montreal. At the time, a player who was not kept on a major league team's roster could be picked up by another team. When Clemente was not called up to the Dodgers by the end of the season, the Pittsburgh Pirates drafted him. He started the 1955 season as the Pirates' official right fielder.

Clemente's career began without great fanfare as he slowly learned the routine in the big leagues. One major obstacle for him was the English language. "He found it difficult to make his feelings clear," said Joe L. Brown, who worked for the Pirates at the time. "He was an emotional person, a very sensitive person, and he was not understood."

## Begins Compiling Superstar Stats

In 1960, however, Clemente began to make his presence known on the field. He hit .314 with 16 home runs and 94 runs batted in.

He helped lead the Pirates to win both the National League pennant and the World Series.

Over the next twelve seasons, Clemente was a dominant force in professional baseball. He was famous for his incredible fielding skills, swift running, and powerful throwing. He thrilled fans by throwing out runners from remote spots in the outfield. Many times he threw strikes to home plate from more than 400 feet in the outfield. He was fearless in pursuit of the ball, diving into the grass and crashing into the wall.

Clemente's batting statistics were impressive as well. He trained to become a "spray hitter," scattering line-drive doubles and triples into the gaps between fielders. He was only the eleventh player in major league history to collect 3,000 hits in a career. His lifetime batting average was .317. For his heroics in the field and at the plate he was elected to the National League All Star team twelve times. After leading the Pirates to victory in the 1971 World Series, he was honored with the series's outstanding player award.

## Misunderstood by Media

In spite of his achievements, Clemente had disappointments during his career. He suffered from numerous injuries and ailments, including back pain, stomach disorders, and tension headaches. Even after diligent study, he never completely mastered English. American sports writers had trouble understanding him, and his quotes in newspapers often contained grammar errors that he found embarrassing and insulting. Because of the language barrier, he believed he and other Hispanic players did not receive the recognition or respect they deserved.

Clemente always promoted Hispanic players and Hispanic pride. He took young Hispanic players under his wing, helping them with their game. His large home in Puerto Rico, where he lived with his wife and three children, often was open to admiring fans. During the off-season he traveled around the island giving baseball clinics for children. "I go out to different towns, different neighborhoods," he was quoted in *Smithsonian.* "I get kids together and talk about the importance of sports, the importance of being a good citizen, the importance of respecting their mother and father."

## Dreams Cut Short

Clemente's dream was to build a sports complex to give Puerto Rican children opportunities to learn and to grow. At the end of the 1972 baseball season, he contemplated retiring from baseball to work full-time to develop his hometown sports camp for kids. Late that year, he was distracted from his decision by a massive earthquake that caused widespread disaster in Nicaragua. After organizing relief efforts from Puerto Rico, he went along to deliver the supplies in person. On December 31, 1972, Clemente died in the crash of a cargo plane that was carrying food to Nicaragua.

The world mourned the death of the great athlete and humanitarian. The Baseball Hall of Fame waived its five-year waiting period after a player's retirement and immediately elected Clemente to membership. His family continues to work on his Sports City in Carolina, Puerto Rico. The 304-acre complex provides children with baseball, basketball, swimming, and track training. Future plans include programs in drama, music, dance, and folklore.

## For More Information

Gilbert, Thomas W., *Roberto Clemente,* Chelsea House, 1991.

O'Connor, Jim, *The Story of Roberto Clemente, All-Star Hero,* Dell, 1991.

*Smithsonian,* September 1993, pp. 136+.

Walker, Paul Robert, *Pride of Puerto Rico: The Life of Roberto Clemente,* Harcourt, Brace, Jovanovich, 1988.

# Francisco Vásquez de Coronado

Spanish explorer
Born c. 1510, Salamanca, Spain
Died September 22, 1554, Mexico City, Mexico

*"Coronado pushed the boundaries of New Spain far to the north, proving there were unimagined amounts of land to develop in America."*

Francisco Vásquez de Coronado was a fearless Spanish explorer who continued Spain's relentless quest for gold into unmapped regions of the New World. He led the first European expeditions into the present-day southwestern United States. His men were the first Europeans to view the geographical wonders of the area, including the magnificent stone walls of the Grand Canyon.

Coronado was born around 1510, the second son of a noble Spanish family. Only the oldest son could inherit the family wealth, so Coronado chose to seek his fortune in the New World. In 1535 he arrived in Mexico (called New Spain by the Spanish) to work for Antonio de Mendoza, the first viceroy (the king's representative) of the region. Shortly afterward, Coronado married Beatriz de Estrada, a wealthy heiress. He successfully completed his first assignment—subduing a revolt by workers in the royal mines. For his deed, he was appointed governor of New Galicia, an area on the west coast of Mexico, in 1538.

The Spanish were still hoping to find gold in the vast, unknown territories to the north. No Europeans had ever ventured into these lands. Another explorer, **Alvar Núñez Cabeza de Vaca** (see entry), had reported hearing of seven great cities in a northern region called Cibola. A Franciscan friar named Fray Marcos de Niza was sent to verify reports of the supposed riches in this area. Upon his return, he claimed to have seen Cibola from a distance. Coronado and Mendoza were convinced they should send an expedition to find and conquer Cibola. Fray Marcos would be their guide.

## Searches for Cities of Gold

In 1540 Coronado led a force of about three hundred Spaniards and one thousand Native Americans northward. They took along herds of cattle, sheep, goats, and swine for food. They marched slowly to Culiacán, the northernmost European settlement in New Spain. The slow pace frustrated Coronado. Once the group reached Culiacán, he chose one hundred men as an advance army and led them ahead. He sent another smaller group to scout westward, and they traveled into present-day California.

Coronado led his group into present-day Colorado, then into present-day New Mexico. He came upon the town Fray Marcos identified as Cibola and quickly captured it. Once there, however, Coronado realized it was no city of riches, only a poor village. He sent Fray Marcos back to Mexico in disgrace.

## Amazing Geographical Discoveries

Thinking there might be other riches ahead, Coronado wanted to explore further. He also dreaded returning to Mexico as a failure. Coronado sent several small expeditions in different directions looking for gold. One group found ancient Hopi villages in present-day northern Arizona. Another arrived, amazed, at the edge of the Grand Canyon. The group tried to climb down its cliffs to the Colorado River. After three days, the Spaniards gave up and turned back.

A third party explored along the Rio Grande River and found an area the Pueblo called Tiguex, near present-day Albuquerque, New Mexico. Coronado joined them at Tiguex and settled down for the winter. Troubles soon developed between the Europeans and Native Americans because the Spanish demanded supplies and Pueblo women. The Pueblo revolted and Coronado spent the winter battling them. In one notorious incident, Coronado ordered two hundred Pueblo prisoners to be burned at the stake.

Francisco Vásquez de Coronado. *Reproduced by permission of Corbis Corporation (Bellevue).*

In the spring of 1541, Coronado set out once more in search of gold. A captured Pawnee guide, whom the Spanish had named "the Turk," had told the Spanish of a land of riches to the east, called "Quivira." Searching for Quivira, Coronado and his men crossed the Pecos River of New Mexico into the Texas panhandle, then moved north into the Great Plains. Local Native Americans often fled as the Spanish approached. They were fearful of the Spanish explorers' horses, animals that were new to the Americas. As the explorers moved through the plains, they were surprised to encounter large herds of animals they called "humpback oxen"— the American bison. Coronado sent his main force back to Tiguex with large supplies of meat from these animals.

## Disappointment and a Long Trip Home

For five weeks, Coronado wandered westward in Texas. He then turned north to explore present-day Oklahoma and Kansas, crossing the Canadian and Arkansas Rivers along the way. When he finally arrived at Quivira, he found neither gold nor silver—only poor Native American camps. Coronado was crushed by disappointment at not finding a city of treasures. He left three missionaries to convert the native people of Quivira to Christianity. He then turned back toward Tiguex. After reaching the area, he was seriously injured in a riding accident. Coronado stayed at Tiguex to recover and to wait out the winter.

Coronado's difficult journey home to Mexico took about six months. Discouraged Spanish soldiers deserted at every opportunity. When Coronado arrived in Mexico City in June 1542, he was accompanied by less than one hundred men. Viceroy Mendoza was angered by what he considered a wasted expedition, but allowed Coronado to continue as governor of New Galicia for a few more years. In 1545 the explorer was tried for cruelty toward Native Americans during his travels. Although cleared of all charges, Coronado lost his governorship. He retired to Mexico City where he died in 1554.

Coronado and his men considered their expedition a failure. However, the journals they kept, along with the reports they sent back to Mexico and Spain, were of great value in the future. Coronado pushed the boundaries of New Spain far to the north, proving there were unimagined amounts of land to develop in America. The maps he had made aided other explorers in their quests to go farther.

## For More Information

*Hispanic,* October 1990, p. 38.

Jensen, Malcolm C., *Francisco Coronado,* Watts, 1974.

Syme, Ronald, *Francisco Coronado and the Seven Cities of Gold,* Morrow, 1965.

Udall, Stewart L., *To the Inland Empire: Coronado and Our Spanish Legacy,* Doubleday, 1987.

Zadra, Dan, *Coronado: Explorer of the Southwest (1510–1554),* Creative Education, 1988.

# Benicio Del Toro

Actor
Born February 19, 1967, San German, Puerto Rico

*"Logically, I feel a great responsibility for being a Latino actor working in Hollywood.... The only thing that I ask is not to be solely seen as a Latino actor. The fact that my name is Benicio Del Toro should not imply that I must be thought of only as a Hispanic actor."*

**W**hen Benicio Del Toro won the Academy Award in 2001 for best supporting actor for his role in *Traffic,* he chose the occasion to publicly thank his father "for showing me the power of caring," his mother "for teaching me never to give up," his brother "for looking out for me," and his godmother "for giving me a million and one reasons to believe."

Family had always been important to the Puerto Rico-born actor, although they were not always supportive of his career choice, thinking instead that he should become a lawyer. Del Toro's mother died of hepatitis when Del Toro was nine years old. Afterward, Del Toro's godmother, Sarah Torres, stepped in to help raise Del Toro and his brother, Gustavo, who is two years older. Gustavo eventually became a doctor and settled in New York City.

## A High Spirited Childhood

A movie fan from an early age, Del Toro especially enjoyed monster movies. It seems he was a bit of a monster himself, quickly establishing a reputation as a troublemaker at the Catholic school he attended as a youngster, the Academy of Our Lady of Perpetual Help. Del Toro's father eventually remarried, and since Del Toro and his stepmother did not get along, at the age of thirteen he was allowed to go to the United States to attend boarding school at Mercersburg Academy in Pennsylvania. Basketball was Del Toro's passion during this time. "In the beginning," he later told the *Miami Herald,* "I had communication problems due to the language barrier. But through sports I could communicate perfectly."

Del Toro thrived in the United States, making friends, rediscovering an enthusiasm for painting, and becoming passionate about rock 'n' roll. But he still caused trouble, once terrorizing a family so badly that they moved out of their house. He was not proud of this later in life.

## The Acting Bug Bites

Since both of his parents and his godmother were lawyers, it was expected the Del Toro would enter the family profession. But the acting bug bit him in his freshman year at the University of California at San Diego. After auditioning for and getting a part in a play to be produced on campus, he

Benicio Del Toro. *Reproduced by permission of AP/Wide World Photos.*

discovered that he would not be allowed to perform unless he declared a theater major. "That's how I changed my major without telling anybody," he told the *Miami Herald.* "Up until that moment I had been a business major, something in which I would have failed."

Del Toro eventually moved to New York City to study at the Circle in the Square Theater School, in spite of the continuing opposition of his family, who saw no future in acting for him. After studying in New York, Del Toro moved to Los Angeles to join his brother, who was then living there. Del Toro won a scholarship to study at the prestigious Stella Adler Conservatory, where he remained for more than three years. While there, he saved money by living with his brother and by helping the acting school construct a new theater.

Two years into his new life as an Angeleno (someone from Los Angeles), Del Toro was cast as a day player on the TV show *Miami Vice.* "That motivated me," Del Toro told the *Miami Herald,* "but I did not get any other parts for quite some time." Del Toro's first film role was that of a circus freak in 1988's *Big Top Pee-wee* featuring Paul Reubens as Pee-wee Herman. The next year, he landed a small part in the James Bond film *License to Kill.* The actor Sean Penn noticed Del Toro in his role as a drug dealer in *Drug Wars: The Camarena Story,* a television miniseries that aired in 1990. Penn was then casting for his film directing debut, *The Indian Runner* and cast Del Toro in the role of an unbalanced Native American unjustly accused of murder. Penn later remembered Del Toro in the *New York Times* as "an acting animal, this guy who comes out of the forest to make movies better. He's fearless, and he has a very distinctive imagination for character. He's one of the few actors who can make flamboyant choices that never just say, 'Look at me.' He's not showy. If he stands out, it's only because the rest of the people haven't risen as high on the bar."

## The First Taste of Fame

But stand out he did, in his role as a petty criminal in *The Usual Suspects* in 1995. Small though the part was, it was the one that gave him his first taste of fame. He took a risk for this role, copping a barely intelligible mumble calculated to either endear him to his audience, or irritate them. The role nabbed him the Independent Spirit Award

for best supporting actor in 1996, and *The Usual Suspects* marked a major turning point in his career. The success of that movie boosted Del Toro's career to the next level, and it directly led to his being cast in four movies in rapid succession, all in a single year. But, he told the *Miami Herald,* "That was too much, since I like to have sufficient time to concentrate on each role I play." He then learned to take time off when he needed it, even to turn down roles he liked.

Del Toro won the Independent Spirit Award again in 1997 for his part in *Basquiat* as the sidekick of the title character. In 1998, Del Toro won critical acclaim in *Fear and Loathing in Las Vegas* as Dr. Gonzo, the main character's sidekick, played by Johnny Depp. (He gained forty-five pounds in nine weeks to look the part of his character.) But it was the movie *Traffic,* released in 2000, that propelled Del Toro into major fame, and gave him his first Academy Award nomination. He won the award in 2001, for best actor in a supporting role. It also marked a new level of maturity for the actor. "With my character in *Traffic,*" he told the *New York Times,* "I knew where I was coming from, what I wanted and where I was going. When you know that, man, it's not easier to play, but it's clear. All you got to do is just be." One of many details he worked on was his accent. He did not want his character of the Mexican cop to sound like a Puerto Rican.

## Traffic

In *Traffic,* Del Toro was in the best possible position to use his talents to the fullest, since the writers of the film wrote Del Toro's part specifically for him. "I've always found him magnetic on screen," *Traffic* director Steven Soderbergh told the *New York Times,* "and we really didn't consider anyone else. The rhythm of his character is slowed down, and what I like best is his attention to detail. The design of the story demands that he play what he's thinking very close to the vest, because the stakes are so high. It's a towering performance."

When he accepted the Oscar for his role in *Traffic,* Del Toro dedicated his Academy Award to the people of the border towns of Nogales, Arizona, and Nogales, Sonora, two of the film's locations. He told the press, "The people were so humble, so beautiful. It made it easier. It's my way of giving something back."

In 2001 *Hispanic Magazine* named Del Toro Hispanic of the Year. In a piece he wrote for *El Nuevo Herald* and posted on his Web site, Del Toro, who does not talk with the media very often, candidly related his thoughts about being a Hispanic actor. "Logically, I feel a great responsibility for being a Latino actor working in Hollywood. For now, though, I am only an actor and cannot feel any type of responsibility for the roles I play. My only responsibility is to do my job well. But if I were a director or a movie producer, my responsibilities would be greater.... The only thing that I ask is not to be solely seen as a Latino actor. The fact that my name is Benicio Del Toro should not imply that I must be thought of only as a Hispanic actor. Logically, I don't have a problem with playing Latino characters, and would play them more frequently if they were better written."

Del Toro appeared in *The Pledge* with Jack Nicholson and the comedy *Snatch* (in which he adopts a Yiddish accent) with Brad Pitt, both 2001 releases, and the 2002 documentary filmed in Puerto Rico *Julia: Toda en mi* (Julia, All in Me). He plays a killer who makes a sport of hunting deer hunters in *The Hunter* (2002) with Tommy Lee Jones playing the FBI agent tracking him down. During the intense shooting of the film, Del Toro broke his wrist. In 2003 he can be seen in *The Assumption of the Virgin,* playing fifteenth-century Italian artist Fra Filippo Lippi, a monk who falls in love with a nun who modeled for many of his religious paintings. He also plays the title role in *Che Guevera: A Revolutionary Life* as well as in the part of Benny in *Bring Me the Head of Alfredo Garcia,* both 2003 releases.

In spite of his obvious success as an actor, Del Toro's family still has a hard time accepting his career choice. "To this day," he told the *New York Times,* speaking of his father, "I don't think he's really convinced about it. My dad is a lawyer, and I'm very close to my godmother, who's a lawyer too. They're always going 'You get up at 11 A.M. every day. If you got up at 8 A.M. and went to school, you could study law, little by little. You could be a great lawyer.'"

The humble actor is determined not to let his fame go to his head. "I prefer not to pay much attention to fame," he told the *Miami Herald.* If you think too much about your fame, he said, "you can enter a vicious circle and think that you really are a superhero. It is at that moment that you are in great trouble."

## For More Information

"Benicio Del Toro," Internet Movie Database. Available at http://us.imdb.com/NewsFeatures/deltoro (accessed June 21, 2002).

"Benicio Del Toro Traffics in Acclaim," CNN.com, March 8, 2001. Available at http://www.cnn.com/2001/SHOWBIZ/Movies/03/08/benicio.del.toro/ (accessed June 21, 2002).

Mejías-Rentas, Antonio, "Bullish Benicio," *Hispanic Magazine,* December 2001.

*New York Times,* January 21, 2001.

"This Is My Life," Benicio Del Toro Zone. Available online at http://www.beniciodeltoro.com/media/1997/miami2.htm (accessed June 21, 2002).

# Cameron Diaz

Actress
Born August 30, 1972 in San Diego, California

*"I have a plan, and this business definitely has a plan for you. You have to have an idea of what you want for yourself, or else you just end up getting used up in their plan. It's been important for me to be happy, enjoy the work that I'm doing, and work with people that I feel I'm going to get something out of."*

A self-described "heavy metal chick," Cameron Diaz began modeling as a teenager thanks to a chance meeting with a photographer. Her acting career began by chance as well, after she answered a casting call for models. Starring in films such as *She's the One* and *There's Something About Mary,* she soon found her niche in independent films that feature ensemble (group) casts. While she professes not to be interested in box-office potential, or how much a money a movie can make, Diaz looks carefully at roles to determine whether they fit into her career plan. The actress explained her career philosophy to *Premiere* contributor Robert Hofler: "I just look for roles that will be fun for me."

## A Southern California Girl

Cameron Diaz was born in San Diego, California, on August 30, 1972. The second child of Emilio and Billie Diaz, she has an older sister, Chimene. Blonde-haired and blue-eyed, Diaz has a diverse cultural background: her father, a foreman for a large oil company, is a second-generation Cuban American, while her mother, an import-export agent, is part English, part German, and part Native American. "I grew up with Cuban food and with the music," Diaz told an Internet Archive interviewer. "I grew up with the hospitality, passion and warmth of the Latin family." Although close to her older sister, she often fought with her sibling. "I adore and love her like nobody ever," she explained. "But we fought like crazy when we were kids. We were maniacal [crazed]—everybody in the neighborhood knew that when we started fighting, to step back. We were like two Tasmanian devils." In spite of the fighting, Chimene Diaz looked out for her younger sister. "I was a total terror to her, and she was patient with me," Diaz concluded. "She took care of me, looked out for me, was the perfect big sister."

Raised in a two-story stucco house in suburban Long Beach, California, Diaz liked to take care of animals and dreamed of becoming a zoologist. "I've always loved animals," she said. "When I was growing up I had two snakes. The bigger one was about six-and-a-half feet, and I raised mice for them to eat. I also had three dogs, three cats, and five birds."

A onetime cheerleader who hung out with the skateboarding crowd, Diaz developed a passion for heavy metal music by her early teens. A die-hard Van Halen fan by the age of thirteen, she attended concerts by Metallica, Ozzy Osbourne, Ratt, and other bands that performed at the Long Beach Arena. Somewhat of a tomboy, she wore the uniform of a heavy metal teen: blue jeans (with a comb in the pocket), flannel shirts, and feathered hair. As a teenager Diaz also started to hang out with a hard-partying nightlife crowd in Los Angeles. At one such Hollywood party, she met photographer Jeff Dunas, who expressed interest in helping her break into modeling. Dunas, she explained, had the ability to spot a diamond in the rough. "I looked hideous," she told Internet Archive. "I was wearing, like, a jump-suit with heels." It was not the first time Diaz had been approached by someone claiming to be a photographer. She recalled the parties where a "bunch of sleazy guys were coming up and saying, 'Hey, baby, wanna be a model? I'm a photographer.'" Dunas, however, gave her a business card, and turned out to be a professional fashion photographer who was genuinely interested in jump-starting her modeling career.

## A Model Teen

After signing a contract with the Elite Modeling Agency, the sixteen-year-old aspiring model told none of her friends, for fear that nothing would come of the agreement. Several months passed before she was

Cameron Diaz. *Reproduced by permission of Archive Photos, Inc.*

given an assignment, an "advertorial" for *Teen* magazine. Earning far less than supermodel wages, she took home $125 for the job. After graduating from Polytechnic High School in Long Beach, Diaz traveled to Japan to find modeling work. Returning to California, she worked as a model for catalogs. "I was successful in L.A. doing catalog," she told *Harper's Bazaar* reporter Chris Mundy. "Not because I was the prettiest girl. I had a good relationship with the people I was working with. That was it. They wanted to know that they'd have a good time and not be stuck with some prima-donna [vain] model."

Magazine and catalog work took Diaz to Europe as well. Although she earned as much as $2,000 a day, Diaz was never—

despite popular rumors—a teenage super-model. "I was a working model," she told *Premiere* contributor Robert Hofler. "I was doing junior ads for newspapers every single day of the week. I never got the work I wanted. I had to become an actress to get the cover of *Vogue*. I worked *twice* when I was in Paris, and I lived there for nine months. From the age of sixteen, I'd been working my ass off. That was my suffering. I was trying to get over that hump of trying to make something of myself."

A member of the heavy-metal skateboarding crowd in high school, Diaz typically wore jeans and flannel shirts After she began modeling, she traveled around the United States, to Japan, and throughout Europe to shoot commercials, magazine ads, and catalogs. Soon after venturing beyond the confines of southern California, she began to develop her own style. "Until I started traveling, I didn't know what my options were," she told Mundy. "I didn't want the [style] I used to have, which was the stoner girl, the metal chick. I had to learn to become girlie. Girlie's a recent thing."

## A Less Ordinary Life

When a Hollywood casting agent put out a call for models, Diaz auditioned for a role in the movie, even though she had never had a burning desire to become an actress. After surviving twelve call-back auditions for the part, she won the role of night-club singer Tina Carlyle in *The Mask,* a 1995 action-comedy starring Jim Carrey. (Although Anna Nicole Smith had been brought in to audition, Diaz won the part because the infamous actress had recently been offered

a part in the feature *Naked Gun 33 1/3*.) Suddenly thrust into the limelight, Diaz won the 1996 ShoWest Award for the "Female Star of Tomorrow."

Following her success in *The Mask,* Diaz hired a movie agent (Nick Styne, of the ICM agency) and a manager (Rick Yorn). Inexperienced in the movie industry, she pondered how best to avoid becoming yesterday's next big thing, a trap into which she'd witnessed too many young performers fall. The actress explained her reasoning to Hofler: "I don't have any experience. I don't want to go straight into leading roles. I have too much to learn."

Turning down parts in mega-budget mainstream films, she decided to take on small—yet deep— roles in low-budget independent films. First in line was *The Last Supper* (directed by Stacy Title), the story of a group of young liberals who decide to poison conservative foes. Although she was originally offered the pretty-girl part of Paulie, she opted to play the more gutsy role of Jude. Next came a string of roles in small movies, including *She's the One*—a film by Edward Burns, the director, writer, and star of *The Brothers McMullen*—and *Feeling Minnesota,* co-starring Keanu Reeves and Vincent D'Onofrio. The story of a bride who realizes—at her wedding—that she is about to marry the wrong man, *Minnesota* was neither a critical nor box-office hit. Other independent film credits included parts in *Head Above Water* and *The Keys to Tulsa,* in which Diaz appears in just one scene as a flighty southern belle. "When you look at the parts I've taken," Diaz told Internet Archive, "they've actually been quite different from one another. My character in *The Last Supper* is a million miles away from the girl in *The Mask,* or the girl in *She's the One.* It's not like I'm really trying to avoid playing pretty girl roles either…. You've just got to find different ways of playing each role."

Working without a break for the first two years of her film career, Diaz stored her possessions and lived in a friend's guest house. Starring opposite Julia Roberts in the 1997 mainstream blockbuster *My Best Friend's Wedding,* she found Hollywood increasingly receptive to her. "It's always good to be in a film that does well," she explained in a Mr. Showbiz interview. *My Best Friend's Wedding* "made it better for me, it opened a few more doors." After spending five months filming *Wedding,* Diaz went straight to work on *A Life Less Ordinary.* Exhausted following her three-month shoot on that movie, she took a long break from work. "I pretty much slept for ten months," she later told *Harper's Bazaar.*

## There's Something About Cameron

Diaz's starring role in the surprise blockbuster, *There's Something About Mary,* earned the actress *Entertainment Weekly*'s "It Girl" approval. Directed by brothers Peter and Bobby Farrelly (the directors of the low-brow comedy *Dumb and Dumber*), the movie follows Mary Jenson, whose unlucky high school prom date (Ben Stiller) hires a private investigator (Diaz's then boyfriend, Matt Dillon) to track her down. A critical success, *Mary* boosted the actress's resume and garnered her a 1999 Golden Globe nomination for Best Actress in a Musical or Comedy. *New York Times* critic Janet Maslin praised Diaz's portrayal as having "a blithe [cheerful] comic style that makes her as funny as she is dazzling." Director Bobby Farrelly shared the public's enthusiasm over Diaz. "Mary is kind of the perfect woman," he told *Harper's Bazaar.* "We rank Cameron in that category. To me there are only a couple other actresses who have that quality where they're luminous [full of light]. It's hard to describe. She's like one of the guys except she's a gorgeous babe."

Diaz followed her success in *Mary* with a characteristically quirky selection of films, including *Being John Malkovich; Very Bad Things,* a black comedy (a comedy that employs dark, or morbid, humor) about a bachelor party gone wrong; and *Any Given Sunday,* directed by Hollywood heavyweight Oliver Stone (whose previous credits include 1986's *Platoon* and 1989's *Born on the Fourth of July*). Diaz found the prospect of working with the legendary director intimidating: "I'm so excited," she told *Premiere.* "I'm terrified at the same time. Terrified that I won't be able to deliver, but I'll take the chance, because, why not. If I fall flat on my face, I'd feel horrible. I'd be doing a disservice to Oliver." On the other hand, she admitted, "I'd be an idiot not to do it."

Diaz went on in the path she had set for herself: to play a tremendous variety of characters in a wide range of film genres. In *Things You Can Tell Just by Looking at Her* (2000), a poetic film set in five sequences, each based around a lonely woman, she plays the blind but gutsy Carol, who has many boyfriends and enjoys telling them how good they look, but who is nevertheless dependent on her sister. In contrast to working in the art film, the same year Diaz played Natalie in *Charlie's Angels,* a 2000 film based on the 1970s television series. *Entertainment Weekly* summarized the film as a "showcase for pretty women in sexy clothing flipping through intricately choreographed, incredibly entertaining fight sequences." In *The Invisible Circus* (2001) Diaz plays a young hippie who kills herself in Portugal in the early 1970s after becoming involved in revolutionary plots. The movie was poorly received by critics and the public.

In a memorable part in 2001 Diaz was the voice of the feisty and unconventional Princess Fiona in the computer-animated film *Shrek.* She won a Nickelodeon Kids' Choice Award for "Best Burp" for this role. Diaz was also in *Vanilla Sky* in 2001 with Tom Cruise and Penelope Cruz. Already well established in comedy, she played a lead in the 2002 film *The Sweetest Thing,* a gross-out slapstick tale of three single San Francisco female roommates. Unlike *There's Something About Mary, The Sweetest Thing* indulges in more bathroom and raunchy sexual humor than most critics wanted to see. Although the movie was almost universally panned, most critics lauded Diaz's memorable portrayal of a ditzy woman.

In May 2002 a twenty-minute special preview of *Gangs of New York* was shown at the Cannes Film Festival in France. The movie, set in the streets of New York in the mid-nineteenth century, was directed by the well-known director Martin Scorsese, who calls it his greatest undertaking ever. Diaz plays a pickpocket in the film, which also stars Leonardo DiCaprio, Daniel Day-Lewis, and Liam Neeson. Because of the extreme care given to the filming, the original release date was postponed by a year and set for December 25, 2002.

Having gotten into acting almost by accident, Diaz is aware that other opportunities are available to her. "Just because I'm an actor now," she told *Harper's Bazaar,* "doesn't mean I have to do it for the rest of my life." She has no immediate plans to abandon her career, however. "I'm not just going to drop out. The more I learn about acting, the more I like it."

## For More Information

Baldwin, Kristen, "Kicking Assets: Drew Barrymore, Cameron Diaz, and Lucy Liu Refashion Charlie's Angels as an Action Candy Confection," *Entertainment Weekly,* March 30, 2001.

"Cameron Diaz: The 50 Most Beautiful People 2002," *People Weekly,* May 13, 2002, p. 112.

"Cyber Profiles: Cameron Diaz," People Online, August 3, 1998. Available at http://www.pathfinder.com/people/profiles/diaz/index.html (accessed June 21, 2002).

Hofler, Robert, "A Year of Living Famously," *Premiere,* December 1998, pp. 98–104.

Maslin, Janet, "'Feeling Minnesota': Attitude Posing for Substance," *New York Times,* September 13, 1996.

Maslin, Janet, "'She's the One': Light, Sardonic Comedy," *New York Times,* August 23, 1996.

Maslin, Janet, "'There's Something About Mary': Slapstick Pursuit of an Old Flame," *New York Times,* July 15, 1998.

Mundy, Chris, "A Fine Romance," *Harper's Bazaar,* August 1998, pp. 114–121.

Wolf, Jeanne, "Q & A with Matt Dillon & Cameron Diaz." E! Online. Available at http://www.eonline.com/Hot/Qa/Diaz98/index.html (accessed June 21, 2002).

# Placido Domingo

Opera singer
Born January 21, 1941, Madrid, Spain

*"Living in Mexico made me feel very much Latin American wherever I went to perform. Whenever I traveled to Puerto Rico, Argentina, Chile, or any Latin country, I felt very much at home."*

Placido Domingo. *Reproduced by permission of AP/Wide World Photos.*

In Spanish, Placido Domingo's name means "peaceful Sunday." In real life, Domingo's schedule is anything but peaceful. As the busiest and one of the most well-known opera tenors in the world, he sings in 80 performances per year and has made more than 150 recordings, 97 of which are full-length operas. He also conducts orchestras and helps organize new opera companies around the world.

Domingo has also starred in films and television productions. He has even recorded popular music with singers like John Denver. He still tries to find time for fun things, like singing the national anthem at a Los Angeles Dodgers baseball game. Because he travels constantly for performances, he has homes in London, Los Angeles, New York, Vienna, and Monaco. One of his favorite possessions is a needlepoint pillow that reads, "If I rest, I rust."

Domingo was born in 1941 into a musical family in Madrid, Spain. His parents, Placido Domingo and Pepita Embil, were professional singers who specialized in *zarzuelas*, Spanish folk operettas (romantic comedies featuring singing and dancing). When Domingo was six years old, his parents moved the family to Mexico City, Mexico, where they organized an operetta company.

Even though his parents made him a Mexican citizen while he was still young, Domingo never forgot his Spanish roots. When he was older, he reapplied for his Spanish citizenship. The years he eventually spent in Mexico, however, had a great effect upon him. He learned about and came to embrace other Hispanic cultures. "Living in Mexico made me feel very much Latin American wherever I went to perform," he related to Rosie Carbo in *Hispanic*. "Whenever I traveled to Puerto Rico, Argentina, Chile, or any Latin country, I felt very much at home."

## Musical Training Starts Early

Domingo's musical training began with piano lessons at the age of eight. By the age of nine he had won a song-and-dance contest and began singing children's roles in his parents' operettas. During his high school years at the Instituto Mexico, he played soccer (a great fan of the sport to this day, he tries to schedule a month off during World Cup competition). He even tried the dangerous sport of bullfighting, performing as an amateur matador at private fiestas.

Domingo then studied at the National Conservatory of Music in Mexico City. He made his first stage appearance at age nineteen with the Mexico City National Opera in the musical comedy *Rigoletto,* by Italian composer Giuseppe Verdi. He started out as a baritone singer, but switched to tenor on the advice of his teachers. He had to force his voice at first to reach certain high notes, but he soon mastered the technique. Singing is a balancing act: a singer must find a blend between vocal sounds, emotions, and intellect. One of the reasons Domingo is so highly esteemed as a musician is because he masterfully achieves this balance of technique and emotional understanding of his art.

In 1961 Domingo met and married Marta Ornelas, a Mexican opera star. The following year the couple joined the Israel National Opera Company in Tel Aviv and spent two years there (Domingo is fluent in several languages, including Hebrew). In 1965 the couple had a son and Marta Ornelas retired from the stage. Domingo then came to the United States to audition for the New

York City Opera. His performances the first season went unnoticed by New York's music critics. The very next year, however, he caught the attention of those same critics for his singing and acting in the ultramodern opera *Don Rodrigo,* by Argentine composer Alberto Ginastera.

## Takes Risks for His Art

Domingo is a risk-taker. At the age of twenty-seven (still young by opera standards) he attempted to sing a very difficult role in the opera *Lohengrin,* by German composer Richard Wagner. The part requires the tenor to sing a tricky combination of musical notes that strain—and can even damage—vocal chords. Domingo succeeded, but it took months for him to recover his voice and confidence.

In 1968 he made his official debut with the prestigious Metropolitan Opera in New York and received excellent reviews. Because Domingo undertook such a breakneck schedule, many predicted that he would burn out. Fortunately, he didn't have to use his voice to practice. Able to memorize his parts, he studied the music at a piano. He knew ninety operas, thirty of them well enough to perform at a moment's notice.

For two days before a performance, he and his wife Marta were in the habit of escaping to a quiet resort in northern New York. There the singer rested, read sports magazines, walked, and swam. To protect his voice on the day of a performance, he did not talk at all. Since Domingo was outgoing, energetic, and friendly, this was the most difficult of sacrifices.

## Talent Carries Over to Acting and Conducting

In 1984 Domingo made his debut as a conductor. He led New York's Metropolitan Opera in a performance of *La Boheme,* by Italian composer Giacomo Puccini. He soon expanded his talents by turning his operatic stage performances into related roles in films. In 1986 he starred in director Franco Zeffirelli's film adaptation of Verdi's opera *Othello.* His performance won rave reviews. He has also starred in Zeffirelli's version of Verdi's *La Traviata* and director Francesco Rossi's film of the opera *Carmen,* by French composer Georges Bizet.

In 1990 Domingo teamed up with tenors Jose Carreras and Luciano Pavarotti for what was meant to be a one-time-only concert commemorating the World Cup Soccer finals. The trio, who would come to be known simply as the Three Tenors, reunited for a concert for the 1994 World Cup soccer finals in Los Angeles, and staged a world tour in 1996. In 1998 they sang in an outdoor concert in Paris. They toured again in 2000 and have shown no signs of stopping. Their concerts are tremendous crowd pleasers, offering light fare along with operatic arias. The less formal setting allows their personalities to shine on stage, in ways they probably had not been able to express before. With huge audiences and high price tickets, they make money like young rock stars and enjoy themselves to boot.

Domingo amazes the music world with his boundless energy and enthusiasm. He is optimistic about his future and avoids talk of retirement. In 1993 he celebrated his twenty-fifth anniversary at the Metropolitan Opera by singing at a gala opening night before a crowd of thrilled fans. He has served as artistic director of the Washington Opera since 1996. He became artistic director of the Los Angeles Opera in 2000. He was one of the Los Angeles Opera's founders, and had been its music adviser and principal guest conductor for years.

Domingo has received many honors over the years, including (by 2002) two Emmy Awards and nine Grammy Awards. His last Grammy in 2000 was for his album *100 Years of Mariachi.* He won Latin Grammy Awards in 2000 and 2001 for best classical albums. He won the Hispanic Heritage Award for the arts in 1999, and musical awards from all over the world that are far too numerous to mention. One award of which he is most proud is the Order of the Aztec Eagle—Mexico's highest honor. He was given the prestigious award by the Mexican government in 1985 for helping to save victims from the rubble left by a devastating earthquake that shook Mexico City. He spent the following year performing nothing but benefit concerts for the many victims who had been left homeless.

## For More Information

Cling, Carol, "Triple Treat: Three Tenors Performance a Showcase for Distinctive Styles," *Las Vegas Review-Journal,* April 21, 2000.

Domingo, Placido, *My First Forty Years,* New York: Alfred Knopf, 1983.

Domingo, Placido, official Web site. Available at http://www.placidodomingo.com/ (accessed June 21, 2002).

*Hispanic,* August 1992, pp. 47–49.

Stefoff, Rebecca, *Placido Domingo,* Chelsea House, 1992.

*Time,* September 27, 1993, pp. 82–83.

# Sheila E.

Singer, songwriter
Born c. 1958, Oakland, California

*"I've always wanted to incorporate a lot of the Latin into the albums, but I didn't know how. I thought that if I put in too much Latin, people wouldn't like it. I think that it was a mistake to think that people wouldn't accept me as I was."*

Sheila E. first achieved fame in the early 1980s as a duet partner with pop superstar Prince. The drummer and singer then found success on her own with her first solo album, *The Glamorous Life*. The 1984 record was a hit. Her 1985 follow-up album, *Romance 1600,* proved Sheila E. was a musician with a wide range. Pamela Bloom pointed out in *High Fidelity* that "Sheila demonstrates on *Romance 1600* how equally at home she is in fusion, funk, pop, and salsa, as well as in the traditional R&B dance mix."

Sheila E. was born Sheila Escovedo sometime in the late 1950s in Oakland, California, to Pete and Juanita Escovedo. Her father was famous for his drum work with the rock group Santana and, later, the Latin band Azteca. Her brothers also became drummers. When Sheila E. was three, she began to watch her father practice his conga drums. She'd sit in front of him and copy him, mirroring his style. Because of this "mirroring," she developed a left-handed style on the drums, which allows her to beat them faster and harder than most drummers.

Her father had hoped she would become a symphony performer and sent her to violin lessons when she was ten. She quit after five years and switched to more popular instruments such as guitar and keyboard. As a teenager she believed she had a greater chance of becoming an Olympic athlete than a successful musician. She spent much of her time playing football with neighborhood boys and challenging her friends to footraces.

## Joins Father's Band

Despite her attraction to sports, Sheila E. kept practicing the drums. While still a teenager, she was offered professional music jobs. Her father, who thought she was still too young to become a professional drummer, eventually let her fill in for an ailing percussionist in his band. In her first appearance with the group, she performed a solo that received an overwhelming response from the audience. "When I heard that ovation," she related to Bloom, "I had this feeling I had never had in my whole life…. It felt like the ultimate." Soon after, she quit high school to concentrate on her musical career.

Sheila E. toured Europe and Asia with her father's band and recorded two albums as part of that group. She also worked as a studio musician for stars such as Lionel Richie, Diana Ross, and Herbie Hancock. In 1978 she met Prince (as he was then called). "When I first saw him, I just thought he was this cute guy standing against the wall," she told Bloom. "But when we met, he was impressed, too, because he had heard of *me*.

Although the two often worked together writing songs, Sheila E. did not record with

Sheila E. *Reproduced by permission of Corbis Corporation (Bellevue).*

Prince until 1984, when she sang a duet with him on his hit single "Erotic City." He showed her how to compose songs faster than she had been doing, helped her create a sexy new image, and advised her to go solo. He even helped produce *The Glamorous Life*. He also gave her more experience and publicity by hiring her as the opening act for his "Purple Rain" tour. She was nervous at first, but soon learned to enjoy her new role in the spotlight.

## Returns to Her Roots

Sheila E.'s next albums were not tremendous hits, but they established her as a songwriter and performer of note. *Romance 1600,* included "Love Bizarre," another duet with Prince that reached near the top of the charts. On her third album, released in 1987 and simply titled *Sheila E.,* she involved her family. Her father, mother, brothers, and sister sang or played backup on many of the songs.

On her 1991 effort, *Sex Cymbal,* Sheila E. returned to her Latin musical roots. "I've always wanted to incorporate a lot of the Latin into the albums, but I didn't know how," she explained to Karen Schoemer in *Interview.* "I thought that if I put in too much Latin, people wouldn't like it. I think that it was a mistake to think that people wouldn't accept me as I was." In 1993 Sheila E. lent her world-renowned percussion talents to another Latin recording,

**Gloria Estefan**'s *Mi Tierra* (see entry). In 1998 she and her band E Train came out with the album *Writes of Passage*.

For most of the 1990s, Sheila E. has been a major studio presence, playing with musical stars such as Herbie Hancock, Lionel Richie, Ringo Starr, Stevie Nicks, Diana Ross, Marvin Gaye, Natalie Cole, and Babyface. She told Larry Getlin of Bankrate.com that music for her is an enterprise: "I'm in the entertainment business, and it's a business first. I can't look at myself as just being a musician—I wouldn't make as much money. I'm an entertainer, and I'm able to produce and compose and arrange for a lot of different artists as well as myself. I've done things for movies and television, and continue to expand. It's not just being a percussion player, it's continuing to expand, having a business."

Besides composing, producing, and playing music, Sheila E. has become well known for her charitable works. She performed at the Pediatric Aids Foundation's concert "For the Children" and at the Aids Project Los Angeles benefit with Barbra Streisand, Patti LaBelle, Natalie Cole, Shirley MacLaine, and Liza Minelli, and has contributed in many other humanitarian projects as well.

## For More Information

Getlin, Larry, "Sheila E. Times the Market," Bankrate.com, November 28, 2001. Available at http://www.bankrate.com/brm/news/investing/20011128a.asp (accessed June 21, 2002).
*High Fidelity,* January 1986, pp. 64–65+.
*Hispanic,* July 1991, p. 54.
*Interview,* March 1991, p. 24.
*People,* May 6, 1991, pp. 29–30.

# Jaime Escalante

Educator
Born December 31, 1930, La Paz, Bolivia

*"It's the only thing I can do."*

In 1982, eighteen students from the mostly Hispanic Garfield High School in East Los Angeles passed the Advanced Placement (AP) calculus exam. This math test enabled them to receive college credit for classes they had taken in high school. It is a very difficult test, and only a small percentage of students in the United States even attempt it. The students' achievement was remarkable because Garfield High was previously known mostly for its gangs, drug use, and low academic standards.

The driving force behind the students' success was Jaime Escalante, a teacher who challenged them to reach their full potential. The achievements of Escalante and his students caught the attention of the nation in 1988 when a popular movie, *Stand and Deliver,* retold their stories. Afterward, U.S. President Ronald Reagan called Escalante a hero on national television.

Escalante was born in 1930 in La Paz, Bolivia. After receiving his education in that country, he became a highly respected mathematics and science teacher in high schools in La Paz. Political unrest in Bolivia, however, forced Escalante, his wife Fabiola, and their son Jaime, Jr., to flee the country in 1964 and settle in California. Escalante wanted to resume his teaching career, but he spoke no English and his teaching license was of no value in the United States. While working as a busboy and later as a cook, Escalante taught himself English. He then became a computer parts tester.

Although Escalante did well at his new job, he missed teaching. For seven years he attended night classes at California State University. In 1974, after receiving a bachelor's degree in mathematics and a teaching license, he was hired as a teacher at Garfield High School.

## Introduces New Math Methods

On his first day at the school, Escalante realized the students were in trouble. Many of them had to count on their fingers when figuring out math problems on the chalkboard. Almost all the students came to class unprepared and without supplies. The toughness of many of the teenagers at Garfield frightened Escalante. Fights between rival gang members were common, and non-students wandered the halls causing trouble. The adult staff was intimidated and discouraged.

To gain his students' interest, Escalante began skipping lectures and resorting to theatrics. To illustrate a point about percentages, he donned an apron and a chef's hat, set an apple on his desk, then chopped it in half with a large butcher's knife. He encouraged his students to scrape the graffiti off their desks. He then invited them to help paint the classroom, decorating it with Los Angeles Lakers posters afterward. In his lessons, Escalante used sports language and business techniques. He often challenged students to handball contests on Saturdays,

Jaime Escalante. *Reproduced by permission of Arte Público Press.*

telling them that if they won, they would receive an automatic "A." If he won, they had to do their homework. The students were shocked to find the aging Escalante won every time—he had been a handball star in Bolivia.

Escalante also got his students' attention by embarrassing them. If a student was tardy to class, he or she was made to sit in a kindergarten-sized chair. If a student's attention wandered in class, he or she was pelted with a little red pillow. Escalante was also quick to give encouragement if his students performed well in class. He fought for money to provide decent breakfasts and summer scholarships for them. He won their respect because he was strict but fair and kept a sense of humor in the classroom. His students began to increase their math skills.

## Hard Work and Determination Win Out

In 1979 Escalante held his first calculus class. Even though only five students attended, four of them went on to pass the difficult AP calculus test. The next two years were even more successful for the teacher and his students. In 1982, however, Escalante suffered a minor heart attack. That same year fourteen of his eighteen calculus students were accused of cheating on the AP test. Because their errors appeared suspiciously similar, they had to take a new, more difficult test. Escalante was angry, but his students were determined to prove they had mastered the work. Two students decided not to attend college, but the other twelve returned to take the new test. All twelve passed.

The incident received much local publicity and caught the attention of film producers. Many believed that the students' scores would never have been questioned if they were not Hispanic and from the poor Garfield High School. Filmmakers approached Escalante about making a movie of his triumphs and he gave them the go ahead. He allowed **Edward James Olmos** (see entry), the actor who was to play him in the movie, to spend eighteen hours a day with him for a month.

The success of the 1988 movie *Stand and Deliver* made Garfield and Escalante symbols of educational and personal achievement in the face of great odds. It helped attract the attention of businesses, which donated $750,000 to the school to help update its teaching materials and equipment.

## Students Continue Academic Success

In the spring of 1988 Escalante watched as seven of the twelve students from his 1982 class graduated from the engineering program at the University of Southern California. Over the years, more of his students have gone on to graduate from University of California campuses and Ivy League schools. Their fields of study have been diverse, ranging from engineering to teaching to law. For his work with these students, Escalante has received many awards, including the 1989 White House Hispanic Heritage Award and the 1990 American Institute for Public Service Jefferson Award.

In September 1991 Escalante began teaching math at Hiram High School in Sacramento, California. He continued to offer support to the Saturday-and-summer training program he started for students and teachers at East Los Angeles College in 1983. In 1991 he also developed an award-winning public television series on math, science, and careers called *Futures*. A video selection from that series, "Math ... Who Needs It?," was the Blue Ribbon winner at the 1992 American Film and Video Festival. When asked by *People*'s Charles E. Cohen why he continued teaching after he has faced so many obstacles, Escalante replied, "It's the only thing I can do."

## Becomes Honorary Chair of Anti-Bilingual Movement

In 1997 California millionaire Ron Unz was actively campaigning to get an anti-bilingual education proposition on the California ballot. The proposition was unpopular with many Hispanic voters who believed it was a step backward from progress made since the 1960s to give Spanish-speaking children equal access to public education. Many observers believed the proposition, which became Proposition 227 on the ballot, was motivated by discrimination. Despite the concerns of many Hispanics, Escalante agreed to become the honorary chairman of Unz's "English for the Children" campaign. He explained to George Skelton of the *Los Angeles Times* that he believes it is in the students' best interest: "It's good to have bilingual teachers who speak two languages. But if you teach the kids in Spanish, you're not preparing them for life. In this country, we negotiate in one language and you have to master that language to be successful. And it's English.... The tendency of the kid is to go to the mother language. I say, 'Only English, man. Outside [class] you can ask me any question in your language. Inside, you learn my language. In here, we're going to have to prepare to beat the Japanese.'"

Escalante retired from teaching in 1998. In that year alone, he received the Presidential Medal for Excellence, the Free Spirit Award from the Freedom Forum, the Andres Bello prize, Organization of American States, and others. He was a 1999 inductee in the National Teachers Hall of Fame.

## For More Information

*Booklist,* January 1, 1993, p. 818.

Byers, Ann, *Jaime Escalante: Sensational Teacher,* New York: Enslow Publishers, 1996.

"Jaime Escalante, Inductee," National Teachers Hall of Fame. Available at http://www.nthf.org/escalante.htm (accessed June 21, 2002).

Mathews, Jay, *Escalante: The Best Teacher in America,* New York: Henry Holt, 1988.

*Newsweek,* July 20, 1992, pp. 58–59.

*People,* September 16, 1991, pp. 111–12.

Skelton, George, "In Any Language, Escalante's Stand Is Clear," *Los Angeles Times,* November 13, 1997, p. 3.

# Gloria Estefan

Pop singer, songwriter, producer
Born 1958, Havana, Cuba

*"You can't sit there and wallow. You weep for what's gone and then you move ahead."*

From her Hispanic roots to the pop music mainstream, Gloria Estefan is an example of the American Dream come true. She started with the Miami Sound Machine, originally a Cuban American quartet that performed popular music with a Latin influence. The band grew from being a sensation in Spanish-speaking countries to international popularity due to the talent and hard work of Estefan and her husband Emilio.

Estefan was born Gloria Maria Fajardo in 1958 in Havana, Cuba. Her mother was a schoolteacher. Her father, José Manuel Fajardo, at the time of Estefan's birth, was a bodyguard to President Fulgencio Batista. The following year Fidel Castro and others overthrew Batista and installed a Communist government in Cuba. The Fajardo family quickly fled to the United States. José Manuel Fajardo was then recruited by the Central Intelligence Agency into a band of anti-Castro Cubans sent to invade Cuba. The invasion took place on April 17, 1961, at the Bay of Pigs. It failed, and Fajardo was taken prisoner. After President John F. Kennedy won the release of the prisoners, Fajardo returned to the United States, joined the U.S. Army, and served two years in the Vietnam War.

As a child, Estefan took classical guitar lessons, but found them tedious. She preferred to write poetry. She had no idea that she would some day become a popular music star, but music played a very important role for her as a teenager. When her father returned from the war, he became ill with the disabling disease of multiple sclerosis, possibly as a result from exposure to the herbicide (something used to kill plants) Agent Orange while in Vietnam. Estefan's mother worked to support the family during the day while attending school at night. Gloria was left to care for her father and younger sister. With little in the way of a social life, she turned to music for distraction.

"When my father was ill, music was my escape," Estefan told Richard Harrington of the *Washington Post.* "I would lock myself up in my room for hours and just sing. I wouldn't cry—I refused to cry…. Music was the only way I had to just let go, so I sang for fun and for emotional catharsis."

## Joins Future Husband's Band

In 1975 Estefan met keyboardist Emilio Estefan, leader of a band called the Miami Latin Boys. When he heard her voice, he asked her to perform as lead singer with his band. At first, she sang only on weekends because she was attending the University of Miami. A year and a half after she joined the group (by then renamed the Miami Sound Machine), they recorded their first album. *Renacer* was a collection of disco pop and original ballads sung in Spanish.

Although Estefan was somewhat plump and very shy when she joined the band, she slimmed down with a rigorous exercise program and worked to overcome her stagefright. Gradually, her professional relationship with Emilio Estefan turned personal, and in 1978 they married. Their son Nayib was born two years later.

Between 1981 and 1983 the Miami Sound Machine recorded four Spanish-language albums made up of ballads, disco, pop, and sambas (the music for a Brazilian dance with African origins). The group had dozens of hit songs in Spanish-speaking countries such as Venezuela, Peru, Panama, and Honduras, but were unknown in the United States.

## Fame in the U.S.A.

The group's first North American hit was the disco single "Dr. Beat" from *Eyes of Innocence,* their first album to contain songs sung in English. "Conga," a rousing dance number from the album, became the first single to crack *Billboard* magazine's pop, dance, black, and Latin charts at the same time. Estefan and the group, whose members changed over the years, prided themselves on the combination of Latin rhythms, rhythm and blues, and mainstream pop that made their music special.

In 1986 the album *Primitive Love,* the band's first recording entirely in English, set off a string of hit singles. "Bad Boys" and "Words Get in the Way" jumped onto *Billboard*'s Top 10 pop chart. Extensive tours and music videos on MTV and VH-1 made the Miami Sound Machine a leading American band. Their next album, *Let It Loose,* released in 1987, had several hit singles: "Betcha Say That," "1-2-3," and the ballad "Anything for You." Estefan gradually became the star attraction, and the group came to be known as Gloria Estefan and the Miami Sound Machine, or sometimes simply Gloria Estefan. Some people said Estefan reminded them of a nice, Hispanic version of Madonna.

Despite the group's popularity with English-speaking listeners, the Estefans have not forgotten their roots. They are always working on Spanish-language projects. The title of their 1989 album, *Cuts Both Ways,* refers to their intention to appeal to both English- and Spanish-speaking audiences. For this album, in addition to singing, Estefan was involved in the planning, producing, and composing of music and the writing of lyrics. In 1993 she released *Mi Tierra,* an all-Spanish album of original melodies that recall classic Afro-Cuban songs.

## Suffers Back Injury

After their son Nayib was born, Emilio Estefan gave up his position as keyboardist with the band. He devoted his energy to publicity, business arrangements, and spending time with his son. A close family, the Estefans arranged to meet as often as possible during tours. In March 1990, while Emilio Estefan and Nayib were traveling with the group, the band's bus was involved

Gloria Estefan. *Reproduced by permission of AP/Wide World Photos.*

in an accident on a snowy highway in Pennsylvania. Nayib suffered a fractured shoulder and Emilio Estefan received minor head and hand injuries. Gloria Estefan suffered a critically broken back.

In a four-hour operation several days later, surgeons repaired Estefan's spine by inserting two eight-inch steel rods for support. Doctors feared she might never walk again, and the Estefans retired to their home on Biscayne Bay in Florida to recuperate. Thanks to extensive physical therapy, intense determination, and the support of her family and fans, she made what many consider a miraculous comeback. "You can't sit there and wallow," Estefan told *People*'s Pam Lambert. "You weep for what's gone and then you move ahead."

Estefan returned to the stage with an appearance on television's American Music Awards in January 1991, and launched a year-long tour to celebrate her comeback album, *Into the Light*.

In 1992 Florida was battered by Hurricane Andrew. Knowing the pain of coming back from injury, the Estefans jumped into the relief effort with energy. They quickly established relief centers in their South Miami studio-office complex. Estefan then released an inspirational ballad, "Always Tomorrow," and donated all proceeds to the hurricane relief. Afterward, the Estefans recruited celebrity friends to join them in a star-studded benefit concert at Miami's Joe Robbie Stadium. The effort raised two million dollars for victims of the disastrous hurricane.

## Back in the Limelight

The impact of Estefan's accident continued to affect her attitudes and outlook on life. "So many people got behind me," she told *People* magazine's Steve Dougherty, "and gave me a reason to want to come back fast and made me feel strong. Knowing how caring people can be, how much they gave me—that has changed me forever."

In the fall of 1995, just before the release of her new Spanish-language album, *Abriendo Puertas* (Opening Doors), Estefan's life was again touched by tragedy. She and her husband were returning from a Sunday afternoon pleasure cruise aboard their boat when a Wave Runner wet bike accidently smashed into the rear of their craft. The driver of the Wave Runner, a twenty-nine-year-old law student at Howard University, had apparently lost control. Thrown off the wet bike and into the propellers of the Estefan's boat, the student was fatally injured.

The following year, Estefan released *Destiny,* an introspective, accoustic album. In 1998 she was back to dance music with *gloria!* Launched at Studio 54 in New York with Estefan performing in full swing and glitter, the upbeat dance music was a huge success with the crowd, and several singles from the album quickly rose up the charts. In 2000 she released *Alma Caribeña,* a fusion of Caribbean beats featuring the single, "No Me Dejes de Querer." At the First Annual Latin Grammy Awards Gloria Estefan took home the award for best music video for "No Me Dejes De Querer," directed by Emilio and her. In 2001 Epic records released Estefan's *Greatest Hits: Volume II.* She has won two Grammy Awards in Latin music categories.

In June 2001 Gloria and Emilio Estefan became the first Hispanics ever to receive the Songwriters Hall of Fame's most prestigious honor, the Sammy Cahn Lifetime Achievement Award.

## For More Information

DeStefano, Anthony M., *Gloria Estefan: The Pop Superstar from Tragedy to Triumph,* Signet, 1997.

"Gloria Estefan," Epic Records Official Web site. Available at http://www.epiccenter.com/EpicCenter/custom/56/main.html (accessed June 21, 2002).

Gonzalez, Fernando, *Gloria Estefan, Cuban-American Singing Star,* Millbrook Press, 1993.

*Hispanic,* September 1993, pp. 102–03.

*People,* October 12, 1992, p. 47; October 9, 1995, pp. 65+.

Stefoff, Rebecca, *Gloria Estefan,* Chelsea House, 1991.

*USA Weekend,* April 1–3, 1994.

*Washington Post,* July 17, 1988.

# Emilio Estevez

Actor, screenwriter, director
Born May 12, 1962, New York, New York

*"My dad taught me to trust myself and to always search for the truth in whatever I was doing."*

In the mid-1980s, a group of young actors came to be known as Hollywood's "Brat Pack." The talented and sucessful—and sometimes brash—group was unofficially led by Emilio Estevez. The young Estevez, who is also a screenwriter and director, grew up in a family loaded with talent. His father, Martin Sheen, and brother, **Charlie Sheen** (see entry), are well-established actors. Mother Janet is a film producer, and siblings Ramon and Renee Estevez are breaking into the business.

Estevez was born in 1962 in New York City, but moved with his family to Malibu, California, six years later. His father, who had been born Ramón Estevez, changed his Spanish name to avoid being typecast in films. Young Estevez, with his sandy hair and blue eyes, kept the original family name because he could easily play mainstream roles. Also, he wanted to earn his own reputation rather than enter the industry on his father's famous name.

Estevez began performing at an early age in school plays and in 8-mm films he made with his brother Charlie and neighborhood friends Chris and Sean Penn. He also began writing at an early age. One effort was a sci-

Emilio Estevez. *Reproduced by permission of Archive Photos, Inc.*

ence fiction story he wrote as a second grader and tried to sell to the producers of television's *Night Gallery* series. The story was rejected, but Estevez wasn't discouraged. He kept writing, and in high school he starred in another play he wrote about Vietnam War veterans. It was titled *Echoes of an Era* and was directed by his friend Sean Penn. Most of Estevez's attention in high school, however, was focused on sports, especially soccer and track.

## First Movie Roles

Knowing he could not compete professionally in sports, Estevez soon returned to acting. "I knew I had an ability to perform from an early age, to really excel at it," he wrote in an early studio biography, as quoted by *Hispanic*'s Elena Kellner. "So I began taking acting lessons seriously and started auditioning." He landed his first professional acting job right after his graduation from Santa Monica High Schol. It was a role in an after-school TV special, *Seventeen Going on Nowhere*. He made his motion picture debut in 1982, playing opposite Matt Dillon in *Tex,* a film based on a novel by best-selling author S. E. Hinton.

In 1983 Estevez appeared in another screen adaptation of a Hinton novel, *The Outsiders,* a story about a teen gang. The movie featured many other up-and-coming actors, including Tom Cruise, Matt Dillon, Rob Lowe, Diane Lane, Ralph Macchio, and Patrick Swayze. Estevez achieved recognition the following year in *Repo Man,* in which he portrayed a punk rocker who takes a job as an automobile repossessor. To prepare for the role Estevez immersed himself in punk rock music and visited punk clubs.

Estevez finally caught the attention of critics in 1985 when he played a very different role, that of a high school jock in *The Breakfast Club*. Directed by John Hughes, the hit film follows five students from different cliques in a suburban Chicago high school who have to spend a Saturday together in detention. At first, the characters want nothing to do with each other and tempers flare. As the day progresses, however, they begin to open up to each other, discussing their families and their dreams. By day's end, having learned to look beyond their teen stereotypes, they reach out to each other and become friends.

Late in 1985, Estevez appeared in *That Was Then...This Is Now,* a film for which he

also wrote the screenplay. The movie is based on another novel by S. E. Hinton that Estevez had read while filming *Tex*. The author herself suggested that Estevez play the starring role in the story about two teenage boys whose friendship is threatened when one of them falls in love. "I came across a project that I became passionate about," he told *Teen* magazine. "I wanted to bring it to the screen because it's a film about young people that's honest."

## Makes Hollywood History

Estevez went on to increase his involvement in film by starring in *Wisdom* with Demi Moore. It tells the story of a young man who travels across the country entering banks and vandalizing mortgage files to stop the banks from foreclosing on farmers' mortgages. Although panned by most critics, the 1987 film made Estevez—at age twenty-three—the youngest person ever to have written, directed, and starred in a major motion picture.

Estevez continued his writing/directing/ starring role in the 1990 comedy *Men at Work*. The film, about California garbage men who become involved with a murder and an ocean-polluting chemical company, also starred his brother Charlie Sheen. Again, critics were unkind in their view of Estevez's work. Ralph Novak, writing in *People,* believed that "finding things to like in this film resembles—what else?— garbage picking. You have to poke through the junk to get to the good stuff."

Estevez's work in three films that spawned sequels, however, was immensely popular. In 1988 he starred in *Young Guns*. The hit film, which follows the exploits of Billy the Kid

(Estevez) and his gang, also featured Kiefer Sutherland and Lou Diamond Phillips. All three actors, along with others, reprised their roles in the 1990 sequel, *Young Guns 2*.

In 1987 Estevez had starred with Richard Dreyfuss and Madeleine Stowe in the comedy/thriller *Stakeout*. The film, about a pair of police detectives who stake out a woman's apartment hoping to find her boyfriend who broke out of prison, was a success. Six years later, Estevez and Dreyfuss teamed up again in *Another Stakeout*. This time they had to keep an eye on a woman who was going to testify against the Mob.

In 1992's *The Mighty Ducks,* Estevez plays a successful lawyer who becomes the coach of a peewee hockey team due to a court order. The film was popular enough to warrant two sequels, one in 1994 and one in 1996. During the 1990s he also starred in several television movies and appeared on the weekly comedy *Saturday Night Live.*

Estevez has directed several movies. In 1996, he decided to pass up payment for his work in *Mighty Ducks 3* and instead received financing for his film *The War At Home,* which he produced, directed, and starred in. The film told the story of a Vietnam veteran's return home after the war, and featured his father, Martin Sheen. In 2000 Estevez directed and starred in *Rated X,* the true story about two brothers who made it big in the pornography business. Playing the other brother in the film was his own brother, Charlie Sheen.

## Faces Pressures of Hollywood

In 1992 Estevez married Paula Abdul, the equally famous dancer/singer. With the media and their fans following their every move, the couple found it hard to lead a private life. The pressures of a Hollywood marriage soon proved to be too great. The couple separated in the spring of 1994 and then divorced.

Estevez tries to keep his fame in perspective. To help him remain grounded, he remembers lessons his father has taught him. Although he realizes his job is no more important than any other, he tries to remain focused on his work. "My dad taught me to trust myself," he said, as quoted by Kellner, "and to always search for the truth in whatever I was doing."

## For More Information

"Emilio Estevez," Internet Movie Data Base. Available at http://us.imdb.com/M/person-exact?Estevez%2C+Emilio (accessed June 21, 2002).

"Emilio Estevez," MovieThing. Available at http://moviething.com/cgi-bac/ecom9990057318529.cgi?itemid=9960057404740&action=viewad&page=1&placeonpage=11&totaldisplayed=25&categoryid=9990057318529 (accessed June 21, 2002).

*Hispanic,* May 1994, pp. 14–18.

*People,* September 17, 1990, pp. 13–14.

*Teen,* September 1982; March 1985; July 1985; February 1991, pp. 34–35.

# José Feliciano

Singer, guitarist
Born September 10, 1945, Lares, Puerto Rico

*"I have tried to change the image of blind performers. I don't wear glasses, just like deaf people don't wear earmuffs."*

José Monserrate Feliciano is a musician who overcame the obstacles of blindness and poverty to excel as a popular performer. He first became a hit with Spanish-speaking audiences in the United States and Latin America in the early 1960s. He then exploded on the English-language pop scene in 1968 with his stylized version of "Light My Fire," a song originally sung by the rock group the Doors. He gained further notice that year when he performed a controversial rendition of the "Star Spangled Banner" at a Detroit Tigers baseball game.

Feliciano has blended rock, soul, jazz, blues, classical, and Latin sounds into his own highly personal style. This, combined with his masterful guitar playing, has won him praise. He is the only performer to have won Grammy Awards in two language categories. Throughout his career, he has downplayed his blindness, never letting the handicap slow him down or overshadow his talent. "I have tried to change the image of blind performers," he told a reporter for the *Grand Rapids Press*. "I don't wear glasses, just like deaf people don't wear earmuffs."

Feliciano was born in Lares, Puerto Rico, in 1945. He was the second of twelve children born to a very poor family. His father was a farmer and a longshoreman. To find a better life, the family moved to a Latino section of New York City in 1950. Feliciano was born with glaucoma, an eye disease that made him blind. Because of his blindness, he was unable to participate in sports and other activities. At an early age he turned to music. He began beating out rhythms on a tin cracker can when he was three years old.

At six he taught himself to play the concertina (a type of accordion) by listening to records for hours each day. He went on to master other instruments, including the banjo, mandolin, harmonica, organ, piano, and drums.

## Combines Influences for a Unique Style

At first, Feliciano's chief musical influence was the Latin American sound his father urged him to imitate. Soon he was drawn to soul music, then rock and roll. He later became familiar with classical music, thanks to school teachers who recognized his talent. As a result, Feliciano developed a truly unique style. A reporter for *Time* once described it as a cross between "Johnny Mathis and Ray Charles with a Latin American flavor and a classical-tinged guitar backing."

Feliciano made his first public performance at the age of nine at El Teatro Puerto Rico in Spanish Harlem (an area of New York City). Soon he was playing at local events, talent shows, and public assemblies. By the age of sixteen he was contributing to the family income by playing pop, flamenco (a Spanish gypsy dance), and folk music in coffee houses. The next year, when his father lost his job, Feliciano dropped out of school to perform full-time to help support his family. He quickly became a hit with audiences throughout the east and midwest.

At seventeen Feliciano signed a recording contract with RCA Records. Because most of his recordings over the next few years were in Spanish, he became a pop sensation in Central and South America. His popularity in the United States came slowly. In 1968, however, he scored his first big English-language hit with his soulful remake of "Light My Fire." *Feliciano,* the album on which the song appeared, rocketed to the top of the charts, and he was in demand for TV programs, concerts, and personal appearances.

Feliciano's success was sometimes coupled with conflict. During a series of concerts in England, the blind performer had pet problems. English law forbade the entry of his seeing-eye dog into the country. It was a problem for the musician not only because he needed the dog for navigation, but also because she had become his onstage trademark. The helpful canine led the singer to his stool in the center of the stage at the beginning of each performance and returned to bow with him at the end. Because of this law, Feliciano did not return to England for several years.

## Star-Spangled Controversy

One of Feliciano's most memorable performances was his unusual, stylized version of the "Star Spangled Banner," sung before a 1968 World Series baseball game at Detroit's Tiger Stadium. He sang a blues-rock version of the national anthem. It was the first truly nontraditional interpretation of the song performed before a national audience. The Tiger Stadium switchboard was flooded with angry calls and the performance became a hotly debated national controversy.

Some listeners were outraged and found Feliciano's "Spanish soul" treatment of the anthem unpatriotic. Others thought he gave the song a refreshing new twist. His follow-up recording of the "Star Spangled Banner"

José Feliciano. *Reproduced by permission of AP/Wide World Photos.*

sold very well. At that year's Grammy Awards ceremonies, he was named best male pop singer and best new artist.

Feliciano continued to enjoy stardom as a recording artist, performer, and composer over the next decade. He wrote the music for several films and television shows, including the theme to *Chico and the Man.* His Christmas song "Feliz Navidad," released in 1970, is now a holiday standard. Even though he released a only a handful of albums during the 1970s, he remained a frequent television guest and a major concert draw.

## Returns to Latin Roots

During the 1980s Feliciano returned to recording Spanish-language albums. The recordings garnered much praise and his international reputation grew. He received Grammy Awards for best Latin pop performance in 1983, 1986, 1989, and 1990. In 1991, at the first annual Latin Music Expo, he was presented with the event's first-ever Lifetime Achievement Award.

In 1991 Feliciano branched out to take a job as a Saturday morning disc jockey for a radio station in Connecticut, not far from his home. Besides playing a mixture of old and new songs, he chats with callers, tells "insider" stories about the music world, and occasionally plays his guitar or sings a song. He makes time for twenty to thirty benefit concerts per year for charity organizations that help the blind. He and his wife, Susan, have two children. To spend more time with his family, Feliciano has given up extended concert tours.

But he did not give up working in the recording studio and has continued to record albums in English and Spanish. In 1997, his album *Americano* was nominated for a Grammy, marking his fifteenth nomination. In 1998, his album *Señor Bolero* became his sixteenth nomination and within a year attained double platinum status in the United States. In all, Feliciano has received six Grammy Awards. In 2002 he was at work on an English-language album being produced by Emilio Estefan and Rudy Perez. New York City honored Feliciano by renaming Public School 155 in East Harlem "The Jose Feliciano Performing Arts School." Among his many awards, Feliciano was presented with the American Latino Media Arts (ALMA) Lifetime Achievement Award in 2000.

## For More Information

*Contemporary Musicians,* Volume 10, Gale, 1994.
*Detroit News,* September 6, 1991, p. B1.
*Grand Rapids Press,* December 20, 1991, p. B6.
"José Feliciano," RollingStone.com. Available at http://www.rollingstone.com/artists/default.asp?oid=3476 (accessed June 21, 2002).
José Feliciano Web site. Available at http://www.josefeliciano.com/bio.htm (accessed June 21, 2002).
*Time,* September 27, 1968, p. 78.

# Joseph A. Fernandez

Educational administrator, former New York City Public Schools chancellor
Born December 13, 1935, East Harlem, New York

*"I'm leaving here with my head held high and I can sleep well at night knowing that I did the best thing for the children of New York."*

Joseph A. Fernandez has devoted his entire professional life to improving educational opportunities for American students. In 1990 he became chancellor (superintendent) of New York City's public schools. With almost one million children, the district is the largest in the United States. At the time Fernandez took over, the city's school system was hurting financially, and its large administration was too slow to respond to the needs of students. Fernandez quickly made changes that pushed the district in a new direction. But the style that won him the job in the first place—high energy, single-mindedness, and a desire to experiment—also cost him his job after just three years.

Fernandez was born in 1935 in East Harlem, New York, to Angela and Joseph Fernandez, Sr., both of whom were of Puerto Rican heritage. His mother worked as a seamstress, then as a maid at Columbia University in New York. His father took whatever work he could find: washing windows, making deliveries, and driving a cab and a bus.

In his youth, Fernandez did not have a great respect for education. Although he attended parochial schools (private schools run by churches or other religious organizations) until the tenth grade, he was ultimately expelled for skipping classes. He then entered a public high school but dropped out before graduating. Most of the time he hung out on the streets of his neighborhood with a local gang, the Riffs. And he did drugs—almost overdosing twice on heroin.

## Gains Education in the Military

Fernandez finally began to turn his life around after joining the U.S. Air Force in the early 1950s. As he wrote in his autobiography, *Tales Out of School,* "I was not yet out of the woods with drugs, but I was on my way to being an educated man." While he was in the service, he spent time in Japan and Korea and completed courses to earn his high school diploma. Fernandez returned home in 1956, married his high school sweetheart, Lily Pons, and entered Columbia University with money from the military. He eventually completed his bachelor's degree at the Uni-

Joseph A. Fernandez. *Reproduced by permission of AP/Wide World Photos.*

versity of Miami in 1963. Immediately afterward he began teaching mathematics at Coral Park High School in Miami, part of the Dade County school system.

"The fourth largest in the nation, the Dade County school system was an ideal training ground for Fernandez," wrote Thomas Toch in *U.S. News & World Report.* Fernandez moved up the academic ladder quickly. After only a year, he became chairperson of the math department. Over the next twenty years, he held a wide variety of positions—principal, contract negotiator, assistant superintendent, and superintendent of the Dade County system.

As superintendent of Dade County public schools from 1987 to 1989, Fernandez showed the creative skills that would later win him the job in New York City. He started Saturday computer and music classes; he persuaded Miami businesses to contribute money and space for school activities; he convinced Miami voters to pass a $980 million school bond issue; and most of all, as Tony Hiss noted in the *New Yorker,* Fernandez constantly found "new ways to teach both inner-city and suburban kids and [gave] them, along with knowledge, self-regard and pride in being citizens."

## Sees Chancellorship as a Challenge

Fernandez took the job in New York City in 1990 because it was the toughest and most challenging in the field of American education. For years the district had been poorly managed. At that time, only about half of the $6,100 New York City spent on each high school student actually went to the schools. Fernandez went to work immediately to cut the waste. "In two weeks," Toch noted, "he cut his 5,200-person central staff by 400, suspended two principals, and ordered a local superintendent fired." He also appointed panels to study everything from classroom curricula to classroom overcrowding.

In his first year, Fernandez introduced two major reform measures. The first ended the building tenure system. Under this system, elementary and junior high school principals could not be fired from their positions if they had served in that capacity at the same school for five or more years—even if they neglected their duties to the students and teachers. Fernandez abolished the system and fired many negligent principals.

The second measure was his School-Based Management/Shared Decision-Making (SBM) program. The program, which he had developed in Miami, decreased the number of high-level administrators in the system and placed control of individual schools (everything from budgets to curriculum) into the hands of the principals, teachers, and parents. This ensured that each school was run by people who had a direct knowledge of a specific region in the district—and a personal interest in the system's overall success. School systems across America now use the SBM program.

## Controversial Programs Lead to Downfall

Fernandez continued to streamline and to improve the New York City school system. When forced to make massive budget cuts, he refused to take away any services for students. Instead, he eliminated more administrative positions. But in 1991 his programs started to come under fire. That year he wanted to start an AIDS education program in high schools. Part of the program included passing out free condoms to students. Although some parents and administrators objected to the practice for religious reasons, Fernandez's program was eventually approved by the New York City Board of Education.

The following year Fernandez faced an even tougher battle over his Children of the Rainbow program, which offered elementary school students a new, multicultural curriculum. The program was designed to expose young people to all of the various ethnic groups and family situations in New York's rich cultural landscape. Fernandez wanted to encourage children to understand and respect racial and cultural differences—and to recognize the beauty of the city's "melting pot" atmosphere. His Children of the Rainbow program was considered controversial, though, because it also focused on families headed by homosexual couples. Many people in New York City thought Fernandez was putting too much emphasis on social issues and not enough on reading, writing, and arithmetic. Fernandez told Hiss in the *New Yorker,* "A lot of people call this a social agenda that's irrelevant to the three R's. But I think it's the fourth R—respect for yourself and others."

Nonetheless, anger over his ideas and his outspoken manner continued. In addition, the publication of his book *Tales Out of School* in early 1993 did little to help his cause. It criticized everyone from the mayor of New York City to the governor of the state for their stand on education. When Fernandez's contract ended in June 1993, the New York City Board of Education voted 5–4 not to renew it.

Even though Fernandez was no longer chancellor of the city's school system, many of his reform programs were accepted and put into practice. The school board approved the creation of his numerous "community schools," which stay open late on weekdays and for six hours on Saturdays, offering activities and classes for students. The schools also have free dental and medical clinics. Fernandez has no regrets about his tenure as chancellor. "I'm leaving here with my head held high," he told Barbara Kantrowitz of *Newsweek,* "and I can sleep well at night knowing that I did the best thing for the children of New York."

## For More Information

Fernandez, Joseph A., *Tales Out of School: Joseph Fernandez's Crusade to Rescue American Education,* Little, Brown, 1993.

*Nation,* May 10, 1993, pp. 631–36.

*Newsweek,* February 22, 1993, pp. 54–55.

*New Yorker,* April 12, 1993, pp. 43–54.

*U.S. News & World Report,* October 1, 1990, pp. 76–77.

# Mary Joe Fernández

Professional tennis player
Born 1971, Dominican Republic

*"I just decided that if I was going to go to school, I was going to do it right. And I wasn't ready to sacrifice being with my friends."*

**M**ary Joe (María José) Fernández began playing professional tennis at the age of fourteen, but only part-time. Despite the lure of more money and quick fame, she chose to wear a neat uniform and attend Carrollton School of the Sacred Heart. She wanted to have normal high school experiences and spend some time with her friends. Fernández was an almost straight-A student throughout her high school years. During that time, she did manage to fit in a scaled-down schedule of tournaments, preparing herself to join the pro circuit in 1990.

Fernández was born in 1971 in the Dominican Republic to José and Sylvia Fernández. When she was six months old, her

Mary Joe Fernández. *Reproduced by permission of AP/Wide World Photos.*

family moved to Miami, Florida. At age three she tagged along when her father and older sister went to play tennis. To keep the young Fernández occupied, her father gave her a tennis racket to bounce balls off a wall. Two years later she began taking lessons from a professional player.

Fernández showed talent right from the start. From the age of ten, she won one tournament after another, beginning with the United States Tennis Association Nationals. By the time she started high school, her coaches were pressuring her to turn professional and play full time. Many players do this in hopes of earning more money, reaching their full potential at an earlier age, and having a longer career.

## Saving Friendships

If she went pro, Fernández would have had to take correspondence courses by mail to complete her high school diploma. She would have had to fit in homework between practices, then fax it to her teachers from her hotel rooms. She decided to postpone the daily competition and travel until after she had graduated. "I just decided that if I was going to go to school, I was going to do it right," Fernández explained to Austin Murphy of *Sports Illustrated*. "And I wasn't ready to sacrifice being with my friends."

When Fernández did miss classes to play in occasional tournaments, her friends helped out by faxing their class notes to her or dictating them to her over the phone. Because she was participating in the French Open at the time of her senior class final exams, her school allowed her to take them in August rather than in June. Unfortunately, she missed graduation ceremonies because of the tournament.

After collecting her diploma, Fernández jumped into the pro schedule full time in 1990. She did well, but soon discovered she had to make up for training time she lost while in school. Although she won forty of fifty singles matches and two tournaments, she suffered several injuries. During the year she was sidelined for a torn hamstring, a back injury, a severe knee sprain, and tendinitis. Her schoolmates teased her for failing to pass the President's Council on Physical Fitness test in high school because she couldn't perform the "arm-hang" well enough. Her coaches believed her lack of stamina and injuries were due to her poor exercise program and weak upper body strength.

Fernández then hired a strength coach and started a consistent aerobic and training schedule. The hard work paid off. During the period between late 1990 and early 1991 she rose from seventh to fourth in the rankings of the top women players. In 1992 she reached the semifinals in the singles at the U.S. Open before losing to future champion Monica Seles. In the 1993 French Open, Fernández fought a courageous battle against Steffi Graf in the final before losing 6–4, 2–6, 4–6. She won a Grand Slam in the 1996 French Open with partner Lindsay Davenport and she was a member of the winning United States's 1996 Fed Cup squad. In 1998, Fernández had surgery on her right wrist and missed the beginning of the season, but she was back in the spring, winning again.

## Olympic Moments

Fernández's brightest moment on the court, however, came in the 1992 Summer Olympics held in Barcelona, Spain. Fernández and doubles partner Gigi Fernández (no relation) captured the gold medal by defeating Spain's own Arantxa Sánchez Vicaro and Conchita Martínez. Watching the match from the stands was Spanish King Juan Carlos. In the 1996 Olympics, Fernández and Fernández took the gold medal for doubles again, defeating Jana Novotna and Helena Sukova of the Czech Republic.

By 1993 Fernández had earned more than $2 million from tournaments and endorsements (allowing companies to use her name to advertise their products). Despite her wealth and fame, Fernández continues to maintain a down-to-earth lifestyle and attitude. When Hurricane Andrew devastated areas of Florida in 1992, leaving many homeless, she helped organize a charity tournament to benefit the victims.

In 2000 Fernández was forced to withdraw from the Australian Open because of the recurring injury to her wrist. She then began a new career as an analyst on women's tennis events for the television stations ESPN and ESPN2.

## For More Information

Cole, Melanie, *Mary Joe Fernández: Real Life Reader Biography,* Childs, MD: Mitchell Lane, 1998.

"Mary Joe Fernández," ESPN.com. Available at http://espn.go.com/espninc/personalities/maryjoe-fernandez.html (accessed June 21, 2002).

*Sports Illustrated,* February 11, 1991, pp. 76–79; June 14, 1993, pp. 26–33.

*Tennis,* June 1994, p. 94+.

*World Tennis,* February 1991, pp. 25–26.

# Andy García

Actor
Born April 12, 1956, in Bejucal, Cuba

*"There's nothing that I cherish more than my culture and what I am. But to call me the great Hispanic actor is ridiculous; it's racism. They don't call Dustin Hoffman the great Jewish-American actor."*

From a young age, Andy García had hopes of growing up to be a professional basketball player. When he was a senior in high school, however, he was benched for weeks after contracting mononucleosis. While recovering from the long-term illness, he began to think about a career in the entertainment industry. Although he had performed in several school plays, he had never really considered acting as a profession. Once he made up his mind to pursue it, though, he never looked back. "From then on," he related to Jennet Conant in *Redbook,* "acting was a hunger in the pit of my stomach, and if I didn't cater to it, it got worse."

Andrés Arturo García Menendez was born in 1956 in Bejucal, Cuba, the youngest of three children. His mother, Amelie, taught English, while his father, Rene García Nuñez, was a prominent lawyer. The family enjoyed a comfortable life in the small town outside the capital city of Havana until the Cuban Revolution broke out in the late 1950s. Rebels led by Fidel Castro and Ernesto "Ché" Guevara sought to overthrow the brutal Cuban dictator Fulgencio Batista. After about two years of fighting, the rebels were victorious, and by December 1959 Castro had risen to power. All private property was then seized by the new government. Having lost all they had, the García family fled to Miami.

García remembers his early years in Florida as difficult ones. He was only five when he came to America, and at that time he could not speak English. His parents took what work they could and began to rebuild life for the family. Even the children helped out. On his way home from school, young García picked up soda pop cans for change. When he grew older, he spent his evenings sweeping out the hosiery factory where his father worked.

## Sports Give Way to Acting

Because he initially had trouble speaking English and was short for his age, García was involved in fights almost every day during his years in grade school. By the time he reached high school, however, his greatly improved English and his athletic abilities helped enlarge his social circle. After he became ill, though, García was forced to change his main goal in life. He took the switch from sports to acting in stride. "Acting is very much like a game of basketball," he explained to Stephanie Mansfield in *Gentlemen's Quarterly.* "There's a moment-to-moment, spontaneous thing about it. You don't know what's going to happen."

García enrolled in Florida International University and majored in theater. He left college without graduating but soon found that Florida offered very few opportunities for a fledgling actor, so he moved to Los Angeles in 1978. While looking for acting parts, he worked at odd jobs—loading trucks and waiting on tables. When he could, García did improvisational comedy at clubs around Los Angeles. His first television role, a small part as a gang member, was on the premiere episode of the long-running television drama *Hill Street Blues* in 1981.

García found roles in motion pictures much harder to come by. Although he had small parts in a few movies in the early 1980s, he was denied many more parts because of his ethnic background. As he told Mansfield, "I was rejected. And in the rudest of ways.... All the racist kinds of things." His first big film role finally came in 1985, when he played a Hispanic detective in *The Mean Season.*

## Commands Attention With Breakthrough Role

The following year García landed the part of a charming but brutal drug dealer in *8 Million Ways to Die*. Although the movie received only lukewarm reviews, his performance stood out, capturing the attention of film critics—and of director Brian De Palma, who wanted García to play the villain in his next movie, *The Untouchables*. Fearing he would always be typecast as a Hispanic bad guy, García convinced De Palma to let him play a good guy FBI agent instead. His performance in the 1987 film won him international acclaim. Subsequent parts in films like *Black Rain* (with Michael Douglas) and *Internal Affairs* (with Richard Gere) also cast García in law enforcement roles, but he proved he was capable of acting out a range of intense emotions. Critics seemed to notice his presence even in small supporting roles in other feature films.

García achieved star status in 1990 with his appearance as the illegitimate nephew of Don Corleone in *The Godfather Part III*. He received an Academy Award nomination for his role and quickly went on to star in other major films, including *Hero,* with Dustin Hoffman and Geena Davis, and a thriller titled *Jennifer Eight*. Each of these films offered García the chance to branch out beyond the kinds of roles he had played almost exclusively earlier in his career: either a cop or a typically "ethnic" character of Hispanic descent. "There's nothing that I cherish more than my culture and what I am," García told Charla Krupp of *Glamour*. "But to call me the great Hispanic actor is ridiculous; it's racism. They don't call Dustin Hoffman the great Jewish-American actor."

Andy García. *Reproduced by permission of AP/Wide World Photos.*

In 1993 García moved behind the camera to direct a Spanish-language documentary film about Cuban musician Israel "Cachao" Lopez. Gary Hentzi praised the film in *Film Quarterly,* noting that it "captures many beautifully executed performances of danzones and descargas, featuring some of the most gifted exponents of Latin music in the United States. More generally, the film … offers a splendidly instructive panorama of Cuban musical genres, from the elegant danzas of Ignacio Cervantes and Ernesto Lecuona to the major African-influenced forms like the son, the conga, the guaracha, and the type of traditional rumba known as the yambu." Hentzi continues that the film goes beyond its musical subject to explore the Cuban American "desire to preserve some sense of imaginative connection to a country from which they have been absent for so long, and it is one of the strengths of Andy García's film that it communicates the force of this desire without falling into strident political posturing."

Throughout the rest of the 1990s and into the 2000s, the question of being typecast into any one kind of role was put to rest for good for García. Even when some of his films have been poorly reviewed, García has been acclaimed for the depth of his understanding of his characters and his tight and intelligent performances. In 1994 he played a kind and understanding husband to an alcoholic Meg Ryan in *When a Man Loves a Woman*. In 1996 he played a slick con man in *Things to Do in Denver when You're Dead*. In *Night Falls on Manhattan* (1997), García played a naive district attorney who begins to discover a scandal in the New York City police department that might involve his father. In the same year he took the role of 1930s gangster Lucky Luciano in *Hoodlum*.

In 1999's *Just the Ticket* García portrayed a ticket scalper. Although the movie received very mixed reviews, Oliver Jones of *Variety* lauded García's performance, saying: "This is the performance that García fans have been waiting for since his breathtaking debut in 1987's *The Untouchables:* As a ticket scalper who has never had an honest job, he's cocky, vulnerable, dangerous and charitable all at once." In *The Unsaid* (2001), García plays a psychologist haunted by his son's suicide. The well-reviewed *The Man from Elysian Fields* was released later that year, in which García plays a down-and-out writer desperate to make a living. At the end of 2001 *Ocean's*

*Eleven* was released, a blockbuster remake of an original "Rat Pack" film starring Frank Sinatra, about a group of thieves stealing from a Las Vegas casino owner played in the remake by García. Starring with him are Brad Pitt, George Clooney, Julia Roberts, and a host of others.

## Family Comes First

In 1982 García married Marivi (short for Maria Victoria), a Cuban exile he met while in college. They had three daughters, and in January 2002, Marivi gave birth to a son, Andres Antonio García-Lorido. García insists that their lives remain very normal despite his stardom and wealth. He has a reputation for being a family man and has refused roles in films that include explicit sex scenes that might embarrass his family. To be near his family, he and his wife purchased a home in Key Biscayne, Florida, in 1991.

Part of the reason García moved back to Florida from Los Angeles is that he wanted his children to grow up in an environment that stresses their Cuban identity. He still considers himself a political exile of Cuba. "I had a great childhood in Miami Beach, but ultimately it's like having a stepmother," he explained to Conant. "If you are ripped from the womb of your real mother at the age of five, you can love your stepmother, but your mother is missing. You can't touch her, only love her from afar."

On May 13, 2002, the Second Annual Crowning Achievement: A Celebration of Stars Who Care honored Andy García, along with actors Hector Elizondo, Laura Elena Harring, and **Elizabeth Peña** (see entry), as exemplary role models and leading contributors to the progress of the Hispanic community.

## For More Information

"Boys Just Want to Have Fun: For Danny Ocean and His Swell Pallies, Easy Does It," *Newsweek,* December 17, 2001.

*Gentlemen's Quarterly,* December 1990, pp. 272–77+.

*Glamour,* January 1991, p. 92.

Hentzi, Gary, Review of *Cachao … Como Su Ritmo No Hay Dos, Film Quarterly,* June 22, 2000.

*Hispanic,* January/February 1994, pp. 14–16.

Jones, Oliver, Review of *Just the Ticket, Variety,* March 1, 1999.

*Redbook,* January 1993, pp. 25–29.

# Jerry Garcia

Singer, songwriter, guitarist
Born August 1, 1942, San Francisco, California
Died August 9, 1995, Forest Knolls, California

*"It's just great to be involved in something that doesn't hurt anybody. If it provides some uplift and some comfort in people's lives, it's just that much nicer."*

In the 1990s Jerry Garcia and his psychedelic 1960s band, the Grateful Dead, were enjoying a comeback. Along with other classic rock musicians, the Dead recycled their hits, hit the concert trail, and made new musical waves. To the legions of "Deadheads" who made festivals of every concert, Garcia was legendary—the big, lovable musician with the high lonesome voice and unique guitar style. Grounded in American roots music, he spearheaded the Dead's fusion of psychedelic rock, blues, soul, country, and bluegrass. Unlike many contemporaries, the Dead often seemed to transcend the commercial music world by keeping in touch with both the styles of the past and the possibilities of the future. Garcia's lengthy guitar solos had some of the daring of free jazz but retained the same striving, hopeful twang that came through in his vocals. "His playing was moody, awesome, sophisticated, hypnotic, and subtle," noted legendary singer-songwriter Bob Dylan—a longtime friend who once recorded an album with the Dead—at Garcia's funeral, numerous sources reported.

## A Musical Background

Garcia was born in 1942 in San Francisco, California, to José and Ruth Garcia. His father was a Spanish immigrant who loved music. He owned a bar and was a respected musician and bandleader around San Francisco. The young Garcia had already begun piano lessons when his father died in a fishing accident in 1952. He gave up the piano shortly after this because of his lack of interest and a physical disfigurement (while chopping wood, his older brother had accidently cut off half of Garcia's right middle finger when Garcia was four).

Garcia's mother, who worked as a nurse, presented him with an accordion for his fifteenth birthday. By this time, however, he was more interested in owning a guitar. "So we took it down to the pawn shop and I got this little Danelectro, an electric guitar with a tiny amplifier, and, man, I was just in heaven," Garcia explained to a reporter for *Rolling Stone.* "I stopped everything I was doing at the time."

Garcia had no interest in school, a problem that caused him to repeat the eighth grade. Matters didn't improve in high school. He cut classes and was regularly in trouble for fighting, drinking, and using drugs. When he was seventeen, he finally dropped out of school to join the army. Military discipline was no easier for him to accept. After nine months, he was discharged on the suggestion of his commander.

## Learns Guitar in the Army

While in the army, Garcia had became interested in traditional American folk and blues music, and in acoustic guitar. "I used to do things like look at pictures of guitar players and look at their hands and try to make the chords they were doing, anything, any little thing," he said in *Rolling Stone.* For the next few years he practiced guitar and hung out with other young musicians who were crowding California college campuses. By 1964 he was part of a jug band called the Warlocks, which included Phil Lesh, Ron McKenna, Bill Kreutzmann, and Bob Weir. When the Beatles invaded American in 1964, the group turned to rock and roll.

Garcia and his band mates fit right in with the San Francisco hippie culture. They performed at concerts throughout the state. Sometime during this period the band changed its name to the Grateful Dead and adopted a skull-and-roses logo. Warner Brothers offered them a recording contract in 1967, and the band issued its first album, *The Grateful Dead.*

Two more albums were released in the next two years, but neither one was a great success. Their first big seller was *Live Dead,* a 1969 recording of one of their live concerts. "Our income doesn't come from records," Garcia told the *Detroit Free Press.* "It comes from [live] work. Making records is a different thing. It's not playing for warm human beings.... In my mind, it's never really been making music."

## Deadheads Keep Band Going

The 1970s brought tough times. After two successful albums were released in 1970, *Workingman's Dead* and *American Beauty,* McKenna died of alcohol abuse. The Dead broke away from Warner Brothers and embarked upon a series of business decisions that were financial failures. They set up a headquarters in a small suburban house, then drifted apart. Garcia worked solo for a while. But Grateful Dead fans just wouldn't let the group die.

In its 1971 release, *Grateful Dead,* the group had inserted a short message: "Dead Freaks Unite. Who are you? Where are you? Send us your name and address and we'll keep you informed." The reaction was overwhelming. By 1972 there were newsletters that kept Deadheads in touch with the band and with each other.

The network grew more sophisticated over the decades. Newsletters changed to telephone hotlines, which then gave way to electronic bulletin boards. By the time of Garcia's death, the Deadhead mailing list contained ninety thousand names in America and twenty-thousand in Europe. Deadheads came from a wide variety of professions and lifestyles—from college professors to bikers. Many bought concert tickets in packages and traveled together from city to city following the band.

## A Deadly Drug Habit

Garcia's long-time drug abuse took its toll in 1985. That year he was arrested in Golden Gate Park in San Francisco and charged with possession of cocaine and heroin. Authorities allowed him to undergo drug rehabilitation treatment rather than serve time in jail. Despite this treatment, his physical condition continued to deteriorate. In 1986 he slipped into a week-long diabetic coma brought on by his drug use. He recovered, but his career was threatened. He had to take lessons to remember how to play guitar.

"There was something I needed or thought I needed from drugs," he explained to a *Rolling Stone* reporter. "I don't know what it was, exactly.... But after awhile, it was just the drugs running me, and that's an intolerable situation."

In 1987, the Grateful Dead released *In the Dark,* the group's first recording in seven years. The album became the group's biggest selling record. One of the singles off the album, "Touch of Gray," became the Dead's first-ever hit. That year the Grateful Dead toured with folk legend Bob Dylan and on its own. Later in the year, Garcia played a two-week stint on Broadway with his own bands. In the early 1990s, the guitarist had trimmed down and began following a better diet and healthier lifestyle. He branched into the clothing business with a line of ties based on his drawings—even though Garcia never wore a tie.

Jerry Garcia. *Reproduced by permission of AP/Wide World Photos.*

But the good health was not to last. In 1992 Garcia canceled his tours to deal with exhaustion. He was still forgetting things and scrambling words from his coma. Garcia had struggled with drugs, alcohol, cigarettes, and weight problems for years and it had taken a tremendous toll on his body. Worse yet, no matter what his intentions, he apparently never got clear of the drugs.

In July 1995, Garcia checked into the Betty Ford Center in California to detox (clear his body of drugs). He spent a few weeks there and went home but soon checked into another small clinic in Forest Knolls, California. He died there on August 9, 1995, of heart failure. He had recently married Deborah Koons (his third wife), who told mourners, *People* reported, that her husband "died in his sleep with a smile on his face. He wanted to make it. He was on an upswing." Many who praised Garcia's artistic achievements—President Bill Clinton among them—saw his passing as an object lesson in the damage done by drugs and other toxins.

## For More Information

*Detroit Free Press,* June 19, 1984.

Gates, David, "Requiem for the Dead," *Newsweek,* August 21, 1995, p. 46.

Jackson, Blair, *Grateful Dead: The Music Never Stopped,* Delilah Books, 1983.

*New Yorker,* October 11, 1993, pp. 96–102.

*People,* August 21, 1995, pp. 64–70; August 28, 1995, pp. 36–39

*Rolling Stone,* July 16, 1987; October 31, 1991, pp. 36–41+.

# Gabriel García Márquez

Writer, journalist
Born March 6, 1928, Aracataca, Colombia

*"I had an extraordinary childhood surrounded by highly imaginative and superstitious people, people who lived in a misty world populated by phantasms."*

Gabriel García Márquez is one of Latin America's most influential writers. He writes best sellers using "magic realism," a technique whereby fantastic happenings are interwoven with realistic, matter-of-fact events. His most acclaimed work is his 1967 novel, *Cien años de soledad* (published in English in 1970 as *One Hundred Years of Solitude*). For that masterpiece and for his entire body of writings, García Márquez was awarded the prestigious Nobel Prize for literature in 1982.

García Márquez was born in 1928 in Aracataca, Columbia, the oldest of sixteen children born to Gabriel Eligio García Márquez and Luisa Santiaga Márquez Iguaran. He lived in the Caribbean part of Colombia, which he has described in interviews as a "fantastic place." The people there were descendants of pirates, smugglers, and slaves, a mixture of cultures given to magical stories and legends. Because his family was poor, he lived with his grandparents until he was eight years old.

## Childhood Filled With Ghosts

García Márquez grew very close to his grandparents. He claims his writing style comes from his grandmother, who would invent fantasies to avoid answering his questions about their life and its often sad realities. "I had an extraordinary childhood surrounded by highly imaginative and superstitious people," he explained to Manuel Osorio in the *UNESCO Courier,* "people who lived in a misty world populated by phantasms."

When his grandfather died in 1936, García Márquez was sent back to live with his parents. He found this change very disturbing at first. However, he soon realized that his parents were a positive influence for him.

Raising many children in extreme poverty resulted in a hard life for his mother. Since García Márquez was the oldest child, his relationship with her was always very serious. He said later that there was nothing they could not tell each other. His father was a telegraph operator who wrote poetry, played the violin, and loved to read. He shared his love of the arts with his oldest son.

Free public schools are uncommon in much of South America. Since García Márquez's family was desperately poor, he had to apply for a scholarship to attend school when he was twelve. To take a qualifying exam for the scholarship, he was forced to undertake a seven-hundred-mile, eight-day voyage by ship and train to the capital city of Bogotá. He was competing with three thousand students for only three hundred scholarships. While on the train, García Márquez met and befriended a shy man. It turned out that this man was in charge of the scholarship program. He awarded a scholarship to García Márquez, whose schooling was thus assured.

## Journalism Versus Creative Writing

By the time García Márquez finished high school in 1946, he had earned a reputation as a writer. Although he next studied law at the University of Bogatá, he began to write short stories. In 1950 he joined the staff of a newspaper. During the day, he worked as a journalist; at night, he worked as a novelist. By 1955 he had completed work on his first book, *La hojarasca* ("Leaf Storm").

In 1958 García Márquez married his childhood sweetheart, Mercedes Barcha.

Gabriel García Márquez. *Reproduced by permission of Alfred A. Knopf.*

After he had first proposed to her when he was thirteen, they maintained a sporadic, casual relationship until they were ready to marry. The couple eventually had two sons, Rodrigo and Gonzalo. García Márquez continued to work as a reporter, covering stories throughout Latin America, including the Cuban Revolution in 1959. By 1961 he had also managed to write two more books, *El coronel no tiene quien le escriba* ("No One Writes to the Colonel") and *La mala hora* ("The Evil Hour").

In 1965 García Márquez left journalism to write fiction full time. He spent eighteen months in Mexico working on *One Hundred Years of Solitude*. When he finished the book, he was so poor he couldn't afford to mail it all at once to his publisher. To raise the money needed for postage, his wife sold their blender. She then divided the bundle of pages into two halves. By mistake she mailed the second half of the book first. Then, when she had raised more money, she sent along the first half. Luckily, the publisher recognized the excellence of the book, no matter in what order he received it.

## Magical Masterpiece Is a Best-seller

*One Hundred of Years of Solitude* is set in an imaginary community on the coast of Colombia and follows the lives of several generations of the Buendia family. Besides describing the complicated family relationships, the story reflects the political, social, and economic problems of South America. The mix of historical and fictitious elements in the book give it its air of "magic realism."

The novel was a best-seller from the day it appeared in 1967. It has been translated into thirty languages and has sold more than ten million copies. *One Hundred Years of Solitude* has been so popular that García Márquez has been offered millions of dollars to have a film version made of the book. He refuses to allow it. "I want readers to go on imagining the characters as they see them," he told interviewer Claudia Dreifus. "That isn't possible in the cinema. In movies, the image is so definite that the spectator can no longer imagine the character as he wants to, only as the screen imposes it on him."

During the 1960s and 1970s, works by Latin American writers were increasingly translated and made available to American readers. *One Hundred Years of Solitude* helped solidify the presence of these writers in the American market. A critic for the *Antioch Review,* quoted in *Hispanic Writers,* wrote that García Márquez's work would also help insure that "Latin America itself will be looked on less as a crazy subculture and more as a fruitful, alternative way of life."

## Nobel Prize in Literature

When García Márquez was awarded the Nobel Prize in 1982, he was praised for his literary talents. The Swedish Academy that presents the prizes noted in its citation the "each new work of his is received by critics and readers as an event of world importance, is translated into many languages and published as quickly as possible in large editions."

The Academy also cited García Márquez for his activities on behalf of the poor and the oppressed in Latin America. The writer is a well-known social activist who uses his fame to promote political goals. García Márquez indicated that the money he received with the Nobel Prize would be used to help political prisoners and leftists in Latin America. His close friendship with Cuban President Fidel Castro and his communist political views eventually caused him to flee Colombia and settle in Mexico City, Mexico. The U.S. government has prohibited García Márquez from spending time in the United States because of his views and his involvement with Castro.

## After the Nobel

García Márquez hasn't rested on his success. He has published numerous books—both fiction and nonfiction—and has written several screenplays for Spanish television. One of his most beloved works is the

1985 novel *El amor en los tiempos del cólera* (published in English in 1988 as *Love in the Time of Cholera*). It is the captivating story of Florentino Ariza's undying love for the woman who rejected him twice. Merle Rubin, writing in the *Christian Science Monitor,* labeled the novel "a boldly romantic, profoundly imaginative, fully imagined work of fiction that expands our sense of life's infinite possibilities."

With *El general en su labertino* (The General in His Labyrinth), first published in 1989, García Márquez told yet another type of story: historical fiction. The novel relates the story of the final months in the life of the great South American revolutionary leader Simón Bolívar (1783–1830), who gained independence for the northern colonies of South America. *The General in His Labyrinth* details Bolívar's renouncing of the Colombian presidency and his final long journey down the Magdalena River to his death near the Caribbean coast in 1830. Applauded for its research, the novel was dubbed "a fascinating literary tour de force and a moving tribute to an extraordinary man," by novelist Margaret Atwood in the *New York Times Book Review.*

In 1992 García Márquez published *Strange Pilgrims,* a collection of a dozen short stories, all set in Europe. His 1995 novel, *Of Love and Other Demons* tells a story he covered as a young journalist, recreating the fabulous life of Sierva Maria, the daughter of wealthy parents who grows up with the African slaves on her family's plantation. Bitten by a rabid dog, the girl undergoes an exorcism.

García Márquez produced a more journalistic book in the 1997 *News of a Kidnap-ping,* which recounts the edge-of-the-seat tale of a series of kidnappings mounted by the drug lords of Colombia in their attempts to avoid U.S. extradition. In 2001 García Márquez came out with a series of short picture books. The illustrated short stories in hard cover books are somber and haunting and not necessarily for children. Among them are *La siesta del martes* (Tuesday's Siesta or Nap), *Maria dos Prazeres,* and *Un senor muy viejo con unas alas enormes,* (A Very Old Man with Large Wings).

As prolific in his senior years as he was as a younger man, it is clear that García Márquez connects with his craft at a level many writers can only hope to achieve. He explained in an interview with the *UNESCO Courier:* "When you are working hard on something, trying to make sense of it, worrying at it, fanning it into a blaze, you reach a point where you control it and identify with it so completely that you feel that a divine wind is dictating it to you. That state of inspiration exists, yes, and when you experience it, although it may not last very long, it is the greatest happiness that anyone could possibly experience."

## For More Information

Atwood, Margaret, review of *The General in His Labyrinth, New York Times Book Review,* September 16, 1990, pp. 1, 30.

*Christian Science Monitor,* May 12, 1988.

Dolan, Sean, *Gabriel García Márquez,* Chelsea House, 1994.

Elnadi, Bahgat; Rifaat, Adel; Labarca, Miguel, "Gabriel García Márquez: The Writer's Craft," *UNESCO Courier,* February 1996, p. 4.

*Hispanic Writers,* 2nd Edition, Gale, 2000.

Lopez, Adriana, "*Tuesday's Siesta,* Review," *Library Journal,* June 1, 2001.

*UNESCO Courier,* October 1991, pp. 8–9.

# Roberto C. Goizueta

Chairman and chief executive officer of Coca-Cola
Born November 18, 1931, Havana, Cuba
Died October 18, 1997, Atlanta, Georgia

*"We are not going to spend long hours sitting down and trying to foretell the future. Instead, we will devote our energies to creating it."*

**W**hen Roberto Crispulo Goizueta became the chief executive officer (CEO) of the Coca-Cola Company in March 1981, the ninety-five-year-old beverage company was worth about $4 billion. At the time, only one cola—the original—carried the name Coca-Cola. Throughout the 1980s, Goizueta streamlined the company's operations while introducing new products to worldwide markets. By the early 1990s, with over half a dozen Coca-Cola products being sold in more than 195 countries around the world, the company had grown to more than $50 billion in value. Despite these achievements, Goizueta was not content to let the company rest. "We are not going to spend long hours sitting down and trying to foretell the future," he told *Financial World*. "Instead, we will devote our energies to creating it."

Goizueta was born in 1931 in Havana, Cuba, to Crispulo Goizueta and Aida Cantera. His father owned a sugar plantation and was wealthy enough to send him to a small preparatory school in New Hampshire. There young Goizueta learned to speak English partly by watching movies. After he graduated as class valedictorian, he attended Yale University in New Haven, Connecticut, to study chemical engineering. He received his bachelor of science degree in 1953, shortly before marrying Olga Casteleiro. The couple eventually had three children. Goizueta returned to Cuba in 1954, but instead of working on his family's sugar plantation, he became the technical director of Coca-Cola's plant in Havana.

## Future Altered by the Cuban Revolution

The Goizueta family's future was soon changed by a social revolution that swept across Cuba. At the time, the country was controlled by Fulgencio Batista, considered by many to be the most brutal dictator in Latin America. A rebel force led by Fidel Castro and Ernesto "Ché" Guevara tried to overthrow Batista. After a few years, the rebels' guerrilla warfare—consisting of quick attacks and ambushes—proved successful, and Castro and his comrades took over the government in 1959. They immediately put banks and other businesses under the control of the government. They also seized the land of wealthy landowners, and Goizueta's family lost all of its money. In 1960 Goizueta fled to Miami, Florida.

Coca-Cola soon made Goizueta an assistant to the senior vice president in charge of research for Latin America. He was based in Nassau, the capital of the Bahamas. In 1964 the company transferred him to its corporate headquarters in Atlanta, Georgia. Over the next fifteen years, he steadily climbed the corporate ladder. By 1980 he had become Coca-Cola's president and chief operating officer.

Coca-Cola's chief executive officer at the time was Paul Austin. Although Coca-Cola was still the number one soft drink company in the world—selling over 1.3 billion cases of Coke a year—Austin had failed to make the company grow. Coca-Cola's share of the soft drink market was gradually declining. Robert Woodruff, the long-term corporate executive who had built Coca-Cola into a powerful firm and who was still the chairman of the company's executive committee, decided a change was necessary. In 1981, he called Goizueta into his office and asked him, as John Huey related in *Fortune,* "Roberto, how would you like to run my company?" Goizueta is said to have responded, "Well, Mr. Woodruff, I'd be flattered."

## Takes Gambles and Wins

The Coca-Cola Company seemed to bounce back as soon as Goizueta took over its top position. He did what no previous executive of the company had dared to do: he took risks. In an effort to focus Coca-Cola's interests primarily on the soft drink market, Goizueta sold off several unrelated businesses the company owned. He also gambled on brand development, making the decision to offer the calorie-conscious public a diet cola worthy of the Coca-Cola label.

Diet Coke was introduced in 1982, and many industry observers were sure it would fail. If it did, then the Coca-Cola name, which had been on only one product for nearly a century, would be dragged down with it. But the gamble paid off. Within a few years, Diet Coke became the world's third most

Roberto C. Goizueta. *Reproduced by permission of Arte Público Press.*

popular soft drink (behind original Coke and its archrival, Pepsi). By 1986 the company's sales of Coca-Cola, Diet Coke, Cherry Coke, Diet Cherry Coke, Caffeine-Free Coke, and Caffeine-Free Diet Coke reached more than 2.2 billion cases per year.

## New Coke Is a Disaster

The introduction of New Coke (called simply "Coke") in 1985 was an idea that never took off—and almost cost the company its lead in the soft drink war against Pepsi. Goizueta thought it was important for Coca-Cola to come out with a sweeter-tasting cola to compete with Pepsi's growing popularity. But consumer complaints about changes to the one-hundred-year-old original cola formula were immediate and loud. Just three months after New Coke hit the shelves, Goizueta had to admit he made a mistake. The original-formula Coke was then brought back as Coke Classic, and it quickly regained its top spot among soft drinks.

Another gamble that almost didn't pay off for Coca-Cola was its purchase of Columbia Pictures in 1982 for $692 million. The beverage company had no experience in managing a movie studio, and Columbia had a long string of box office losers after the hit movie *Ghostbusters* was released in 1984. But Goizueta had also used Columbia to invest in television programs, such as game show favorites *Wheel of Fortune* and *Jeopardy.* The money made through those shows quickly offset the money lost by the movies. In 1989 Coca-Cola sold its share in Columbia Pictures to the Sony Corporation for $1.55 billion.

"We used to be an American company with a large international business," Goizueta remarked to Huey in *Fortune.* "Now we are a large international company with a sizable American business." With the fall of communist regimes throughout Eastern Europe in the late 1980s and the early 1990s, the worldwide soft drink market opened up. Coca-Cola was there, investing $1 billion in the region. It helped build million-dollar bottling plants in cities such as Warsaw, Poland, and St. Petersburg, Russia. In 1993 Coca-Cola's name was on four of the five top-selling soft drinks in the world.

Goizueta managed the Coca-Cola Company through one of the most successful periods in its history. He continued to serve as CEO until his death at the age of sixty-five

from complications of lung cancer. In his obituary, *U.S. News and World Report* quoted a part of a speech he had given two years before his death: "My story boils down to a single, inspiring reality ... the reality that a young immigrant could come to this country, be given a chance to work hard and apply his skills, and ultimately earn the opportunity to lead not only a large corporation but an institution that actually symbolizes the very essence of America and American ideals."

## For More Information

*Barron's,* May 9, 1994, pp. 29–33.
*Business Week,* April 13, 1992, pp. 96, 98.
*The Chronicle of Coca-Cola Since 1886,* Time, Inc., 1950.
"Coca-Cola," *Encyclopedia of Consumer Brands,* Volume 1: *Consumable Products,* edited by Janice Jorgensen, Gale, 1994.
*Financial World,* April 4, 1989, p. 78.
*Fortune,* October 26, 1987, pp. 46–56; May 31, 1993, pp. 44–54.
Mallory, Maria, "A Single, Inspiring Reality," (obituary), *U.S. News and World Report,* November 3, 1997, p. 15.
*Wall Street Journal,* April 22, 1994, p. B12.

# Henry Barbosa Gonzalez

U.S. congressman
Born May 3, 1916, San Antonio, Texas
Died November 28, 2000, San Antonio, Texas

*"If a bill violates the constitutional rights of even one person, then it has to be struck down."*

Henry Gonzalez, Democratic congressman from Texas, was the first Mexican American elected to the U.S. Congress. He won his first political election in 1953 when he ran for San Antonio's city council. Three years later he became the first Mexican American in over one hundred years elected to the Texas state senate. In 1961 Gonzalez began his service in the House of Representatives in Washington, D.C. Over the years, his fiery speeches against what he saw as corruption or evil in government brought him much attention. Those members of Congress who disagreed with his stand often labeled him an eccentric or a stubborn fool. No one, however, ever questioned his reputation for honesty and independence in all the thirty-seven years he held office.

Henry Barbosa Gonzalez was born in 1916 into a family that traces is roots in Mexico back hundreds of years. In the sixteenth century his ancestors voyaged from southern Spain to help settle the northern Mexican state of Durango. In the early 1900s, his father, Leonides Gonzalez, was mayor of the town of Mapimi in Durango. He and his wife, Genoveva Barbosa, were forced to flee to San Antonio during the 1911 Mexican Revolution, which pitted farm peasants against wealthy landowners and the Mexican government.

While Gonzalez was growing up, he was surrounded by talk of politics. His close-knit family also stressed education, and the young Gonzalez became an avid reader, spending many hours at the local library. After attending San Antonio pub-

Henry Barbosa Gonzalez. *Reproduced by permission of AP/Wide World Photos.*

lic schools, he enrolled in San Antonio Junior College, studying there for two years. He then entered the University of Texas at Austin to study engineering and law. Short on money, he had to return to his hometown after only two years. He eventually earned his law degree in 1943 from St. Mary's University School of Law in San Antonio.

Gonzalez did not begin his career as a lawyer. Instead, he ran a Spanish-English translation service and worked as a probation officer in the county's juvenile court system. In 1950 he began working for the San Antonio Housing Authority. As part of his job, he helped resettle families into new homes after they had been evicted from their previous ones.

## Elected to First Office

In 1953 Gonzalez entered the world of politics, winning a seat on San Antonio's city council. One of the laws he helped enact during his term was one ending segregation in city buildings. Three years later he became the first Mexican American Texas state senator in 110 years. He attracted national attention as an outspoken defender of equal rights for minorities. At one point, he spoke on the floor of the Texas senate for twenty-two continuous hours against thirteen bills he thought were racist. He told Christopher Hitchens of *Harper's* magazine years later, "If a bill violates the constitutional rights of even one person, then it has to be struck down."

In 1960 Gonzalez was elected to Congress for the first time, as a Democrat representing the Twentieth Congressional District. Again, he broke new ground, becoming the first Mexican American congressman from Texas. Although his district is mainly Hispanic, Gonzalez's work in Congress has been for people in all ethnic groups. As Carlos Conde noted in *Hispanic,* Gonzalez "believes that using ethnicity as a crutch only invites more typecasting."

## Witness to Recent Events in American History

Reelected by overwhelming margins at each election for the thirty-seven years he was in Congress, Gonzalez has seen many events that have become part of American history. In 1963 he rode with President John F. Kennedy on Air Force One (the president's plane) just minutes before Kennedy was assassinated in Dallas. In 1972 he wanted to question President Richard Nixon's admin-istration about its possible role in the burglary of the Democratic national headquarters in the Watergate apartment complex. He was denied the chance. And in the mid-1970s, he tried to bring attention to the safety problems surrounding nuclear plants. In 1979 the Three Mile Island nuclear plant in Pennsylvania suffered a partial melting of its uranium core, releasing some radioactivity into the surrounding land and water.

Gonzalez ruffled a few feathers in Congress and in the White House with his views over the years. He considered himself a moderate in the fight for Mexican American civil rights and opposes radical militants. Still, he fought for many Mexican American goals, including protection for farm workers, better education and housing for the poor, and the defeat of the bracero program (recruitment of Mexican laborers by U.S. agents).

Gonzalez's reputation as an eccentric stemmed from several causes: his fondness for wearing "electric blue" suits; his habit of delivering very long, rambling speeches; and his tendency to wait until evening to deliver those speeches to a mostly empty House chamber. His speeches, though, always seem to correctly predict scandals lurking just ahead. Even though no members of Congress bothered to stay around to listen, Gonzalez knew that a cable television network was broadcasting every minute of his speech to the American people who tune in.

## Battles Two Presidents

During the 1980s, Gonzalez fought against President Ronald Reagan and his administration. Gonzalez tried unsuccessfully to have the administration fund programs to build more low-cost housing. He also attacked Reagan for intervening in the affairs of other countries and for abusing the power of the presidency. Gonzalez called for Reagan's impeachment in 1983 after the United States invaded Granada. In 1987 he again wanted Reagan impeached for his possible involvement in the arms-for-hostages scandal with Iran.

In 1988 Gonzalez was named chairman of the powerful House Committee on Banking, Finance, and Urban Affairs. His committee helped find a remedy for the failing savings and loans associations across the country in the late 1980s. Gonzalez showed his independence from the politics of Washington when he brought about a formal investigation of five senators who might have had improper dealings with people involved in the savings-and-loan scandal. Four of those five senators were Democrats.

In January 1991 Gonzalez again called for the impeachment of a president, this time of George Bush. That month the United States started the Persian Gulf War against Iraq for its invasion of Kuwait. Gonzalez believed Bush did not rightly seek permission from Congress to start the war. He also tried to show that the Bush administration sold weapons to Saddam Hussein, the Iraqi president, months before the war.

Although mocked by some of his fellow members of Congress and unsuccessful in his attempts to impeach two recent presidents, Gonzalez remained committed to his ideal—serving the people who have elected him. Hitchens quoted Wisconsin Republican Toby Roth: "[Gonzalez] has the stick-to-it-iveness of an English bulldog. He's a genuine old-fashioned public servant."

In 1999, Gonzalez retired and his son, Charlie Gonzalez, succeeded him in Congress. Gonzalez died on November 28, 2000, in San Antonio. He was eighty-four years old.

## For More Information

*Harper's,* October 1992, pp. 84–96.

"Henry B. Gonzalez," *Texas Monthly,* January 2001, p. 204.

"Henry Gonzalez, 84: Served 37 Years in House," *New York Times,* November 29, 2000, p. A33.

*Hispanic,* October 1989, pp. 13–14.

*Nation,* June 1, 1992, pp. 740–41.

*New York Times,* March 24, 1994, p. A18.

# Juan Gonzalez

Professional baseball player
Born October 16, 1969, Vega Baja, Puerto Rico

*"When my playing days are over, I will be focused on serving the people of Puerto Rico, not from a political platform but from a social platform."*

T he children of Puerto Rico call baseball superstar Juan Gonzalez their hero. He grew up hitting bottlecaps with a broomstick bat and, at a young age, went on to become major league baseball's home run champion in 1992 and 1993. He spends the off-season visiting Puerto Rican schools to speak to children. After his baseball career ends, he plans a career in social work.

Gonzalez was born in 1969 in Puerto Rico. He was raised in an area called Alto de

Cuba—a tough neighborhood where the narrow streets are now filled with crime, abandoned houses, drugs, and poverty. Shopkeepers there remember the young, barefoot Gonzalez playing baseball in those streets. Today Gonzalez deplores the condition of his old barrio (Spanish-speaking neighborhood). When he can, he tries to encourage the children there to escape as he did.

"It makes me feel bad and sad at the same time," he related to Tom Verducci in *Sports Illustrated*. "The youth is losing its future to drugs. But I also blame the government authorities for not caring for the people of the barrio. There is not a baseball field or a basketball court for them."

## Signs with Rangers at Sixteen

When Gonzalez was thirteen, his father, a high school math teacher, moved the family to a safer neighborhood. There he played baseball on organized teams. His coaches immediately recognized his remarkable talent for hitting home runs. When Gonzalez was sixteen, a scout from the Texas Rangers offered him a professional baseball contract worth $75,000. His father had to sign it because Gonzalez was still under age.

Gonzalez weighed only 170 pounds when he started with the Rangers, and he spent his first seasons playing on their minor league teams. He began lifting weights to increase his strength. Late in the 1989 season, he was brought up from the minors and hit his first major league home run. He was nineteen years old. The next year, his first full season in the big leagues, he smashed 27 homers.

In 1992 Gonzalez hit 43 home runs and drove in 109 runs, capturing the major league

home run title. When he flew home to Puerto Rico after the season ended, five thousand fans met him at the airport in San Juan. One hundred thousand more lined the road he took to his hometown. The people love him because of his success and because he hasn't forgotten his roots. "Juan Gonzalez is the perfect guy that, if I was a youngster, I'd want to emulate," Hall of Fame pitcher Jim Palmer said, as quoted by *Washington Post* reporter David Mills. "He hasn't been caught for speeding. He hasn't taken a gun through a metal detector. He's done everything he possibly can to be the best player he can, and also be a responsible citizen."

## Has High Social Concerns

Gonzalez took this responsibility to heart. He believed it was his duty to be a role model for the youth of Puerto Rico and to help the people of his neighborhood. He paid electric, water, and medical bills for the needy in Alto de Cuba. He bought vitamins for the boys who worked out with him in the neighborhood gym. He treated residents of the neighborhood to a Christmas party in the streets. During the off-season, he visited more than fifty Puerto Rican schools. He signed autographs and talked to students, encouraging them to avoid drugs and to stay in school.

The children of Puerto Rico called Gonzalez "Igor," a nickname he earned at age ten when his hero was a professional wrestler called "The Mighty Igor." They lined up for his autograph and imitated his lifestyle. When not playing baseball, Gonzalez lived with his parents, and resumed his own education. In 1992 he began taking English lessons. Since Spanish is his native tongue, he needed an interpreter to help him with questions from

American reporters. Some sports writers say his inability to speak English helped him avoid unwanted interviews and publicity.

Gonzalez is a fierce competitor who hates to strike out. He has been criticized for throwing his bat and helmet when his hitting has been off. After a strong 1993 season, in which he hit 46 home runs, Gonzalez started the 1994 season poorly. By mid-June he was hitting only .258. He claimed to be hampered by a number of injuries, but many people felt these injuries were not that serious. However, by the time the season came to an early end in August because of the players' strike, Gonzalez had raised his average to .275 and had batted in 85 runs.

Gonzalez won the Most Valued Player award with the Texas Rangers in 1996 and 1998. He was with the Rangers for eleven years and scored more than 40 home runs in five different seasons.

In 1999, when Gonzalez was at the end of his contract with the Rangers, they decided to trade him to the Detroit Tigers. The Tigers offered him a huge deal: an eight-year contract paying a whopping $151.5 million. Gonzalez did not like Detroit's Comerica Park and hesitated to sign. In 2000 injuries kept him down to 115 games and he played poorly. Unhappy with the Tigers, Gonzalez looked into getting back to the Rangers, but they had just signed Alex Rodriguez for a lot of money. Gonzalez signed a one-year contract with the Cleveland Indians for 2001. Almost instantly, he was playing like his old self, thrilling the Indians fans and helping to put Cleveland at the top of the American League Central. He had a great season and hoped to stay with the Indians, but their budget for 2002

Juan Gonzalez. *Reproduced by permission of AP/Wide World Photos.*

was limited and Gonzalez was once again a very valuable player. In January 2002 he signed a two-year contract to go back to the Texas Rangers for $24 million.

Even with his career on the rise, the muscle-bound power hitter had definite post-baseball plans. "When my playing days are over, I will be focused on serving the people of Puerto Rico, not from a political platform but from a social platform," he told Verducci. "God gave me a good mind and the ability to succeed in baseball. I understand that I have to give back for what God has given me."

## For More Information

Pearlman, Jeff, "The Power of Juan: After a Miserable Season in Detroit, Juan Gonzalez Has Gone

Gaga over Cleveland," *Sports Illustrated,* September 3, 2001, p. 56.

*Sacramento Bee,* January 9, 2002.

*Sport,* May 1993, p. 61+.

*Sports Illustrated,* April 5, 1993, p. 60+; June 13, 1994, pp. 74–75.

*Washington Post,* August 23, 1993, p. B1.

# Rodolfo "Corky" Gonzalez

Former professional boxer, social and political activist
Born June 18, 1929, Denver, Colorado

*Gonzalez's epic poem* I Am Joaquín *had a tremendous social influence, uniting Mexican American youths in their own quest for identity.*

**R**odolfo "Corky" Gonzalez is a dynamic and colorful personality whose interests range from boxing to poetry to politics. He played a large part in the Chicano movement of the late 1960s and early 1970s. (The word "Chicano" comes from *Mechicano,* the same Nahuatl, or ancient Aztec, word from which the country of Mexico derived its name.) Young Mexican Americans involved in the Chicano movement not only struggled for civil rights but also sought to understand their cultural roots. To help provide his people with a sense of identity, Gonzalez wrote *I Am Joaquín / Yo Soy Joaquín.* Many people consider this work the classic epic poem of the Chicano movement.

Gonzalez was born in the Mexican barrio (a Spanish-speaking neighborhood) of Denver, Colorado, to a poor family of migrant workers. While growing up, he attended public schools in Denver. In the springs and summers of his youth, he worked alongside family members in the Colorado sugar beet fields. Before graduating from high school, Gonzalez became interested in boxing as a way to earn extra money and escape farm work. His boxing skills developed quickly and, while still a teenager, he became a Golden Gloves winner. He began his professional boxing career in 1947 and went on to win 65 of his 75 matches. Before he quit boxing, he was ranked as a contender for the World Featherweight title.

Gonzalez left boxing in the late 1950s and ran a neighborhood bar full time. He soon turned his attention to politics. In 1957 he became the first Mexican American chosen as district captain of the Denver Democratic party. Three years later he coordinated the John F. Kennedy presidential campaign in Colorado.

## Tries to Help Mexican American Youths

Gonzalez was greatly disturbed by the poor conditions under which Mexican Americans lived in the Southwest. He was especially concerned with Mexican American youths and their seemingly unjust treatment by government officials and police officers. In 1963, hoping to solve some of these problems, Gonzalez organized Los Voluntarios ("The Volunteers"), a group that fought to give Mexican Americans a greater political voice. Over the next few years, he also helped direct antipoverty and youth employment programs in Denver.

In 1966, however, a Denver newspaper published an article accusing Gonzalez of discriminating against African Americans and whites in the youth program. Angered over the accusation, Gonzalez resigned from the boards of the government programs and left the Democratic party.

Gonzalez was still determined to help young Mexican Americans but refused to do so through standard political organizations. Instead, he developed an organization called the Crusade for Justice in 1967 to raise political and ethnic awareness among Chicano youths and to help in the fight for their civil rights. The following year he converted an old school and church building in Denver into a Crusade school, theater, gym, nursery, and cultural center. The school was named after the ancient Aztec city of Tlatelolco, located near the Aztec capital of Tenochtitlán (now Mexico City). In addition to offering classes from kindergarten through the twelfth grade, the Crusade school taught students about the cultures of their Spanish and native Mexican ancestors.

## Writes I Am Joaquín

It was during this time that Gonzalez wrote his long poem *I Am Joaquín / Yo Soy Joaquín*. In the poem, the hero Joaquín journeys into the past to view and take part in important events in Aztec, Mexican, and Mexican American history. The journey is both historical and spiritual. As Joaquín travels back to the present, he comes to terms with who he is. Gonzalez's epic poem had a tremendous social influence, uniting

Rodolfo "Corky" Gonzalez. *Reproduced by permission of Corbis Corporation (Bellevue).*

Mexican American youths in their own quest for identity. *I Am Joaquín,* written in both English and Spanish, was read aloud at rallies, performed as a drama by street theaters, and was even made into a film by leading Mexican American director **Luis Valdez** (see entry).

In the summer of 1968, the Crusade for Justice took part in the historic Poor People's March on Washington, D.C. Here Gonzalez announced the "Plan of the Barrio," which demanded improved education, housing, and land reform for Mexican Americans. The following year the Crusade for Justice sponsored the first national Chicano Youth Liberation Conference in Denver. The main theme of the conference was cultural identity and pride. At the end of

Gonzalez in the ring. *Reproduced by permission of AP/Wide World Photos.*

five days, participants produced a document titled *El Plan Espiritual de Aztlán* ("The Spiritual Plan of Aztlán"; Aztlán is the mythical home of the Aztec.) The conference members declared that the American Southwest would be the new Aztlán, a new cultural home for Mexican Americans.

## Forms Political Party for Mexican Americans

In 1970, at the next Chicano Youth Liberation Conference, Gonzalez formed the Colorado La Raza Unida ("United Race") party to help elect Mexican Americans to political office in the state. His political ideas soon spread as the party sprang up in other states. However, at a national convention of La Raza Unida in 1972 in El Paso, Texas, Gonzalez lost his bid to become the party's permanent chairperson.

Gonzalez then returned to Denver to continue his work with the Crusade for Justice. He supported the drive for Mexican American rights and the efforts of **César Chávez** (see entry) to organize a union for Mexican American migrant farm workers in California. As the 1970s wore on, though, Gonzalez's influence on the national level declined.

In the late 1970s, while remaining head of the Crusade for Justice, Gonzalez became involved again in boxing, this time helping to train amateurs. He turned his attention to professional boxers a few years later. In 1987, however, Gonzalez was involved in a serious automobile accident. His recovery was slow and his work with young Mexican Americans was hampered as a result of his injuries, but his overall impact on the fight for Chicano rights remains unquestionable.

## For More Information

Gonzalez, Rodolfo, *I Am Joaquín / Yo Soy Joaquín,* Bantam, 1972.

Marín, Christine, *A Spokesman of the Mexican American Movement: Rodolfo "Corky" Gonzales and the Fight for Chicano Liberation, 1966–1972,* R and E Research Associates, 1977.

Steiner, Stan, *La Raza: The Mexican Americans,* Harper and Row, 1969, pp. 378–92.

# Antonia Hernández

MALDEF president and general counsel
Born May 30, 1948, Coahuila, Mexico

*"When I came to the United States, I was very proud of who I was. I was a Mexican. I had an identity. I had been taught a history, a culture of centuries of rich civilization so I had none of the psychoses of people who don't know who they are."*

**A**s president of the Mexican American Legal Defense and Educational Fund (MALDEF), Antonia Hernández is an advocate (defender and spokesperson) for the nation's large and growing Hispanic population. Her opinions and advice on how legal or educational issues affect Hispanics in the United States are featured in newspapers, magazines, radio, and television talk shows across the country.

MALDEF is an organization that supports and defends Hispanic Americans. As its president, Hernández attempts to correct discrimination against her people through negotiation, compromise, or legal action. Her special areas of concern are immigrant rights, employment discrimination, unequal education opportunities, and voting and language rights.

Hernández was born in the Mexican state of Coahuila in the town of Torreón in 1948. When she was eight, her family immigrated to the United States, settling in East Los Angeles, California. Her father, Manuel, was a gardener and laborer. Her mother, Nicolasa, was a homemaker who raised six children and worked odd jobs whenever possible. As the oldest child, Hernández was often called upon to watch over her younger brothers and sisters. "I grew up in a very happy environment but a very poor environment," Hernández told an interviewer from *Parents* magazine.

Hernández credits her early upbringing in Mexico with instilling pride in her Mexican roots. "When I came to the United States, I was very proud of who I was," she told the *Los Angeles Daily Journal.* "I was a Mexican. I had an identity. I had been taught a history, a culture of centuries of rich civilization so I had none of the psychoses [mental disorders] of people who don't know who they are."

## Wants to Follow a Noble Profession

Hernández's parents taught their children that working for the public good was a noble thing to do. Hernández was working toward a postgraduate degree in education when she decided she could be more useful to her community with a law degree. She already had a bachelor's degree and a teaching certificate from the University of California at Los Angeles (UCLA). She realized that she could help children more by changing the laws she believed were holding them back.

Hernández's professors encouraged her to attend Harvard University, but she chose to remain at UCLA so she could be near her family. Since her parents were sacrificing to help her with school costs, she felt it would be best to stay at home and help them with the rest of the family when she had the time.

Hernández was not a straight-A student in law school, but her professors remember she was bright and well-spoken. She was respected for being able to make her point without angering others. She explained that she cared more about her organizations and issues than earning top grades. During law school she worked for several Chicano (Mexican American) student organizations. She wanted to be a well-rounded person and intended to work in public service law. She received her law degree in 1974.

## Fights for State and Federal Laws

Hernández's first job as a lawyer was for the East Los Angeles Center for Law and Justice. She handled criminal and civil cases, which often involved police brutality. She went on to direct a Legal Aid Foundation office where she helped defend those who did not have enough money to hire a lawyer. She also fought for the passage of state laws that would help minorities and the poor.

In 1977 Hernández married Michael Stern, a fellow lawyer. The following year, she was offered a job as an attorney for the United States Senate Judiciary Committee. While in Washington, D.C., she gained valuable experience. She helped write laws and advised government officials on immigration and human-rights issues.

Her time spent in Washington, D.C., also gave Hernández a broader understanding of the diversity within the U.S. Hispanic community. She came to know the problems facing Cuban Americans, Puerto Rican Americans, and other Hispanic groups. Since that time, she has sought to increase cooperation among civil rights groups across both racial and ethnic lines. The key to doing this, she believes, is through education. "We don't know ourselves," Hernández explained to Roger E. Hernandez in *Hispanic*. "For instance, we Mexican Americans have to understand the Puerto Rican experience, the Cuban experience. We don't have a good enough grasp about these things."

## Begins Working for MALDEF

In 1980 MALDEF asked Hernández to join their staff as a staff attorney in the Washington office. She worked her way up through the ranks, returning to Los Angeles in 1983 to direct the organization's lawsuits on unemployment issues. She became its president and general counsel in 1985 and remained in that position into the 2000s.

At MALDEF, Hernández supervised all pending court cases and advocacy programs and planned the organization's long-range goals and objectives. She has played a key role in a number of MALDEF's major undertakings, including defeating a bill in Congress that would have required Latinos to carry identification cards and challenged questionable school and voting district boundaries. She has also been involved in MALDEF's ongoing efforts to promote affirmative action (programs and policies designed to improve employment and educational opportunities for minorities and women) in both the public and the private employment sector.

Hernández is often called upon by professional, civic, and religious groups to discuss MALDEF's view on issues of particular importance to Latinos. She has delivered talks on subjects such as discrimination, bilingual education, voting rights, and even U.S. Census Bureau policies and statistics. But perhaps the hottest topic she has addressed in recent years is immigration.

In elections held during the fall of 1994, Californians were asked to vote on a bill known as Proposition 187. This controversial measure sought to ban illegal immigrants from benefitting from a wide variety of public services, including public education, welfare, and nonemergency health care. Additonally under the terms of Proposition 187, doctors, teachers, and others coming into contact with people they thought might be illegal immigrants were required to report their suspicions to the authorities. Hernández and MALDEF campaigned against the

Antonia Hernández. *Reproduced by permission of Arte Público Press.*

bill. When it passed, she led the opposition and vowed to fight against what she considered unfair laws designed to lash out at the immigrant community. "Everyone is governed by the same laws; everyone is entitled to the same justice," has been her motto throughout her years at MALDEF.

After the 2000 Census results were made public, some voting districts in California were called into question because they discriminated against Latinos. One in question was in the San Fernando Valley near Los Angeles, California. MALDEF claimed that the congressional district maps cut across a heavily Latino community, separating it into two separate districts. This meant that Latino votes could be rendered ineffective as minority dissent votes rather than the majority that they were. Other districting problems arose in San Diego. MALDEF filed a suit in federal court against the state of California in October 2001. Hernández explained the reason for the lawsuit: "It is unacceptable and illegal to jeopardize the voting rights of historically disenfranchised minority voters [people who have not in the past had the right to vote due to race or ethnicity]. The district lines compromised the basic principles of community and the electoral process and are illegal." The suit, however, was not successful in the lower courts and stands little chance with the Supreme Court if appealed.

Community involvement is important to Hernández. She continues to work for a number of organizations, including Quality Education for Minorities Network and the Latino Museum of History, Art, and Culture. After the 1992 riots in Los Angeles in the wake of the Rodney King court decision, Los Angeles Mayor Tom Bradley appointed Hernández to a commission to oversee the reconstruction of the city. She is a member of the board of directors of the Los Angeles branch of the Federal Reserve Bank of San Francisco, Los Angeles 2000, Innovations in State and Local Government, Rebuild LA,, and California Leadership.

Hernández won the prestigious Hispanic Heritage Award in 1999. In 2000 she was awarded the Mujer Award by the National Hispanic Leadership Institute.

## For More Information

Eliash-Daneshfar, Meyling, "MALDEF Sues State of California for Violating Voting Rights Act and Constitution with Redistricting Plans," October 1, 2001, MALDEF Web site. Available at http:// www.maldef.org/news/press.cfm?ID=85 (accessed June 21, 2002).

*Hispanic,* December 1990, pp. 17–18; September 1991, pp. 18–22.

*Los Angeles Daily Journal,* September 3, 1985, p. 1.

*Parents,* March 1985, pp. 96–100+.

*Vista,* August 1992, pp. 6, 28.

# Guillermo "Willie" Hernandez

Former professional baseball player
Born November 14, 1954, Aguada, Puerto Rico

*"A lot of people make mistakes. I believe I made a good mistake."*

Guillermo Hernandez was a left-handed relief pitcher who was known in the world of baseball for working only the last couple innings of a game, often when the game was on the line. In baseball jargon, he was known as a "stopper" or "short man." In 1984, Hernandez recorded 32 saves in 33 appearances, an almost-unheard-of statistic. That year he helped the Detroit Tigers to victory in the World Series. He was named the Most Valuable Player in the American League and was honored with the Cy Young Award as the league's best pitcher. Few pitchers in baseball history have had so successful a season.

Hernandez was born in 1954 in Aguada, Puerto Rico. He was the youngest of nine children born to his father, a sugarcane worker, and his mother, a housekeeper.

While growing up, he did odd jobs to help his family. "My parents would buy me things," he related to a reporter for the *Detroit Free Press,* "but I could help pay for the bills."

Hernandez played baseball from a young age, although he started out as a rarity in the sport—a left-handed third baseman. It was an accident that he soon became a pitcher. As a teenager he played semiprofessional ball on Sundays. The day before the game, he would often pitch batting practice to his team. "I got a good fastball and a good breaking ball," he told a *Detroit Free Press* reporter. "But I don't know how to pitch. One time, somebody got suspended, somebody else got hurt. We don't have a pitcher. My manager give me the ball."

Even though Hernandez's team eventually lost 1–0, he pitched seven scoreless innings. His career on the mound was underway. After pitching with his team for a month and a half, he traveled to Italy as a member of the Puerto Rican national team. They beat the United States for the first time, but lost the championship to Japan.

## Major League Career Starts Slowly

In 1974 the Philadelphia Phillies signed Hernandez to a professional contract, but kept him on their minor league team for three seasons. The Chicago Cubs then drafted him during the winter of 1976. The following season marked his rookie year in the majors. For most players, making the majors is the end of a long and difficult journey, but Hernandez felt his troubles were only beginning.

Guillermo (Willie) Hernandez. *Reproduced by permission of Corbis Corporation (Bellevue).*

As a reliever for the Cubs, Hernandez never had more than four saves during each of his first five seasons. "People were talking behind my back, saying I'm through," Hernandez told a reporter for the *Detroit Free Press.* He felt he was not appreciated in Chicago and was always in the shadow of more well-known pitchers. By 1981 he was back to the minors. He finished the season with a losing record and a bad attitude.

In 1982 Hernandez asked the Cubs for a release. They granted his wishes by trading him to the Philadelphia Phillies. In a new city and with a new organization, his pitching improved. With his first winning season since 1978 (he finished the year 8–4), he helped Philadelphia to the World Series. Even though the Phillies eventually lost to

Hernandez in action. *Reproduced by permission of Corbis Corporation (Bellevue).*

the Baltimore Orioles, Hernandez ended the season on a good note: he signed a three-year contract worth $1.7 million.

## Carries Tigers to a Banner Year

Hernandez's performances caught the attention of the Detroit Tigers. For three years they tried to trade for him, but were unsuccessful. Finally, during the last week of spring training in 1984, Philadelphia agreed to a trade and Hernandez put on a Tigers uniform.

Nineteen eighty-four was a banner year for the Detroit Tigers. They won 35 of their first 40 games—a major league record. The team also accomplished the rare feat of spending the entire season in first place. One of the main reasons for the team's success was Hernandez. His late inning trips to the mound were a familiar sight. Batters dreaded seeing the 6-foot-2-inch, 185-pound pitcher with the menacing look and macho mustache. His walk from the bullpen became a sure sign that the Tigers were going to win.

Hernandez had a terrific season in 1984. In addition to his 32 saves, he compiled a 9-3 record with 112 strikeouts and a 1.92 earned-run average. But even though he collected a shelf-full of awards and had a contract that ran through the following season, he was dissatisfied. He threatened to leave the club unless he was given a new contract worth more money. He negotiated with team officials for three months. Finally, in January 1985, the Detroit Tigers offered him a baseball contract worth more than $1 million a year, the richest contract in Tiger history to that point.

## Problems With the Media

During the late 1980s Hernandez encountered some difficulties in dealing with the media. During 1988 spring training, he dumped a bucket of ice water on *Detroit Free Press* sports columnist Mitch Albom, who had written articles criticizing Hernandez. He later apologized for the incident, but only half-heartedly. "A lot of people make mistakes," he was quoted as saying by *Sports Illustrated.* "I believe I made a good mistake."

That same year Hernandez asked fans and writers to call him Guillermo instead of Willie (the name he had previously used in his baseball career). He explained that he wanted to show respect for his ethnic roots by returning to his Latin name. He pitched well that year, but it was to be his last successful season.

Hernandez injured his elbow late in the 1989 season and had to have surgery in September of that year. The Tigers then released him. A month later, he signed a contract with the Senior Professional Baseball Association. In the spring of 1990, the Oakland Athletics picked him up, but released him shortly afterward. His arm had never fully recovered from the injury. His pitching days over, he retired to Puerto Rico to live with his wife and two sons.

## For More Information

*Detroit Free Press,* March 26, 1984; August 26, 1984; January 10, 1985.
*Sporting News,* March 5, 1990, pp. 23–24.
*Sports Illustrated,* March 14, 1988, p. 14.

# Carolina Herrera

Fashion designer
Born 1939, Caracas, Venezuela

*"I am never satisfied. I'm a perfectionist. When I see the show is ready and the collection is out and they're quite nice, I still say, 'I could do much better.'"*

Carolina Herrera is one of the most respected fashion designers in the United States. Born to a wealthy South American family, she was a member of fashionable society even as a child. She began her business in 1981 at the insistence of friends and business people who admired the elegant clothes she designed for herself. Since that time she has dressed some of the world's most famous women.

Maria Carolina Josefina Pacanins y Nino (her full Spanish name) was born in Caracas, Venezuela, in 1939. She was the daughter of Guillermo Pacanins, who served as an officer in the Venezuelan Air Force and, later, as the governor of Caracas. Her parents enjoyed hosting lavish parties in their glamorous homes and loved to wear the latest fashions. As a young girl, Carolina designed clothes for her dolls. As she grew

Carolina Herrera. *Reproduced by permission of Carolina Herrera.*

older, she began to design them for herself and her friends.

When Herrera married her childhood friend Reinaldo Herrera, she found even more reason to dress glamorously. Her mother-in-law, a wealthy sponsor of artists, owned an enormous, historic house in Caracas that was built in 1590. Herrera dressed herself to fit in with her new elegant surroundings. She first made the annual Best Dressed List in 1971 and has not been off it since. Ten years later she won a spot in the Fashion Hall of Fame.

## Hobby Turns Into a Career

Herrera and her husband had four daughters—Mercedes, Ana Luisa, Carolina, and Patricia. She began her professional career in 1981 when her children were grown and she wanted to try something new. "I have always liked fashion," Herrera told Mary Batts Estrada in *Hispanic,* "and I thought I was capable of doing it, so I said, 'Why not try it?'"

By this time the Herrera family had moved to New York where her husband was special projects editor at *Vanity Fair* magazine. Herrera told a reporter for *Newsweek* that once she opened her House of Herrera design firm, she "changed from being a mother with nothing to do but arrange flowers and parties to being a professional who works twelve hours a day at the office."

Her first collection stunned the fashion world. Many expected Herrera to be a frivolous socialite with nothing of real substance to contribute to the fashion business. She proved them wrong when her glamorous dresses and gowns—of many different fabrics, layers, and lengths—appealed to other socialites like herself.

## Dresses the Rich and Famous

Within two years, Herrera received worldwide acclaim. Many well-known political figures and celebrities began to wear her creations. Among her customers were former U.S. First Ladies Jacqueline Onassis and Nancy Reagan, Princess Elizabeth of Yugoslavia, Spain's Duchess of Feria, and American actress Kathleen Turner. Traveling in the same international social circles as these famous people, Herrera understands their lifestyles and designs clothes to fit their needs and desires.

The fine quality and unique designs of Herrera's clothes make them much in demand in spite of their exceptional prices. In 1982, a luncheon suit by Herrera cost anywhere between $1,500 and $3,800. Silk pajamas made especially for lounging at the pool were tagged at $1,200. Her exquisite gowns ranged from $2,100 to $4,000. Fortunately for the rest of society, other designers have copied her styles and made their imitations available at lesser prices.

In 1987 Herrera won the MODA award as the Top Hispanic Designer from Hispanic Designers, Inc. Previous winners include the famous designers Aldolfo and Oscar de La Renta. In the late 1980s Herrera branched out to design a sportswear line for younger women, a leather and fur collection, and a less expensive line of clothing that she named "CH." She also introduced her own perfumes, "Carolina Herrera," and "Flore." The jasmine and tuberose fragrance of "Carolina Herrera" reminds Herrera of her happy childhood—a jasmine vine grew in the family garden and scented her bedroom.

In 2000 Herrera opened the first Carolina Herrera/New York boutique on Madison Avenue in New York. In the early years of the new century she planned to open forty new shops while continuing her fashion line and bringing out new fragrances and cosmetics. Her closest assistant in the business was her daughter, Carolina. In 1997 Carolina, who had been working in filmmaking, had the idea for a new perfume called 212, which she brought to her mother. She then became involved with all aspects of launching this new perfume for her mother's company. Released to the market in 1998, 212 was a grand success and mother and daughter had found they worked well together.

Despite her wealth and worldliness, Herrera leads a simple life. She walks to her New York office each day, accompanied by her dog, Alfonso. She works an eight-hour day, and often attends a charity event in the evening. Even though she has earned her place as a distinguished fashion designer, Herrera continues to work hard. "I am never satisfied," she told an interviewer for *Hispanic*. "I'm a perfectionist. When I see the show is ready and the collection is out and they're quite nice, I still say, 'I could do much better.'"

## For More Information

*Americas,* September/October 1990, pp. 30–35.

"Carolina Herrera," Virtual Runway. Available at http://www.virtualrunway.com/designh/Carolina-Herrera/CarolinaHerrera.htm (accessed June 21, 2002).

*Hispanic,* March 1989, pp. 28–32; October 1989, pp. 36–37.

*Newsweek,* June 30, 1986, pp. 56–57.

Tapert, Annette, "Carolina Herrerra: Profile of a Fashion Designer," Las Mujeres, September 1997. Available at http://www.lasmujeres.com/carolina-herrera/designer.shtml (accessed June 21, 2002).

*Vogue,* January 1991, p. 132.

# Oscar Hijuelos

Writer
Born August 24, 1951, New York, New York

*"What I want to do is entertain and give readers something that can help them live more happily, just like characters in a song of love."*

In 1990 Oscar Hijuelos became the first Hispanic writer to publish a book that received the Pulitzer Prize for fiction, America's highest literary award. His novel *The Mambo Kings Play Songs of Love,* which won the award, explores the lives of two Cuban brothers who seek fame as musicians in the United States during the 1950s. Hijuelos's book portrays the impact of Hispanic influences on American popular culture in a way that American fiction has neglected in the past.

Hijuelos was born in New York City in 1951. His parents, Pascual and Magdalena Torrens Hijuelos, had immigrated from Cuba to the United States in 1943. The family owned some farmland and two factories in their homeland, but Hijuelos's father lost what money they had after they went to America. "He was very generous, trusting to a fault," Hijuelos related to Dinitia Smith in *New York,* adding, "Occasionally, he liked to drink too much."

Although they lived in a culturally rich neighborhood that included people of Jewish, Italian, Irish, and African American descent, the Hijuelos family spoke only Spanish at home. When he was three years old, Hijuelos visited Cuba with his family. He contracted nephritis—a serious infection of the kidneys—during the trip, and after returning to the United States he was sent to a hospital for terminally ill children in Connecticut. Hijuelos spent two years there before finally recovering. During this time, he learned to speak English.

After high school, Hijuelos attended Bronx Community College. He later transferred to the City College of the City University of New York, where he earned his bachelor's degree in English in 1975. The following year he received his master's degree in creative writing. While enrolled in City College's distinguished graduate writing program, he studied creative writing with noted author Donald Barthelme, who is best known for his short stories.

## Follows His Dream

Hijuelos then obtained a job with Transportation Display Inc., an advertising firm in New York that creates ads for subways and buses. At night, he pursued his dream of being a writer, penning short stories and sending them to magazines for publication. His fiction quickly gained notice, and he was awarded grants, fellowships, and scholarships from such prestigious writing associations as the Breadloaf Writers Conference.

By 1983 Hijuelos had written enough material to publish his first novel, *Our House in the Last World.* The book follows the lives of the Santinios, a Cuban family, as they immigrate to America in the 1940s. As they struggle to adapt to life in the United States, the Santinios also try to hold on to their cultural past and maintain their identities as Cubans in America.

Critical reaction to *Our House in the Last World* was enthusiastic. Many reviewers saw Hijuelos's writing style as elegant and moving, and praised the book for its vivid and compassionate depiction the immigrant experience—especially of the sense of alienation so often felt by people who leave their homeland to settle in a foreign country. Both the National Endowment for the

Arts and the American Academy and Institute of Arts and Letters awarded the author fellowships for his book. The money from these awards allowed him to quit his day job and devote his time completely to writing.

## Second Novel Focuses on Two Brothers

Hijuelos finished work on his second novel, *The Mambo Kings Play Songs of Love,* in 1989. The novel tells the story of Cesar and Nestor Castillo, two musician brothers who leave Cuba in 1949 and seek their fortune on New York's nightclub circuit. Latin dance music was catching on in the United States by the early 1950s, and Hijuelos captures the mood of the era in his narrative.

The Castillo brothers form an orchestra to play in nightclubs where people dance the mambo, a rhythmic dance set to horns and drums. Their only big hit is "Beautiful María of My Soul," a romantic song Nestor has rewritten twenty-two times about his love for a woman he left behind in Cuba. The highlight of the brothers' career occurs when they are invited by bandleader **Desi Arnaz** (see entry) to perform their song on the hit television show *I Love Lucy.*

Soon after this, the Latin dance craze begins to fade and the brothers' lives spiral downward. Though he is married to another woman, Nestor cannot forget his lost love. With each passing year, he becomes more withdrawn and eventually dies of a broken heart. Cesar, a heavy drinker and womanizer, ends his days as a superintendent of a run-down hotel. In a drunken haze, he dreams of his past glory days.

Oscar Hijuelos. *Reproduced by permission of AP/Wide World Photos.*

## Mambo Kings Wins Top Award

Farrar, Straus & Giroux, the publisher of *The Mambo Kings Play Songs of Love,* made the book its lead fall title in 1989. It was the first time a major publishing house had ever invested heavily in a Hispanic writer. The book became a bestseller and was nominated for both the National Book Award and the National Book Critics Award, two of America's top literary awards. In 1990 *The Mambo Kings* was awarded the Pulitzer Prize. A film version of the novel, starring Armand Assante and Antonio Banderas and featuring the music of **Tito Puente** (see entry), was released in 1992.

Despite the somber ending of *The Mambo Kings* and the main characters' seemingly tragic preoccupation with the past, Hijuelos believes his role as a novelist is to enlighten and uplift his readers. "People live this dream and then they hit real life again.… What I want to do is entertain and give readers something that can help them live more happily," he told an interviewer in *Publishers Weekly,* "just like characters in a song of love."

## Subsequent Novels

Hijuelos's third novel, *The Fourteen Sisters of Emilio Montez O'Brien,* was published in 1993. Set in the United States at the beginning of the twentieth century, the story centers on the lives of fourteen sisters, their Cuban mother, and their Irish father. Through the book, Hijuelos tries to present "a pure appreciation of the *female* principle of life, the nurturing things," he explained to Smith in *New York.* "The things that are the most beautiful in the world are mostly female."

In his fourth novel, *Mr. Ives' Christmas,* Hijuelos returns to New York for his most spiritual work to date. The title character was adopted as a young child and has few cultural roots, though Hijuelos implies that Ives is Hispanic, as he is drawn time and again to New York's Hispanic community. Ives's successful marriage and professional life are thrown into disarray when his son is killed in a random act of violence. The book focuses on Ives's coming to terms with this death.

Hijuelos's 1999 novel, *Empress of the Splendid Season,* is set in Spanish Harlem. It is an intimate portrait of a cleaning lady, a proud woman who has had a difficult life and to whom Hijuelos gives depth of character and identity. In 2002 Hijuelos pub-

lished another novel, *A Simple Habana Melody (from when the world was good),* about a Cuban composer who is mistaken for a Jew in France during the Nazi occupation in the 1940s and sent to a concentration camp. Moving between Havana and Paris, as well as back and forth in time between the 1920s and the post-World War II era (after 1945), the novel hits many of Hijuelos's major themes—identity, family, love, culture, art, and beauty—and conveys a rich sense of the historical background of the two cities. *A Simple Habana Melody* was praised for its emotional depth, passion, and imagination, but most critics agreed that it is bogged down with too many different elements. Celia McGee observed in the New York *Daily News:* "Hijuelos won the Pulitzer Prize for his incandescent [brilliant] first novel, *The Mambo Kings Play Songs of Love,* and he has not quite been able to match its originality and verve since then."

The blending of Cuban and American cultural traditions makes Hijuelos's novels unique. Readers escape to a different culture and a different time through the lush imagery and language contained within the pages of his works. Ironically, much criticism of Hijuelos's work concerns his knowledge of Cuban culture as an American-born citizen. As he once said of his first novel's concern with cultural identity (as quoted in *Contemporary Popular Writers),* "Although I am quite Americanized, my book focuses on many of my feelings about identity and my 'Cubanness.' I intended for my book to commemorate at least a few aspects of the Cuban psyche [as I know it]."

## For More Information

*Contemporary Popular Writers,* St. James Press, 1997.

*Detroit News,* September 3, 1989.

*Hispanic Writers,* 2nd Edition, Gale, 2002.

McGee, Celia, "Cuban Blowout: Latest Hijuelos Novel Is Overstuffed with Interesting Ideas," *Daily News,* (New York), p. 19.

*Newsweek,* August 21, 1989.

*New York,* March 1, 1993, pp. 46–51.

*New York Times,* September 11, 1989.

*New York Times Book Review,* August 27, 1989, pp. 1, 30; June 23, 2002, p. 11.

*Publishers Weekly,* July 21, 1989.

Santiago, Fabiola, "Oscar Hijuelos," review of *A Simple Habana Melody, Miami Herald,* May 30, 2002.

*Washington Post,* August 20, 1989.

# Dolores Huerta

Labor leader, social activist
Born April 10, 1930, Dawson, New Mexico

*"I think we brought to the world, the United States anyway, the whole idea of boycotting as a nonviolent tactic. I think we showed the world that nonviolence can work to make social change."*

D olores Huerta is the most prominent Chicana (Mexican American woman) labor leader in the United States. She is cofounder and first vice president of the United Farm Workers union. For more than forty years she has dedicated her life to the struggle for justice and dignity for migrant farm workers. Honored with countless community service, labor, Hispanic, and women's awards, Huerta is a role model for Mexican American women.

Dolores Fernández Huerta was born in 1930 in the small mining town of Dawson in northern New Mexico. She was the second child and only daughter of Juan Fernández and Alicia Cháves Fernández. Her mother's parents were born in New Mexico, while her father's parents had immigrated to the United States from Mexico. When Huerta was a toddler her parents divorced, and she moved to California with her mother and two brothers.

As a single parent during the Great Depression (severe economic slowdown in America during the 1930s), Alicia Cháves Fernández had a difficult time supporting her young family. While she worked at a cannery at night and as a waitress during the day, her father helped watch the children. Young Dolores enjoyed a close relationship with her grandfather. "My grandfather used to call me seven tongues," she related to Margaret Rose in *Notable Hispanic American Women,* "because I always talked so much." As Huerta grew older, her mother encouraged her to get involved in youth activities. She took violin, piano, and dance lessons. He also sang in the church choir and was an active Girl Scout.

During the 1940s her family's financial situation improved. Huerta's mother, who had remarried, now owned a restaurant and a hotel. Huerta and her brothers helped run these establishments. She believes she learned to appreciate all different types of people while growing up and working in an ethnically diverse neighborhood. Her community included Japanese, Chinese, Jewish, Filipino, and Mexican families.

## Inspired by Father's Accomplishments

Although Huerta was separated from her father, she did not lose contact with him. His work activities inspired her. To supplement his wages as a coal miner, he joined the migrant labor force, traveling to Colorado, Nebraska, and Wyoming. He was unhappy with working conditions and became active in labor unions. He eventually returned to school to earn a college degree. In 1938 he won election to the New Mexico state legislature where he worked for better labor laws. Huerta was proud of her father's education, his union activism, and his political achievements.

Huerta attended schools in her hometown of Stockton, California. Then, unlike most Hispanic women of her generation, she went on to college. She earned a teaching certificate, but was frustrated with the limitations of the job. She realized she wanted to do more than just teach children. She wanted to help those who came to school barefoot and hungry.

Huerta soon found her niche in community work and social activism. In the mid-1950s, she began to work for the Community Service Organization (CSO), a Mexican American self-help association founded in Los Angeles. She registered people to vote, organized citizenship classes for immigrants, and pressed local governments for improvements in barrios (Spanish-speaking neighborhoods). As a result of her skills, the CSO sent her to the California capital of Sacramento to work as a lobbyist (a person who persuades legislators to vote for certain laws). Then, during the late 1950s, Huerta became concerned about the living and working conditions of farm workers.

Since before World War II, life for migrant farm workers had been incredibly harsh. They worked in the hot sun for hours, picking crops such as grapes, tomatoes, and cotton. During the often cool nights, they slept in run-down shacks or in their cars if they could not afford a room. Farm owners paid the workers poor wages. Sometimes workers were paid only fifty cents for every basket they picked; other times they were paid only twenty cents. Some owners paid even less, subtracting from a workers' pay for any water he or she drank in the fields during the hot day. Many of the workers were Mexicans or Mexican Americans who knew little English. Farm owners often took advantage of this, swindling the workers out of the money they had rightfully earned for their day's hard labor.

## Chávez and the UFW

Huerta joined the Agricultural Workers Association, a community interest group in northern California. Through her work with the AWA, she met **César Chávez** (see entry), the director of the CSO in California and Arizona. Chávez shared her deep interest in farm workers. Unhappy with the CSO's unwillingness to form a union for farm workers, Chávez and Huerta eventually branched off to found the National Farm Workers Association in Delano, California, in 1962. After 1972 this influential union would be known simply as the United Farm Workers (UFW).

As second-in-command to Chávez, Huerta helped shape and guide the union. In

1965, when Delano grape workers went on strike, she devised the strategy for the strike and led the workers on the picket lines. Afterward, she became the UFW's first contract negotiator. In the late 1960s, she directed the grape boycott on the east coast, the primary distribution point for grapes. Her work there helped bring about a successful grape boycott across the nation.

Huerta's style was forceful and uncompromising. However, she succeeded in bringing together feminists, community workers, religious supporters, Hispanic associations, student protestors, and peace groups. All were united to fight for the rights of migrant farm workers. Victory finally came in 1975 when California Governor Jerry Brown signed the Agricultural Labor Relations Act. This was the first bill of rights for farm workers ever enacted in America. It legally allowed them to form a union that would negotiate with farm owners for better wages and working conditions.

## UFW Activities Prove Dangerous

Over the years, Huerta has committed her energies to the UFW as a leader, speaker, fund raiser, negotiator, picket captain, and advisor to government leaders. In the 1980s she helped found KUFW—Radio Campesina, the union's radio station in California. She continued testifying before state and federal committees on a range of issues, including the use of pesticides on crops and other health matters facing migrant workers.

Many of Huerta's activities on behalf of the UFW have placed her in personal danger. She has been arrested more than twenty

Dolores Huerta. *Reproduced by permission of AP/Wide World Photos.*

times. In 1988, during a peaceful demonstration in San Francisco against the policies of presidential candidate George Bush, Huerta was severely injured by baton-swinging police officers. She suffered two broken ribs and a ruptured spleen. In order to save her life, she had to undergo emergency surgery. This incident outraged the public and caused the San Francisco police department to change its rules regarding crowd control and discipline.

After recovering from her life-threatening injuries, Huerta resumed her work on behalf of farm workers. During the 1990s, UFW influence was declining due in part to changes in the economic and political climate at state and national levels. The death of César Chávez in 1993 also dealt a blow to the organization, which struggled to keep his spirit alive as well as increase membership. The UFW had a true fighter in Huerta, who remained active into the early 2000s. In 2002, at the age of seventy-one, Huerta was touring the nation, speaking about women's rights, amnesty for undocumented workers, and bilingual education. The same year, a congressional resolution paid honor to Huerta for her "commitment and dedication" in promoting the rights of farm workers.

## For More Information

De Ruiz, Dana Catharine and Richard Larios, *La Causa: The Migrant Farmworkers' Story,* Raintree Steck-Vaughn, 1992.

"Dolores Huerta and Farm-Labor Activists Remember Their Leader," Associated Press, March 16, 2002.

Dunne, John Gregory, *Delano: The Story of the California Grape Strike,* Farrar, 1976.

"Homage Bill Seeks to Honor Latino Leader Huerta," EFE News Service, February 19, 2002.

*National Catholic Reporter,* September 30, 1988, p. 12.

*Notable Hispanic American Women,* Gale, 1993.

# Julio Iglesias

Singer, songwriter
Born September 23, 1943, Madrid, Spain

*"The biggest problem in my job is that you get afraid to lose it. One day you are a winner, but the next, no matter how big of a star you are, you can be a loser."*

**S**panish singer Julio Iglesias has sold more albums than any other singer in the world—more than 250 million as of 2000. His fame first began when his Spanish songs and romantic style won audiences in his homeland and in Latin American countries. When Iglesias started singing in Portuguese, Italian, French, German, Japanese, and English, his fan club quickly spread around the world.

Julio José Iglesias de la Cueva was born in 1943 in Madrid, Spain, to Julio Iglesias, Sr., a wealthy gynecologist, and his wife, Rosario. He had a comfortable childhood. While growing up, he attended Catholic schools, where his grades were mediocre and he couldn't sing well enough to join the school choir. One thing he did excel at, however, was soccer. After he graduated from high school, he briefly studied law at the University of Madrid, but gave it up to become goalie for Real Madrid, Spain's premier pro-soccer team.

## Accident Ends Soccer Career

Iglesias's athletic career was cut short in 1963 when he was almost killed in an automobile accident. After his car had been forced off the road by a runaway truck, it rolled over several times. Iglesias's spine was injured in the accident. For a week, he was in a coma. For the next year, he was paralyzed from the chest down. Iglesias knew his sports career was over, but he was determined not to spend his life in a wheelchair. He underwent physical therapy for the next three years. To help keep his mind off his disabilities during his long recovery, his soccer teammates gave him a guitar. After learning a few chords, he began to play along with songs on the radio. Soon he was composing songs of his own.

Iglesias regained the use of his legs but was left with a slight limp. Since playing soccer was out, he focused on singing as a career. On a trip to England to improve his English, he composed the song "La Vida Sigue Igual" (Life Goes on Just the Same). He performed it at the 1968 Festival de la Canción, a national singing competition in Spain, and won first prize. He then recorded the song and it became a hit on Spanish radio. To please his parents, Iglesias completed law school, but then concentrated his energy on music. By 1971 he had signed a recording contract with Alhambra Records, and his voice hit the airwaves throughout Europe, Japan, and Latin America.

That same year, Iglesias married Isabel Preysler, who came from a wealthy Filipino family. The couple eventually had three children: Chabeli, Julio José, and Enrique. Although Iglesias and Preysler divorced in 1979, Iglesias has remained close to his children. His career, however, is his main passion. "He was always into his work," Chabeli explained to Cynthia Sanz in *People*. "When he had the time, he was with us, but family was never his strong point."

## Perfectionist in the Studio

Iglesias, who spends up to nine months a year in the recording studio, earned a reputation as a workaholic and a perfectionist. It was not uncommon for him to sing a particular song over and over in the studio until he was satisfied. His dedication to his craft paid off: By 1973 he had sold ten million albums. In 1980 his album *Hey* was the number one album in eighty countries.

Julio Iglesias. *Reproduced by permission of AP/Wide World Photos.*

In 1983 Iglesias had six albums on the pop charts, a feat managed previously only by Elvis Presley and the Beatles. That year, he earned a spot in the *Guinness Book of World Records* for having sold one hundred million records in six languages (Iglesias is fluent in Spanish, French, Italian, Portuguese, and English).

Despite having switched to the larger CBS International record company in 1980, Iglesias still found it difficult to reach an English-speaking audience. Finally, British tourists in Spain in the early 1980s took note of his popularity and brought his records home to British disc jockeys. Iglesias soon became the first Hispanic singer to have a number one song in England—the Spanish-language version of Cole Porter's

"Begin the Beguine." CBS began to release his albums in English and book him on talk shows in the United States.

## Duets Bring Him a U.S. Audience

Iglesias's first album in English was the 1984 release *1100 Bel Air Place.* The record, which featured duets with American stars Diana Ross, the Beach Boys, and the Pointer Sisters, sold four million copies in the United States. He then went on to earn a country-western audience when his duet with Willie Nelson, "To All the Girls I've Loved Before," became a hit.

After the 1994 release of Iglesias's album *Crazy,* a *New York Times* critic noted that "Whatever Mr. Iglesias sings, he communicates variations of the same sentiment: I may be the ultimate cosmopolitan smoothie … but my heart is lonely unto breaking." *Newsweek* characterized Iglesias's appeal this way: "Using every technique of the modern recording studio and his own diaphanous voice, he has taken the Mediterranean pop ballad and raised it to a spectacular new pitch of melodramatic grandeur." "What Iglesias has done, more than any other performer," observed a critic for *Time,* "is bring back to popular music the romantic style of the '40s and '50s." *Billboard*'s Diane Patrick, reviewing an Iglesias concert in 1991, declared: "Iglesias sings well, he sings songs, in many languages, about feelings, and he has charm and grace. That is the very simple 'secret' of his popularity." By 2000, in fact, he had 2,650 gold and platinum albums recorded in six different languages.

Even though Iglesias has remained more popular outside of the United States, he has come to embrace the country. "This is an incredible country," he told Achy Obejas in *Hispanic.* "It's very special to me. But perhaps it's something else too. People who don't have a home can make a home anywhere." Iglesias mirrors this feeling of goodwill by supporting many charities around the world. Since the beginning of his career, he has donated more than $20 million to health and social service organizations. In the United States, he supports the American Paralysis Association, the Red Cross, and Casita Maria, a New York-based organization for Hispanic unwed mothers.

Iglesias performs about two hundred stage shows per year, jetting between countries in his private plane. He had performed more than forty-seven hundred shows on five continents by the year 2000. That year he was named the highest paid entertainer in Europe by *Eurobusiness* magazine. He owns a ranch in Argentina and a mansion in Miami. Despite his many fans and successes, however, Iglesias knows that the fame he has achieved over the years can one day suddenly fade away. Memories of his accident remind him of this. "The biggest problem in my job is that you get afraid to lose it," he explained to Dougherty. "One day you are a winner, but the next, no matter how big of a star you are, you can be a loser."

Iglesias was honored as the 2001 Latin Academy of Recording Arts and Sciences (LARAS) person of the year, the second person to be so honored.

## For More Information

*Billboard,* February 23, 1991, p. 87; July 27, 1991, p. 28; June 27, 1992, p. 17.

*Hispanic,* August 1988, pp. 26–30; May 1991, pp. 20–26.

Lannert, John, "The International Superstar Who Needs No Introduction," *Billboard,* May 27, 2000, p. 72.

*Newsweek,* July 11, 1983, p. 69.

*New York Times,* June 13, 1991, p. C14; June 3, 1994, p. C3; June 19, 1994, sect. 2, p. 25.

*People,* August 29, 1988, pp. 50–54; November 23, 1993, pp. 63–64; May 23, 1994, p. 23.

*TV Guide,* November 24, 1990, pp. 20–22.

*Time,* September 10, 1984, p. 60.

# Raul Julia

Actor
Born March 9, 1940, San Juan, Puerto Rico
Died October 24, 1994, Manhasset, New York

*"I like to explore. I always have the sense that there must be something more ... that there are possibilities we don't even know about."*

Raul Julia was an actor well known for his broad range of talents. From his work in classic stage productions such as William Shakespeare's tragedy *Othello* to zany film comedies like *The Addams Family,* Julia earned praise from critics—and from audiences of all ages. Whatever role he took on, he felt compelled to probe his character's background, feelings, and beliefs; such attention to detail became his trademark in the industry. What was most important for Julia, though, before his early death, was constantly testing his own acting abilities. "I love diversity in acting," he explained to

Raul Julia. *Reproduced by permission of AP/Wide World Photos.*

Phoebe Hoban in *New York* magazine, adding that he was most interested in "trying to do things I'm not sure I can do."

Raul Rafael Carlos Julia y Arcelay was born in San Juan, Puerto Rico, in 1940, the oldest of four children of Raul and Olga Julia. Before Julia was born, his father studied electrical engineering in the United States. After returning to San Juan, the elder Julia opened a gas station, then a chicken and pizza restaurant. Both of his parents wanted their young son to grow up to become a lawyer, but he had a different idea early in life.

Julia had his first role on the stage at the age of five, playing the devil in a school play. From that moment on he was hooked.

While attending parochial schools in San Juan, he performed in every school play that was staged. After he graduated from high school, he enrolled in the University of Puerto Rico, eventually earning a bachelor of arts degree. He then moved to New York City in the mid-1960s to study acting. For a while, he had to live on money his parents sent to him. After he won his first role in the Spanish play *Life Is a Dream,* he was able to support himself, but times remained tough.

## Brings Shakespeare to Hispanic Neighborhoods

To save money, Julia shared a tiny apartment with another actor. Because he could not get work in the theater, he often performed in small plays on the street. More than once he was hit with eggs and bottles from rude, unappreciative audiences. In 1967 he landed a role in a Spanish mobile-theater production of Shakespeare's *Macbeth.* He and the rest of the cast traveled through New York neighborhoods in a truck that turned into a stage. Julia was happy not only to have work but to bring theater to people who didn't have the time or the money to see plays in New York's theater district.

This role led to others, but Julia still had a hard time earning money. For a while he tried to sell magazines and pens, but his heart wasn't in it. He then worked as a house manager for the New York Shakespeare Festival. He was happy to do anything connected with theater. Occasionally he was even allowed to play a small role in the Festival's productions.

Julia's big break came in 1971 when he received the role of Proteus in a production of Shakespeare's *Two Gentlemen of Verona.* Originally staged in New York City's Central Park, the production became a hit after it moved to Broadway. Julia's performance caught the attention of theater critics, and he was nominated for a Tony Award (the equivalent of the film world's Academy Award). Over the next decade, he played larger, more demanding roles in such theatrical productions as Shakespeare's *Hamlet* and Kurt Weill's *Threepenny Opera*. His work brought three more Tony Award nominations.

## Researches His Roles Thoroughly

During this time Julia began branching out into television and motion pictures. For a while, his work in movies was limited to small roles that did not attract much attention. In 1985, however, he achieved stardom for his portrayal of a South American political prisoner in *Kiss of the Spider Woman,* a film that also starred William Hurt. To ready himself for the role, Julia talked to Brazilians who had actually been imprisoned or tortured because of their political beliefs. "I needed to know what the feelings and emotions were of a person who had gone through that," he noted in the *New York* interview with Hoban. "You feel humiliated. You feel anger. And you cannot express it."

Similarly, Julia has spent countless hours preparing for other roles. When he portrayed a lawyer in the whodunit *Presumed Innocent,* he spent days in court with a criminal attorney to become familiar with the legal system and the courtroom environment. And for his role as Archbishop Oscar Romero of El Salvador in the film *Romero,* he listened to the priest's actual taped sermons and diaries.

Julia's in-depth research often changed his outlook on his own life—affecting him even after the cameras had stopped rolling. He was, for example, raised a Catholic but had drifted away from his religion as he grew older. His research for *Romero* required him to delve back into Catholicism and brought about a renewal of his faith. After filming was completed, Julia became a practicing Catholic once again.

Julia was married to Merel Poloway, and they had two sons, Raul Sigmund and Benjamin Rafael. When not acting, Julia worked for Project Hunger, a group devoted to finding ways to end world hunger by the year 2000. With each new role on the stage, on television, and in films, he continued to receive acclaim. His only requirement for himself as an actor was that he never stand still. "I like to explore," he told Hoban. "I always have the sense that there must be something more … that there are possibilities we don't even know about."

The world was shocked when it was revealed that Julia, only fifty-four, had fallen into a coma after sustaining a stroke on October 16, 1994. He died twelve days later. Though many knew him primarily through his role as Gomez Addams, he is remembered by his peers as a gifted actor who never stopped striving for excellence in the variety of roles he tackled.

## For More Information

*America,* February 25, 1989, p. 164.
*New York,* November 25, 1991, pp. 52–56.
*New York Times,* October 24, 1994, p. B15.

Stefoff, Rebecca, *Raul Julia: Puerto Rican Actor,* Chelsea House, 1994.

# Bartolomé de Las Casas

Missionary, historian
Born 1474, Seville, Spain
Died 1566, Madrid, Spain

*"The more I thought about it the more convinced I was that everything we had done to the [native people] so far was nothing but tyranny and barbarism."*

For fifty years, Spanish missionary Bartolomé de Las Casas fought the inhumane treatment of the native people of the New World by Europeans through his writings, sermons, and example. Because of his efforts, laws were enacted to protect their rights, although many abuses continued. His book, *The Devastation of the Indies,* is an eyewitness account of life in the early Spanish settlements of the West Indies.

Not much is known about Las Casas's childhood. He was born sometime in 1474 in the city of Seville in southern Spain. Some of the details of Las Casas's childhood are sketchy. His father, Pedro, was a merchant and his mother, who is thought to have been Isabel de Sosa, owned a bakery. It is known that his father and three of his uncles sailed on Christopher Columbus's second voyage to the New World in 1493. As a result, his father acquired some property in Hispaniola (an island in the present-day Caribbean Sea divided between the Dominican Republic on the east and Haiti on the west), and lived there for a while. During this period, Las Casas remained in Spain, studying theology and law at the University of Salamanca, northwest of the capital city of Madrid.

## Joins Spanish Colonists on Hispaniola

By 1502 Las Casas had traveled to Hispaniola to live. The young man, fascinated by the native people of the island, studied their cultures and languages. Despite his understanding of the natives, he joined his fellow Spanish colonists in abusing them. Las Casas used the native Hispaniolans as slave workers to farm the land his father had given him. He saw nothing wrong with this practice.

The Spanish believed that Columbus had conquered Hispaniola and the land and its people now belonged to Spain. Queen Isabella of Spain ordered the explorers to convert the natives to the Catholic faith and to teach them to read and to write. She also insisted that the native Hispaniolans be put to work to cure what she thought was their idleness. The explorers, however, were more interested in the gold and other treasures the New World had to offer than in converting the native people to the Catholic religion. In their greed for wealth, the explorers enslaved the natives to do the mining and the farming. Las Casas shared their desire for riches.

Disruption of the native Hispaniolans' hunting and food gathering practices—unchanged for thousands of years before the Spanish arrived on Hispaniola—caused famine among the tribes. Europeans brought diseases to the New World against which the native people had no natural defenses. Thousands died of smallpox, measles, and influenza. The natives tried to fight against this European invasion, but their primitive bows and arrows were no match for the swords the Spaniards wielded on horseback. Hundreds of thousands of natives died each year. Those who remained were quickly enslaved in their own lands.

## Comes to New Understanding of Native People

Most Spaniards had no concept of the cultural and religious richness of the native Hispaniolans. They believed their treatment of the native people of the New World was morally correct—that it was, in fact, their religious duty to subdue and convert the "godless" natives to Christianity. Gradually, however, some recognized the suffering of the natives and began to speak out against the injustice. At first, Las Casas, who had been ordained a priest in 1512, was not sympathetic to those who spoke out. But in 1514, while reading a passage in the Bible, he experienced his own conversion. As he wrote later in his book, "The more I thought about it the more convinced I was that everything we had done to the [native people] so far was nothing but tyranny and barbarism."

Las Casas began to fight for the rights of native Hispaniolans. He gave up his land, freed his slaves, and began delivering angry sermons to the Spanish settlers. He also traveled back and forth to Spain to report to its rulers the injustices suffered by the native peoples.

In 1520 King Charles V of Spain granted Las Casas, who was now a bishop, some land to set up peaceful, free villages where native Hispaniolans could live and work with Spanish peasants. Under Las Casas's plan, the peasant families were to instruct the native people in European work as well as in Catholicism. The experiment quickly failed when the native Hispaniolans rebelled and the peasants deserted to join the other colonists. Las Casas was so discouraged that he returned to Spain and isolated himself in a monastery for nearly ten years.

## Writings Bring About Change

During his stay at the monastery, Las Casas began working on his book, *The Devastation of the Indies: A Brief Account*. Published in 1542, it described the cruelties and tortures the Spanish had inflicted on native peoples since they had arrived in the New World. Europeans were shocked by the horrific stories of native women raped in front of their husbands, of native children thrown into rushing rivers, and of young men slowly burned alive. As a result, Charles V established the New Laws, which forbid the future enslavement of native Hispaniolans and gave guidelines for the proper treatment of those already working for Spanish landowners.

The settlers were outraged by the New Laws. While some returned to Spain rather than obey the laws, most simply disregarded them. Distance and the lack of communication between Spain and the New World hampered their enforcement. Under pressure, Charles V repealed the New Laws in 1545.

Bartolomé de Las Casas. *Reproduced courtesy of the Library of Congress.*

Las Casas continued to fight on behalf of native Hispaniolans for the rest of his life. His book, translated into English, French, Dutch, German, and Italian, was read throughout Europe. For hundreds of years, the rest of Europe used the book to politically condemn Spain for its enslavement of the native peoples of the New World.

Those Europeans who came to colonize America did not embrace Las Casas's condemnation of all slavery. Earlier in his life, Las Casas had written that Africans should be substituted as slaves for native Hispaniolans because they were stronger. After he wrote his book, though, Las Casas changed his view, stating that enslavement of Africans was as unjust as enslavement of native Hispaniolans. However, for hundreds of years some Americans used his earlier words to support their policy of slavery, choosing to ignore his later views.

## For More Information

*America,* July 18–25, 1992, pp. 30–32+.

Hanke, Lewis, *Bartolomé de Las Casas: Bookman, Scholar, and Propogandist,* University of Pennsylvania Press, 1952.

Las Casas, Bartolomé de, *The Devastation of the Indies: A Brief Account,* translated by Hans Magnus Enzenberger, Seabury Press, 1974.

Wagner, Henry Raup, *The Life and Writings of Bartolomé de Las Casas,* University of New Mexico Press, 1967.

# Aliza Lifshitz

Doctor, medical journalist
Born c. 1947, Mexico City, Mexico

*"I would basically like in some way to leave this world a little bit better than what I found it."*

**A**liza Lifshitz's patients call her an old-fashioned doctor who listens to them and takes the time to explain medical terms. Yet she is also a physician who skillfully uses the media to educate Hispanic viewers on present-day advances in health and medicine. In 1992 she served as the president of the California Hispanic American Medical Association, which has thirteen hundred members. She was also one of the first Hispanic woman physicians to have become actively involved in the struggle against AIDS.

Lifshitz was born in Mexico City, Mexico, sometime in the late 1940s. Her Jewish father was an engineer and a classical pianist; her Mexican mother was an artist. Her parents enrolled her in the American elementary school in Mexico City so she could experience cultural diversity and learn English. She then attended both Jewish and Catholic schools. After having graduated from high school, Lifshitz enrolled in the Colegio Israelite de Mexico, earning her bachelor's degree with honors in 1969.

## Healing Through Communication

Lifshitz decided she wanted a career that would allow her to be both creative and helpful to others. She chose medicine. "I've always seen medicine as an art that is based on a science," she explained to Diana Martínez in *Notable Hispanic American Women.* "The greatest majority of the healing that we do is actually through listening to the patient and communicating with them." Lifshitz enrolled in the Universidad Nacional Autónoma de México. After she graduated in 1976, she completed her medical training in the United States at the University of California at San Diego.

As a physician specializing in internal medicine, Lifshitz has worked with community-based organizations to make sure poor patients receive the treatment they need. She has been paid with knitting, hand-made decorations, cookies, and fruit. She says she truly enjoys helping her patients and is happy with whatever they bring her.

Many of Lifshitz's patients admire her for her compassion. She attributes this trait to her parents, especially to her mother. "My mother had a tremendously big heart for people," Lifshitz told Martínez. "I remember her taking care of everything from a limping dog on the street to making sure she bought food for people who she saw needed it. That's what my mother was all about."

## Explores Health Issues Through the Media

In 1986 Lifshitz appeared on a live, thirty-minute call-in program on a southern California television station. After having received and answered hundreds of calls, she realized she could reach out to many more people in her community through the media than through her office practice alone. Since that time, she has became the health reporter for Univisión, a Spanish-language television network in Los Angeles. She is also the medical editor of *Más,* a national Spanish-language magazine, and editor-in-chief of *Hispanic Physician.*

Lifshitz is the medical editor of *Primer Impacto,* Spanish-language television's highest-rated news magazine. She has been a columnist for the women's magazine *Latina,* the teen magazine *Latingirl* and the men's magazine *Oye.* She is also the health columnist for the Spanish language newspaper *La Opinión.* and the health reporter for Radio Unica, a national Spanish-language radio network. Her book, *Mamá Sano, Bebé Sano/Healthy Mother, Healthy Baby (A Spanish/English Guide to Pregnancy, Prenatal Care, Childbirth, and Early Infant Care),* was published by HarperCollins in 1999.

One of the main issues Lifshitz focuses on through her media outlets is the lack of

Aliza Lifshitz. *Reproduced by permission of Aliza Lifshitz.*

information available to the Hispanic community regarding AIDS (Acquired Immune Deficiency Syndrome) and HIV (Human Immunodeficiency Virus that leads to AIDS). "In very many instances it has been said ... that Hispanics are not interested in preventive health," she explained to Martínez. "But many times it's simply because Hispanics don't have access to that information. Once data are made available to them, they are very interested." Lifshitz devotes about one-third of her practice to the treatment of patients who are HIV-positive.

Lifshitz is also concerned with the need for universal health care. "We need to be able to provide basic health care for everyone in a country that is supposed to be a developed country," she pointed out to

Martínez. "If we are going to rate how civilized a country is according to how they treat their poor, I think we're becoming more and more uncivilized." In addition, Lifshitz believes more attention should be paid especially to women's health issues and to the position of women in medicine. Lifshitz notes that women have made significant contributions to health care—beyond traditional nursing—that the world should readily recognize.

Lifshitz has received numerous honors for her work in educating the public on health matters. In 1992 the University of Southern California Los Amigos De La Humanidad of the School of Social Work bestowed its Distinguished Contributor to Social Welfare award on her. She was selected the same year by the American Medical Association to kick off its 1992 Medical Ethics Consumer Information Campaign. *Hispanic Business* magazine recognized her as one of the 100 most influential Hispanics in 1999. She also received the 1999 C. Everett Koop Media Award from the American Heart Association as well as the Avance Human Services "Daniel Lara" AIDS Award, and the 2000 Latino Tribute Award from the American Diabetes Association.

Lifshitz is motivated in her hard-working efforts by one strong desire, as she explained to Martínez: "I would basically like in some way to leave this world a little bit better than what I found it."

## For More Information

"Aliza Lifshitz," Women in Balance. Available at http://www.wibwomeninbalance.org/camp_lifshitz.html (accessed June 21, 2002).
*Hispanic,* October 1991, p. 15.
*Notable Hispanic American Women,* Gale, 1993, pp. 229–31.
*Unidos,* April 1992, pp. 16–18.

# Jennifer Lopez

Actress, singer, dancer
Born July 24, 1970, New York, New York

*"I want everything. I want family. I want to do good work. I want to love. I want to be comfortable. I want it all."*

I've had a career, I swear, like no other actress—Latina or not," Jennifer Lopez once told *Vibe* magazine. "When I think of who I've worked with—Jack Nicholson, Francis Ford Coppola, Sean Penn—I freak out." From the time she was a young child, Lopez wanted to be a star—in spite of the near absence of Latina role models in Hollywood. Driven and ambitious, Lopez worked hard to be taken seriously as a leading lady and struggled to overcome the barrier of being typecast in ethnic roles. "There aren't a lot of parts for [Latinas], and we're not generally considered for other roles that aren't race specific," she explained to Jeffrey Ressner of *Time* magazine. "It's starting to change a little bit, but we're still treated like foreigners who just got here because we're not white." Now the most handsomely paid Latina in Hollywood history, Lopez has put a great deal of thought into making the right career choices. "I've been careful with what I've selected," she explained in an E! Online interview. "There were projects I could've done for the money because I was broke, but I always felt I had a chance at a better, longer career."

## From Fly Girl to Elephant Woman

Jennifer Lopez was born on July 24, 1970, in the Bronx, New York (one of the five boroughs of New York City). Both of her parents—David, a computer specialist for an insurance company, and Guadalupe ("Lupe"), a teacher—are Puerto Rican. The second of three children, she has an older sister, Leslie, and a younger sister, Lynda. After graduating from Holy Family School, where her mother teaches kindergarten, she enrolled in Baruch College in New York City. Having decided to pursue a career in dance, she dropped out after one semester. Hoping eventually to appear in Broadway shows, she studied ballet and jazz dance. Lopez appeared in two productions that toured abroad (*Golden Musicals of Broadway,* which toured in Europe, and *Synchronicity,* which toured in Japan) prior to winning a spot in 1990 as one of **Rosie Perez**'s "fly girl" dancers on the Fox comedy *In Living Color* (see entry). After winning the part—for which she competed with over two thousand other performers—Lopez moved to Los Angeles, California. In a later interview with *Women's Wire,* Lopez said of the experience, "That was cool, but I didn't like to be anyone's backup."

Although she never expected to remain in Los Angeles, Lopez enjoyed good fortune in her new home. Shortly after becoming a "fly girl," she was cast in *South Central,* a television pilot written and directed by the

Jennifer Lopez. *Reproduced by permission of Archive Photos, Inc.*

husband of one of her fellow dancers. Although the series failed, Lopez had begun to attract the attention of other producers. In 1992 she appeared on *The Tonight Show* with Jay Leno. The following year she played the role of Melinda Lopez on the television series *Second Chances,* and portrayed Rosie in the made-for-television movie *Nurses on the Line: The Crash of Flight 7.* She also had a part in the short-lived television series *Hotel Malibu* before making her big-screen debut in 1995, as Maria Sanchez, a Mexican American mother, in *My Family.* The sprawling story of generations of a Latino family also starred Jimmy Smits (who is perhaps best known for his role as Bobby Simone in the successful television series *NYPD Blue*).

Next Lopez was cast as Grace Santiago, a New York City transit cop, in the 1995 action comedy *Money Train.* The following year, she played Miss Marquez, a sweet fifth-grade teacher, in *Jack,* directed by Francis Ford Coppola and starring Robin Williams. In 1997 she played the role of Gabriela in *Blood and Wine,* a film noir thriller starring Jack Nicholson. Although critics took little notice of Lopez's role in the film, Henri Behar wrote in *Film Scouts Interviews* that "her swishing hips all but stole a couple of scenes from Jack Nicholson and Stephen Dorff." Also that year Lopez played Terri Flores, a first-time filmmaker, in the action thriller *Anaconda. Rolling Stone* reporter Peter Travers referred to her role as doing "hard screen time dodging snakes." The role proved to be physically demanding, and Lopez enjoyed the challenge. "I'm tough that way," she explained to *Cosmopolitan* reporter Dennis Hensley. "Some actresses are like, 'Get my stunt double, I don't want to have to run.' But I'll do anything…. I was like the Elephant Woman from the hips down. It was a major bruise movie." The movie was bruising in more ways than one: it took a beating at the box office and from the critics.

## The New Queen of Tejano

Lopez's biggest break came when she landed the title role in *Selena,* written and directed by Gregory Nava (whose previous credits included *My Family).* The movie portrays the brief life of Mexican American singer Selena Quintanilla Perez, the so-called Queen of Tejano music, who was shot and killed in 1995 at the age of twenty-three by the president of her fan club.

(Tejano—pronounced *tay-HA-no*—is a form of music, originated in the borderland between Texas and Mexico, that combines traditional Mexican folk music with polkas, country-and-western, and even rock and roll.) Out of a field of twenty-two thousand women who auditioned for the title role, seven were chosen for a final screen test.

"When I started preparing for the audition and really learning about Selena, I really wanted to play her," Lopez explained in *Vibe.* After winning the part, she moved to Corpus Christi, Texas, where she lived with Selena's sister, Suzette, and watched tapes of the Tejano artist's performances and studied her every move. Lopez spoke to Selena's family and friends in an attempt to learn more about the private side of the popular singer's life. "I didn't want to merely impersonate or caricature her," Lopez told *Time* reporter Jeffrey Ressner. "I wanted to capture her personality, down to the tiniest details—even the way she rubbed her nose." In order to look like the flamboyant singer, Lopez spent two hours every day having make-up applied. The colorful costumes she wore (fifty in all) were sewn by Selena's seamstress—from the original patterns. On the advice of the singer's sister, she even wore Selena's favorite nail polish, L'Oreal Sangria.

Not everyone was pleased that Lopez—a New Yorker of Puerto Rican descent—had been cast as a Mexican American. Some charged that Warner Brothers (the studio producing the film) had used the talent search, which included nonprofessional actresses, to generate publicity. Some even suggested that Lopez, who had previously appeared in a film by director Nava, had never even auditioned for the part. Lopez took the pressure in stride. "I had to do a good job not just for me, but for Selena, her family, her fans, and her legacy," she explained in *Vibe*. "It was a big responsibility, and I took that on without thinking twice."

Although *Selena* received lukewarm reviews, the critics praised Lopez's turn as Selena. Richard Corliss, writing in *Time*, noted that Lopez "gives a feisty, buoyant performance that could set her on a star path similar to the singer's." Behar wrote in *Film Scouts,* "Nothing quite prepares you for what she does in—AS—Selena in Gregory Nava's film. Beyond getting the deceased singer's moves right, she creates a character on whose shoulders the entire film practically rests." For her portrayal of Selena, Lopez won the Imagen Foundation Lasting Image Award, the Lone Star Film & Television Award, and an Alma Award, which recognizes Latino contributions to the television and movie industry. She was nominated for a Golden Globe and MTV Movie Award. And she reportedly became the first Latina actress to earn $1 million for one role.

Like the character she portrayed in *Selena,* Lopez has been hailed as a crossover artist. It is a label she prefers not to embrace. "I was born in the Bronx," she explained in a *Film Scouts* interview. "'Crossover' is when you cross over from one market to another. I've always been in this market.... If it's convenient for them to say I'm doing the crossover thing, so be it. I prefer to say I'm Latin, I'm an actor, and I'm having some success."

## Marriage and Other U-Turns

With the completion of *Selena* came another turning point in Lopez's life. At a party to celebrate the completion of the movie, her boyfriend, Ojani Noa, proposed. The two had met while he was waiting tables in Miami. "All of a sudden Ojani takes the mike," she told *Cosmopolitan* reporter Dennis Hensley, "and I'm thinking he's going to say something about how hard I worked. He comes up to my table and in Spanish he says, 'I just want to say one thing: Jennifer, will you marry me?' Everybody just burst out in applause. I started crying. Then he gets down on one knee and puts the ring on my finger. It was very, very romantic." The couple was married about a year later, in February 1997, but were divorced sometime in 1998.

Taking no break after filming *Selena,* Lopez flew to a new location to begin work on Oliver Stone's *U Turn,* starring Nick Nolte and Sean Penn. (Stone had to rearrange the production schedule in order to cast Lopez in the film.) "I didn't expect it to happen like this, wrapping one film and flying out to do a new one the next day," she told E! Online. "But I'm fresh enough and ambitious enough to stay up all night for the sake of a job. I'm not gonna take it easy. I want to do so much more when I'm getting these great opportunities." Director Oliver Stone had nothing but praise for Lopez, who plays the role of a Mexican-Apache femme fatale (seductive woman) in *U Turn*. "She's striking, strong, and has an extremely enthusiastic attitude," he told *Time* magazine's Richard Corliss. "She's there at 7 in the morning, ready to rehearse, knows all her lines, and is fearless about doing her own stunts, whether it's climbing a mountain or tussling in a fight scene." As it turned out, *U Turn* was a box-office failure. It did, however, allow Lopez to work with some of the biggest names in Hollywood, which, for a young, up-and-coming star, is an invaluable opportunity and learning experience.

## Beyond Out of Sight

Lopez—who provided the voice of Azteca in the 1998 animated movie *Antz*—was a hit starring with George Clooney in the 1998 crime story *Out of Sight*. In the role of Karen Sisco, a U.S. marshal, Lopez is kidnapped by bank robber Jack Foley (Clooney), a nonviolent and gentlemanly crook who resorts to kidnapping only after Sisco interferes with his jail-escape plan. The unlikely duo develops a romantic attraction. As the tough but sexy federal officer, Lopez impressed the critics. Janet Maslin, for example, wrote in the *New York Times,* "Ms. Lopez has her best movie role thus far, and she brings it both seductiveness and grit. If it was hard to imagine a hardworking, pistol-packing bombshell on the page [in the original Elmore Leonard novel], it couldn't be easier here."

In spite of her apparent success, Lopez observed to Knight Ridder reporter Rene Rodriquez (printed in the *Arizona Republic*) that being Latina is still an issue in casting for some directors—and that it poses a constant barrier with which she must contend. *Out of Sight* director Steven Soderbergh, however, claimed that he did not take into account Lopez's background. "I just thought she was the best actress for that part," he explained. "Jennifer is ebullient [lively], very positive and effervescent. She's really unique, because she can do just about anything, and it's not often you find someone with that kind of range."

Lopez took a year off from acting to work on a new project: music. She released her first album, *On the 6,* in 1999. *On the 6,* named after a subway train she often took as a girl, explores a variety of musical styles, though the whole album has a Latino flavor. Lopez co-wrote one of the songs, "If You Had My Love"; sang a duet, "No Me Ames (You Don't Love Me)," with Marc Anthony; and recorded a song by her boyfriend, hip hop singer and producer Sean "Puffy" Combs.

## Scandal and Enterprise

At the end of 1999 Lopez and Combs were involved in a shooting at a Manhattan night club when a member of Combs's entourage allegedly shot at three bystanders. Combs and two others were charged with criminal possession of a 9-mm handgun. Combs and Lopez evidently led the police on a high speed chase and both were arrested. One of the guns from the shootout was found in the sport utility vehicle they were riding in. Lopez spent fourteen hours in jail, but she was cleared of criminal wrongdoing. Combs, however, faced weapons charges.

Lopez's relationship with Combs would come to an end in early 2001, mainly because of career demands. They had been together since 1998. He had helped out on some of the production work in one track of her first album; on her second album, *J.Lo,* he worked on several tracks. Lopez, never one to sit on the sidelines, was co-executive producer of the second album and co-wrote seven of its songs. The album was a huge success, selling a million records after only two months of release, and going on to double that within a year.

Besides her movie and music work, Lopez started a fashion line called Sweetface Fashion Company, making women's and girls' clothing and eventually branching off into cosmetics and perfume. She opened a Cuban restaurant in Pasadena, hiring her ex-husband Ojani Noa to run it for her. She got more and more involved in movie production.

## A Full Schedule

In rapid succession, hit movies starring Jennifer Lopez hit the theaters. In the 2000 horror movie *The Cell,* Lopez plays the role of a psychologist who is able to travel inside her patients' minds. She is asked to go into the mind of a deranged psychotic serial killer, with terrifying results. Already the highest-paid Latina actress in Hollywood, Lopez was awarded $5 million for the role. Her next movie, *The Wedding Planner* (2001), is a romantic comedy in which Lopez plays a hard-working business executive in the wedding planning business who, inevitably, meets the man of her dreams while she plans his wedding to someone else. Many critics reviewed this film harshly, but it was a big hit at the box office. Notably, the same week that the film hit the number one position at the box office her album *J. Lo* was number one on the *Billboard* Top 200.

Later in 2001, the mystery *Angel Eyes* was released. In this film, Lopez plays a detective working the tough streets of Chicago. Lopez received some high praise for her work in the film, as in this review by

Richard Schickel from *Time* magazine: "Mostly, though, the movie works because Lopez gives such a terrific performance. She's a vulnerable hard-ass, lonesome but damned if she'll admit it, forgiving in some relationships, unforgiving in others. It's an intense, complex performance in unexpected circumstances." In 2002, in the thriller *Enough,* Lopez plays an abused wife who learns the martial arts in order to defend herself. Once again, though many critics found fault with the plot of the movie, most applauded Lopez's performance.

Lopez married dancer Cris Judd in 2001. In February 2002, her remix album, *J To Tha L-O! The Remixes,* took the number one spot on the *Billboard* Top 200, marking the first time a remix album had ever taken that spot. The album contains a new song written by Lopez and Judd, *Alive.* Unfortunately, Lopez and Judd separated in 2002.

Lopez started filming *Uptown Girl,* directed by Wayne Wang, in the spring of 2002. The film is a romantic comedy co-starring Ralph Fiennes, about a politician who falls in love with a hotel maid. Lopez was also in production with *Gigli,* in which she stars with Ben Affleck. She is scheduled to start shooting another film with Affleck as her co-star, *Jersey Girl,* in the summer of 2002.

In the spring of 2002 Lopez signed a contract to star in the movie version of *Carmen,* nineteenth-century French composer George's Bizet's opera about a Spanish soldier who falls in love with a gypsy. The script for the film was written by *Moulin Rouge* co-writer Craig Pearce. In an interview with hip-hop's Redman, Lopez admitted to being particularly eager to take on this role: "I'm very excited about that because we'll be able to incorporate some singing and dancing and also acting and that's always what I wanted, something like 'The Rose' or 'The Bodyguard,' those kind of movies. It would be great if I could incorporate the two together."

Lopez attributes her success in Hollywood to hard work and preparation. "[It's] about being prepared when your opportunity comes, about being able to perform under pressure," she told Rodriguez. "If you're going in to audition for Oliver Stone or Francis Ford Coppola, are you gonna choke? If you have a good day that day, then it's not luck. It's because you made it happen."

## For More Information

Behar, Henri, "Jennifer Lopez on 'Selena,'" *Film Scouts* Interviews. Available at http://filmscouts. com/scripts/interview.cfm?ArticleCode=680 (accessed June 21, 2002).

Corliss, Richard, "¡Viva Selana!" *Time,* March 24, 1997.

Duggan, Dennis, "A Rising Latina Star Wows Them in the Bronx," *Newsday,* March 20, 1997.

Fitzpatrick, Eileen, "Selena," *Billboard,* April 5, 1997.

Handelman, David, "A Diva Is Born," *Mirabella,* July/August 1998, pp. 82–84.

Hensley, Dennis, "How Do You Say 'Hot' in Spanish? Jennifer Lopez," *Cosmopolitan,* April 1997.

*In Style,* May 1, 1997.

"Jennifer Lopez: Articles," RollingStone.com. Available at http://www.rollingstone.com/mv_people/ articlelist.asp?oid=8272 (accessed June 21, 2002).

Maslin, Janet, "'Out of Sight': A Thief, a Marshall, an Item," *New York Times,* June 26, 1998.

Ressner, Jeffrey, "Born to Play the Tejano Queen," *Time,* March 24, 1998.

Rodriguez, Rene, "*Too Latin* Jennifer Lopez Answers with Her Talent," *Arizona Republic,* June 26, 1998.

Sessums, Kevin, "Bronx Belle," *Vanity Fair,* July 1998.

Schickel, Richard, "Good Deeds: Jennifer Lopez Saves a Guy's Life, and This Movie," *Time,* May 28, 2001, p. 84.

Smith, Kyle, et al., "Shaking It Up," *People,* September 13, 1999, p.71.

Travers, Peter, "Selena," *Rolling Stone,* April 17, 1997.

*USA Weekend,* June 21, 1998.

Wuntch, Philip, "*Out of Sight* review," *Dallas Morning News,* June 26, 1998.

# Nancy Lopez

Professional golfer
Born January 6, 1957, Torrance, California

*"I've always felt like a role model for the Hispanic people. I hope that I stand for honesty."*

**N**ancy Lopez was one of the youngest women golfers to achieve professional success. Since 1978, she consistently ranked among the top women players. She has won over forty tournament victories. In 1987 she became the youngest woman ever to be named to the Ladies Professional Golf Association (LPGA) Hall of Fame.

Lopez was born in 1957 in Torrance, California, but raised in Roswell, New Mexico. She learned to play golf when her parents, Domingo and Marina Lopez, took up the game for her mother's health. By the age of eleven, she was a better golfer than either of her parents, and her father was convinced that she should pursue the sport as a career. The family tried to scrape up the money to pay for her lessons and practice. However, the Lopezes were hindered not only by finances but also by prejudice. "My dad worked so hard to do so much for me," she recounted to Annette Alvarez in *Hispanic,* "and a lot of doors were shut in our faces because he couldn't afford to get me into the country club so I could play golf there."

## Perseverance Brings Early Success

Lopez's struggle against these barriers quickly paid off. At the age of twelve, she won the New Mexico Women's Open. She then went on to become the only female member of her high school golf team. In 1972 and 1974, she won the U.S. Girls Junior title, and while still in high school placed second in the U.S. Women's Open golf tournament. She won a golf scholarship to the University of Tulsa, where she won the intercollegiate golf title before dropping out to turn professional.

Her first year of professional play—1978—was a whirlwind for Lopez. She broke several records and won nine tournaments, including the famed Ladies Professional Golf Association (LPGA) title. It was her year for collecting trophies—she was named Rookie of the Year, Player of the Year, Golfer of the Year, and Female Athlete of the Year. She also set a new record for earnings by a rookie, winning over $200,000.

## Dominates Her Sport

Lopez continued to mow down her opponents the following year. She won eight more tournaments, which brought her two-year-old career victory total to seventeen. It was a feat Bruce Newman of *Sports Illus-*

Nancy Lopez. *Reproduced by permission of Corbis Corporation (Bellevue).*

*trated* called "one of the most dominating sports performances in half a century." Lopez proved she was a true sports superstar by continuing to overshadow many of her fellow golfers during the 1980s. Her best year was 1985—her eighth on the pro circuit. That year she won five tournaments and earned over $400,000

Lopez began balancing the demands of her sports career with the role of wife and mother when she married New York Mets third baseman Ray Knight in 1982. Over the years, the couple has had three daughters: Ashley, Erinn, and Torri. Many sports writers and observers have marveled at what has come be called a model marriage. Lopez explained to Jaime Diaz of *Sports Illustrated* that her marriage to Knight has given her peace of mind. "I'm so happy with my life, that now when I play, there is no pressure. It's just all fun, and when it's fun, you perform better."

Happiness at home indeed seemed to enhance Lopez's career. In 1987 she was named to the LPGA Hall of Fame. The LPGA has some of the most difficult requirements for entry of any sports Hall of Fame: nominees must have thirty tournament victories, of which two must be major titles. By the end of 1987, Lopez had passed the $2 million mark in golf-related earnings. That same year she also authored a book, *Nancy Lopez's The Complete Golfer.*

## Focus Extends Beyond Golf

Lopez has achieved greatness in her career through hard work and self discipline. Yet she has never forgotten that any sport is meant to be fun, and she has maintained a cheerful and positive approach. As Alvarez noted, "Lopez has a tremendous following because, regardless of how busy she is, Lopez will find time to give an autograph, do an interview, pose for pictures, give a smile, and shake hands."

As her family has grown, so has Lopez's commitment to issues outside the golfing world. When she can, she volunteers her time to Aid for the Handicapped, an organization that helps children with physical disabilities. And she has never forgotten her community and the hardships she overcame as a child. "I've always felt like a role model for the Hispanic people," she told Alvarez. "I hope that I stand for honesty." Her status as a role model was confirmed in 1991 when the Roswell, New Mexico, school

board changed the name of Flora Vista Elementary School (her old school) to Nancy Lopez Elementary School.

## Fitting Golf Into the Day

With her other commitments, Lopez's golf game suffered. In the thirty-seven events in which she participated in 1994 and 1995, she did not have one victory. She gained weight and became so frustrated with her game that in 1996 she was about to retire. But she could not give up quite so easily and, instead, went to work to get her game back. She got into shape and got motivated and went into the 1996 U.S. Women's Open with some wins behind her. In 1997 she came in second in the Open; it was the fourth time she had come in second out of twenty-one tries. She continued to play well over the next few years with her many fans and peers always in her corner.

In March 2002, Lopez announced that the 2002 season would be her last full season on the LPGA tour. "This will be my last year committed to the LPGA as a full-time touring professional, but I am not walking away from golf," Lopez announced, as quoted on the LPGA Web site. "I am at the beginning of a brand new chapter in my golf career. You will see me because I will be participating in corporate golf events, television, golf course design and working with Women's Golf Unlimited to develop new ideas for my namesake club line. I still have the fire, so I plan to compete in some events during the years after the 2002 season. Although this change in my career makes me sad, I know that it is time to make my commitments to new projects, my wonderful sponsors, AIM for the Handicapped, and my family."

## For More Information

*Hispanic,* June 1989, pp. 15–16.

"Legendary Golfer Nancy Lopez To Make 2002 Her Final Full Season on LPGA Tour After 25 Years," Ladies Professional Golf Association (LPGA) Web site, March 13, 2002. Available at http://www.lpga.com/news/index.cfm?cont_id=100033 (accessed June 21, 2002).

Lopez, Nancy, *Nancy Lopez's The Complete Golfer,* Contemporary Books, 1987.

Shipnuck, Alan, "Open and Shut," *Sports Illustrated,* July 21, 1997, p. 44.

*Sports Illustrated,* August 4, 1986, p. 34–35+; February 9, 1987, pp. 84–85.

*Women's Sports and Fitness,* August 1985, pp. 15–16.

# Los Lobos

Mexican American roots/rock band

*"At the heart of the Los Lobos sound is the traditional music of their Mexican parents and grandparents and the mainstream pop music they grew up with in the 1960s."—Mark Holston, Hispanic*

Los Lobos reached commercial stardom in 1987 when it recorded the successful soundtrack for film *La Bamba,* which retold the life story of Mexican American singer **Ritchie Valens** (see entry). The band had been together for fourteen years before that, combining country swing, rock and roll, Mexican folk songs, and rhythm and blues into a sound that is both old and new. "At the heart of the Los Lobos sound," Mark Holston wrote in *Hispanic,* "is the traditional music of their Mexican parents and grandparents and the mainstream pop music they grew up with in the 1960s."

The four original members of Los Lobos—David Hidalgo, Cesar Rosas, Louie Pérez, and Conrad Lozano—have known each other since their high school days in the same Los Angeles area neighborhood. Until 1973 they had all played in various bands. Tired of playing Top 40 songs over and over, they decided to join together to explore their Mexican roots and to learn the folk songs they were raised on but had taken for granted at the time.

## Folk Music and New Instruments

Taking the name Los Lobos (Spanish for "the wolves"), the members began by collecting as many old recordings of Mexican folk music as they could find. They then studied each song carefully in order to play it properly. Many of the songs required instruments—such as the *vihuela,* a sixteenth-century Spanish guitar similar to the lute—that the members of the group had never even played before. They started playing at parties, weddings, and other small events. They landed their first full-time professional job in 1978 at a Mexican restaurant in Orange County, California.

"It wasn't even a real Mexican restaurant," Rosas told an interviewer in *Guitar World.* "One of those tourist joints. We were working there because we had come to a point where we had to either make more money from music or find other jobs; some of us had gotten married, and we weren't kids anymore."

For its first eight years, Los Lobos was an all-acoustic group playing only traditional music. The members had accumulated over 30 different folk and classical instruments, taking time to learn how to use each one properly. They then began adding other instruments, like the accordion, and their own electric guitars and amplifiers. Their two-year job at the restaurant ended when the owner complained that their music had become too loud.

In 1978 the group had also recorded its first album, *Just Another Band from East L.A.* Financed by the members themselves, the album sold poorly. After a while, they decided to try recording again, but this time with their own material. As Los Lobos's songs were heard more and more around Los Angeles, their reputation grew until they signed a recording contract with Slash/Warner Bros. Their musical hobby quickly became more serious. In 1983 they released a recording called ...*And A Time To Dance.* Music critics praised it. A song off the album, "Anselma," won a Grammy Award for best Mexican American performance.

## Extensive Musical Ability

The members of Los Lobos have an impressive range of musical ability. From the very beginning, instead of hiring additional musicians to play the different instruments, the four members split the instruments among themselves. Pérez had begun playing drums only years after he joined the group. He was originally a guitarist, having picked up the instrument when he was twelve. In his mid-twenties, he was elected to play drums when Los Lobos began to go electric. Pérez, along with Hidalgo, also writes most of the group's songs.

Hidalgo began playing guitar when he was eleven years old. He launched his career as a drummer in the early 1970s by playing in a Christian rock band. He also plays violin, accordion, and drums. "You have to understand, the group does work and evolve around David," Lonzano said of Hidalgo, as quoted by a reporter in *Musician.* "His playing is so strong; his talent is still being tapped."

Lozano, who plays both electric and acoustic bass, began playing rock and roll when he was sixteen. He juggled his time between two bands before jumping to Los Lobos in 1973. Rosas is from Sonora, Mexico. He immigrated to Los Angeles with his family when he was seven. Basically a self-taught guitar player, he took some lessons in order to learn chords and musical theory. He also plays the mandolin and the vihuela.

Steve Berlin joined the group in the early 1980s after working on one of their recordings. His full tenor and baritone saxes add another dimension Los Lobos's sound. Berlin also co-produced the group's first full-length album, *How Will the Wolf Survive?* Released in 1984, the record features a wide variety of styles, from Tex-Mex polkas to New Orleans rhythm and blues.

## Success

Los Lobos's follow-up album, *By The Light of the Moon,* released in 1987, showed the group expanding even more. In addition to superb musicianship, the album featured songs whose lyrics offered social commentary. That same year, Los Lobos recreated the original recordings of the late Ritchie Valens for the movie *La Bamba.* Many thought their recreations were better than the

Los Lobos. *Reproduced by permission of AP/Wide World Photos.*

originals, and their version of the title track reached number one on the pop music charts. The soundtrack album also spent two weeks at number one. The group's new audience stretched across the country.

The instant popularity, however, almost proved to be too much for the band. "That kind of eclipsed everything else we had done up to that point," Pérez explained to Jay Cocks in *Time.* "[But] we didn't know if we were going to be an alternative novelty thing or just a flavor of the month."

To remain centered, the members of Los Lobos returned to what was most important to them—the folk songs of their youth. In 1988 they released *La Pistola y El Corazón,* an album composed wholly of those folk songs. The recording earned the group it's second Grammy Award. Describing the album in *Guitar World,* critic Harold Steinblatt wrote, "It is a stunning personal statement of musical faith by a band at the height of its creative powers."

Since that time, Los Lobos has continued to bridge the gap between mainstream American music and its Mexican roots. *The Neighborhood* (1990) showcased their smooth blend of rock, jazz, and Mexican folk songs. Other prominent musicians, like Ry Cooder and Paul Simon, have tapped Los Lobos's talents for various projects of their own. In 1992 the group also lent its sound to the recording for *The Mambo Kings,* the film adaptation of the Pulitzer Prize-winning novel by **Oscar Hijuelos** (see entry).

## Yet Another Masterpiece

In 1992 the band came out with what many critics and fans think is their best record, *Kiko*. On the record, they mixed their roots music with a glossy, atmospheric production. The record made "album of the year" in newspapers across the country, including the *Los Angeles Times* and the *Chicago Tribune*.

The band celebrated 20 years together by releasing a two-CD compilation, *Just Another Band from East L.A … A Collection,* including material from live shows, out-takes, and material from their early indie (independent label) records. Before regrouping for their next big release, the members of Los Lobos worked on various side projects. They put out the children's record *Papa's Dream* and worked on songs for the 1996 movies *Desperado* and *Feeling Minnesota.* Hidalgo and Pérez teamed up to create the Latin Playboys, an avant-garde roots band.

## On to Colossal Head

The band recorded their 1996 album *Colossal Head* quickly, trying to catch the first sparks of inspiration. "We were working really fast," said Pérez in a press release for the album. "We couldn't second guess ourselves. I would be writing something in the studio lounge, and it was like 'Are you ready to record that yet?' But I really think that the first thought is usually the best thought."

Unfortunately, many critics didn't agree. *Entertainment Weekly* gave the record a "B–," saying they "waste too much time groaning leaden beat-generation platitudes." *Rolling Stone* was even harsher, giving the record two out of five stars and saying the band was "still searching for the right balance between experimentation and craftsmanship, and between concepts and passion."

For three years after *Colossal Head,* the band members were busy but the band itself seemed to disappear. Hidalgo and Pérez prepared to release their second album as the Latin Playboys. Cesar Rosas did a solo album. And Hildalgo did another side project. The band also got a new label, moving from Warner Bros. to Hollywood. In 1999, all of the side projects were released at the same time that the band released a new album called *This Time,* which showcased the many new sounds all of the individual Los Lobos members had been working on. In 2000 the band came out with *El Cancionero/Mas y mas* and in 2002 another album, *Good Morning Aztlán,* was released.

Throughout their twenty-five-year career together, the members of Los Lobos have experimented in a wide variety of sounds and styles, but they have returned time and again to the traditional music of their Mexican American roots. Asked about this in Digital Interviews David Hidalgo responded: "We have a responsibility, since we're in whatever position we're in. If we can say something, or pay tribute to someone, we will, because we have a lot of respect for the people that we listened to growing up, and the people that taught *us* how to play."

## For More Information

Andrews, Jon, "Colossal Head," *Downbeat,* June 1996, p. 58.

Eddy, Chuck, "Colossal Head," *Entertainment Weekly,* March 22, 1996, p. 75.

Forte, Dan, "Los Lobos," *Guitar Player,* July 1995, p. 38.

*Guitar World,* September 1986; February 1989.

Himes, Geoffrey, "Colossal Head," *Rolling Stone,* April 18, 1996, p. 70.

*Hispanic,* March 1994, p. 48.

Hochman, Steve, "Los Lobos," *Rolling Stone,* October 1, 1992, p. 34.

"Los Lobos," Digital Interviews. Available at http://www.digitalinterviews.com/digitalinterviews/views/lobos.shtml (accessed June 21, 2002).

Morris, Chris, "Los Lobos, Biography," Rollingstone.com. [6–12–02.] Available at http://www.rollingstone.com/artists/bio.asp?oid=221&cf=221 (accessed June 21, 2002).

*Musician,* April 1987.

Thompson, Art, and Ellis, Andy, "Flex Mex: New Twists from Los Lobos," *Guitar Player,* October, 1996, p. 68.

*Time,* November 26, 1990, pp. 88–89.

# Wendy Lucero-Schayes

Broadcaster, former Olympic athlete
Born June 26, 1963, Denver, Colorado

*"The success I've had in sports overcoming those people who didn't think that I could [succeed] has made me like myself better.... Hopefully I can share that with others."*

When she was a young girl, Wendy Lucero-Schayes dreamed of being an Olympic athlete. She trained as a gymnast and as a figure skater before finally settling on diving. She was a member of the U.S. Diving National Team for eight years. During that time, she won nine national titles, three U.S. Olympic Festival titles, and several medals in international competition. In 1988 she competed in the summer Olympics in Seoul, Korea. She then went on to begin a career in television broadcasting.

Lucero-Schayes was born in 1963 in Denver, Colorado, to Dan and Shirley Lucero. Her father, the son of Spanish immigrants, worked as an electrician. Her mother, of Irish heritage, worked at home, raising the three Lucero children. Growing up in an athletic family, Lucero-Schayes began swimming and dancing at an early age. She later learned gymnastics, tennis, and diving while tagging along to her older sister's lessons.

Sports soon became an activity at which the tomboy Lucero-Schayes excelled. Part of the motivation behind her success was her fierce desire to compete against her older sister. "I would always strive to be the best I could be," Lucero-Schayes explained to Diane Telgen in *Notable Hispanic American Women,* "because I wanted to grasp what my sister was attaining—but I wanted it now, even though I was two years younger."

## Skating Star Inspires Dream

Lucero-Schayes first dreamed of competing in the Olympics when she was nine years old. She thought she would compete in gymnastics, but soon realized that her late start in the sport would severely limit her chance of success. After watching Dorothy Hamill win the gold medal in figure skating in the 1976 winter games in Innsbruck, Austria, Lucero-Schayes was inspired to become a skater. After competing for four years, however, she again realized that she had begun the sport too late. In addition, her family did not have the finances necessary for her to compete nationally.

In high school, Lucero-Schayes returned to the sport of diving. Her gymnastics training helped her excel at springboard events. At the end of her senior year in high school, she competed in the Junior Olympic Championships, finishing sixth in the three-meter event. For her success in this competition and others that year, she was named 1981's Hispanic Athlete of the Year. Cited as an Academic All-American, she received a scholarship to the University of Nebraska.

Lucero-Schayes's parents placed a high value on education. They encouraged her to work hard at her studies, as well as at diving. After two years at the University of Nebraska, Lucero-Schayes transferred to Southern Illinois University, where she had more chances to compete on a national level. She won the 1985 National Collegiate Athletic Association championship and earned her first national titles. She was also named an Academic All-American for her academic performance.

Even then, Lucero-Schayes wanted to be more than just a diver. After earning her bachelor's degree in 1986 in television sales and management, she sought out opportunities in broadcasting and television production. "As I was training for the Olympic Games in 1988 and the few years before that," she related to Telgen, "I would try to be a production assistant for golf tournaments, horse tournaments, Monday Night Football—anything I could do." She worked as a sportscaster for television networks and hosted a talk show, "Focus Colorado," in her hometown of Denver.

## Olympic Training Marred by Mother's Illness

Lucero-Schayes encountered two problems during her training for the 1988 U.S. Olympic trials. First, her mother, who had always encouraged her, developed breast cancer and had to undergo chemotherapy treatments. Second, her coach undermined her self-confidence, telling her she probably would not make the Olympics. Lucero-Schayes switched coaches and focused on training for her mother's sake.

Lucero-Schayes's mother soon recovered and was able to watch her daughter compete in the trials. Lucero-Schayes was greatly motivated by the presence of her mother. She turned in one of the best performances of her career and finished second, qualifying for the U.S. Olympic team. Her victory was especially sweet because she had beaten competitors who were guided by her former coach.

At the 1988 Summer Olympics in Seoul, Lucero-Schayes finished sixth. Although she didn't win a medal, she enjoyed the experience of meeting and competing against other athletes from around the world. After the Olympics, Lucero-Schayes continued her work in communications. She increased her involvement in public speaking, visiting schools and speaking at charity events and conferences. She served as a spokesperson for the American Cancer Society, and often appeared as a motivational speaker in front of groups, passing on what she has learned. "The success I've had in sports overcoming those people who didn't think that I could [succeed] has made me like myself better…. Hopefully I can share that with others," she related to Telgin.

Lucero-Schayes met her husband, professional basketball player Dan Schayes, at a charity benefit where they both spoke. Finding sports to be a bond, they married in 1991. They not only train together but also give each other understanding and support during the stress and strain of competition.

## U.S. Female Diving Athlete of the Year

Nineteen ninety-one was a banner year for Lucero-Schayes. In the national indoor championships that year, she placed first in both the one-meter and the three-meter springboard events. In the outdoor championships, she won the one-meter event and placed second in the three-meter event. At the Sixth World Championship and at the Alamo International competition, she received silver medals. At the end of the 1991 season, Lucero-Schayes was voted the U.S. Female Diving Athlete of the Year (she had also won the award the previous year).

A severe intestinal infection kept Lucero-Schayes from training properly for the 1992 U.S. Olympic trials. At the competition, she finished third—one place short of qualifying for her second Olympic team. Her greatest disappointment was in not having the chance to compete in Barcelona, Spain, the country of her ancestors. Overall, Lucero-Schayes was still satisfied with a sporting career that paid for her college education and enabled her to travel around the world.

Wendy Lucero-Schayes. *Reproduced by permission of Wendy Lucero-Schayes.*

Lucero-Schayes's long-term plans include returning to Denver to continue her work in communications. Her athletic career over, she hopes to inspire others through a different medium, as she explained to Telgin: "I always felt that communications—whether radio and television, or through newspapers and journalism—it's going to shape our world, it is the up-and-coming future."

## For More Information

*Atlanta Constitution,* July 28, 1989, p. F3; August 2, 1990. p. F7.
*Detroit Free Press,* April 14, 1992, p. D1.
*Notable Hispanic American Women,* Gale, 1993, pp. 242–45.

# Manuel Lujan, Jr.

Utilities executive, former congressional representative, former secretary of the U.S. Department of the Interior
Born May 12, 1928, San Ildefonso, New Mexico

*Manuel Lujan's term as the secretary of the U.S. Department of the Interior was marked by considerable controversy.*

In 1968 Manuel Lujan, Jr., became the first Hispanic Republican ever elected to the U.S. House of Representatives. For twenty years, Lujan served quietly in the House as a representative of the state of New Mexico, working on issues that best benefited those people in his home district. In 1988 he decided to retire from politics, but then-president-elect George Bush convinced Lujan to become a member of his cabinet. Lujan's term as the secretary of the U.S. Department of the Interior was marked by considerable controversy. Many environmentalists disagreed with almost all of his wildlife and wilderness policies and believed his programs damaged the very lands he was supposed to protect.

Lujan was born in 1928 in San Ildefonso, a small town on the Rio Grande River in northern New Mexico. He was the eighth of Manuel and Lorenzita Romero Lujan's eleven children. His father, who owned a successful insurance agency, had served three terms as the mayor of the nearby city of Santa Fe.

While growing up in San Ildefonso, Lujan attended parochial schools (private schools run by churches or other religious organizations). He graduated from high school in 1948, then enrolled in St. Mary's College in San Francisco. In November of that year he married Jean Kay Couchman; the couple eventually had four children.

Following one year at St. Mary's, Lujan transferred to the College of Santa Fe, where he earned his bachelor's degree in business administration in 1950. After college, he helped run his father's business. In the early 1960s, he became active in politics, serving for a while as vice chairman of New Mexico's Republican party. Lujan ran for the representative's seat in New Mexico's First Congressional District in 1968. He appealed to the district's Hispanic voters, who normally voted Democratic, and was elected. While serving as a representative, Lujan worked mostly on measures that directly affected his constituents. He was re-elected by overwhelming margins throughout his twenty years in Congress. His only serious threat came in the early 1980s, when he was accused by his Democratic opponents of voting on issues that benefited his family's insurance business.

## Poor Environmental Record in Congress

Beginning in 1969, Lujan served on the House Interior and Insular Affairs Committee, which handles issues regarding the nation's natural resources. His work on the committee, however, earned him low marks with environmentalists. He cosponsored a bill that would have allowed oil and gas companies to begin drilling in the Arctic National Wildlife Refuge. This ecologically sensitive area in northeast Alaska is America's largest wildlife refuge. In addition, he voted to support the nuclear power industry while cutting federal energy conservation funds. He did, however, vote in 1987 to override President Ronald Reagan's veto of a clean water bill.

President Reagan, who served from 1981 to 1988, twice considered Lujan for the top spot in the Department of the Interior but passed him over both times. In 1988, at the end of his tenth term in Congress, Lujan decided to retire. He believed he had served long enough. President-elect Bush, however, thought Lujan would be perfect for the Interior Department position. "Manuel knows the issues," Bush said, as quoted by Bruce Reed in the *New Republic*. At first, lacking interest, Lujan declined the job. Only after Bush personally appealed to him did Lujan accept the offer.

The Department of the Interior is responsible for managing almost 450 million acres of wilderness in the United States. The department also directs the Bureau of Land Management and the National Parks Service. The job of the secretary of the interior is to balance environmental protection with the need for the development of natural resources. As energy needs have increased and energy sources have declined over the past decades, the secretary's balancing act has become harder and harder to manage.

## Questions Nation's Environmental Policies

The day after he was sworn in as secretary of the interior, Lujan proposed that oil companies be allowed to explore in the Arc-

Manuel Lujan, Jr. *Reproduced by permission of AP/Wide World Photos.*

tic National Wildlife Refuge. From the beginning, Lujan questioned the need for the strict Endangered Species Act, which was passed by Congress in 1973. He did not think it was necessary for every type of animal to be protected over the needs of industry. "Nobody's told me the difference between a red squirrel, a black one, or a brown one," Lujan said, according to Ted Gup of *Time*.

Environmentalists believed Lujan was ill-suited for his job. Many thought he knew nothing about the situation facing endangered species and wilderness areas. One example was his lack of concern about wetlands, where almost half of all endangered species live. While biologists and other experts have found it difficult to define exactly what wetlands are, Lujan offered a simple approach. "I take the position that there are certain kinds of vegetation that are common in wetlands—pussy willows or whatever the name is," Gup quoted him as saying. "That's one way you can tell. [Another is] if it's wet."

As secretary, Lujan did introduce a number of measures that almost everyone agreed with. He helped upgrade schools on Native American reservations (Native American lands fall under the jurisdiction of the Department of the Interior), protected historical battlefields that were threatened by developers, and raised the government's earnings from private food stands in federal parks. He also increased the number of minorities hired by the Department of the Interior.

## Speeches Land Him in Trouble

What angered many people, however, were Lujan's seemingly inappropriate public remarks on environmental issues. One instance occurred after the *Exxon Valdez* oil spill in March 1989. The environmental disaster was the worst in American history. The tanker spilled eleven million gallons of oil into Prince William Sound off the southern coastline of Alaska, killing much wildlife and threatening to destroy the area's fishing industry. Lujan appeared on Alaskan television a few months after the incident and compared it to the massive fires that destroyed much of Yellowstone National Park the previous year. "If the same experience holds true for Alaska that held for Yellowstone," he said rather sarcastically, as quoted by Reed, "your tourism should increase this year."

During his four years as secretary of the interior, Lujan claimed that he tried to maintain a balance between environmental concerns and economic development. After Bill Clinton defeated Bush in the 1992 U.S. presidential race, Bruce Babbitt was named the new secretary of the Department of the Interior.

Lujan survived one heart attack in 1986 and another mild one in 1992. In April 1994 he became a director of the Public Service Company of New Mexico, a utility company based in Albuquerque. He has continued to serve on corporate boards and provided business consultation in the early 2000s.

## For More Information

*New Republic,* October 16, 1989, pp. 20–22.
*Time,* May 25, 1992, pp. 57–59.
*Wall Street Journal,* April 12, 1994, p. B8.

# Sonia Manzano

Actress, writer
Born June 12, 1950, New York, New York

*"I think it has a terrible impact when you don't see yourself reflected in the society because then you get the feeling you don't exist."*

**W**hile she was growing up in the United States, Sonia Manzano never saw any Hispanic images in children's books or in the media. Today things are very different—thanks in part to Manzano. She portrays the character "Maria" on the long-running, award-winning children's show *Sesame Street*. Manzano thinks her character, beyond being a positive role model, is important for Hispanic children across the country simply because she exists. "I think it has a terrible impact when you don't see yourself reflected in the society," she explained to Luis Vasquez-Ajmac in *Notable Hispanic American Women,* "because then you get the feeling you don't exist."

Manzano was born in New York City in 1950. She is one of four children born to Bonifacio Manzano, a roofer, and Isidra Rivera, a seamstress. Of Puerto Rican descent, Manzano was raised in the South Bronx (a section of New York City) as part of a very close-knit, Spanish-speaking community.

Manzano never thought of pursuing a career in show business until she was a junior in high school. With the encouragement of a teacher, Manzano went to the famous High School for the Performing Arts in New York City. After graduating, she earned a scholarship to attend Carnegie Mellon University in Pittsburgh, Pennsylvania, where she majored in drama.

## How She Got to Sesame Street

While in college, Manzano was cast in the musical *Godspell*. She was later part of the original cast when the popular play came to Broadway. A theatrical agent noticed her talent during one of her *Godspell* performances and helped her win an audition for a role on *Sesame Street*.

When Manzano began working on *Sesame Street* in 1972, the emphasis of the TV series was on helping black inner-city children. With its endearing muppet charac-

Sonia Manzano. *Reproduced by permission of Getty Images.*

ters, fast pace, and catchy tunes, the program was so appealing that preschool children of almost every ethnic group across the nation began to watch it. The quick humor, original presentation, and educational themes made *Sesame Street* a favorite of parents as well. With the addition of the character "Maria," Manzano introduced a new role model for Hispanic children.

Maria was a teenager when Manzano took on the role. The character has grown and changed quite a bit over the years. Manzano has portrayed her through various stages—from a hippie to a radical feminist. She has also taken Maria through a courtship and into a marriage.

After having portrayed the outspoken, warm-hearted, multi talented Maria for ten years, Manzano began writing scripts for the show. She hoped to make her character more visible and realistic, and to help erase racial-ethnic stereotypes. Manzano also wanted to blend Hispanic culture into the story lines. She often wrote material based on her own real-life experiences.

## Maria's Baby

Along with numbers, letters, and social skills, *Sesame Street* has taught American children about life. Kids learned about families when Maria and fellow character "Luis" married on the show in 1988. When Manzano became pregnant in real life, writers included the pregnancy in Maria's story line. As Manzano pointed out to *Newsweek*'s Jean Seligmann, the pregnancy "gave us an opportunity to deal with something kids really face." By watching the show, children learned how a fetus develops, eats, and breathes inside a mother, and how a mother's body changes during pregnancy. They also heard the baby's heartbeat and watched the parents prepare for its arrival in 1989. Manzano's own child plays the couple's baby.

Manzano has earned seven Emmy Awards as a member of the *Sesame Street* writing staff. In 1991 she won an award from the Hispanic Congressional Caucus in Washington, D.C. Manzano has no interest in leaving *Sesame Street*. She is very content acting and writing for the top-rated children's show. By enriching children's lives and expressing her ideas, Manzano believes that she has been a positive influence. Married since 1986, Manzano especially enjoys working with her own daughter, Gabriela, on *Sesame Street*.

Beyond her *Sesame Street* career, Manzano has been in the cast of the plays *The Living Room* and *Happy New Year,* and directed and starred in *Appearing in Person Tonight: Your Mother.* She has also appeared in the films *Death Wish* (1974) and *Firepower* (1979). In 1999 she played Maria in a collaboration between Jim Henson Films and the Children's Television Workshop, *The Adventures of Elmo in Grouchland.* She is also a popular public speaker.

## For More Information

*Children Today,* September/October 1989, pp. 20–22.

*Newsweek,* May 15, 1989, p. 71.

"Latina Actress Breaks Television Barriers," *Ithaca College News,* September 28, 1998. Available at http://www.ithaca.edu/icnews/vol21/21-03/latina.htm (accessed June 21, 2002).

*Notable Hispanic American Women,* Gale, 1993, pp. 249–50.

# José Martí

Cuban revolutionary, writer, journalist
Born January 28, 1853, Havana, Cuba
Died May 19, 1895, Dos Rios, Cuba

*"Freedom is dearly bought and either we resign ourselves to living without it or we resolve to have it at its price."*

J osé Martí was a Cuban poet and patriot who led a revolution on his island homeland during the 1800s. Banished from Cuba because of his political beliefs, he lived in Spain, Mexico, and the United States, using his writings to raise support for the cause of his people. Throughout his time in exile, he always passionately planned to return to Cuba. Martí championed understanding and respect between cultures, and gave his life for freedom.

Martí was born José Julián Martí y Pérez, the son of a retired Spanish army sergeant. The elder Martí worked as a night watchman to supplement his army pension, but his earnings were barely enough to provide his family with the bare necessities. Despite growing up in poverty, Martí became an excellent student. At the age of four, he traveled with his parents to Spain where he began his education. After he returned to Cuba in 1859, he completed his primary education. He then was admitted to the prestigious Institute of Havana, a college "prep" school.

Cuba had been a Spanish-controlled colony since the 1500s, and for over three hundred years slavery existed on the island. During the 1860s, many Cuban intellectuals began to call for social reforms and complete political independence. From the time he was a young boy, Martí had seen the brutality of slavery. Despite his father's continued loyalty to Spain, he soon joined the growing revolt against Spanish rule. By the age of sixteen, he was writing articles and poems critical of the Spanish government and helping to edit a new journal, *La Patria Libre* ("The Free Homeland"). Outspoken and defiant, he eventually came to the attention of the intolerant police. He was arrested for disloyalty, sentenced to six months of hard labor, then deported to Spain.

## Studies Law and Starts a Family

While in Spain, Martí earned literature and law degrees and became even more com-

José Martí. *Reproduced courtesy of the Library of Congress.*

mitted to Cuban independence. He wrote a pamphlet about the suffering of Cubans to motivate the people of Spain to bring about changes in their government's control of Cuba. In 1875 he moved to Mexico to work as a journalist, submitting political articles to newspapers. He traveled to Guatemala two years later and was made a professor of literature at the Central School. All the while, he continued writing essays and articles on behalf of Cuban independence and worked with other Latin American reformers to bring about change. While in Guatemala, he met and married Maria Garcia Granados.

By 1878 the authorities had gained control over the revolt in Cuba. For the moment, peace returned to the island. Accompanied by his new wife, Martí returned to Cuba hoping to practice law. Government officials still considered him dangerous, however, and would neither grant him a law license nor allow him to teach. While Martí struggled to find work, his wife gave birth to their son, Ismael. To support his new family, he turned to his writing. Once again, his antigovernment views led Cuban leaders to deport him to Spain. After just two months in Spain, Martí traveled to New York City.

## Moves to U.S. and Plans Invasion

Many exiled Cubans lived in New York, and Martí joined with them to gather support from Americans for a rebellion against Spain. Martí longed for a nonviolent solution to Cuba's problems. During the 1880s he was extremely busy working toward that end. His articles calling for Cuban independence appeared in leading Latin American newspapers such as *La Opinión Nacional* of Caracas and *La Nación* of Buenos Aires, Argentina. His writings made him well known throughout North and South America. In 1881 Martí went to Venezuela to work for the renowned newspaper *Revista Venezolana*. His political articles, though, were deemed too radical by the country's dictator, Antonio Guzmán Blanco, and Martí was forced to leave Venezuela after only five months.

Upon his return to New York, Martí continued to submit articles to American newspapers. Not all of his writings, however, were political. He wrote a Spanish magazine for children and became editor of New York's Spanish-language newspaper, *La America*. He not only translated Spanish works for New York publishers, but also translated into Spanish the works of such American writers as the essayist Ralph Waldo Emerson and the poet Walt Whitman. His writing output was tremendous and included novels and poems that were highly praised by literary critics. Believing poetry was only successful if it could be understood by everyone, Martí developed a clear poetic style. His best-known volume of poems, *Versos sencillos* ("Simple Verses"), published in 1891, focused on the themes of love and friendship. By the early 1890s, Martí was perhaps the most famous Latin American writer.

Even though Martí's experiences in Mexico, Guatemala, Venezuela, and the United States led him to work toward Hispanic unity and solidarity, his commitment to Cuban independence remained strong. In 1892 he stopped all his other activities to concentrate fully on organizing a revolution. He founded the Cuban Revolutionary Party. A rousing speaker, Martí urged Cubans and Puerto Ricans in the United States to join him or contribute to the cause. In 1895 he launched a carefully planned invasion of Cuba from the coast of Florida. Once in Cuba, he was named Major General of the Army of Liberation. His followers feared for his safety and tried to convince him to return to the United States to continue to gain support for their cause. Prepared to die for independence, Martí would not leave his homeland again.

## Martí's Name Lives on in Cuba Today

On May 19, 1895, Martí rode into a battle on a white horse and was shot down. The forty-two-year-old leader was one of the first to die in the revolution that, three years later, gained Cuba its freedom from Spain. He is credited with making the free world aware of Cuba's problems and gaining the support and help of the United States in its fight. His political writings and stories of immigrant life in New York are still quoted and studied today.

Many consider Martí to be the author of the revolution that is still being fought today against the Communist government of Fidel Castro. In 1982 Cuban Americans won approval for the creation of a Voice of America radio station that beams news and music from the United States to Cuba. Television transmissions followed in 1990. Organizers honored Martí by naming the stations Radio Martí and TV Martí.

## For More Information

*American History Illustrated,* July/August 1990, pp. 56–59+.

Appel, Todd M., *José Martí,* Chelsea House, 1992.

Gray, Richard Butler, *José Martí: Cuban Patriot,* University of Florida Press, 1962.

Kirk, John M., *José Martí: Mentor of the Cuban Nation,* University Presses of Florida, 1983.

Martí, José, *Major Poems,* translated by Elinor Randall, edited by Philip S. Foner, Holmes & Meier, 1982.

# Eduardo Mata

Conductor
Born September 5, 1942, Mexico City, Mexico
Died January 4, 1995, near Mexico City

*"Classical music, like great painting, like all the arts and humanities … belongs to everybody."*

**O**ne of Mexico's most outstanding symphonic conductors, Eduardo Mata dedicated his entire life to music and gained international recognition in the process. For sixteen years he was music director of the Dallas Symphony Orchestra (DSO) in Texas, and he was credited with bringing the music of Hispanic composers to the rest of the world through his recordings with the symphony. During his lifetime Mata traveled widely, conducting orchestras from Japan to Australia to Germany. He explored the works of such diverse composers as nineteenth-century French experimentalist Claude Debussy and twentieth-century American Aaron Copland.

Mata was born in Mexico City, Mexico, in 1942. Although his parents were not musicians, the family home was filled with the sounds of classical music. Mata learned to play the guitar as a child, but his real dream was to become a conductor. At the age of eleven, he entered the National Conservatory of Mexico in Mexico City to study composition, piano, and conducting. When he was eighteen, he studied privately for four years with Mexican composer Carlos Chávez. He also received advanced training in conducting at the Tanglewood School, a renowned musical institute in Massachusetts.

In 1964, when he was only twenty-two years old, Mata was named musical director of the Guadalajara Symphony Orchestra in Mexico. Two years later he helped organize the Orquestra Filarmonia of the National University of Mexico City. He remained the ensemble's music director and conductor for the next ten years. During this time, he received invitations to conduct South American orchestras and smaller orchestras in the United States. By 1973 Mata had also become principal conductor of the Phoenix Symphony Orchestra in Arizona. The following year he made his London debut, conducting a performance by the London Symphony. He then accepted the position of music director with the Dallas Symphony Orchestra (DSO) in 1977.

## Rebuilds Struggling Dallas Symphony

"I aim to give the Dallas Symphony a much more European sound than it has now," Mata told Sue Regan in *Gramophone* in 1978. He explained that "the typical sound of an American orchestra is more aggressive, more edgy and direct" than that of orchestras in Europe. But before he could change the sound of the Dallas Symphony, Mata had to reverse its dismal financial situation. When he took over the DSO, it was struggling back from bankruptcy. He set out to strengthen the ensemble by adding top-notch musicians. Knowing that a recording contract would increase the value of the DSO, he negotiated a deal with RCA Records. Dallas citizens began to take pride in the orchestra, and within ten years the DSO's audiences increased fourfold.

Mata's reputation spread across the United States and throughout the world. He served as a guest conductor with notable American orchestras in Atlanta, Boston, Chicago, Cleveland, Detroit, and San Francisco. In 1989 he became the principal guest conductor with the Pittsburgh Symphony. He also performed with symphony orchestras in Rotterdam (the Netherlands), Stuttgart (Germany), and Stockholm (Sweden).

Despite Mata's international travels, he did not forget the music of his homeland. "The great Hispanic composers [were] staples of his repertoire," Matthew Sigman observed in *Symphony,* "and he [brought] them to Dallas with great fervor." Mata realized, however, that bringing the music of these composers to the concert hall would not be enough. He knew that many people in the Hispanic communities of Texas could not afford the cost of symphony tickets. To reach them, he scheduled free outdoor concerts with the DSO. After Dallas's new Meyerson Symphony Center was built in 1989, Mata organized frequent open houses to encourage a more diverse audience to experience the magic of the symphony.

## Brings Hispanic Music to the World

In 1985 Mata led the DSO on its first European tour, playing concerts in England, Germany, France, and Spain. In addition to a standard repertoire of American and European compositions, his recordings with the orchestra from this time showcase the works of Hispanic composers such as Antonio Estevez of Venezuela and Carlos Chávez, who is considered by many music critics to be Mexico's leading composer of the twentieth century.

For his work in championing Hispanic music, Mata received many awards. In Mexico he was honored with the Elías Sourasky Prize in the Arts, the Golden Lyre Award from the Mexican Union of Musicians, and lifetime membership in the prestigious Colegio Nacional—one of Mexico's highest honors. The president of Mexico awarded Mata the Mozart Medal in 1991.

That same year, he was honored at the White House in Washington, D.C., with the Hispanic Heritage Award.

## Recordings Offer Range of Composers

Mata has conducted and recorded many pieces by European and American masters. His continued interest in presenting a broad and varied range of compositions stems from his firm belief in the universal nature of music: according to *Hispanic,* he once told a Dallas reporter that "classical music, like great painting, like all the arts and humanities … belongs to everybody." During his years with the DSO, Mata performed works by famous European composers such as Maurice Ravel, Jean Sibelius, Peter Ilyich Tchaikovsky, and Sergey Rachmaninoff. In 1993 he and the DSO released an all-American program of works by Aaron Copland, Leonard Bernstein, and Roy Harris. "The musicmaking is something to cheer about," commented Richard Freed in *Stereo Review.*

In June 1994 Mata retired from his position with the Dallas Symphony Orchestra. His sixteen-year tenure with the ensemble was one of the longest among present-day conductors. At the time of his retirement, Mata indicated he would still do freelance work with other orchestras. As a certified pilot, he also planned to spend more time in the cockpit of his plane. "Now that I'll be freelance," he told Sigman in the *Symphony* interview, "I'll probably be able to fly more."

Sadly, just six months after his retirement Mata was killed when the plane he was piloting crashed at Cuernavaca Airport near Mexico City. He was fifty-two years old.

Eduardo Mata. *Reproduced by permission of AP/Wide World Photos.*

## For More Information

*American Record Guide,* March/April 1993, pp. 78–79.
*Audio,* April 1988, pp. 97–98.
*Billboard,* (obituary) January 21, 1995, p. 11.
*Gramophone,* May 1978, pp. 1841–42.
*Hispanic,* September 1991, pp. 41–43.
*Stereo Review,* January 1993, p. 96.
*Symphony,* November/December 1991, pp. 53–54.

# Rachel McLish

Bodybuilder, actress
Born 1958, Harlingen, Texas

*"If I was going to portray a Hispanic, it was going to be a Hispanic that I could relate to.*

*Every Hispanic person that I know has something good going for them."*

**R**achel Livia Elizondo McLish is the woman who brought glamour to women's bodybuilding. Through her campaign against steroid abuse and her unique image as a "feminine bodybuilder," she became a role model for many women. She helped make weight-training and body shaping one of the fastest growing exercise activities for women in the 1980s. Although she still promotes physical fitness, she has turned her attention to acting, writing, and the fashion world.

McLish was born in 1950 in Harlingen, Texas, to Rafael and Rachel Elizondo. Her father, who came from a Spanish background, was a neon sign-maker. Her mother, of Mexican-German heritage, was a homemaker. McLish's interest in fitness was first sparked by her study of ballet and by her father's weight-lifting hobby. Even as a child, she was fascinated with the strength and grace of the human body. The two very different activities led her to believe that a woman with muscles could be both feminine and attractive.

During her high school years, Mclish found herself forced to choose between cheerleading and ballet. Even though she had dreamed since childhood of becoming a professional dancer, she opted for cheerleading. It seemed to offer popularity and a full social life. By the time she enrolled at Pan American University in Texas, however, she regretted giving up her dream. At age seventeen, she believed she was already too old to pursue dancing again.

## Misses Active Lifestyle

While studying at Pan American University in Edinburg, Texas, McLish missed the physically active lifestyle she had known all her life. She decided to work with weights. At the time, weight-training wasn't very popular with the general public, and exercise clubs were scarce. McLish eventually found a place to work out called the "Shape Center." She loved the atmosphere there. Since her finances were already strained by college expenses, she couldn't afford the membership dues. McLish solved the problem by applying for a job teaching exercise classes at the center. She eventually became the center's manager.

In 1978 McLish earned her college degree in health and physical education and married her college sweetheart, John McLish. After the couple split up the following year, she formed a partnership with others to build the "Sport Palace," the first and largest health club facility in south Texas. The club was so successful it expanded to two other locations in Texas.

In 1980 McLish read about the first U.S. Women's Body Building Championship being held in Atlantic City. She was interested for two reasons: to promote her fitness centers, and to become a positive "feminine" example of a bodybuilder. She entered and won easily. Later that year she won the Ms. Olympia title—the highest award a female bodybuilder can receive.

As the first female bodybuilding champion, McLish was a new female role model. She appeared on magazine covers and television programs worldwide. She traveled and lectured on physiology (the study of the human body), diet, and beauty. Her dedication and effort paid off when she won the Ms. Olympia title again in 1982. She also won the World Championship that year.

## Fights Against Steroid Use

By the mid-1980s, the emphasis in female bodybuilding shifted from muscle tone to massive muscular development. The use of steroid drugs for quick muscle growth became widespread. McLish stopped competing and campaigned against steroid and other drug use. "My goal has always been systematic weight training to enhance my body—to build muscles to become more womanly and sensual," McLish related to Lisa Saenz in *Hispanic*. "Without steroids there is no way a woman can achieve [that] degree of muscularity."

In 1984 McLish published *Flex Appeal,* a book on health, fitness, and nutrition (her second book on fitness, *Perfect Parts,* was published in 1987). Shortly after *Flex Appeal* appeared in bookstores, McLish became the spokesperson for the Health and Tennis Corporation of America. In 1990, McLish joined with K-Mart department stores to create a line of bodywear for active women. McLish took a hands-on approach to the fashion project and was actively involved in the construction of the garments. Her collection, "Rachel McLish for the Body Company," accounted for 28 percent of the total sales of sportswear in the United States in 1991.

McLish's career in film began in 1985, when she had a starring role in *Pumping Iron II: The Women,* a documentary movie about the world of women's bodybuilding. She also starred in the 1991 CBS prime-time television special *Women of the 21st*

Rachel McLish. *Reproduced by permission of Corbis Corporation (Bellevue).*

*Century,* a documentary exploring women's commitment to a physical lifestyle.

## Refuses Demeaning Roles in Films

When McLish first tried to pursue roles in feature films, she received offers to play "a female robojock, a female boxer, the typical roles you'd expect for a female bodybuilder," she explained to Saenz. She promptly turned them all down. She has also turned down roles that she finds demeaning to women or Hispanics. One such role was that of the character Vasquez in the 1986 hit *Aliens.* "Every other word was profane," McLish told Saenz, describing the role, "and if I was going to portray a Hispanic, it was going to be a Hispanic that I could relate to. Every Hispanic person that I know has something good going for them."

McLish's motion picture debut came in the 1992 film *Aces: Iron Eagle III,* which also featured Academy Award-winner Louis Gossett, Jr. In the film, McLish portrays Anna, a Peruvian woman who fights against a local drug lord who controls her hometown. She also starred in the 1996 action-adventure film *Ravenhawk.* In 1995 she made an exercise video called *In Shape with Rachel McLish.*

While continuing to pursue a film career, McLish also sets aside time to give speeches at high schools. She emphasizes the importance of education and urges students to attend college. In addition, she has set up scholarship funds for Hispanic students at Texas State Technical College in her hometown of Harlingen and at Pan American University, her alma mater.

## For More Information

*Hispanic,* September 1992, pp. 50–54.

McLish, Rachel, and Bill Reynolds, *Flex Appeal by Rachel,* Warner, 1984.

McLish, Rachel, and Joyce Vederal, *Perfect Parts,* Warner, 1987.

*People,* June 29, 1992, p. 68.

# Nicholasa Mohr

Writer, artist
Born November 1, 1935, New York, New York

*"As a writer I have used my abilities as a creative artist ... to establish a voice for my ethnic American community and our children."*

**A**s a young girl, Nicholasa Mohr used her imagination to escape the poverty of her dismal neighborhood. As an adult, she uses this same creativity to express her feelings as a woman and as a Puerto Rican American. Mohr began her career as a fine arts painter and printmaker, then became a writer and illustrator of her own award-winning books.

Mohr was born in a barrio (a Spanish-speaking neighborhood) in New York City in 1935. Her parents, Pedro and Nicholasa Golpe, had migrated from Puerto Rico to America shortly after the beginning of the Great Depression in 1929. When she was eight years old, her father died. Poverty and prejudice constantly threatened to tear the family apart, and Mohr's mother struggled to keep it together. As the only girl of seven children, Mohr had to help her mother with the housework. Often stuck in her family's crowded apartment, she found freedom and adventure by drawing and painting.

Mohr's artistic talents brought her much praise in school. This in turn gave her extra confidence. Still, some of her classmates remained prejudiced against her because she was Hispanic. She was further humiliated when her high school counselor told her that, as a Puerto Rican girl, she should learn to sew rather than continue on with her education. Mohr refused to listen. After graduating high school in 1953, she managed to enroll in the Arts Students' League, an art school in New York. While studying there, she supported herself by working as a waitress, a factory worker, and a translator.

## Mexico Inspires Art

At first, Mohr wanted to study art in Europe. After reading about the work of Mexican artists such as **Diego Rivera** (see entry) and Jose Clemente Orozco, she decided instead to travel to Mexico City in 1956 to study their murals and paintings. The colors, figures, and methods of the Mexicans inspired her. She was especially drawn to the way those artists tried to bring about social change through their powerful artwork.

Mohr returned to the United States the following year and enrolled in the New School for Social Research where she met her future husband, psychologist Irwin Mohr. In 1959 she started taking classes at the Brooklyn Museum of Art School. She continued to work at her craft, developing her artistic style. Her life's experiences began to shape her work. Using bold letters and symbols, she told stories through her paintings.

## Turns From Painting to Writing

This technique caught the eye of a publisher in New York. He tried to convince Mohr she had the ability to become a writer. At first, she was reluctant to switch from painting to writing, but soon wrote several short stories about growing up in a barrio. She was excited by the challenge of writing, a craft she found similar to painting. Writing allowed her the chance to draw pictures with words. After reading her stories, however, the publisher turned them down. Disappointed, Mohr returned to painting. A short while later, another publisher read her stories and offered her a book contract. Mohr then began work on her first novel.

Nicholasa Mohr. *Reproduced by permission of Nicholasa Mohr.*

Mohr's first book, *Nilda,* which contained eight illustrations by Mohr, was published in 1973. The novel traces the life of a young Puerto Rican girl, Nilda, growing up in Spanish Harlem (a New York City neighborhood) during World War II. She has to endure not only her family's poverty but prejudice from people outside her family. While the book focuses on the problems Nilda faces as she grows up, it also depicts her joys: spending time at summer camp, finding a hidden garden, drawing. Many critics praised *Nilda* as a powerful yet sensitive story. Among the awards the book received was an outstanding book award in juvenile fiction from the *New York Times.*

In 1975 Mohr published *El Bronx Remembered,* a collection of short stories set in the Puerto Rican neighborhoods of New York City. The stories present the lives of many different characters—from a teenage Puerto Rican girl to an elderly Jewish man—and touch on the delicate subjects of death, incest, sexuality, and teen pregnancy. Reviewers applauded the stories for their realism and optimism. Like *Nilda, El Bronx Remembered* also received many awards, including being named a finalist for the prestigious National Book Award.

Two years later Mohr published another collection of short stories for young adults, *In Nueva York*. Mohr again focused on characters in Hispanic neighborhoods who had to confront poverty, racism, drugs, street gangs, and other problems. This time, however, she presented many of them in more than one story. Reviewers believed this gave readers a more intimate look into the lives of the characters, making them appear more real as they struggled to succeed. The American Library Association bestowed their Best Book Award in young adult literature on *In Nueva York*.

## Explores the Character of Felita in Two Novels

Mohr wrote for a younger audience with the novel *Felita*, published in 1979. The book tells the story of a young Puerto Rican girl whose parents move to a nicer part of town, hoping to give their family a better life. Felita quickly misses her friends, and the rest of the family is soon discouraged by the discrimination they face there. After her family moves back to the old neighborhood, Felita still has problems with her classmates, but her grandmother helps her cope.

Mohr wrote about Felita once more in *Going Home,* which she published in 1986. In the novel, Felita is eleven years old, has a new boyfriend, and goes on vacation with her parents to Puerto Rico. Problems arise when her friends become jealous of her boyfriend and Felita becomes homesick while on vacation. By the end of the novel, however, she has learned to make new friends in Puerto Rico.

## Other Projects

Mohr turned away briefly from fiction in 1993 when she published *All for the Better: A Story of El Barrio,* a biography of Evelina Lopez Antonetty. Because of the economic effects of the Great Depression, Lopez Antonetty had to move away from her family in Puerto Rico to live with an aunt in Spanish Harlem (El Barrio) in New York City in 1933. Over the years, she worked to improve not only her life but the lives of the people in the Hispanic community around her. She eventually founded the United Bronx Parents Group to work for solutions to the problems facing her community.

In 1995 Mohr published a collection of three stories, *The Song of El Coqui: And Other Tales of Puerto Rico,* illustrated by Antonio Martorell. Each story is about an animal that represents one of the culture groups of Puerto Rico. A *Publisher's Weekly* review praised the book: "Together, stories and art afford an unusually engaging introduction to Puerto Rican culture and history." Her 1997 collection of seven short stories, *A Matter of Pride and Other Stories* focus on a variety of Hispanic women, in New York, the Dominican Republic, and Puerto Rico. A *Library Journal* reviewer said of this collection: "Mohr is funny, sad, poignant, and, ultimately, hopeful."

Although the majority of Mohr's writing has been directed at teenagers, she has stated in interviews that she doesn't write for them alone. She feels the characters and ideas in her works can appeal to people in all age groups. Mohr has no plans to change from writing to another art form. She believes writing has given her a chance both to express herself creatively and to address social issues that are important to her ethnic community. Mohr continues to entertain readers of all ages and to challenge them to view the world with eyes open to new ideas and viewpoints. She was a Hispanic Heritage Award Honoree in 1997.

## For More Information

*Authors and Artists for Young Adults,* Volume 8, Gale, 1992, pp. 161–67.

Blicksilver, Edith, "Nicolasa Mohr," *Biographical Directory of Hispanic Literature in the United States,* edited by Nicolás Kanellos, Greenwood Press, 1989, pp. 199–213.

*Hispanic Writers,* 2nd Edition, Gale, 2000.

*Publishers Weekly,* July 10, 1995, p. 56.

*School Library Journal,* May 1993, p. 118.

# Mario Molina

Chemist, educator
March 19, 1943, Mexico City, Mexico

*"It's clear to me that one of the important needs for global environmental issues is the participation of scientists from all over the world."*

 ario Molina is an important figure in the development of a scientific understanding of our atmosphere. Molina earned national prominence by theorizing, with fellow atmospheric chemist F. Sherwood Rowland, that chlorofluorocarbons (CFCs) deplete Earth's ozone layer, a layer in our atmosphere that lies about twenty or thirty miles above us and protects the lower atmosphere from the Sun's ultraviolet radiation. Their work earned them, along with Dutch scientist Paul Crutzen, the 1995 Nobel Prize in chemistry. In his years as a researcher at the Jet Propulsion Laboratory at the California Institute of Technology (CalTech) and a professor at the Massachusetts Institute of Technology (MIT), Molina has continued his investigations into the effects of chemicals on the atmosphere.

## Begins Career as Chemist in Mexico

Mario José Molina was born in Mexico City, Mexico, on March 19, 1943. He is the son of Roberto Molina-Pasquel and Leonor Henriquez. Following his early schooling in Mexico, he graduated from the Universidad Nacional Autónoma de México in 1965 with a degree in chemical engineering. Immediately upon graduation, Molina went to West Germany to continue his studies at the University of Freiburg, acquiring the equivalent of a master's degree in polymerization kinetics (the study of the motion and energy involved in chemical reactions in which smaller molecules join to form larger molecules) in 1967. Molina then returned to Mexico to accept a position as assistant professor in the chemical engineering department at the Universidad Nacional Autónoma de México.

## Studying the Ozone in California

In 1968 Molina left Mexico to further his studies in physical chemistry at the University of California at Berkeley. He received his Ph.D. in 1972 and became a postdoctoral associate that same year. His primary area of postdoctoral research was the laser measurement of energy changes during certain chemical reactions. The following year, 1973, was a turning point in Molina's life. In addition to marrying a fellow chemist, Luisa Y. Tan (the couple have one son, Felipe), Molina left Berkeley to continue his postdoctoral work with physical chemist F. Sherwood Rowland at the University of California at Irvine.

Molina and Rowland had a common interest in the effects of chemicals on the atmosphere. In particular, they looked at the stratosphere, the outermost section of the atmosphere that extends from about seven miles above Earth to about thirty miles. In the stratosphere, a thin layer of ozone gas (a compound made up of three oxygen atoms) encircles the planet, acting as a filter that screens out much of the Sun's most damaging ultraviolet radiation. (Human beings can only see light with long wavelengths: red wavelengths are longest and violet are the shortest that we can respond to. Light with wavelengths too short for the human eye to see is called ultraviolet [beyond violet] light. Ultraviolet [UV] light is contained in the range of wavelengths produced by the Sun.)

Without the ozone shield to reflect back the ultraviolet radiation, life could not survive on Earth. Just a few years earlier, in 1970, Dutch atmospheric chemist Paul Crutzen had shown that a chemical compound naturally produced by bacteria in the soil, nitrous oxide, could drift up into the stratosphere of Earth, where it would react with and break down ozone molecules. Molina and Rowland wondered if man-made compounds released into the atmosphere could have a similar effect.

Both scientists were well aware that every year millions of tons of pollutants (things that contaminate) were pumped into the atmosphere from industrial processes (the activities of manufacturing the things we use to live, some of which take place in factories and plants). What impact did these various chemical discharges have on the envelope of air that surrounds Earth? Molina and Rowland decided to conduct experiments to determine what happens to chemical pollutants that reach both the atmosphere directly above us and up in the stratospheric levels.

They concentrated their research on the impact of a specific group of chemicals called chlorofluorocarbons, commonly known as CFCs, which are widely used in such industrial and consumer products as aerosol spray cans, pressurized containers, and refrigeration and air conditioning coolants. They found that when CFCs are subjected to massive ultraviolet radiation they break down into their most basic chemical parts: the elements chlorine, fluorine, and carbon. It was the impact of chlorine on ozone that alarmed them. They found that each chlorine atom could destroy as many as one hundred thousand ozone molecules before becoming inactive. With the rapid production of CFCs for commercial and industrial use—millions of tons annually—Molina and Rowland were concerned that the impact of CFCs on the delicate ozone layer within the stratosphere could be life threatening.

## Ozone Report Leads to CFC Reduction

Molina published the results of his and Rowland's research in *Nature* magazine in 1974. Their findings had startling results. Molina was invited to testify before the House of Representatives Subcommittee on Public Health and Environment to help determine what should be done about the problem. Suddenly CFCs were a popular topic of conversation. Manufacturers began searching for alternative propellant gases (gases that are kept under pressure in cans and bottles so that the containers' contents will be expelled when the pressure is released) for their products. The U.S. government felt that the problem was so serious that in 1976 it enacted a temporary ban on the use of aerosol sprays after 1978.

The world community eventually followed the example of the United States after the discovery of "holes" in the ozone layer in the 1980s. In 1985, a group of British researchers found that during certain seasons of the year, weather conditions help increase the rate of ozone destruction over the South Pole, resulting in an area where the ozone is much thinner than usual—what is commonly referred to as a "hole." Molina became interested in these findings and went on to help solve the puzzle of why this hap-

Mario Molina. *Reproduced by permission of Archive Photos, Inc.*

pens. He suggested that when the ice crystals in the air over the Antarctic combine with leftover compounds from CFCs that have already broken down, such as chlorine nitrate and hydrochloric acid, the resulting substances are strong ozone destroyers. Due largely to the continued appearance of ozone holes since the 1980s, an international agreement banning the production of CFCs was put into effect on January 1, 1996.

## Cal Tech and MIT

In the years that followed the landmark 1974 paper, Molina continued to work with Rowland; they published additional data on CFCs and the destruction of the ozone layer in such publications as *Journal of*

*Physical Chemistry, Geophysical Research Letter,* and *Science.* In 1976 Molina was named to the National Science Foundation's Oversight Committee on Fluorocarbon Technology Assessment. Molina became a member of the technical staff at the Jet Propulsion Laboratory at CalTech in 1982; two years later he was named senior research scientist, a position he held for an additional five years. In 1989, Molina left the West Coast to accept the dual position of professor of atmospheric chemistry at MIT's Department of Earth, Atmosphere, and Planetary Sciences and professor in the Department of Chemistry. In 1993, he was selected to be the first person to hold the chair established by the Martin Foundation, Inc., at MIT "to support research and education activities related to the studies of the environment."

In the mid-1990s, Molina reported in a *Physics Today* article that his current work involved continued research on the effect of CFCs on the northern hemisphere, the impact of small particles from volcanoes on the ozone layer, and the potential effects of supersonic transport aircraft that the United States was once again considering for use. Molina has published more than fifty scientific papers, the majority dealing with his work on the ozone layer and the chemistry of the atmosphere. In 1992, Molina and his wife, Luisa, wrote a paper titled "Stratospheric Ozone" that was published in the book *The Science of Global Change: The Impact of Human Activities on the Environment.* The Public Broadcasting System (PBS) televised a six-part series on science entitled *The Changing Face of Science in America,* in 1996. Molina was one of the

scientists featured in this series that celebrated the contributions of minorities in the various fields of science and specifically his Nobel Prize-winning work on the ozone.

## Shares Nobel Prize for Critical Discovery

Molina is the recipient of many awards, including the 1987 American Chemical Society Esselen Award, the 1988 American Association for the Advancement of Science Newcomb-Cleveland Prize, the 1989 NASA Medal for Exceptional Scientific Advancement, and the 1989 United Nations Environmental Programme Global 500 Award. In 1995, Molina, Rowland, and Crutzen received the scientific community's highest honor, the Nobel Prize, in the field of chemistry. In announcing the award, the Royal Swedish Academy of Sciences stated that by showing the effects of human activity on the delicate balance of the atmosphere, "the three researchers contributed to our salvation from a global environmental problem that could have catastrophic consequences." Molina was selected as an Institute Professor at MIT in 1997, an honor that is awarded to a few outstanding faculty members. In 2000 Pope John Paul II named Molina to the Pontifical Academy of Sciences.

Molina donated $200,000 of his Nobel prize money to help scholars from developing nations conduct environmental research at MIT. He was quoted in the February 14, 1996 *Boston Globe:* "It's clear to me that one of the important needs for global environmental issues is the participation of scientists from all over the world." He is the first Mexican American to win a Nobel

Prize and the first person born in Mexico to win in the sciences.

Molina has spent less time in labs and more time in policy-making and teaching in the last decade. In 1994 President Bill Clinton appointed him as a science advisor to his administration. With real concerns about environmental issues, Molina has attempted to communicate his knowledge to people who can make a difference. And he is preparing the next generation of concerned scientists to do the same. In an autobiographical essay Molina provided to the Nobel e-Museum, he looked ahead to a future of teaching and rethinking ideas: "Although I no longer spend much time in the laboratory, I very much enjoy working with my graduate and post-doctoral students, who provide me with invaluable intellectual stimulus. I have also benefitted from teaching; as I try to explain my views to students with critical and open minds, I find myself continually being challenged to go back and rethink ideas. I now see teaching and research as complementary, mutually reinforcing activities."

## For More Information

Howe, Peter J., "Chemist Donates Nobel Winnings, Part of Prize to Fun Ecology Work at MIT," *Boston Globe,* February 14, 1996, p. 46.

Levi, Barbara Goss, "Nobel Chemistry Prize Gives a Stratospheric Boost to Atmospheric Scientists," *Physics Today,* December 1995, pp. 21–22.

Lipkin, R., "Ozone Depletion Research Wins Nobel," *Science News,* October 21, 1995, p. 262.

"Mario J. Molina: Autobiography," Nobel e-Museum. Available at http://www.nobel.se/chemistry/laureates/1995/molina-autobio.html (accessed June 21, 2002).

Nemecek, Sasha, "Profile: Mario Molina: Rescuing the Ozone Layer," *Scientific American,* November 1997, pp. 40+.

"Pope Names U.S. Environmental Scientist to Pontifical Academy," *America,* Nov 25, 2000, p. 4.

Service, Robert F., "Uncovering Threats to the Ozone Layer Brings Rewards," *Science,* October 20, 1995, pp. 381–82.

---

# Pat Mora

---

Poet, writer
Born January 19, 1942, El Paso, Texas

---

*"I take pride in being a Hispanic writer. I will continue to write and to struggle to say what no other writer can say in quite the same way."*

When she was young and growing up in El Paso, Texas, Pat Mora was ashamed of her Mexican American heritage. In school she tried to look and act "American." At home she spoke Spanish only to her grandmother and her aunt, and she hated the Mexican music her father played on the radio. As she grew older, however, Mora realized she was denying a part of her identity, an essential part of who she was. She decided to accept herself fully and to share that acceptance with other Hispanics through her writings. "I take pride in being a Hispanic writer," she wrote in *Horn Book.* "I will continue to write and to struggle to say what no other writer can say in quite the same way."

Mora was born in El Paso in 1942 to Raul Antonio Mora and Estella Delgado. Her father worked as an optician while her mother cared for the family at home. The city of El Paso sits on the U.S. border with Mexico, across the Rio Grande River from the Mexican city of Juarez. The influence of Mexican culture in her hometown was strong, and Mora desperately tried to escape it while she was growing up.

After graduating from high school, Mora attended Texas Western College, earning her bachelor's degree in 1963. That same year she married William H. Burnside; the couple had three children before divorcing in 1981. During the mid-1960s, Mora taught in the El Paso Independent School District. In 1967 she earned her master's degree from the University of Texas at El Paso (UTEP), and within four years she was teaching English and communications part-time at El Paso Community College.

## Learns the Value of Her Heritage

The early 1980s were important years in Mora's life. In 1981 she became the assistant to the vice president of academic affairs at UTEP. Around the same time, she finally realized that she could no longer deny her Mexican American heritage. This acceptance gave her a different outlook on life. She commented on her new approach in the *Christian Science Monitor:* "I revel in a certain Mexican passion not for life or about life, but *in* life, a certain intensity in the daily living of it."

Mora began writing poetry to express her new and intense feelings. Her desire to write, however, was not for herself alone. She felt American literature was missing the voices of Hispanic writers, and she wanted to help preserve her culture in that litera-

ture. "We need to be published and to be studied in schools and colleges," she wrote in *Horn Book,* "so that the stories and ideas of our people won't quietly disappear."

The quality of Mora's poetry was recognized quickly. In 1983 she won the Creative Writing Award from the National Association of Chicano Studies. The next year brought both personal and professional triumph for Mora. In addition to marrying her second husband, archaeologist Vernon Lee Scarborough, her first poetry collection, *Chants,* was published by the Arte Público Press of the University of Houston. The volume surveys the desert landscape around which Mora grew up. In many of the finely crafted poems, Mora depicts the desert as a woman; other times she presents women as the embodiment of the desert's strength. *Chants* received the Southwest Book Award, given by the Border Regional Library Association to outstanding works of literature about the Southwest.

In 1986 Arte Público published Mora's second book of verse, *Borders.* It, too, won the Southwest Book Award. The poetry in this collection explores all types of borders—including those between the United States and Mexico, and those between women and men. Many of the poems draw their inspiration from Mexican folk customs and the wisdom of native healers.

## Hailed as a Poet and an Educator

While Mora was gaining fame as a poet, she was also receiving recognition for her work as an educator. In 1987 she received the Chicano/Hispanic Faculty and Professional Staff Association Award for helping Hispanic students advance at UTEP. The following year she became director of the university's museum, as well as the assistant to the university's president.

In the autumn of 1989, Mora left the desert environment of El Paso and moved to the midwestern pastures of Ohio. At first, the loss of her Mexican American surroundings was unsettling to her. In an article she wrote for the *Christian Science Monitor,* Mora related that whenever she heard someone speaking Spanish in the Midwest, she automatically focused on the speaker: "I listen, silently wishing to be part of that other conversation—if only for a few moments, to feel Spanish in my mouth."

However, Mora quickly adapted to her new environment and expanded her artistic vision in the process. As she explained to Norma Alarcón in *Nuestro,* poetry taught her to use her "senses more keenly." In her third book of poetry, *Communion,* she examines larger themes, such as the way she relates to other women around her—and also to other people around the world. In 1995 she came out with *Agua Santa: Holy Water* a collection of poems that feature the voices of Latin American women and children from the past and present. *Aunt Carmen's Book of Practical Saints* (1997) is a book of poems that are conversations between the feisty Aunt Carmen and the saints as she tries to understand the nature of faith.

## Work Becomes Important Part of American Literature

Mora's desire to have the works of Hispanic writers included in the mainstream of

Pat Mora. *Reproduced by permission of Pat Mora.*

American literature was finally realized in 1992. Harcourt Brace Jovanovich, the nation's largest textbook publisher, issued a high school English textbook titled *Mexican American Literature.* The seven hundred-page book covers the works of Hispanic writers from colonial times to the present. Mora's work is included. Her poems are also featured in *The Norton Anthology of American Literature,* another highly respected textbook. Mora has been involved in compiling several collections of poetry as well.

In the early 1990s Mora took on writing projects outside of poetry. In 1993 she published a book of essays, *Nepantla: Essays from the Land in the Middle.* These autobiographical essays describe her childhood in the desert around El Paso and how she has grown as a poet. In 1997 she published a portrait of her family, living and dead, called *House of Houses.* In this book, says Paul Trachtman in a *Smithsonian* review, "Mora turns her family's old adobe casa, built along the Rio Grande between El Paso and Santa Fe, into a place where present and past tense are one, a realm where memory and imagination are fused in the style of magic realism." Although several critics noted that the book becomes confusing in places, it was highly acclaimed for its vision and its developed portraits of ordinary people.

Beginning in 1992 with *A Birthday Basket for Tia,* Mora published a series of about fifteen children's books, including *The Desert Is My Mother/El Desierto es Mi Madre* (1994); *The Race of Toad and Deer* (1995), a Guatemalan version of the tortoise and the hare fable; *Thomas and the Library Lady* (1997) the true story of Tomas Rivers, the son of migrant workers who loved to go to the library to read as a child and later became the president of the University of California; and *This Big Sky* (1998) a book of poems about the Southwest.

Mora was selected for the Garrey Carruthers Chair in Honors, Distinguished Visiting Professor at the University of New Mexico in the fall of 1999. She was a judge and recipient of the poetry fellowships from the National Endowment for the Arts and an advisor and recipient of the Kellogg National Leadership Fellowships. Among her many prestigious awards are the Ohioana Award, the Pellicer-Frost 1999 Bi-national Poetry Award, four Southwest Book Awards, and the Premio Aztlán Literature Award.

Mora believes her mission is to uphold her cultural identity, both for herself and for younger generations of Hispanic people. The best way she can do that, she explained in *Horn Book,* is through her gift of writing: "I want to give to others what writers have given me, a chance to hear the voices of people I will never meet."

## For More Information

*Christian Science Monitor,* July 18, 1990, pp. 16–17.
*Hispanic Writers,* 2nd Edition, Gale, 2002.
*Horn Book,* July/August 1990, pp. 436–37.
*Nation,* June 7, 1993, pp. 772–74.
*Nuestro,* March 1987, pp. 25–27.
*Publishers Weekly,* March 24, 1997, p. 68.
Trachtman, Paul, *House of Houses* review, *Smithsonian,* December 1997, p. 154.

# Rita Moreno

Actress, singer, dancer
Born December 11, 1931, Humacao, Puerto Rico

*"I have crossed over, but never, not for one minute, have I forgotten where I came from, or who I am. I have always been very proud to carry the badge of honor as a Hispanic."*

Rita Moreno has brightened movie screens and theater stages with her talent since she was a teenager. In the beginning, she often had to accept stereotypical, ethnic roles in order to make a living, but she knew she was capable of more challenging parts. When she finally won an Academy Award in 1962 for her portrayal of the character of Anita in *West Side Story,* she became one of the few Hispanics who was recognized an international star. Since that time, she has won a Tony Award, a Grammy Award, and two Emmy Awards, making her one of the only two women in the world to have received show business's four most prestigious honors (Barbra Streisand is the other).

Moreno was born Rosita Dolores Alverio in 1931 in the small town of Humacao, Puerto Rico. Her parents, Paco Alverio and Rosa María Marcano Alverio, divorced soon after her birth. Her mother left her with relatives in Puerto Rico and went to New York City to work as a seamstress. When Moreno was five years old, her mother returned for her. Along with other family members, Moreno traveled with her mother to live in New York City.

Moreno began dance lessons around this time, and attended New York Public School 132. She soon began performing in the children's theater at Macy's Department Store, at weddings, and at bar mitzvahs. By the time she was thirteen, she had dropped out of school to pursue the life of an actress. She performed in nightclubs in New York, Boston, and Las Vegas. She also gained work in film, dubbing in Spanish for such actresses as Elizabeth Taylor and Margaret O'Brien.

## Frustrated by Stereotypical Roles

Moreno's role in her first film, *So Young, So Bad* (1950), caught the eye of Hollywood mogul Louis B. Mayer. He immediately offered her a contract with his studio, Metro-Goldwyn-Mayer. Under the names Rosita Moreno (her stepfather's surname) and, later, Rita Moreno, she found parts in

Rita Moreno. *Reproduced by permission of AP/Wide World Photos.*

some twenty-five films during the 1950s, playing mostly ethnic roles. She became known as "Rita the Cheetah" because of the parts she played and because of her highly publicized romances in real life. She was disheartened not only by the unfair nickname but also by the weak, stereotypical parts she was forced to play. She worked very hard to shed both.

Moreno's first satisfying acting role came in 1956. That year she played a slave girl in the hit musical *The King and I,* which starred Deborah Kerr and Yul Brynner. In the film Moreno had several scenes in which she acted well and sang beautifully. Despite this professional success, however, her career stalled in the late 1950s. She made few movies between 1956 and 1960.

She returned to performing on the theater stage and was received well by critics. But she could not handle the mounting frustrations over her career—she attempted suicide with sleeping pills. When she awoke in a hospital, however, she realized that she wanted to live and went on to recovery.

## Finds Success Through West Side Story

In 1961 Moreno landed her most famous role: Anita in *West Side Story.* Loosely based on William Shakespeare's play *Romeo and Juliet,* the musical follows two rival gangs in New York—the Sharks (Hispanics) and the Jets (Anglos)—as they fight for turf. Two characters in the musical, Tony and Maria, fight to maintain their love in the face of their ethnic differences. Moreno lit up the screen with her singing, dancing, and convincing acting in *West Side Story.* The musical was an instant success. It won ten Academy Awards, one of which was Moreno's for best supporting actress.

Moreno's performance in *West Side Story* propelled her to international stardom, and she began to receive roles over the next decade that were not based on her ethnicity. Even though she became a mainstream actress, she did not forget her roots. "I have crossed over, but never, not for one minute, have I forgotten where I came from, or who I am," she explained to Javier Bustillos and Anthony Chase in *Hispanic.* "I have always been very proud to carry the badge of honor as a Hispanic."

In 1965 Moreno met and married Dr. Leonard Gordon, a cardiologist. Their successful marriage has lasted to this day. In 1971 Moreno began to work in television. She appeared on *The Electric Company,* a television series for older children. For her participation in the show's soundtrack recording, she won a Grammy Award for the best recording for children in 1972.

## Pokes Fun at Stereotypes

In 1975 Moreno was a hit in the Broadway play *The Ritz.* She portrayed her character—a Puerto Rican singer named Googie Gómez—in an outrageously comic manner to poke fun at all the stereotypes she had played over the years. Some worried that her performance would offend Hispanics, but Moreno thought otherwise. "The Spanish people who come backstage say they love what I'm doing," she told a reporter for the *New York Times.* "Of course, some *Latins* might take offense, but I don't want to meet them. I don't want to talk to anyone who doesn't have a sense of humor about themselves." For her portrayal of Googie, Moreno won a Tony Award in 1975 for best supporting actress in a play.

Displaying her trademark versatility, Moreno returned to television and won an Emmy Award in 1977 for her guest appearances on *The Muppet Show.* She won another Emmy the following year for her appearance on an episode of the detective show *The Rockford Files.* In the later 1970s, she developed a nightclub song-and-dance act that she performed on cruise ships and in cities across the country.

Throughout the 1980s, Moreno continued her acting work, especially on the stage. Despite her hectic schedule, she made time to promote Hispanic causes and to appear

Moreno in a scene from *West Side Story. Reproduced by permission of AP/Wide World Photos.*

before Hispanic groups. For her positive portrayal of Hispanics on film and in the theater, Moreno was named one of ten Hispanic Women of the Year by *Hispanic* magazine in 1989. The following year she was awarded the White House Hispanic Heritage Award.

Moreno continues to expand her career as a star of television, stage, and screen with roles that reflect her many talents. She has acted in television shows from the 1990s detective show *B. L. Stryker* to many seasons of *The Rockford Files* to the HBO prison drama *Oz*, in which she played the part of Sister Peter Marie Reimondo for several seasons beginning in 1997. For her part in *Oz* she has won the ALMA Award twice. In 1996 Moreno took to the stage in *Sunset Boulevard*, a play about an aging actress who has not had a part in twenty-five years. In 1998 she was in the acclaimed film *The Slums of Beverly Hills*. In 2000 she starred with Ben Gazarra in the film *Blue Moon*, about a long-married couple who take a vacation to try and rekindle the spark of romance in their love for each other. In 2001 Moreno played the part of the mother in

*Piñero* and in 2002 she starred with Darryl Hannah, Mary Steenburgen, and Lili Taylor in *Casa de los Babys,* a film about women trying to adopt South American babies who are forced by the law to live there.

Moreno celebrated her seventieth birthday in December 2001, just as she looked forward to starting her fifth season in the television series *Oz.* She told Valerie Menard of *Hispanic Magazine,* "I can't explain it. I'm just like the Energizer Bunny. I keep going and going and going."

## For More Information

*Hispanic,* October 1989, pp. 30–33; September 1990, p. S6.

Menard, Valerie, "Radiant Rita," *Hispanic Magazine,* December 2001. Available at http://www.hispanicmagazine.com/CurrentIssue/Cultura/ (accessed June 21, 2002).

*Ms.,* January/February 1991, pp. 93–95.

*New York Times,* March 1975.

Suntree, Susan, *Rita Moreno,* Chelsea House, 1992.

# Joaquín Murieta

Folk hero, bandit
Born c. 1830, Sonora, Mexico
Died July 1853, California

*"The facts surrounding the life and times of Joaquín Murieta are few, but the legends, tall tales, and rumors are many."*

**F**ollowing the gold rush fever of 1848, the hills of California were filled with luckless gold diggers turned bandits. Stories of the notorious antics and eventual death of one, Joaquín Murieta, grew into a folk tale. This was due mainly to the 1854 publication of John Rollin Ridge's book, *The Life and Adventures of Joaquín Murieta, the Celebrated California Bandit.* In 1881 the novel was published in serial form by the Santa Barbara newspaper *La gaceta,* lending some substance to the myth. The facts surrounding the life and times of Joaquín Murieta are few, but the legends, tall tales, and rumors are many.

Born in the Mexican state of Sonora around 1830, Murieta (often spelled Murrieta) reportedly came to California in search of farm land and a better life. When gold was discovered, he quickly gave up farming for mining. For reasons lost to history, bad-hearted Americans abused Murieta's family. His wife was assaulted, his brother was hanged, and Murieta was beaten. Murieta retaliated in the only way he knew how—by becoming a horse thief in 1851. He reportedly committed his crimes in the name of ethnic honor and revenge, which gained him some sympathy and fame among Californians.

## Hunted by Rangers

Murieta and his band of outlaws repeatedly terrorized the California countryside with murders and robberies. Local authorities posted a $1,000 reward for his capture. At least one member of his group had also achieved notoriety—an unfortunate accident led Jack García to be known as Three-Fingered Jack. In the spring of 1853, the California legislature hired a group of rangers to track down Murieta and put an end to his misdeeds. Led by Captain Harry Love, a Mexican-American War veteran, the group was given three months to stop the crime wave.

A few days before the deadline, Love and his rangers surprised a band of Mexican horsemen near Tulare Lake in south-central California. The rangers insisted that one of the horsemen was Murieta. Furious gunplay followed and the Mexicans were killed. To prove their success and claim their reward, the rangers cut off Murieta's head and García's three-fingered hand and preserved them in alcohol. The morbid souvenirs were later placed on exhibit by the businesslike Captain Love.

From the very beginning, there has been some doubt that the infamous head actually belonged to Murieta. This led to more speculation on his whereabouts and his further adventures. Murieta's legend began in 1854 with the publication of Ridge's book, which romanticized the bandit's supposed deeds. Over the years, his legend grew as it was rewritten and expanded upon in subsequent books, poems, and ballads. Much later, Hollywood used the stories passed down about Murieta as a basis for the colorful but more law-abiding characters of the Cisco Kid and Zorro.

## For More Information

Latta, Frank Forrest, *Joaquín Murrieta and His Horse Gangs,* Bear State Books, 1980.

Neruda, Pablo, *Splendor and Death of Joaquín Murieta,* Farrar, Straus, and Giroux, 1972.

Ridge, John Rollin, *The Life and Adventures of Joaquín Murieta, the Celebrated California Bandit,* University of Oklahoma Press, 1955.

*Sports Afield,* July 1989, pp. 81, 97–98.

# Antonia Novello

Doctor, former surgeon general of the United States
Born August 23, 1944, Fajardo, Puerto Rico

*"I hope that being the first woman and minority surgeon general … enables me to reach many individuals with my message of empowerment for women, children, and minorities."*

Antonia Novello was the first female and first Hispanic appointed surgeon general of the United States. As a former pediatrician, her focus was on the health concerns of children and youth. As leader of the sixty-five hundred employees of the Public Health Service, she directed the nation's attention to AIDS-infected children, the perils of smoking, teenage drinking, and women's health issues.

## Childhood Illness

Antonia Coello Novello as born in 1944 in Fajardo, Puerto Rico, to Antonio Coello and Ana Delia Coello. When she was eight years old, her father died, and she and her brothers were raised by their mother, a school teacher. As a child, Novello suffered from a painful chronic illness of the colon (a section of the large intestine). She was hospitalized every summer for treatments for the disease, and learned what it is like to be a helpless patient. Her condition was finally corrected by surgery when she was eighteen years old. These experiences convinced her to pursue a career in medicine.

She wanted to help other children who were suffering as she had.

Novello earned her bachelor of science degree from the University of Puerto Rico in 1965. She continued her studies at the university, earning her medical doctor (M.D.) degree in 1970. That same year she married Joseph Novello, a U.S. Navy flight surgeon. The two then moved to Ann Arbor, Michigan, to continue their medical training at the University of Michigan Medical Center. Novello worked in the pediatric nephrology unit, treating children with kidney diseases. For her skilled and caring treatment of patients, Novello was honored with the Intern of the Year award by the center's pediatrics (children's health) department. She was the first woman to receive the award.

Novello continued her medical training at Georgetown University in Washington, D.C. In 1982 she earned a master's degree in public health from John Hopkins University in Baltimore, Maryland. In 1986 she became deputy director of the National Institute of Child Health and Human Development. In this position, she took a special interest in children with AIDS (Acquired Immune Deficiency Syndrome). At the same time, Novello served as a professor of pediatrics at Georgetown University Hospital.

Novello earned a reputation in the medical field and in Washington as a cooperative, dedicated, and quiet physician. In the early 1980s, she had served on a Congressional staff, giving advice to lawmakers on such medical issues as organ transplants and cigarette warning labels. President George Bush, elected in 1988, was impressed by her ideas on many medical-legal issues. In the fall of 1989 he nominated Novello to be the country's next surgeon general.

## Appointed Surgeon General

The role of surgeon general—the symbolic doctor for all Americans—is a public one. Instead of seeing individual patients, the surgeon general tries to inform the public about problems or trends in medicine. The surgeon general is also head of the United States Public Health Service. This organization, associated with the U.S. Navy, is composed of medical professionals who hold military ranks. They serve on Native American reservations and in other areas of the country where there is a shortage of doctors. In her position, Novello held the rank of Vice Admiral and wore a military uniform trimmed with gold braid.

Each month, the surgeon general receives several hundred invitations to speak about medical issues. The opportunity to influence common people on health matters is great. Shortly after her appointment, Novello visited her birthplace in Puerto Rico. "When I got off the plane, kids from my mother's school lined both sides of the road handing me flowers," Novello related to a reporter for the *Washington Post.* "I went to the [veterans] hospital to speak. When the veterans saw my gold braid they all stood and saluted.... I realized that for these people, for women, I have to be good as a doctor, I have to be good as a surgeon general, I have to be everything."

During her term as surgeon general, Novello attempted to solve many problems. Concerned about the dangers of teenage drinking, she met with some of the largest beer and wine companies in the country and asked them to stop aiming their advertising at young people. She criticized the tobacco industry and lectured the public on the dangers of smoking. She was particularly disturbed by rising lung cancer rates among females. During her hectic schedule, she found time to visit many hospitals to give hugs and encouragement to children and AIDS victims.

AIDS and his long-term effect on children was an especially important issue for Novello. "AIDS is the only epidemic in the world where children will survive their parents," she told Carol Krucoff in the *Saturday Evening Post.* "By the year 2000, we might have as many as 10 million children who are orphans of this epidemic. We've got to do the best we can for all children."

When she was chosen to be surgeon general, Novello told Tonya E. Wolford of *Hispanic,* "I hope that being the first woman and minority surgeon general … enables me to reach many individuals with my message of empowerment for women, children, and minorities."

## Moving Forward in Her Career

Novello left her post as U.S. surgeon general in June 1993, five months after President George Bush left office. She served as the special representative for health and nutrition for UNICEF, the United Nations organization devoted to children and their needs until 1996. From 1996 to 1999 Novello was the visiting professor of health policy at Johns Hopkins School of Hygiene and Health, and special director of community health policies. She worked on

Antonia Novello. *Reproduced by permission of AP/Wide World Photos.*

a doctorate in Health Policy at the same time. In 1999 New York Governor George Pataki nominated Novello to be New York State's health commissioner. Her nomination was confirmed by the Senate and Novello stepped into the position ready to continue her pursuit of health care for everyone.

## For More Information

"Governor Pataki Nominates Dr. Novello As Health Commissioner," State of New York press release, June 3, 1999. Available at http://www.state.ny.us/governor/press/year99/june3_99.htm (accessed June 21, 2002).

Hawxhurst, Joan C., *Antonia Novello: U.S. Surgeon General,* Millbrook Press, 1993.

*Hispanic,* January/February 1990, p. 20; October 1991, p. 15.

*People,* December 17, 1990, pp. 109–10.

*Saturday Evening Post,* May/June 1991, pp. 38–41, 93.

*Washington Post,* October 18, 1989; October 24, 1989; May 8, 1990.

# Ellen Ochoa

Astronaut
Born May 10, 1958, Los Angeles, California

*"If you stay in school, you have the potential to achieve what you want in the future."*

As a little girl in California, Ellen Ochoa wasn't sure what she wanted to be when she grew up. Even in college, she changed her major five times. She went from music to business to journalism to computer science, before finally settling on physics. Her career choice proved to be the right one. Before the age of thirty-three, she had received three patents in optical processing (patents are documents issued by the government legally recognizing the creation of a invention or product). The year she turned thirty-three, she become America's first female Hispanic astronaut.

Ochoa was born in 1958 in Los Angeles, California, to Rosanne Deardorff and Joseph Ochoa. Her father, a native Californian, was of Mexican descent. Her parents divorced when she was in junior high school. Ochoa, her sister, and her three brothers were then raised by their mother in La Mesa, California. Ochoa's mother instilled the value of education in all her children at an early age.

Ochoa took her mother's advice to heart. She was always an excellent student, but did exceptionally well in math and science. When she was thirteen, she won the San Diego County spelling bee. In junior high school she was named outstanding seventh and eighth grade girl. Consistently at the head of her class, Ochoa graduated valedictorian from her high school in La Mesa. She repeated that feat at San Diego State University where she earned her bachelor of science degree in physics in 1980.

While in school, Ochoa also won honors for her musical ability. She was named her high school's top musician. In 1983 she was a student soloist winner with the Stanford Symphony Orchestra. With her many achievements in the field of music, she considered playing the flute for a career, but decided science would be a more stable field. She continues playing the flute as a hobby.

## Research Developments Earn Patents

Ochoa continued her education at Stanford University in California. She earned a master's degree in electrical engineering in 1981 and a doctorate degree in that field in 1985. Following her graduate studies, she became a research engineer at Sandia National Laboratories in Livermore, California. Scientists, inventors, and artists sometimes struggle all their lives to develop ideas or inventions that they can patent and claim as their own. Ochoa's three patents for processes she developed in the field of optics (the study of light and vision) came within a few years after she had begun working at the laboratory.

It was a combination of Ochoa's many talents that won her a job with the National Aeronautics and Space Administration (NASA). She had first applied to the astronaut program in 1985. Two years later she was named one of the top one hundred finalists. She began her work at NASA as a researcher, then became a supervisor of over forty other scientists. In 1989 she received the Hispanic Engineer Achievement Award for the most promising engineer in government. The following year she became one of twenty-three new astronauts chosen by NASA for the Space Shuttle program. She reached another milestone in her life in 1990 by marrying Coe Fulmer Miles.

Ochoa takes her status as a role model for young Hispanics very seriously. Since her selection as an astronaut, she has often spoken to Hispanic students and community groups. Her message to them is simple: "If you stay in school you have the potential to achieve what you want in the future," she told Kim Bergheim in *Hispanic*. "Education increases career options and gives you a chance for a wide variety of jobs."

## Space Musician and Scientist

In 1993 Ochoa became the first Hispanic female to travel in space. On the space shuttle Discovery, she and other crew members undertook the ATLAS 2 mission. ATLAS stands for Atmospheric Laboratory for Applications and Science. During her nine days in space, she orbited Earth 148 times.

While in orbit, Ochoa became the first astronaut to play a flute in space. She entertained her crewmates with military and

llen Ochoa. *Reproduced courtesy of the National Aeronautics and Space Administration (NASA).*

national anthems and some classical music. She also held a space-to-ground ham radio conversation with students in her hometown of La Mesa, California. She told them what it felt like to float in space and explained the primary goal of the ATLAS 2 mission, which was to study Earth's atmosphere. The astronauts on the mission were particularly concerned with studying the ozone layer to find any depletion in it.

Ochoa's most important job during the mission, however, was to operate the shuttle's 50-foot robot arm to send a 2,800-pound satellite into space. The satellite was programmed to gather information about solar wind and the Sun's corona. The world watched as Ochoa captured the satellite a day later and returned it to the cargo bay so scientists on Earth could study the data it collected.

## More Space Flights

In November 1994 Ochoa flew a second time in space, this time aboard the space shuttle *Atlantis* on a ten-day mission with a total crew of six, including a French representative of the European Space Agency. The Sun was again the focus of attention as mission specialists gathered data on changes in its energy output and the impact such variations have on the Earth and ozone levels in the atmosphere. Ochoa once again used the remote robotic arm to retrieve a satellite that had performed atmospheric research.

Her next space shuttle flight began on May 27, 1999, and culminated on June 6 of that same year. During her stay aboard the *Discovery,* whose seven-person crew included representatives from the Canadian Space Agency and the Russian Space Agency, Ochoa served as both a mission specialist and flight engineer. May 29 was a particularly momentous day during the journey in that it marked the first time the shuttle docked with the International Space Station. Ochoa's responsibilities included coordinating the transfer of nearly two tons of supplies such as clothing, sleeping bags, medical equipment, spare parts, and water from one craft to the other to prepare for the arrival in 2000 of the first crew to live on board the space station. She also operated the remote robotic arm during a lengthy space walk by two of her fellow astronauts.

By the end of 1999, Ochoa had logged nearly 720 hours in space. The veteran of three shuttle flights and countless hours of training compares the astronaut experience to the life of a student. "Being an astronaut allows you to learn continuously, like you do in school," she remarked in an article published in the *Stanford University School of Engineering Annual Report, 1997–98*. "One flight you're working on atmospheric research. The next, it's bone density studies or space station design." But she readily admitted that other components of space flight such as the launch, weightlessness, and seeing Earth from afar have a strong appeal as well: "What engineer wouldn't want those experiences?"

Between space shuttle flights, Ochoa has held a variety of other technical support positions with NASA at the Johnson Space Center in Houston. She has, for example, verified flight software, served as crew representative for robotics, and worked at Mission Control as spacecraft communicator. As assistant for space station to chief of the Astronaut Office for two years, Ochoa directed the crew involved in the international space station project, a high priority for NASA in 2000 and beyond.

Ochoa's contributions to the space program have garnered her several awards, including two Space Act Tech Brief Awards in 1992, Space Flight Medals in 1993, 1994, and 1999, an Outstanding Leadership Medal in 1995, and an Exceptional Service Medal in 1997. A number of other honors have come her way as well, among them the Women in Aerospace Outstanding Achievement Award, the Hispanic Engineer Albert Baez Award for Outstanding Technical Contribution to Humanity, and the Hispanic Heritage Leadership Award. In addition, Ochoa has served as a member of the Presidential Commission on the Celebration of Women in American History.

Ochoa is frequently asked to speak to students and teachers about her career and the success she has enjoyed as NASA's first Hispanic female astronaut. She regards this part of her job as an unexpected bonus and relishes the many chances she has had to inspire young people to study mathematics and science. "I never thought about this aspect of the job when I was applying, but it's extremely rewarding," she noted in the *Stanford University School of Engineering Annual Report, 1997–98.* "I'm not trying to make every kid an astronaut, but I want kids to think about a career and the preparation they'll need." As a parent herself (she and her husband, Coe Fulmer Miles, have two sons), and the daughter of a woman she has described as a "supermentor," Ochoa is very much aware of her status as a role model, particularly among women and Hispanics. "I do as much speaking as I am allowed to do," she explained to Lydia Martin of Knight-Ridder Newspapers. "I tell students that the opportunities I had were a result of having a good educational background. Education is what allows you to stand out."

## For More Information

"Biographical Data," National Aeronautics and Space Administration, Lyndon B. Johnson Space Center. Available at http://www.jsc.nasa.gov/Bios/html bios/ochoa.html (accessed June 21, 2002).

*Hispanic,* May 1990, pp. 18–19.

*Knight-Ridder*/Tribune News Service, December 1, 1993.

*Latina,* May 1998.

*Notable Hispanic American Women,* Gale, 1993, pp. 296–99.

Romero, Maritza, *Ellen Ochoa: First Hispanic Woman Astronaut,* New York: Rosen Publishing Group, 1997.

*San Diego Union-Tribune,* May 12, 1993, p. A1.

*Sol de Texas,* May 20, 1993.

"STS–56," *Space Shuttle Mission Chronology.* Available at http://www-pao.ksc.nasa.gov/kscpao/chron/sts-56.htm (accessed June 21, 2002).

"STS–66," *Space Shuttle Mission Chronology.* Available at http://www-pao.ksc.nasa.gov/kscpao/chron/sts-66.htm (accessed June 21, 2002).

"STS–96," *Space Shuttle Mission Chronology.* Available at http://www-pao.ksc.nasa.gov/kscpao/chron/sts-96.htm (accessed June 21, 2002).

# Edward James Olmos

Actor, director, social activist, philanthropist
Born February 24, 1947, Los Angeles, California

*"I come from a dysfunctional family, I'm a minority, I have no natural talent, but I did it. If I can do it, anybody can do it. I take away all the excuses."*

Edward James Olmos is an actor with a very active social conscience. He has created memorable characters on television, in plays, and in movies. But his greatest enjoyment comes from influencing young people to do something good with their lives. Each year Olmos makes time to give more than one hundred speeches to groups of disadvantaged kids. He encourages them to get an education and to take control of their own destinies. He has been involved in humanitarian causes throughout the Americas and promotes cultural understanding and human dignity in his acting career as well as his charitable and political works.

Olmos's passion for education is a gift from his parents. He was born in 1947 in East Lost Angeles, California, to Pedro Olmos and Eleanor Huizar. His father had left Mexico City, Mexico, at the age of twenty-one with nothing more than a sixth-grade education. After having settled in Los Angeles, his father returned to school and eventually earned a high school degree. Olmos's mother left school after the eighth grade, but she, too, returned to school to complete her education after her children had grown.

Olmos's parents divorced when he was eight years old. It was a traumatic time for him, and he responded by concentrating on baseball. He explained that baseball was the only thing that made him stop thinking about his own problems. He practiced the sport every day, and he won the Golden State (California) batting championship while he was still a schoolboy. Through his concentration on baseball, he developed a tremendous sense of self-discipline that has remained with him as an adult.

## Baseball to Music to Acting

Olmos's father was certain that his son would become a professional ball player. At the age of fifteen, however, Olmos suddenly changed his goals. Instead of becoming a ball player, he decided he would be a singer and dancer. By the time he graduated from high school, he was earning money as the leader of a band called Pacific Ocean. The group played regularly at top nightclubs in Los Angeles.

"I sang terrible," Olmos told *New York*'s Pete Hamill, "but I could scream real good

and I could dance. So I'd dance for five minutes, then come back and sing a couple more screams, then dance again."

During the day, Olmos attended East Los Angeles College. At night, he brought his books along on Pacific Ocean's jobs and studied during breaks. He eventually earned an associate's degree in sociology. Hoping to improve his singing, Olmos returned to the college to take a drama course. Before long, he fell in love with acting and decided to make it his career goal.

## Starts Out as a "Bad Guy"

By the time he was twenty-five, Olmos was married to Kaija Keels, and had two sons, Mico and Bodie. (He and Keels eventually divorced and Olmos married actress Lorraine Bracco in 1991.) At this time, Olmos supported his family by running an antique furniture delivery business. To satisfy his acting desires, he found work with experimental theater groups at night. At the same time, he also tried out for small roles on television. He frequently won bit parts on TV police shows, often playing the role of the "bad guy."

In 1978 Olmos won the role that changed his life as an actor. It was a part in *Zoot Suit,* a musical drama written by **Luis Valdez** (see entry). The story was based on an actual 1942 case in which a group of Hispanic youths were wrongly convicted of murder in Los Angeles. Olmos played the macho "El Pachuco," the narrator of the story. Strutting across the stage, Olmos delivered a powerful, attention-getting performance. *Zoot Suit* electrified Los Angeles and awakened the city to its Chicano (Mexican American) community. Scheduled for a ten-day run, the play actually ran for a year and a half. It then moved to Broadway, where Olmos was nominated for a Tony Award for his performance.

After *Zoot Suit* Olmos no longer had to fight for one-line parts on TV shows. He was offered feature roles in major films. Worried about becoming locked into stereotyped Hispanic roles, however, he selected his projects carefully. One of his memorable roles from this time was in the 1982 science fiction thriller *Blade Runner,* which starred Harrison Ford.

## Portrays Mexican Folk Hero

Olmos's next film, *The Ballad of Gregorio Cortez,* was deeply meaningful to him. It was the tale of a Mexican folk hero who traditionally had been portrayed as a fierce bandit. Through research, however, Olmos discovered that Cortez was actually a poor rancher and dedicated family man. He had became the subject of the largest manhunt in Texas history simply because of a misunderstood word. Olmos decided to portray Cortez as an ordinary man who was victimized because of discrimination and ignorance.

Olmos spoke Spanish in *The Ballad of Gregorio Cortez,* which carried no English subtitles (translation). Although the film appeared on public television, no major movie studio chose to distribute it. In response, Olmos rented a Hollywood theater and showed the film every Saturday morning for free. He traveled extensively to promote the film. During this period, he turned down film and television roles because he felt they would take up too much of his time. One of those roles was on the popular television series *Hill Street Blues.*

Edward James Olmos. *Reproduced by permission of Archive Photos, Inc.*

One television role Olmos eventually agreed to play was that of Lieutenant Martin Castillo in *Miami Vice.* This immensely popular series, which began its five-year run in 1985, made Olmos's face known nationwide. Although unhappy with the series as a whole (he thought it had no good storylines), Olmos found his character interesting. "He embodies concepts," Olmos explained to Marcia Seligson, "that I think are essential to getting to the highest level of understanding oneself—discipline, determination, perseverance, and patience." For his riveting performance on the series, Olmos was honored with an Emmy Award for best supporting actor in a dramatic series in 1985 and a Golden Globe Award in 1986.

## Dives into Role of Math Teacher

Olmos was more enthusiastic, however, about his role in the 1988 film *Stand and Deliver.* The movie presents the true story of **Jaime Escalante** (see entry), a Bolivian-born math teacher who came to a gang-filled Los Angeles high school. There, he inspired eighteen students to take—and pass—an advanced placement calculus test. Along the way, Escalante also taught them to have pride in themselves and to take control of their own futures.

"The film is really about the triumph of the human spirit," Olmos told Seligson. "It's about something we've lost—the joy of learning, the joy of making our brains develop." To prepare for his role as Escalante, Olmos attended the teacher's classes, studied Escalante's mannerisms, and gained forty pounds. For his realistic portrayal, Olmos received an Academy Award nomination.

Next, Olmos directed and starred in *American Me,* a 1992 film about rising street crime in the Los Angeles barrio (Spanish-speaking neighborhood) where he grew up. *American Me* presented the brutal, realistic story of a gang member's life, in and out of prison. "The film is not for one race, one subculture, one age range," Olmos told Jack Kroll in *Newsweek.* "Gangs teach a distorted discipline, a distorted familial bonding, a distorted sense of pride and power."

## Starring Roles

Among Olmos's next projects was *Menendez: A Murder in Beverly Hills,* which aired in May 1994 on CBS. Olmos played Jose Menendez, the real-life father of Lyle and Erik Menendez, who was allegedly killed by his sons due to years of sexual and mental abuse. In his review for *People,* David Hildbrand praised Olmos's performance: "Edward James Olmos is outstanding as Jose Menendez, the driven, demanding father, who spits at both his sons at one time or another, 'You disgust me!'"

Olmos followed that riveting performance with another in *The Burning Season.* The made-for-television movie, which aired on HBO in September 1994, presented the life of Brazilian labor unionist Chico Mendes. Actor **Raul Julia** (see entry) portrayed the late union leader in the film. For his work in the award-winning production, Olmos was presented a Golden Globe Award for best supporting actor in a television movie by the Hollywood Foreign Press Association in January 1995.

Olmos's commitment to meaningful productions was evidenced again by his role in the 1995 film *My Family/Mi Familia* directed by Gregory Nava. The critically acclaimed movie traced the trials of three generations of a Mexican American family living in Los Angeles. One of three brothers in the Sanchez family, Olmos's character becomes a writer and supplies the film's narration. Jimmy Smits and Esai Morales portrayed the other two brothers in this impassioned drama.

In 1997 Olmos starred with **Jennifer Lopez** (see entry) in *Selena,* a film about the murder of the Tejano singing star, to high critical acclaim. That same year he also had roles in *The Disappearance of Garcia Lorca, 12 Angry Men,* and *Hollywood Confidential.* He went on to star in *The Wall* (1998) a 1999 documentary, *Bonanno: A*

*Godfather's Story,* and a film called *Gossip.* In 2000 he appeared in the films *The Princess and the Barrio Boy* and *The Road to El Dorado,* and in 2002 he starred in the film version of Dominican American writer **Julia Alvarez**'s novel *In the Time of the Butterflies* (see entry).

In 2001 Olmos could be seen on PBS television weekly in the highly acclaimed drama series *American Family,* which entered its second season in 2002. *American Family,* created and produced by Gregory Nava, was the first drama series featuring a Latino cast ever to air on broadcast television. The series was originally financed by CBS, but the network decided at the last moment not to air it. PBS then picked up the series. Starring with Olmos were **Raquel Welch** (see entry), Sonia Braga, and Esai Morales.

Olmos has been involved in other projects as producer and director. In 1999 he launched a multimedia project called *Americanos: Latino Life in the United States,* a documentary that celebrates the heritage of Latino-Americans in the arts, music, politics, education, and religion. The project includes a five-year traveling photography exhibition organized by the Smithsonian Institution Traveling Exhibition Service and the Smithsonian Center for Latino Initiatives. Also included is a music CD featuring Latino artists; an HBO documentary; and a book of essays and photos by notable Hispanics.

## Dedicated to Public Service

Anyone interested in Latino issues will find the name of Edward James Olmos connected to a huge variety of Hispanic concerns. He is said to be the voice of Latinos in Hollywood and throughout the nation, and he speaks and campaigns for justice and equal opportunity at a breakneck pace. Throughout his career, Olmos has dedicated his time to public service work. He has helped to make peace between Los Angeles's warring gangs, has worked with disabled and sexually abused children, and has spoken out against drug abuse. After the 1992 Los Angeles riots resulting from the court decision in the Rodney King beating trial, Olmos was one of the first people to appear on the streets of Los Angeles to begin the clean-up. He then met with local and state officials to develop plans for rebuilding. As a member of the Rebuild LA Committee, he was intimately involved in the process. He is also the U.S. Goodwill Ambassador for UNICEF (a United Nations organization devoted to helping children worldwide) and a national spokesperson for the Juvenile Diabetes Foundation.

In the spring of 2001 Olmos joined other demonstrators from the mainland United States and Puerto Rico on Vieques Island, Puerto Rico. They were there to protest the U.S. Navy's bombing of the island for the purpose of tests and training that has been going on in Vieques since just after World War II in 1945. The Navy's tests are destroying the environment and the health and living conditions of many of the island's inhabitants, and in 1999 one civilian on the island was killed by a stray bomb. Like many other protestors, Olmos was arrested for trespassing during the demonstration and was sentenced to prison time—he served his twenty-day sentence in San Juan, Puerto Rico, in August 2001.

Olmos continues his social activities, often visiting children in juvenile halls, in inner-city schools, and on Native American reservations. He brings them the message that it is possible to improve one's lot in life, even against heavy odds. He is proof of that. "I come from a dysfunctional family, I'm a minority, I have no natural talent, but I did it," Olmos explained to Kroll. "If I can do it, anybody can do it. I take away all the excuses."

## For More Information

"Edward James Olmos," Keppler and Associates. Available at http://www.kepplerassociates.com/olmos.htm (accessed June 21, 2002).

"Field Museum and Mexican Fine Arts Center Museum Hold Joint Preview of New Photo Exhibition on Latino Life in US; Actor Edward James Olmos to Speak," *PR Newswire,* August 16, 2000.

*Hispanic,* September 1988, pp. 29–33.

*Newsweek,* March 30, 1992, pp. 66–67.

*New York,* September 29, 1986.

*Washington Post,* March 21, 1992, p. B1.

# Sandra Ortiz-Del Valle

Basketball referee, educator
Born April 23, 1951, New York, New York

*"Many think I am into [being a basketball referee] for the novelty. The players and coaches who know me recognize that I am serious and respect me."*

In the early 1990s Sandra Ortiz-Del Valle was a rarity—a woman working in the world of men's professional sports. She quietly tried to break down boundaries in the male-dominated sporting world by becoming one of the few women basketball referees working in the United States Basketball League. Her skills and discipline earned her a spot in the Naismith Basketball Hall of Fame. But the resistance to women in the traditionally male field was strong. Eventually, Ortiz-Del Valle, denied the chance to referee, filed a lawsuit against the National Basketball Association (NBA). In doing so she drew attention to the problem of gender discrimination in sports and may have paved the way for women referees in the future.

Ortiz-Del Valle was born in New York City in 1951 to Esteban and Delia Ortiz. Her father worked as an electrician, while her mother served as the only Hispanic on the local school board. From her Puerto Rican parents, Ortiz-Del Valle learned the importance of self-improvement and determination.

## Sports Kept Her Straight

As a child, Ortiz-Del Valle turned to sports as a way to stay out of trouble. She got hooked on basketball while in high school. In 1974 she graduated from New York's City College with a bachelor of science degree in education. She earned her master's degree in administration and supervision from the college in 1983. It was while playing women's college basketball that Ortiz-Del Valle first started refereeing, beginning with youth games in 1978.

Ortiz-Del Valle quickly became attracted to a possible career as a referee. To increase her skills, she took courses. In 1984 she started working in semiprofessional leagues. By 1989 her ability and reputation caught the attention of the USBL and they offered her a job.

The USBL is composed of some of the best basketball players in the United States. A number of players in the league could make it to the National Basketball Association (NBA). Ortiz-Del Valle's ultimate goal was to work as a referee in the NBA.

## Fighting the NBA

Ortiz-Del Valle met with resistance in the male-dominated sport. She was able to referee a USBL game in 1991 and a few preseason scrimmages in 1992, but never received an NBA referee position. "When I am faced with people new to the idea of a woman referee in a men's league, they think I have to pay my dues, and many think I am in it for the novelty," she explained to Robyn Kleerekoper in *Notable Hispanic American Women.* "The players and coaches who know me recognize that I am serious and respect me."

The NBA gave Ortiz-Valle a variety of reasons that they were unwilling to hire her as a referee even though it was clear that she had the credentials to do the job. Finally, she filed a lawsuit against the league, citing gender discrimination. In 1999 a jury agreed that she had been the victim of discrimination and awarded her $100,000 in damages for lost wages, $750,000 for emotional distress, and $7 million in punitive damages (fines that serve as punishments). This was the first time the NBA had lost a discrimination case.

The court eventually reduced the damages to $250,000 in punitive damages, $76,926 in

Sandra Ortiz-Del Valle. *Reproduced by permission of AP/Wide World Photos.*

lost wages, and $20,000 in emotional distress, finding that there had indeed been discrimination but that the damages figures were too high. The NBA is appealing (asking for the case to be taken up by a higher court). Notably, it hired two female officials after Ortiz-Del Valle filed the lawsuit.

In addition to her basketball career, Ortiz-Del Valle has been a full-time physical education teacher in New York. She also coaches bowling and boys' baseball.

## For More Information

"Female Referee's Award Reduced in Her Gender Discrimination Suit vs. NBA: Ortiz-Del Valle v. National Basketball Association, 42 F. Supp. 2d 334 (S.D.N.Y., 1999)," Findlaw Sports. Available at http://sports.findlaw.com/sports_law/makethe-call/summer99/ortiz/ (accessed June 21, 2002).

*Notable Hispanic American Women,* Gale, 1993, pp. 306–07.

# Elizabeth Peña

Actress
Born September 23, 1959, Elizabeth, New Jersey

*"I've never thought of [being Hispanic] as an obstacle. I think it's good. There are certainly enough five-foot-seven blonds."*

Elizabeth Peña never considered her ethnic looks or heritage an obstacle to her goals. She was shocked in high school to lose a the role of a midwestern farm girl in a school production because she just didn't look the part. Through determination and hard work combined with a gift for acting, Peña has proven herself a versatile and sought-after actress.

Peña was born in 1959 in Elizabeth, New Jersey (her parents named her after the town). She was the first daughter of actor, writer, and director Mario Peña and producer Estella Marguerita Toirac Peña. Four months after her birth, her parents took her back to their home country of Cuba. At the time, the Cuban Revolution was underway. Fidel Castro and others had overthrown Fulgencio Batista, the brutal dictator who had ruled Cuba throughout the 1950s. The Peñas believed Cuba would become a land of greater opportunity under Castro's government.

Unfortunately, Mario Peña was sent to a Cuban prison upon his return. Castro's Communist government disapproved of his poems and political views. When he was finally released, he had no choice but to leave the country and return to the United States. Peña, her mother, and younger sister were not allowed to follow him until 1968.

## Mother Opposes Career Choice

After being reunited, the family settled in New York City. Peña's parents founded the city's Latin American Theater Ensemble, and became respected and well-known figures in New York's theater community. The young Peña was inspired to pursue acting by her parents' example, even though her mother wished she would try a more stable career. Against her mother's wishes, Peña enrolled in New York's famous School of Performing Arts. After she graduated from the school, she continued to study acting and clowning with various theater groups and private teachers.

Peña's determination eventually convinced her mother that she was in the right field. Beginning in 1979, it also earned her a number of small roles on the stage and in movies. In the theater, she played such roles as Juliet in *Romeo and Juliet* and Beba in *Night of the Assassins.* In movies, she played opposite actors such as James Caan in *Thief* (1981) and **Rubén Blades** (see entry) in *Crossover Dreams* (1985).

## Moves to Hollywood

Success in New York spurred Peña to move to Hollywood to search for larger roles. She wanted a role in *Down and Out in*

*Beverly Hills,* a 1986 film starring Richard Dreyfuss and Bette Midler. She decided to flood the casting director's office with her pictures and messages. The ploy worked: Peña managed to earn a screen test and won the role of a maid in the film. Critics praised her sexy and funny portrayal, and her Hollywood career was launched.

Nineteen eighty-seven was a busy year for Peña. She won a role in *La Bamba,* the film biography of the late Mexican American singer **Ritchie Valens** (see entry). In the hit film, Peña played the part of the abused-yet-loyal-wife of Ritchie Valens's older brother. That same year, she earned a role in the television series *I Married Dora.* However, the situation comedy, about a man who marries his Central American maid so she won't be deported, was panned by critics. Peña then finished out the year with a role in a Steven Spielberg film, *\*batteries not included.*

In 1988 Peña took a break from acting to marry William Stephan Kibler, a movie agent turned junior high school teacher. That year she accepted a number of awards, including the Hispanic Women's Council Woman of the Year award, the New York Image Award, the U.S. Congressional Award, and the Nosotros Golden Eagle Award.

## Biggest Role Comes in Eerie Picture

Peña resumed her acting career in 1990. She landed her biggest role to date in the movie *Jacob's Ladder.* She played the part of Tim Robbins's mysterious girlfriend in the eerie picture about a Vietnam veteran struggling to hold onto reality. Her part was

Elizabeth Peña. *Reproduced by permission of AP/Wide World Photos.*

not originally written for a Hispanic actress, but Peña was able to convince the producers of the film to change it. Her persistence paid off once again. A reviewer for *Newsweek* magazine called her performance "warm and gritty."

That same year, Peña was cast as a client/secretary of a heartbroken lawyer in the television show *Shannon's Deal.* Critics treated the show unkindly, but gave Peña high marks for her work. The *Washington Post*'s Tom Shales, quoted in *People,* maintained that Peña was "assertive and gutsy.... Maybe the show should be about *her.*"

For several years Peña brightened many productions, including the television shows *Hill Street Blues, TJ Hooker, Cagney and Lacey, As the World Turns, Tough Cookies,* and *Saturday Night Live,* the made-for-television movies *Drug Wars: The Camarena Story* and *Found Money,* and the movies *Blue Steel* and *Fat Chance.* She had a role in the 1995 sequel *Free Willie II: The Adventure Home,* and several other films in the 1990s, but was frequently frustrated when filmmakers cast her only in roles they saw fit for Hispanics.

## Lone Star Performance Praised

Then in 1996, Peña took on the starring role of Pilar Cruz in *Lone Star,* directed by John Sayles. The movie centers on a border town in Texas and the hidden history of the relations between the Anglos and the Mexican Americans. Pilar is a high-school teacher trying to change the version of Texas history taught in the schools, to make it encompass the Mexican American experience. The movie was highly praised by critics, and most noted the outstanding performance by Peña. *Time* critic Richard Schickel wrote that "the beautiful Elizabeth Peña invests [the character of Pilar] with the most touching vulnerability."

Peña had a role in the popular 1998 Jackie Chan martial arts flick *Rush Hour.* In the 2001 film *Tortilla Soup,* she played the leading role of Leticia Naranjo, a born-again Christian chemistry teacher, the daughter of a Los Angeles chef played by Hector Alizando. For Peña, playing the repressed schoolteacher was a challenge: "I've never played anyone who was, 'tucked in.' That's the best word. She keeps tucking herself in. So it was exhausting trying to sedate my own energy more than anything."

In the early 2000s Peña was known to most film viewers as a skilled professional who has played challenging roles with intelligence and grace. She believes, though, that American movie makers remain slow in casting Hispanics. "I like who I am," she is quoted in *Dictionary of Hispanic Biography,* "I don't have a problem with it; I think everybody else does. That's part of *their* growing up." She went on to add: "I've never thought of [being Hispanic] as an obstacle. I think it's good. There are certainly enough five-foot-seven blonds."

## For More Information

*Contemporary Theater, Film, and Television,* Volume 5, Gale, 1988.

*Dictionary of Hispanic Biography,* Gale, 1996.

*Newsweek,* November 12, 1990, pp. 77–78.

*People,* May 13, 1991, pp. 107–08.

Schickel, Richard, *Lone Star,* review, *Time,* July 22, 1996, p. 95.

Sperling, Seana, "An Interview with Elizabeth Peña," Acid Logic, October 16, 2001. Available at http://www.acidlogic.com/elizabeth_pena.htm (accessed June 21, 2002).

# Federico Peña

Former secretary of energy, former secretary of transportation, and former mayor of Denver, businessperson
Born March 15, 1947, Laredo, Texas

*"It's taken me time to understand there will always be someone who opposes me. I have had to learn to be a little more thick-skinned, yet not become an insensitive armadillo."*

Federico Peña served in President Bill Clinton's cabinet (group of advisors on policy) in two different capacities in a short period of time. As secretary of energy, he was responsible for the regulation, production, and conservation of energy in the United States. As secretary of the U.S. Department of Transportation, Peña was responsible for the smooth operation of the nation's highways, airports, and railroad networks. These jobs followed his earlier work as the first Hispanic mayor of Denver, Colorado. While mayor for two terms, he revitalized the city through major construction projects, including the building of a new airport. His many accomplishments in all his positions were achieved in the face of controversy and criticism, which he faced rationally and with dignity.

Federico Fabian Peña was born in 1947 into a Texas family whose ancestors had been politicians. His great grandfather were mayor of Laredo, Texas, during the American Civil War. Peña was the third of six children born to Gustavo and Lucia Peña. Theirs was a strict family. While growing up, the Peña children addressed their parents as "sir" and "ma'am," and were punished for disrespect or swearing.

Peña and his brothers were altar boys at the Sacred Heart Catholic Church and attended St. Joseph's Academy high school. Standard achievement tests were not easy for Peña. He had to study long hours to earn good grades in school. Still, he managed to graduate with honors, and his classmates voted him "most likely to succeed." He attended the University of

Federico Peña. *Reproduced by permission of AP/Wide World Photos.*

Texas at Austin where he was active in campus politics and took part in Vietnam War protests. After graduating with a bachelor's degree in 1969, he enrolled at the University of Texas Law School. He earned his law degree in 1972.

## Moves to Denver and Enters Politics

Peña joined his brother Alfredo in Denver to form a law partnership, Peña and Peña. In addition, he worked for the Mexican American Legal Defense and Educational Fund (see **Antonia Hernández** entry), and for the Chicano Education Project. As the legal advisor for this last group, he pushed for better schools in Hispanic neighborhoods. Through his activities in the Hispanic community, he became interested in politics. In 1978 he made a successful run for the Colorado House of Representatives. Peña was so committed to his work in the House that his colleagues named him outstanding legislator of the year in 1981.

In 1983 Peña surprised political analysts by winning the election for mayor of Denver. He replaced the man who had held the job for fourteen years. This was especially notable since the Hispanic population of the city was relatively small. But Peña had captured the interest of most of the voters with his campaign slogan, "Denver: Imagine a Great City." At age thirty-six, he became one of the youngest mayors in the United States and the first Hispanic mayor of Denver.

Like many older American cities, Denver was suffering from a slow economy, air pollution, and inner city decay. Peña had a tough job convincing businessmen, citizens, and politicians that drastic change was needed to save the city. During his first four-year term, he made little progress and was harshly criticized.

## Barely Escapes Recall

"It's taken me time to understand there will always be someone who opposes me," Peña explained to Ann Carnahan in the *Rocky Mountain News*. "I have had to learn to be a little more thick-skinned, yet not become an insensitive armadillo." Peña had to fight hard to win re-election in 1987. A few months after his victory, he was almost ousted from office when citizens started a

petition drive to recall him. The drive fell two thousand signatures short.

Peña was finally able to convince diverse groups of citizens to cooperate with his plans during his second term in office, and Denver began to make an economic comeback. Peña arranged for the construction of the new $2.3 billion Denver International Airport—the largest airport in the world—and a convention center. He had city workers clean up neighborhoods, plant thousands of trees, and repair streets and bridges. He introduced pollution controls that dramatically improved the city's air. For his accomplishments, Peña received the City Livability award from the U.S. Conference of Mayors in 1990. In 1991 he received the American Planning Association's Distinguished Leadership Award.

In 1988 Peña had married Ellen Hart, a lawyer and former English teacher. They have two daughters. To spend more time with his family and to seek new challenges in his life, Peña decided not to run for a third term as mayor of Denver in 1991.

## Invited to Washington

In 1992 President Bill Clinton offered Peña the challenge he was seeking. Clinton invited Peña to become a member of his cabinet as the new head of the Department of Transportation (DOT). Peña's reputation as a successful mayor and his work as a member of Clinton's transition team on transportation issues helped earn him the job. In 1993 Peña took charge of the country's transportation systems and the 110,000 people who operate them.

While in office as secretary of transportation, Peña faced a number of crises and controversies. In October 1994, for example, he caused a stir when he overruled a National Highway Traffic Safety Administration (NHTSA) recommendation for the first time in the DOT's history. At issue were as many as six million General Motors (GM) pickup trucks some consumer groups claimed had a tendency to burst into flames following side-impact collisions. Although the NHTSA concluded that the risk of death in a pickup truck crash was no greater in GM trucks than other makes, Peña decided to go ahead with a recall anyway.

Airline troubles took up much of Peña's time as well. On several occasions, he had to find ways to help airline companies on shaky financial ground obtain tax relief and loan guarantees in order to head off takeovers by foreign investors. Airline safety was on everyone's minds, particularly because air disasters resulted in many deaths in 1994. Maintenance and inspection practices, flight crew training, air traffic control procedures, and weather monitoring all came under public scrutiny.

In response to the disturbing increase in air crash-related deaths, Peña called for a safety check of the nation's airlines and announced a "zero accident" goal. His boldest move, however, was to propose that the country's air traffic control operations no longer be supervised by the Federal Aviation Administration (FAA). Instead, he suggested that they should be run by a type of public-private partnership in an effort to improve efficiency and reduce costs.

## From One Post to Another

With a shrinking budget, Peña also made extensive plans to reorganize the DOT. With these plans in place, he resigned his post as secretary of transportation in December 1996. Although he planned to seek a job in the private sector, when President Clinton asked him to serve in his cabinet as secretary of energy for the president's second term, Peña agreed.

Upon accepting the top position, Peña again faced turmoil, particularly in the area of nuclear waste disposal, nuclear arms testing, and nuclear weapons plant clean-ups. He resigned his position after two years, on June 30, 1998, citing personal and family reasons for his departure. He then became an investment banker with Vestar Capital Partners in New York. He was named managing director of the company in 2000. He still participates in the nation's public policies through his corporate work. He served on the board of directors of govWorks, an company that provides a wide variety of Internet-based services for interactions between government agencies, citizens, and businesses, and he serves on a diversity panel for Toyota.

## For More Information

*American Planning Association,* March 1991.
*Distribution,* February 1993, p. 14.
*New York Times,* December 25, 1992, p. A24; March 16, 1993.
*PR Newswire,* April 7, 2000; January 11, 2002.
*Rocky Mountain News,* August 6, 1989.
"Statement of U.S. Secretary of Energy Federico Peña," Brookhaven National Laboratory, April 6, 1998. Available at http://www.bnl.gov/bnlweb/pubaf/pr/1998/doest040698.html (accessed June 21, 2002).
*Washington Post,* January 7, 1993, p. A14.

# Maggie Peña

Entrepreneur
Born January 29, 1959, Bogota, Colombia

*"As Hispanics, we need to take a more aggressive leadership role with respect to finding and contributing to a solution to [the problem of Hispanic education]."*

In 1988 Maggie Peña cofounded the National Society of Hispanic MBAs (NSHMBA). Since that time, she has worked to increase the number of Hispanic business students in graduate schools. She has also led the fight to improve Hispanic advancement in the business world. In 1991 Peña served as president of NSHMBA. During her presidency, she helped the society launch a scholarship program for Hispanic pupils. "Much has been written about the sad state of Hispanic education," she wrote in an article in *Hispanic*. "As Hispanics, we need to take a more aggressive leadership role with respect to finding and contributing to the solution to this problem."

Peña was born in 1959 in Bogota, Colombia. When she was seven years old, she moved with her family to Los Angeles, California. She attended school in Los Angeles until the eleventh grade, then completed her last two years of high school in Colombia. "My parents wanted me to get in touch with my cultural roots," she explained to Michelle Vachon in *Notable Hispanic American Women*.

In 1976 Peña won a four-year California State scholarship. She chose to attend Immaculate Heart College in Los Angeles and graduated with a bachelor's degree in biology in 1980. For the next few years she worked as a biology lab assistant and as a high school chemistry teacher. She also managed to run her family's juice business.

## MBA Provides Opportunities

At first, Peña planned on a career in scientific research. After working in a lonely laboratory for three years, however, she decided to change careers. She returned to school, enrolling in the University of California at Los Angeles. By 1986 she had earned a master of business administration (MBA) degree in marketing and finance.

The MBA opened up a world of opportunities for Peña. She worked as a financial analyst for the video division at Paramount Pictures Corporation. She managed Paramount's multimillion-dollar budget. "My experience in the corporate world opened my eyes to what was an unknown to me: the mysterious world of big business and big money," she told Vachon. Through her work at Paramount, Peña learned how to handle large business projects. More than that, she became confident in her own abilities.

## Shares Skills with Hispanic Community

In 1988 Peña helped launch the NSHMBA. She and other educated Hispanics felt there was not enough support for Hispanics who wanted to study business in graduate school. By 1991 NSHMBA had grown to seven chapters across the country, and its members had raised $500,000 for educational opportunities for Hispanics. During her presidency of NSHMBA, Peña also established a summer enrichment program for junior high school students in Chicago, Los Angeles, and Washington, D.C.

"My work with the society proved extremely rewarding," Peña related to Vachon. "I developed a stronger sense of my Latino roots and discovered the tremendous network of Hispanic leaders nationwide." Peña believes that many people are more than willing to help others. They only need a person or an organization to show them where to begin. This is the function of a group like NSHMBA.

## Moving On

NSHMBA, after starting out with just seven chapters and a few dedicated people, grew tremendously throughout the 1990s and into the early 2000s. It now has twenty-three chapter groups and nearly three thousand members.

In 1991 Peña left Paramount Pictures to join her family's business—The Juice Fountain. Having taken over the reins of the business from her mother, Peña has expanded the business into three fresh-squeezed juice outlets in Los Angeles.

In addition to her work with NSHMBA, Peña also volunteers for charitable, fine arts, social, and political organizations. Her plans don't end here. In the future, she wants to work with youth groups to reduce school absenteeism and gang problems in Los Angeles. Peña also hopes to raise money to help poor children in Colombia, the country of her birth.

## For More Information

*Hispanic,* July 1991, p. 66; March 1992, p. 20.

*Hispanic Business,* February 1991, p. 21.

National Society of Hispanic MBAs Web site. Available at http://www.nshmba.org/home.asp (accessed June 21, 2002).

*Notable Hispanic American Women,* Gale, 1993, pp. 315–16.

# Rosie Perez

Actress, dancer, choreographer
Born 1964, Brooklyn, New York

*"Hispanics, we're not even in the running. There are no roles. I'm stealing the roles written for non-minorities."*

In just a few short years, Rosie Perez switched from being a college student to a professional dancer to a busy actress. Her energy and talent for business have earned her jobs as a choreographer for a television show and a tour manager for a rap group and as the star of some top films. Perez is not slowing down. "I'm very happy with the way things are going for me right now," she explained to Frank Spotnitz in *Entertainment Weekly,* "but I still feel like they're going too slow. I want it all."

Rosa Mary Perez was born in Bushwich, a mostly Puerto Rican district of Brooklyn. The exact year of her birth is her closely guarded secret. At one time she would admit only to being "under 25." She is the daughter of Ismael Serrano, a merchant marine, and Lydia Perez, who used to be a singer in Puerto Rico. When Perez was just a toddler, her mother placed her in a New York convent home. When she turned nine, she went to live with her father's sister, Anna.

Perez's family (which includes ten children) was on welfare, but that was no drawback to life in her neighborhood. "On the block where I grew up, everybody was in everybody's business," she told Mim Udovitch of *Vibe*. "You had no money so you couldn't go anywhere, and all your friends were there, so you just hung out. It was kind of cool because no one could act like they were better than anybody else."

## Dances Her Way Onto Television

Although shy, Perez was a good student in school. She excelled at science, but had to take remedial speech classes—she called herself "Wosie" until sixth grade. As a teenager, she was also overweight, but eventually slimmed down through diet and exercise. Perez moved to Los Angeles at age eighteen to attend college, where she studied marine biology. While dancing one night in a Latino club in Los Angeles, she was spotted by a scout for the television show *Soul Train*. She was invited to become a dancer on the show and her entertainment career took off.

Perez soon danced her way into choreography. While she stayed with *Soul Train* for only a few shows, she made contacts that quickly led to other jobs. She created video and stage dance arrangements for singer Bobby Brown and rappers Al B. Sure, LL Cool J, and Heavy D & the Boyz. These in turn led her to the Fox television program *In Living Color*, where she became choreographer of the Fly Girls.

## Moves to the Big Screen

During this period, while dancing at a Los Angeles club, Perez came to the attention of director Spike Lee. He offered her a part in his 1989 film, *Do the Right Thing*. She played the role of Tina, an unwed Puerto Rican mother with a quick temper. Some Hispanic groups criticized her for playing a stereotype, but she explained to Martha Frase-Blunt in *Hispanic* that she was playing an authentic role: "I was not portraying something that's not really out there."

Perez's performance soon brought her other projects. She appeared in television roles in such series as *21 Jump Street, Criminal Justice,* and *WIOU*. In almost all of these roles, however, she played the same type of character, and she was determined to branch out as an actress.

Her big break came with the 1992 hit film *White Men Can't Jump*. In the movie she played Woody Harrelson's feisty girlfriend, a character who originally was to have been a white woman from an Ivy League college. After Ron Shelton, the film's writer-director, heard Perez audition for the role, he rewrote it for her, but only slightly. "I finally played someone," Perez told Charles Leerhsen in *Newsweek,* "who had it together, who wasn't a victim or messed up by the ghetto." In quick succession, Perez landed parts in *Night on Earth,* a small independent film, and *Untamed Heart,* starring Christian Slater and Marisa Tomei.

## Lands First Starring Role

Perez played her very first starring role in *Fearless,* released in 1993. In the film, which also starred Jeff Bridges, Perez played a young mother who survives a plane crash but blames herself for her young son's death. Once again, the role was not written with a Hispanic in mind, and noted actresses Jodie Foster and Winona Ryder both tried for the part. And once again, Perez had to fight for the role she eventually won. As Tony Bill, her director in *Untamed Heart,* explained to Leerhsen, "She has such a naturalness and a genuineness about her, that her way of doing something becomes the right way, the only way." Because Perez was so convincing in her role in *Fearless,* she was nominated for an Academy Award for best supporting actress.

In the summer of 1994 Perez was on the big screen again, playing opposite Nicholas Cage and Bridget Fonda in *It Could Happen to You.* She was the executive producer and played in ten episodes of the 1997 HBO series *Subway Stories.* She played a new and busy working mother in the poorly reviewed 1999 film *24 Hours.*

Perez has been involved in a wide variety of ventures in the new century. On January 6, 2000, she joined a demonstration in Manhattan against the U.S. Navy's testing on the Puerto Rican island of Vieques. Along with many of the protestors, she was arrested for disorderly conduct. That same year the animated Disney movie *The Road to El Dorado,* was released. When sixteenth century explorers (voices by Kevin Kline and Kenneth Branagh) arrive in the New World, they are greeted by native Chel (voice by Perez). *Maclean's* observed that Perez as Chel "has to be the most risque sexpot ever to vamp through a Disney-style animated feature." In 2001 she took to the stage in the play by Jose Rivera "References to Salvador Dali

Rosie Perez. *Reproduced by permission of AP/Wide World Photos.*

Make Me Hot" and was highly praised for her work.

Despite her successes, however, Perez has had to continue to fight against the narrow options open to Hispanic entertainers. "Hispanics, we're not even in the running," she told Udovitch. "There are no roles. I'm stealing the roles written for non-minorities."

## For More Information

*Entertainment Weekly,* April 3, 1992, p. 11.
*Essence,* October 1993, p. 63.
*Hispanic,* April 1993, pp. 14–16.
*Newsweek,* May 4, 1992, pp. 64–65.
"Pop Quiz with Rosie Perez," *People Weekly,* January 24, 2000, p. 20.
*Vibe,* December 1993/January 1994, pp. 65–68.
"Yukatan Yuk-Fest," *Maclean's,* April 3, 2000, p. 61.

# Paloma Picasso

Fashion designer
Born April 19, 1949, Paris, France

*"The most important thing is to know yourself. You should always be the same person. Style is how you conduct yourself, the silly things you do as well as everything else."*

Paloma Picasso is the daughter of Pablo Picasso, one of the twentieth century's most famous and influential artists. She has emerged from her famous father's shadow to establish an artistic reputation of her own—in the competitive world of fashion design. She has also launched an international company to sell her designs. Her work is whimsical and modern, and her use of color is dramatic and bold. Both reflect her own personality and style.

Picasso was born in Paris, France, in 1949. As the daughter of two artists, the Spanish Pablo Picasso and French Françoise Gilot, it is not surprising that she chose a career in the arts. She was named Paloma (Spanish for "dove") after the peace symbol her father created for the 95th World Peace Conference held in Paris at the time of her birth. Although Picasso's parents lived together for ten years, they never married because Pablo Picasso had been married before in Spain, and the law there did not permit divorce.

Pablo Picasso's genius and fame were an obstacle for his daughter. She was drawn to a career in art, but feared that her work would always be compared to that of her father. "From the time I was fourteen," she explained to Mary Batts Estrada in *Hispanic,* "I stopped drawing completely. I didn't want to hear, all day long, 'Oh, you're going to become a painter like your father.'" Instead, she decided to concentrate on fashion, and studied jewelry design in France.

## Begins Designing for Yves St. Laurent

By the time she was a teenager, Picasso had already made her mark on the French fashion scene. She wore unusual, trendsetting clothes that she often bought in flea markets or antique stores. One of Picasso's friends at the time was the famous fashion designer Yves St. Laurent. In 1969 he asked her to design jewelry for his fashion show that year. Her creations began to be noticed, and soon she was asked to design bold pieces of costume jewelry for use in films and in stage plays.

Picasso stopped designing for a while after her father's death in 1973. She spent time arranging his estate. She also helped develop a new museum in his honor in Paris, the Musée Picasso. After meeting the Argentine playwright Rafael Lopez-Cambil, Picasso began to work again, designing costumes and sets for his productions. Their business relationship soon became personal and they married in 1978. Lopez-Cambil left the theater to become his wife's business partner.

According to Picasso, she provides the creative inspiration while her husband maps out the business plan. "I'm not disciplined at all," she admitted to an interviewer from *Harper's Bazaar.* "I'm very messy, yet I manage to do a great deal. I'm a terrible businesswoman, but Rafael, as a playwright, can envision all the parts and how to make them work together."

## Expands Her Design Line

In 1980 Picasso designed her first collection of fine jewelry for Tiffany & Company in New York City. Her creations were chunky, large, bright, and expensive. She framed brilliant gems in blocks of gold, or hung large stones or pendants from simple cords. Her "hugs and kisses" jewelry (stylized Os and Xs in gold and silver) continue to be especially popular. They are often copied by other designers. Prices for Picasso's jewelry range from the low hundreds to a half million dollars.

Picasso introduced her own fragrance, called Paloma, in 1984. This was a natural move, since her grandfather, Emile Gilot, was a chemist and perfume manufacturer. Her scent took months to define, and she designed the packaging herself. The bottle is circle-shaped, and the surrounding red and black box is as bold and bright as some of Picasso's jewelry.

Picasso's face is familiar to many people because she often models her own fashions in full-page, glossy magazine ads. She makes a strong impression with her pale skin, dark hair, and deep-set, expressive eyes. Her looks are enhanced further by her own trademark deep red lipstick (only one color is available—*Mon Rouge*).

## Leads a Jet-Set Life

Since creating her perfume, Picasso has added accessories to her line of products.

Paloma Picasso. *Reproduced by permission of AP/Wide World Photos.*

They include leather handbags, scarves, cosmetics, china, bathroom tiles, fabrics, and wallpaper. Her company has offices in New York, and stores in Paris and Tokyo. She travels regularly to Italy, where many of her products are made. To ease her busy life, Picasso speeds around the world in the supersonic Concorde jet. Her schedule is computerized, and she keeps a fax machine handy to send design ideas to her office.

Despite her hectic life, Picasso makes time to volunteer for a variety of Hispanic organizations. She devotes whatever time she can to help the fight against AIDS (Acquired Immune Deficiency Syndrome). Picasso tries to live by one simple rule: "The most important thing is to know yourself," she told Estrada. "You should always be the same person. Style is how you conduct yourself, the silly things you do as well as everything else."

## For More Information

*Harper's Bazaar,* December 1989, pp. 144–50; January 1991, pp. 123–26.
*Hispanic,* December 1988, pp. 28–33.
*House Beautiful,* March 1992, pp. 74–77.
*Vogue,* January 1990, pp. 190–97.

# James Plunkett

Former professional football player
Born December 5, 1947, San Jose, California

*"When a quarterback has been around, booed, cheered, and benched, he can feel good. He has lasted. Because every lasting quarterback experiences all of that in some order."*

**P**erhaps better than anyone in professional sports, James William ("Jim") Plunkett has known the joy of victory and the agony of defeat. After a spectacular college career, he was named the National Football League's Rookie of the Year in 1971. Over the next few years, however, his career began to fall apart. He was injured several times and was traded. But Plunkett did not waver. He fought back to win the starting quarterback position with another team, eventually leading them to two Super Bowl victories. Plunkett explained to Tom Callahan in *Time,* "When a quarterback has been around, booed, cheered, and benched, he can feel good. He has lasted. Because every lasting quarterback experiences all of that in some order."

Plunkett was born in 1947 in San Jose, California. He was the youngest child and only son of blind Mexican American parents, William and Carmen Plunkett. His father managed a newsstand in San Jose, and the young Plunkett helped with family finances by selling newspapers and working as a grocery clerk and gas station attendant. Even in grade school, it was apparent that he was a great athlete. By junior high, he was a standout player in baseball, basketball, wrestling, and track.

Plunkett led his high school team to championships and was offered a number of college football scholarships. He chose to attend Stanford University because it was close to home. He majored in political science and maintained a B average while setting records on the football field. During his junior year he threw passes for 2,671 yards and 20 touchdowns. He was named to the Associated Press's All-American second team, and won the Voit Memorial Trophy as the Pacific Athletic Conference's outstanding player.

## Wins Heisman Trophy

During Plunkett's senior year at Stanford, he became the first major college football player to surpass 7,000 yards on offense, setting the National Collegiate Athletic Association's career total offense mark. He led his team to victory in the Rose Bowl championship game on New Year's Day. At the end of that season, he won the Heisman Memorial Trophy, an annual award given to the best college football player in the United States.

After graduating from Stanford in 1971, Plunkett became the first pick in the National Football League (NFL) draft. He was chosen by the New England Patriots. He continued his spectacular play that first season, passing for 2,158 yards and 19 touchdowns. Even though the Patriots did not advance to postseason play, Plunkett capped off the season with the NFL Rookie of the Year award.

## Career Spirals Downward

Then the bottom fell out. The Patriots were a weak team with an even weaker offensive line. Plunkett received no protection in the pocket and was battered by defensive linemen. Between 1972 and 1974, he was sacked 97 times. He underwent several knee and shoulder operations and lost his confidence. "The second year was miserable," he told Callahan. "I had never been on a losing team in my life, or experienced such negativism all around me." After Plunkett led the Patriots to a 3–11 season in 1975, the team lost its confidence in him. He was traded to the San Francisco 49ers.

Plunkett was pleased with the trade, as he was now closer to his recently widowed mother. His situation with the 49ers, however, soon proved worse than it was with the Patriots. In a 1978 preseason game, he attempted 11 passes, completing none. San Francisco released him. "That's when I thought I was done," he explained to Rick Telander of *Sports Illustrated*. "I didn't think that I could play the game anymore."

Plunkett contemplated quitting the game he had excelled at his whole life, but his competitive drive was too strong. In 1978 he

James Plunkett. *Reproduced by permission of Corbis Corporation (Bellevue).*

joined the Oakland (now Los Angeles) Raiders as a free agent. He spent the next two years sitting on the bench, letting both his injuries and his confidence heal.

## Comeback of the Year

In the fifth game of the 1980 season, starting Raiders quarterback Dan Pastorini suffered a broken leg. Plunkett assumed control of the team and led it to victory throughout the rest of the season. He then guided the Raiders to victory in the 1981 Super Bowl. He was named the Super Bowl's Most Valuable Player and the NFL's 1980 Comeback Player of the Year.

Injured the following season, Plunkett lost his starting quarterback position.

Again, he was forced to sit on the bench. Once again, he fought back. In 1983 he regained the quarterback spot and guided the Raiders to another successful season. In Super Bowl XVIII, he led the Raiders in a 38–9 blowout of the Washington Redskins. For Plunkett, it was the best season of his career: 230 completions for 1,935 yards and 20 touchdowns.

Injuries sidelined Plunkett over the next few years, and he was never able to recover. His football career came to an end when the Raiders released him in August 1988. Now retired, Plunkett passed for a total of 25,882 yards and 164 touchdowns during his long and inspiring career.

## For More Information

Buck, Ray, *Jim Plunkett, the Comeback Kid,* Children's Press, 1984.

Plunkett, Jim, *The Jim Plunkett Story: The Saga of a Man Who Came Back,* Arbor House, 1981.

*Sports Illustrated,* January 24, 1984, pp. 44–49.

*Time,* December 26, 1983, p. 78.

# Juan Ponce de León

Spanish explorer
Born 1460, Santervas de Campos, Spain
Died July 1521, Havana, Cuba

*"Beneath this stone repose the bones of the valiant Lion whose deeds surpassed the greatness of his name."—Inscription on gravestone*

J uan Ponce de León was the first European to visit Florida and explore its coastline. He is also remembered for his exploration and subsequent appointment as governor of Puerto Rico. Although a legend claims that he came to the New World in search of the mythical "fountain of youth," it is more likely that Ponce de León—like most Spanish explorers—came looking for gold and other riches.

Born in 1460 into a poor but noble family in Spain, Ponce de León spent his boyhood as a page (a young person in training) to a powerful nobleman. During adolescence, he began his military education. He later fought with the Spanish army against the Moors (Muslims) in southern Spain. His bravery led to an assignment to travel with Christopher Columbus on his second voyage to the New World in 1493.

In 1502 Ponce de León traveled to Hispaniola (the Caribbean island presently occupied by the Dominican Republic and Haiti). In 1504 he helped stop a revolt by Native Americans in the province of Higuey, on the eastern part of the island. As a reward, King Ferdinand of Spain made him governor of Higuey.

A few years later, a Native American from the neighboring island of Borinquen (later renamed Puerto Rico by the Spanish) arrived in Higuey with a large nugget of gold. The Spanish were always hoping to find the precious metal, and Ponce de León immediately led an expedition to investigate the island. His army conquered the island, and he was named governor of the new Spanish possession of Puerto Rico.

## The "Fountain of Youth"

Ponce de León was removed from this appointment in 1511 when Diego Columbus (the son of Christopher) was given authority over all of Spain's possessions in the Caribbean. By this time, Ponce de León was a wealthy man and accepted his loss of power calmly. Having heard stories of a rich island called Bimini just north of Cuba, he sought the right to find and settle the island. Bimini supposedly contained a mysterious spring that restored youth to all who drank its waters. Most historians don't believe Ponce de León actually believed the myth. Many stories, legends, and romantic tales, however, have persisted about his quest for the spring. It is more likely that Ponce de León was simply searching for more wealth in the New World.

In 1513 Ponce de León left Puerto Rico with three ships and sailed north to San Salvador. Hunting for Bimini, he and his men moved on until they sighted land. When they went ashore, Ponce de León named the place *Florida* ("flowery" in Spanish). It is unclear whether he chose this name because of the colorful beauty of the land, or because it was the feast of Easter, which is *la pascua florida* in Spanish. In the name of King Ferdinand, he took possession of the new land near the present-day city of St. Augustine on the eastern coast of Florida.

## Discovers Gulf Stream

Ponce de León's expedition then headed south, but its boats were slowed by a heavy current. This was the Gulf Stream. The discovery of this strong current opened a new route for Spanish travel from the Caribbean to North America. The Spanish ships

Juan Ponce de León. *Reproduced by permission of Corbis Corporation (Bellevue).*

dropped anchor at points along the shore, but several unfriendly encounters with Native Americans encouraged Ponce de León to continue on. He and his men followed the shoreline around the southern tip of Florida and past the Florida Keys. Ponce de León then came upon a group of islands where he and his men captured 170 turtles. As a result, he named the islands *Tortugas* ("turtles" in Spanish). This small group of islands are presently known as the Dry Tortugas.

The expedition sailed north along the Gulf coast of Florida as far as Sanibel Island, then turned and headed back toward Cuba. Ponce de León sent one ship on in search of Bimini. That ship reached Andros Island in the present-day Bahamas. Upon rejoining Ponce de León, that ship's navigator admitted he found no "fountain of youth."

Ponce de León returned to Puerto Rico where he was again involved in settling Native American rebellions. After restoring order, he sailed back to Spain where King Ferdinand rewarded him for his explorations by naming him Captain General. He was then ordered to continue his search for Bimini. The king also commanded him to start a settlement on Florida, which the Spanish still believed was an island.

### Fatally Wounded by Native Americans

Ponce de León returned to Puerto Rico where he stayed five years before setting out on a final adventure. In 1521 he undertook a second journey to find Bimini with two ships, about two hundred men, fifty horses, and many domestic animals. Included in his group were several priests to help spread Christianity among the native people. After landing on the west coast of Florida, the group was immediately attacked by Native Americans. Ponce de León was wounded and taken back to his ship, which then sailed to Cuba. There Ponce de León died in July 1521. His body was shipped to Puerto Rico for burial.

Ponce de León died without really knowing the importance of his discoveries. The fearless warrior and explorer was laid to rest under the alter in a San Juan church. Today, many places in Puerto Rico and Florida bear his name. The inscription on his gravestone reads, "Beneath this stone repose the bones of the valiant Lion (*León* is "lion" in Spanish) whose deeds surpassed the greatness of his name."

## For More Information

Blassingame, Wyatt, *Ponce de León*, Chelsea House, 1991.

*Hispanic,* December 1990, p. 54.

King, Ethel M., *The Fountain of Youth and Juan Ponce de León,* T. Guaus' Sons, 1963.

Peck, Douglas T., *Ponce de León and the Discovery of Florida: The Man, the Myth, and the Truth,* Pogo Press, 1993.

# Tito Puente

Musician
Born April 20, 1923, New York, New York
Died May 31, 2000, New York, New York

*"I don't like titles. If you're called the king of something—the King of Boogaloo or the King of Rock—once the music dies, then the king dies, too."*

For years, Tito Puente has been known as *El Rey*—the King. He would rather be known as a regular musician. "I don't like titles," he told Larry Birnbaum in *Down Beat.* "If you're called the king of something—the King of Boogaloo or the King of Rock—once the music dies, then the king dies, too." Puente's reign as the

"King of Latin Music," however, is well assured. His career as a bandleader, composer, and percussionist spanned almost fifty years, during which time he recorded over one hundred albums—a feat unmatched in the music industry. Sadly, the King did not live as long as his music.

Puente was born Ernest Anthony Puente, Jr., in 1923 in the Spanish Harlem section of New York City. His parents, Ernest Anthony and Ercilia Puente, had immigrated to the United States from Puerto Rico just a few years before. From a young age, Puente knew he wanted to be a musician: "I was always banging on cans and boxes," he told Birnbaum. His musical education started with piano lessons. After five years, he began taking trap drum lessons at the New York School of Music. In addition to his music classes, Puente received formal training in dance.

Not all of Puente's musical influences and training came from a classroom. While growing up, he listened for hours to the music of big band leaders such as Artie Shaw, Duke Ellington, and Benny Goodman. When he was older, his father took him to weekend dances, where he sat in with various bands. He especially enjoyed accompanying the new and innovative Latin bands, whose music was based on Afro-Cuban rhythms. During his apprenticeship, Puente learned to play the timbales—a pair of tuned, open-bottomed drums played with sticks. They were to become the instrument of his career.

## Influenced by Cuban Music

At the age of fifteen, Puente dropped out of high school and traveled to Miami Beach

Tito Puente. *Reproduced by permission of AP/Wide World Photos.*

to play with a Latin band. At the time, travel to Cuba from the United States was allowed, and Puente went there often. "I picked up a lot of music, listened a lot to the radio, and met a lot of musicians," he related in the interview with Birnbaum. After a few years, he traveled back to New York City to play with Latin bands, which were quickly gaining popularity there.

During World War II, Puente served three years in the U.S. Navy aboard an aircraft carrier. When he could, he jammed with other musicians on the ship. He also taught himself how to play the saxophone during his off-hours. After his discharge in 1945, he enrolled in the prestigious Juilliard School of Music in New York City on the G.I. Bill (money given by the U.S. government to members of the military to attend school). While at Juilliard, Puente studied composition and orchestration. The leading Latin orchestras of that time soon began to play his compositions and arrangements. In 1949 he formed his own orchestra, the Picadilly Boys.

## Leads the Mambo Craze

In the late 1940s and early 1950s, a new type of dance music swept across the eastern United States. It combined Latin beats with elements of American jazz and would later evolve into a musical form known as *salsa*. (Puente was a leader in the creation of the salsa sound, which reached new heights in the 1970s after fusing with harder-edged rock sounds.) In the 1950s, the early form of this rich musical blend was being played in ballrooms in big cities throughout the United States, where people danced the *mambo*, a rhythmic Cuban dance set to horns and various percussive instruments. Puente's orchestra, with its shrill horn section and his heavy drums, became the greatest mambo group in the nation. Its home was the famed Palladium Ballroom in New York City, a place where everyone danced together, regardless of ethnicity. "The place was a big melting pot," Puente recalled in an interview with Lorenzo Chavez for *Hispanic*. "Jews, Italians, Irish, Blacks, Puerto Ricans, Cubans, you name it. Everyone was equal under the roof of the Palladium."

Puente and his orchestra always tried to bring fresh music to their listeners. When new compositions came out of Cuba, Puente arranged them to fit his group's style. Aside from playing in ballrooms across the country, the orchestra also played in jazz clubs.

"I was always trying to find a marriage between Latin music and jazz," Puente told Birnbaum. "I was trying to play jazz but not lose the Latin-American authenticity." Over the years, Puente has recorded with such jazz greats as Lionel Hampton, Woody Herman, and Dizzy Gillespie.

In the late 1950s another blend of musical styles was also arising—rock 'n' roll. It soon changed national music tastes, and the popularity of Latin dance music declined. Throughout the 1960s, Latin orchestras disbanded or switched to playing other musical styles. Even though he didn't have the audience he once had, Puente continued to play his trademark music in clubs and record album after album during this period.

## Rocker Revives His Career

Puente's career received a boost in 1970 when rocker **Carlos Santana** (see entry) and his band recorded "Oye Como Va," one of Puente's early compositions. The song became a hit for Santana. In the process, it also introduced Puente and his Latin jazz to a whole new audience. Sales of his albums increased and his popularity grew. In 1978, for his recording *Homenaje a Beny More,* he was given his first of his five Grammy Awards, the music industry's highest honor. The next year, President Jimmy Carter invited Puente and his group to perform at the White House. It was the first time a Latin orchestra had played before a U.S. president.

Since that time, Puente's public exposure has increased steadily. In 1990 he was awarded a star on the Hollywood Walk of Fame, joining a select list of other Hispanics so honored by the entertainment industry. In addition, he has recorded with a variety of pop stars and other musicians, and has made guest appearances on the large and small screens. In 1992 he played a small role in *The Mambo Kings,* the film adaptation of **Oscar Hijuelos**'s Pulitzer Prize-winning book (see entry). Puente also served as the film's musical director.

Puente's musical talent and warm, outgoing personality have made him a favorite among young and old. He has been featured on the popular television sitcom the *Bill Cosby Show,* in a Coca-Cola commercial, and even a 1995 episode of *The Simpsons.* Burger King has used Puente's tune "I Like It like That" in their ads, and he has hosted his own show on Spanish-language television. At the closing ceremony following the 1996 Olympic games in Atlanta, Puente joined B. B. King, Wynton Marsalis, Stevie Wonder, and **Gloria Estefan** in an extraordinary finale. Puente's joyous participation in this event helped to rekindle everyone's spirits and proved that Latin music had truly achieved international recognition. Puente was a mentor to many aspiring young musicians, among them **Marc Anthony** (see entries) and India.

As Puente's celebrity status grew, so did his generosity and social concern. In 1989 he staged a benefit concert that raised $150,000 to help Puerto Rican victims of Hurricane Hugo. He also started the Tito Puente Scholarship Fund at Juilliard. The fund makes it possible for minority students in New York City to receive a musical education. Puente explained to Birnbaum that he started the fund to give "a young Latin percussionist an incentive to learn how to read music.... It's not only what you learn in the streets—you've really got to go and study."

On May 31, 2000, at the age of seventy-seven, Tito Puente died from complications after open heart surgery. Thousands lined up outside the funeral home in Manhattan for his funeral. Salsa legend Celia Cruz, who had known Puente since the 1950s, spoke of her grief and the loss to the music world in a *Billboard* tribute: "Our world is in mourning because one of the souls of Latino music has died."

## For More Information

*Américas,* November/December 1990, pp. 56–57.
Burr, Ramior, "Puente's Life, Artistry Praised by Admirers," *Billboard,* June 17, 2000, p. 5.
*Down Beat,* January 1984, pp. 27–29+; May 1991, pp. 20–21.
*Hispanic,* March 1991, pp. 46–48.
Loza, Steven Joseph. *Tito Puente and the Making of Latin Music,* Urbana: University of Illinois Press, 1999.
*New York,* June 15, 1992, pp. 10A–13A.
*Village Voice,* March 14, 1977, p. 39.

# Anthony Quinn

Actor, artist
Born April 21, 1915, Chihuahua, Mexico
Died June 3, 2001, Boston, Massachusetts

*"His Latin looks were not of the soft, gleaming, sensuous kind—more like the glare of the bandido who would kill you for making fun of him."—David Denby,* Premiere

In the 1940s and 1950s, Anthony Quinn made his mark in Hollywood playing Latin roles in such movies as *Viva Zapata!*, the 1952 film about the Mexican revolutionary **Emiliano Zapata** (see entry). Since that time, however, Quinn has become one of the few but increasing number of Hispanic actors whose careers have not been limited to Hispanic roles. His most famous role came in the 1964 film *Zorba the Greek*, in which he played the title character. He also played a biblical character in *Barrabas* (1961), an Arab in *Lawrence of Arabia* (1962), and a Russian pope in *The Shoes of the Fisherman* (1968).

Quinn was born in the Mexican state of Chihuahua in 1915. At that time, the country was in the grips of the Mexican Revolution. To avoid the conflict, Quinn's Mexican mother and Irish Mexican father smuggled him to the United States as an infant. When he was nine, his father was killed in an automobile accident. The young Quinn then had to help support his mother and younger sister. He worked an assortment of jobs, including custodian, boxer, and migrant farm worker. Unable to finish his high school education, he continued to learn through reading and travel.

## Begins Acting During the Depression

During the Great Depression (a period in the 1930s when the nation suffered from an extremely slow economy and widespread unemployment), Quinn joined a Federal Theater Project. This program was one of many sponsored by the government at the time to help people find work. While involved with the project, Quinn came to realize his love for acting. He then polished his acting skills by working with local theater groups. In 1937 he made his motion picture debut, playing a Native American in *The Plainsman,* directed by the famous filmmaker Cecil B. DeMille.

Quinn then married Katherine DeMille, the filmmaker's adopted daughter. For the next ten years he managed to find steady work in supporting roles portraying Native Americans, Latin lovers, Mexican villains, and other ethnic types. In 1947 he became a U.S. citizen. That same year he made his Broadway (New York) stage debut.

## Award-Winning Roles

In 1952 Quinn finally achieved star status with his role in *Viva Zapata!* The screenplay was written by Nobel Prize-winning novelist John Steinbeck. The film presents the life of Emiliano Zapata as he leads the peasant revolt in Mexico beginning in 1910. Marlon Brando portrayed Zapata while Quinn portrayed Zapata's brother, Eufemio Zapata. Quinn's flawless performance in the film earned him an Academy Award in 1952 for best supporting actor.

At that time, Hollywood often cast Hispanic actors for their leading-man looks, but Quinn was cast for his acting ability. "[His] Latin looks were not of the soft, gleaming, sensuous kind—more like the glare of the bandido who would kill you for making fun of him," David Denby wrote in *Premiere.*

In 1956 Quinn received his second Academy Award for a best supporting actor performance in *Lust for Life.* The absorbing film biography presents the life of Vincent van Gogh from his first paintings to his death. Kirk Douglas played the tortured Dutch painter in the film. Quinn gave a stunning performance as the French painter Paul Gauguin.

## Portrays Zorba

Perhaps Quinn's best-known film was *Zorba the Greek.* He seemed well-suited to the role of a crude but sensitive Greek peasant—a simple, intelligent man who accepts life's ups and downs and makes the most of them. Based on the novel by Nikolai Kazantzakis, the film follows the talkative, outgoing Zorba as he meets a young English writer. During the course of the film, Zorba teaches the serious young man to accept and enjoy the simple things in life. In a climactic and symbolic scene, the two link arms and do a boisterous peasant dance on the beach. Quinn's performance was again recognized by Hollywood: he received an Academy Award nomination for best actor in 1965.

Quinn acted in more than one hundred films. Between 1983 and 1986, he toured the country in a musical version of *Zorba.* After undegoing successful bypass heart surgery in 1990, he continued to work. In the early 1990s he has starred in such notable films as *Revenge,* with Kevin Costner, and *The Last Action Hero,* with Arnold Schwarzenegger.

Like some of the characters he played, Quinn lived an expansive life. He married three times, marrying his third wife in 1997. He had two children with her while in his eighties, and was the father of eleven other children, four of them out of wedlock. Along with acting, he was an accomplished

Anthony Quinn. *Reproduced by permission of AP/Wide World Photos.*

painter and sculptor with several very successful one-man exhibitions of his work. In 1972 he published his autobiography, *The Original Sin.*

Quinn died in a Boston hospital of respiratory failure on June 3, 2001. He was eighty-six years old.

## For More Information

Amdur, Melissa, *Anthony Quinn,* Chelsea House, 1993.

"The Mighty Quinn: The Late Actor Had Many Faces, and a Lust for Life," Entertainment Weekly, June 15, 2001, p.10.

"Mighty Quinn: Macho Actor Anthony Quinn Made Passion His Compass," *People Weekly,* June 18, 2001, p. 92.

*People,* September 6, 1993, pp. 80.

*Premiere,* September 1992, pp. 43–45.
Quinn, Anthony, *The Original Sin: A Self-Portrait,*
Little, Brown, 1972.

# Diego Rivera

Artist
Born December 8, 1886, Guanajuato, Mexico
Died November 24, 1957, San Angel, Mexico

*"Rivera devoted his artistic talents to the portrayal of injustice toward the workers of Mexico and other countries."*

**D**iego Rivera was a famous Mexican painter whose large-scale, intricate murals tell the history of his people. Combining symbols of his own strong political beliefs with unmistakable elements of folk art, Rivera created works that champion the cause of struggling workers throughout the world. Although some of his paintings were destroyed by people who disagreed with his politics, most of his works remain for the enjoyment and education of future generations of artists and art lovers.

Rivera was born in 1886 in the city of Guanajuato, located almost two hundred miles northwest of Mexico City. His parents, Maria and Diego Rivera, had invested much of their money in the silver mines surrounding Guanajuato, but the mines had long since given up all their silver. Left with little money, Rivera's father found work as a grade school teacher and then as a local government official.

Rivera's artistic talent surfaced early. By the age of three, he was drawing all over the house—on furniture, on walls, in record books, and on any loose papers. To stop his son from marking up the entire house, the elder Rivera put canvases on the walls of a small room in their home. Young Diego was free to draw on anything in his very first artistic studio.

While Rivera was growing up, Mexico was governed by Porfirio Diaz. Under his tyrannical rule, the rich land owners in Mexico prospered while the poor and the lower classes suffered. Rivera's father started a weekly newspaper in Guanajuato that called attention to the plight of the poor. In turn, the newspaper came to the attention of inhabitants of Guanajuato who were loyal to Diaz, and the Rivera family was forced to move to Mexico City in 1893.

## Inspired by Mexican Folk Art

A year later, Rivera began his education. His mother was a devout Catholic and insisted he attend a parochial school. Although he did not share his mother's religious convictions, Rivera did extremely well in the school, graduating with honors in 1898. In addition, for two years he took art classes during the evenings at the famous Academy of San Carlos. After his graduation from grammar school, he decided to attend the academy full time. Here he improved his technique, learning the basic laws of drawing; he also learned and adhered to the strict rules of classical European art. Rivera's own artistic tastes, however, were drawn more to the free-flowing native designs and folk art of Mexico.

In 1903 Rivera took part in a student protest against the Diaz government. All the students involved were expelled from the Academy of San Carlos and then later readmitted, but Rivera never returned. He had been unhappy with the academy's insistence on an almost photographic realism in the students' work. Wandering the countryside, he painted and drew what he saw. Although he had very little confidence in his work, others quickly recognized his talent.

In 1907—with money from sales of his works and from admirers like Teodoro A. Dehesa, the governor of the Mexican state of Vera Cruz—Rivera sailed to Europe to study the works of the artistic masters. He traveled to Spain, Belgium, Holland, England, and Italy before finally settling in Paris. For the first time in his life, he read a vast number of books. The writings of Karl Marx, the Prussian social philosopher whose ideas led to the development of communism, made a lifelong impression on him. (Communism is a political theory based on the elimination of private ownership of property and the formation of a classless society.) Among artists, Rivera was greatly influenced by the works of Paul Cézanne of France, and Francisco Goya and El Greco, both of Spain. He copied their works, learning their choice of color and line. Throughout his travels in Europe, however, his love of Mexico remained evident in his own works.

## Begins His Mexican Murals

In 1922 Alvaro Obregón, then president of Mexico, encouraged Rivera to return to his homeland to participate in a national popular art movement. Government leaders invited

Diego Rivera. *Reproduced by permission of AP/Wide World Photos.*

him to paint murals on many public buildings. These murals allowed Rivera a chance to depict the new ideas that he had developed in Europe about the history and the social struggles of Mexicans. He pictured the cruelties of the Spanish conquistadors, the heroes of the Mexican Revolution, the sorry state of the nation's lower-class farm workers (commonly referred to as "the peasantry"), and the need for radical changes in society.

Rivera then spent some time in the mid-1920s traveling throughout the rural areas of Mexico. He studied the native history, life, and culture of his country. His work developed a bold, earthy warmth and a simple folk style that was appropriate for his subjects. Rivera's paintings did not demean the peasants, but gave them a proud and

Rivera standing on a scaffold before his mural at the Hotel Reforma in Mexico in 1936. *Reproduced by permission of AP/Wide World Photos.*

intelligent air. Filled with religious and historical imagery, his paintings told fascinating stories. Most art critics agree that Rivera created his greatest works during this period. In 1926, at the Agricultural School in the city of Chapingo, he painted a mural on thirty panels that tells the story of Mexican land reform and depicts scenes of a better society where common laborers, the middle class, and government come together.

During the 1930s Rivera was invited to produce work in the United States. Officials in several American cities asked him to paint murals on the walls of their public buildings. In 1931 he completed *Allegory of California,* a 30-foot-high mural at the San Francisco Stock Exchange. The following year, he painted a fascinating mural depicting the history of the automobile industry on the walls of the Garden Court in the Detroit Institute of Arts. After *Detroit Industry* was completed, some observers demanded that it be removed, saying it depicted automobile workers merely as part of the large machines. Workers in Detroit, however, defended the mural and it was saved.

## Rockefeller Mural Destroyed

Rivera's next piece met a sad fate. In 1932 the artist began work on a mural for the RCA Building in Rockefeller Center in New York City. Even before the painting was completed, it created controversy. New Yorkers were furious to see Rivera include in his mural of workers and leaders a portrait of Vladimir Lenin, the Russian revolutionary and founder of the Soviet Union. The Rockefeller family asked Rivera to remove Lenin's face, but he refused. Rivera was then dismissed from the project and the mural was destroyed. Undaunted, Rivera returned to Mexico City in 1934 and recreated the mural in the Palace of Fine Arts.

Rivera's work continued to create controversy, even in his own country. In 1948 his mural for the Del Prado Hotel in Mexico City caused a riot in the streets around the building. This time the anger was directed at a scroll in the mural that contained the words "God does not exist." Catholic students raided the hotel and damaged the work. The mural was eventually restored and in 1960 moved to the main lobby of the Del Prado.

Rivera continued to be artistically and politically active until his death from heart failure on November 24, 1957. He had devoted his artistic talents to the portrayal of injustice toward the workers of Mexico and other countries. His technique—mixing soft lines and earthen tones with sharp lines and harsh colors—had an enormous influence on art in Mexico and the United States in the twentieth century. Rivera's murals and paintings are carefully preserved wherever they have survived around the world.

## For More Information

Cockcroft, James, *Diego Rivera,* Chelsea House, 1991.

Detroit Institute of Arts Founders Society, *Diego Rivera: A Retrospective,* Norton, 1986.

Hargrove, Jim, *Diego Rivera: Mexican Muralist,* Children's Press, 1990.

Rivera, Diego, *My Art, My Life,* Citadel Press, 1960.

Wolfe, Bertram D., *The Fabulous Life of Diego Rivera,* Stein and Day, 1960.

# Geraldo Rivera

Broadcast journalist, talk-show host
Born July 4, 1943, New York, New York

*"I invented sleaze.... But I'm also the guy who democratized the news-gathering process in this country. I brought passion and compassion to journalism."*

Geraldo Rivera is one of the most controversial television journalists in the business. He has worked as a lawyer, reporter, writer, and talk-show host. Critics question his objectivity and unorthodox style of reporting. Even so, Rivera's programs have drawn large audiences, making him one of the most visible and successful Hispanics in the media and entertainment field.

Rivera was born in 1943 in New York City to Cruz Rivera and Lilly Friedman. As the son of a Puerto Rican father and Jewish mother, Rivera had a difficult time handling his two distinct identities while he was growing up. He was not a great student in high school—he was more interested in sports and street gangs. Rivera spent two years in the U.S. Merchant Marine Corps before attending college.

When Rivera attended the University of Arizona, he felt especially isolated. He tried to fit in with the other students, but was never accepted. He even tried to hide his ethnic identity, going by the name Jerry Rivers. Still, he was not accepted because of the way he looked and spoke.

After graduating from the University of Arizona, Rivera studied law at Brooklyn Law School. He eventually received his law degree from the University of Pennsylvania. He then focused on helping the poor. He worked for the Harlem Assertion of Rights and for the Community Action for Legal Services. For a short while he represented a gang of Spanish-speaking youths called the Young Lords. He convinced the gang to turn their energy away from fighting and violence to more useful projects such as organizing day care centers. However, Rivera grew restless with the slow process of law and turned to a flashier job.

## Switches From Law to Journalism

In 1970 Rivera took advantage of new minority hiring policies and applied for a job as a newscaster with a television station in New York City. For three months he studied journalism intensively at Columbia University's Graduate School of Journalism. Rivera then made his debut on the station's *Eyewitness News* program. As a rookie reporter he was assigned to routine stories such as fashion shows and charity functions.

One day, while on the way to cover a feature story, he encountered a drug addict who was threatening to jump from a rooftop. Rivera tape-recorded a dramatic and emotional plea for help from the junkie's brother while the camera crew filmed the entire event. The story was aired on the evening news. The gripping story captured the attention of the station's producers, and Rivera was assigned more serious stories afterward.

Rivera's popularity grew quickly, especially among young viewers, and he received honors and awards for his work. Rivera gained national publicity for his 1972 news story, "Willowbrook: A Report on How It Is and Why It Doesn't Have To Be That Way." He had smuggled a camera crew into the Willowbrook State School for the Mentally Retarded in New York to expose the terrible conditions in which the patients lived. The report was emotional and heartbreaking, and catapulted Rivera to celebrity.

Reaction was strong to the Willowbrook story. Donations poured in, and Rivera helped create a fund-raising project to benefit mentally disabled people. He volunteered many hours working for the group he named "One-to-One." Today he is chairman of the association.

Rivera explained his reasons for donating his time and effort to helping others in an article he wrote for *Esquire:* "I love being a newsman. Given enormous power and responsibility by the network, I have tried to use my position to make the world a slightly better place.... Sometimes the reporter has to become involved in helping society change the things he is complaining about."

## Reporting Style Is Aggressive and Subjective

This desire to change the world has earned Rivera both praise and criticism. He has been accused of exaggerating facts and distorting the news he reports. Also, he has been criticized for having become too involved in the stories he reports. While interviewing people, he often reacts with emotion and tears, drawing attention toward

Geraldo Rivera. *Reproduced by permission of AP/Wide World Photos.*

himself. Many in the national news establishment are embarrassed and angered by his lack of objectivity. They say he injects his own opinions into stories, which prevents him from presenting issues fairly.

Rivera disagrees with his critics' ideas of what makes a good newsperson. For him, subjectivity means caring. "Soul is the missing ingredient in television journalism," he wrote in a *TV Guide* article. "Coolness has become synonymous with objectivity, aloofness with professionalism. [Network news] is seldom courageous or involved and almost never passionate."

During the 1970s and early 1980s, Rivera traveled the globe aggressively for ABC News, covering many political and social events that have shaped our world. He gave on-site reports from such areas as war-torn Afghanistan and the crime-ridden streets of Guatemala. In 1983 he covered the Israeli-Palestinian conflict from Tripoli in northwest Lebanon. While sitting safely in a car, Rivera and his crew saw an explosion wound a young Palestinian soldier. Rivera raced from the car, pulled the soldier to safety, tended his wound, then helped him into a nearby ambulance. Although the story aired on the evening news, network executives cut Rivera out of the tape that was shown.

The incident soured the relationship between Rivera and executives at ABC. Over the next two years, the argument over his brand of personal journalism worsened. Finally, in 1985, ABC fired him.

## The Opening of Al Capone's Vault

Rivera soon found that being let go was the best thing that could have happened to his career. In 1986 he began producing and hosting a series of news specials. The first was called *The Mystery of Al Capone's Vault*. After a two-hour buildup, nothing more than a few dusty bottles were discovered in the late mobster's vault. Although Rivera was embarrassed by the incident, a huge audience had watched the live TV show, leading to calls for him to lead other specials.

In 1987 Rivera launched his hour-long talk show, *Geraldo*. The show typically focuses on offbeat, even lurid topics. *Geraldo* earns the same praise and criticism that Rivera's work has always attracted. In 1988, during a show titled "Teen Hatemongers," a violent fight broke out between the guests—white racists and black activists. Fists, bodies, and chairs flew across the stage. Even members of the audience joined in. Rivera attempted to calm the free-for-all, but received a broken nose when he was hit by a chair. Police were called in to subdue the crowd, and a dramatic, bloody Rivera concluded the show.

Critics called Rivera's work "tabloid" or "trash TV." Rivera simply pointed to his growing audiences, and insisted he was giving them useful information. "I invented sleaze.... But I'm also the guy who democratized the news-gathering process in this country," Rivera was quoted as saying in the *Detroit Free Press*. "I brought passion and compassion to journalism."

No matter how controversial the *Geraldo* show became, Rivera remained extremely popular with the public. He won seven Emmy Awards and the prestigious Peabody Award as well as many broadcast journalism citations and honorary doctorates.

Rivera came out with an autobiography in 1991. On the book's jacket, he cited a former NBC News president who said, "Geraldo Rivera should be arrested for exposing himself." To counter the remark, Rivera titled his book *Exposing Myself*. True to its title, the book provides a highly personal and sometimes shocking portrait of the complex and controversial television personality.

During the 1990s, Rivera made his way back from his King of Tabloid reputation and was once again perceived by the networks and by many viewers as a serious investigative journalist and reporter. His CNBC series *Rivera Live,* which explored court cases and legal matters was very successful. In 1997 Rivera was being wooed by the big networks when he signed a new six-year contract with NBC worth more than $30 million.

## War Correspondent Becomes the News Story

In the fall of 2001, Rivera left his prime time show on CNBC after seven years. He then joined the FOX News Channel in order to become a war correspondent in Afghanistan after the United States launched its war on terrorism there. He quickly created controversy by carrying a gun in Afghanistan, a rare occurrence among war correspondents, who prefer to draw a distinction between themselves and the soldiers around them. But the criticism Rivera drew for being armed was light compared to the scandal that followed. In a report from Afghanistan in December 2001, he gave a report in which, with his voice choked, he claimed to have been on "hallowed ground" where "friendly fire took so many of our, our men and the mujahedeen yesterday" (as quoted by the *Baltimore Sun*). As it happened, he was hundreds of miles from where the incident had occurred and his explanation for this when questioned did not add up. Rivera was recalled from Afghanistan later that month, and went on to Beirut, Lebanon, to report on the conflict between the Palestinians and the Israelis.

## For More Information

*Detroit Free Press,* September 19, 1994, p.
*Esquire,* April 1986.
Folkenflik, David, "Reports of War Draw Fire to Fox," *Baltimore Sun,* December 15, 2001,

SunSpot.net. Available at http://www.sunspot.net/entertainment/tv/bal-to.geraldo15dec15.story?coll=bal-artslife-tv (accessed June 21, 2002).
Rivera, Geraldo, *Exposing Myself,* Bantam, 1991.
*TV Guide,* April 18, 1987; March 26, 1988.

# Gloria Rodríguez

Founder and president of Avance Family Support and Educational Program
Born July 9, 1948, San Antonio, Texas

*"Children from a strong family [have] a better chance at surviving. Parents must be in the front line of preparing kids for success."*

Teaching parents how to raise their children was unheard of in 1973. Yet Gloria Rodríguez turned the idea into a career by providing low-income Hispanic mothers in Texas with basic parenting skills. As founder and director of Avance (Spanish for "advance"), Rodríguez has helped thousands of women break the cycle of poverty, ignorance, and abuse through classes and special programs. Avance is considered a unique national success story among social service organizations in the United States.

Born in 1948, Rodríguez grew up in a poor Hispanic neighborhood in San Antonio, Texas. Her father, Julian Garza, died when she was two. Her mother, Lucy Villegas Salazar, was left to rear eight children alone. To help raise money for the family, Rodríguez and her sisters sold their mother's homemade jewelry. At age nine, Rodríguez got a job cleaning a neighbor's house. When she started high school, she worked as a clerk in a department store. Rodríguez excelled in school. A popular cheerleader and beauty queen, she graduated in 1967 with good grades.

Rodríguez wanted to be a teacher, but she knew she could not afford college. Her life changed when she was selected for a possible scholarship from Project Teacher Excellence. This government program was designed to give disadvantaged students a chance to study bilingual education. In exchange, the students chosen are expected to return to their communities to teach. Rodríguez competed against three hundred other students for the scholarship. She almost lost her chance when her high school principal wouldn't recommend her—he did not think she was "college material." Rodríguez persuaded the committee to give her a chance, and she set out to prove the principal wrong.

"I knew college would be difficult," Rodríguez explained to a reporter for the West Side Sun. "Other college students were better prepared academically and could express themselves better in the English language." To help get through the troubling times at school, Rodríguez relied on her deep religious faith. She credits her grandfather, who came to live with the family after her father died, with giving her this faith. "I went daily to the chapel to pray," she told the same reporter. "I vowed that if I did well, I would use my training to help others."

## Links Parenting to School Success

Rodríguez completed her bachelor of arts degree in elementary education and bilin-

gual education from Our Lady of the Lake University in 1970. Three years later she earned her master of education degree. She was then hired to be San Antonio's first bilingual teacher. Her first class was a group of thirty-five first graders labeled "problem learners." She found that her poor students had difficulties in Spanish as well as in English. She remembered that her own family was poor, yet it had managed to instill respect, independence, and determination in herself and her siblings.

"It was like a light bulb went on: it all starts with the family," Rodríguez told a reporter for the Dallas Morning News. "Children from a strong family [have] a better chance at surviving. Parents must be in the front line of preparing kids for success."

From then on, Rodríguez focused on educating parents. She believed that education begins at home—the first and most important teachers are parents. When she found out that a company was willing to fund a new education program called Avance in San Antonio, she went after the job. Rodríguez was immediately hired as the director. She set up her first program in the Mirasol Housing Projects, a few blocks from her childhood home.

## Survival Training for Families

Avance had humble beginnings. Rodríguez and three assistants went from door to door encouraging parents to take part in the program. A handful of skeptical women signed up. Almost all of them were high school dropouts and single mothers living on public assistance. Rodríguez discovered that family problems often started with overwhelming financial and social conditions. Many parents are under the stress of simply trying to survive. Sometimes they take their fear and despair out on their children.

Avance's nine-month program gives mothers and their preschool children a support system that many of them have never known. The parents and their children meet every week for three hours in a clean and friendly environment. While the children play in supervised groups, their mothers learn about child development, discipline techniques, problem-solving skills, nutrition, and safety. Together, parents and children take field trips, plant gardens, build friendships, and learn to communicate.

"This is a prevention program," Rodríguez told an interviewer for *Vista* magazine. "Before the 1970s, all treatment went to the child. But you can't separate the child from the environment, so you start with the family."

## Expands Avance Programs

Rodríguez persuaded area businesses, governments, and charities to contribute money to Avance. She expanded its programs to include prenatal (before birth) services for pregnant women and a Fatherhood Project similar to the mothers' classes. In addition, Rodríguez had Avance offer literacy (reading) programs and job placement services for parents.

In the three decades since Rodríguez founded Avance it has grown immensely, from one center to nine chapters with eighty family resource centers in south Texas, Kansas, and soon to be in California as well.

Gloria Rodríguez. *Reproduced courtesy of Dr. Gloria Rodríguez.*

The organization estimates that about seven thousand adults and children benefit from the project annually, people from families that have lived in poverty for generations.

In the early 2000s, Rodríguez reflected about the focus of the organization. The one special night for people in the Avance program is graduation night, which celebrates the achievement of a whole family. Rodríguez describes the event on the Avance Web site: "The parents walk across the stage with their children, who are dressed in caps and gowns. The fathers who go through our fatherhood program then walk with their wives and children; the parents get a certificate and the children get books. Finally, the graduates who have earned their GED walk across the stage, and the other parents get to see where they can go with the next level, how they can strengthen their family even further. We hardly have a dry eye in the house."

Rodríguez married engineer Salvador C. Rodríguez, Jr., in 1972. The couple has three children. Over the years, Rodríguez continued her own education, earning a doctorate degree in early childhood education from the University of Texas at Austin in 1991. She has received numerous honors and awards for her work, including the Temple Award for Creative Altruism from the National Institute of Noetic Science in 1993. Rodríguez has also been inducted into both the San Antonio and the Texas Halls of Fame.

## For More Information

Avance Web site. Available at http://www.aecf.org/familiescount/community.htm (accessed June 21, 2002).

*Business Week,* February 20, 1989, p. 151.

*Dallas Morning News,* February 16, 1992, p. 41A.

*Vista,* May 20, 1990, p. 16.

*West Side Sun* (San Antonio), August 30, 1979; October 5, 1989; May 16, 1991.

# Juan "Chi Chi" Rodríguez

Former professional golfer, philanthropist
Born October 23, 1935, Río Piedras, Puerto Rico

*"I just feel like I'm in heaven, the peace of God comes over me, when these kids touch me on the shoulder and say, 'Uncle Chi Chi.'"*

Juan "Chi Chi" Rodríguez is famous for his successful golf game and his entertaining attitude on the course. Fans love to follow the Puerto Rican senior player to witness his playing skills and to laugh at his jokes. His charitable efforts are equally impressive. He helps run a foundation for troubled children in Florida, contributes to a children's hospital in Puerto Rico, and gives golf clinics for underprivileged children.

Rodríguez was born in 1935 in Río Piedras, Puerto Rico, to Juan and Modesta Rodríguez. He grew up in poverty. His father was a laborer who worked in sugarcane fields and never earned more than $18 a week to support his family of six children. Once, when he had a heart attack, he was fired from his job. Rodríguez claims that his small size (5 feet 7 inches) is a result of childhood illnesses caused by poor nutrition.

While growing up, Rodríguez was more interested in sports than in school (he earned his childhood nickname from his hero, Puerto Rican baseball star Chi Chi Flores). Lacking the money to buy his own golf equipment, he took a job as a golf course caddy. For practice, he hit tin cans with a guava stick.

When he turned nineteen, Rodríguez enlisted in the U.S. Army. During his two-year service, he joined the army's golf team to keep up his skills. After returning to Puerto Rico, he worked as an orderly in a psychiatric clinic helping to care for the mentally ill. "It gave me more satisfaction than winning golf tournaments," Rodríguez related to Doris Lee McCoy of the *Saturday Evening Post*. "Of course, I wanted to do better in life, so I went into golf after that."

## Begins Professional Golfing Career

In 1957 Rodríguez got a job at the Dorado Beach Country Club and took lessons to improve his game. By 1960 he was good enough to join the Professional Golf Association (PGA). Three years later he won his first tournament, the Denver Open. He went on to enjoy a moderately successful, twenty-five-year career with the PGA, earning over one million dollars. His last tournament victory came in 1979. After that, his career went downhill, and he contemplated quitting. "Older players cannot compete with young guys," he explained to Ira Wolfman in *New Choices*. "The worst thing you can do is play and have someone feel sorry for you."

Rodríguez's career turned around—and real success happened—when he toured with the Senior PGA. In his second season in 1987, he set a record by winning seven tournaments. In just two years, he matched his lifetime earnings. By 1993 he had won twenty-one tournaments on the PGA Senior Tour. His earnings have now rocketed past the three million dollar mark. He was inducted into PGA's World Golf Hall of Fame in 1992.

After 1993 Rodríguez's health began to fail and his golf game suffered. In October 1998, Rodriguez had a heart attack just as he was about to play in a Senior PGA Tour event in California. After the heart attack he had surgery to clear a blocked artery and

Juan "Chi Chi" Rodríguez. *Reproduced by permission of the PGA Tour, Inc.*

recovered from what could have been a fatal condition.

## Devotes Life to Helping Children

Rodríguez still loves golf, but his real passion is working with the Chi Chi Rodríguez Youth Foundation in Florida. The foundation helps disadvantaged and troubled kids, ages five to fifteen. The kids receive free counseling and tutoring, and they participate in sporting activities. Rodríguez started the foundation in 1979 after he visited a Florida detention center and wanted to do something to help the young inmates. "Seeing those kids trapped like animals inside cells broke my heart," he told Sue Cronkite in *Life.*

Since the foundation's beginning, hundreds of children have benefited from its training. The governments of Nepal and Costa Rico have expressed an interest in expanding the Chi Chi Rodríguez Foundation to their countries. For his work, Rodríguez is lauded everywhere he goes. In 1986 he became the first athlete to receive the prestigious Horatio Alger Award for humanitarianism. Among many other awards, in 1997 he won the secretary of state's Hispanic Achievement Award and the International Network of Golf Award (the first "Chi Chi Rodriguez Humanitarian Award"), and in 2000 the Boys and Girls' Club of Florida Humanitarian of the Year Award.

Although Rodríguez is flattered by the praise he receives, his rewards for the work he does with the foundation come directly from the children. "I just feel like I'm in heaven," he told Tim Rosaforte of *Business Week,* "the peace of God comes over me, when these kids touch me on the shoulder and say, 'Uncle Chi Chi.'"

## For More Information

*Business Week,* February 10, 1992, pp. 53–58; February 8, 1993, pp. 71–77.

"Chi Chi Rodríguez," Sports Stars USA Web site. Available at http://www.sportsstarsusa.com/golf-speakers/rodriguez_chi_chi.html (accessed June 21, 2002).

"Juan 'Chi Chi' Rodríguez," Latino Legends in Sports. Available at http://www.latinosportslegends.com/chi-chi.htm (accessed June 21, 2002).

*Life,* August 1989, pp. 48–61.

*New Choices,* June 1989, pp. 40–46.

*Saturday Evening Post,* March 1989, pp. 52–53.

# Paul Rodríguez

Comedian, actor
Born c. 1955, Mazatlán, Mexico

*"Comedy was my secret weapon. It saved my life many times. I wasn't the meanest dude in the barrio, but I was the funniest."*

Paul Rodríguez is one of the most recognized Hispanic comedians in the United States. His face first became familiar to Americans in the mid-1980s through comedy specials on cable television and comedy series on network television. He became known as a stand-up comedian for his characteristic way of making fun of Hispanics. Upon deeper examination, though, his humor exposes the limited, stereotypical view many Americans have of Hispanics and Hispanic life. After years as a comedian, Rodríguez began to take his acting seriously as well, and he has been in demand in the movies in the 1990s and into the 2000s.

Rodríguez was born around 1955 in the Pacific seaport town of Mazatlán in the Mexican state of Sinaloa. With little money, his family immigrated to the United States when he was just a child. They settled in a rough East Los Angeles barrio (Spanish-speaking neighborhood). Rodríguez recalled his childhood to a reporter in *People:* "Comedy was my secret weapon. It saved my life many times. I wasn't the meanest dude in the barrio, but I was the funniest."

Members of his family struggled to make a living as migrant farm workers. Although the rights of farm workers were improving slightly in the 1960s (see **Cesar Chavez** and **Dolores Huerta** entries), the working conditions they faced were still harsh. Even so, Rodríguez's parents were happy to have any job to support their family. They disapproved of his childhood fantasies. "My family never thought that being a comedian or an actor was an obtainable goal," he said in *Hispanic American Almanac.* "Being farmworkers, all they wanted for their children was a steady job. But I knew I had to give it a chance."

## From the Air Force to Comedy Clubs

In 1977 Rodríguez enlisted in the U.S. Air Force and served as a communications specialist. During his four-year stint, he lived in thirty-three countries around the world, including Iceland. After his discharge, he entered Long Beach City College and earned an associate arts degree. He then enrolled in California State University with plans to become a lawyer. During theater classes at the university, Rodríguez's comic talent so impressed his professor that he took Rodríguez to amateur night at the Comedy Store nightclub. Rodríguez's career was launched. He dropped out of school and began performing at colleges and at Spanish and English clubs throughout Los Angeles.

Rodríguez's sharp-edged humor soon caught the attention of television producers. In 1984 he was cast as the lead in *a.k.a. Pablo,* a situation comedy developed by Norman Lear that aired on ABC. The show centered on Rodríguez's character, but also focused on his Hispanic family and their

Paul Rodríguez. *Reproduced by permission of AP/Wide World Photos.*

daily routines. The show was canceled, however, after only six episodes aired. Many Hispanic groups objected to Rodríguez's jokes, which they found offensive to Mexicans and Hispanics in general.

The criticism did not stop Rodríguez from continuing his act. To this day, he is unfazed by what other people think of him. "I never read reviews written about me," he explained to Jane Marion in *TV Guide,* "because in reality I'm never as good as they say I am, and I'm never as bad as they say I am. I know who I am."

## Wins Parts in Motion Pictures

Rodríguez found 1986 to be a busy year. He played supporting roles in three motion pictures: *Miracles, Quicksilver,* and *The Whoopee Boys.* Of the three, *Quicksilver* had the greatest box-office appeal. The movie starred Kevin Bacon as a young stockbroker who loses everything, then becomes a city bicycle messenger. That same year, Rodríguez also released his first comedy album, *You're in America Now, Speak Spanish.*

Rodríguez was given a second chance at a television series in 1988. CBS offered him the chance to play in the situation comedy *Trial and Error.* Rodríguez portrayed the character of Tony, a T-shirt salesman. He rooms with John (played by Eddie Vélez), a newly graduated Puerto Rican lawyer working in an established law firm. Although the show was also broadcast in Spanish on Spanish-language radio stations, it never attracted a sizable audience and was canceled.

In 1993 Rodríguez played a supporting role in the comedy *Made in America,* which starred Whoopi Goldberg and Ted Danson. Rodríguez made his directorial debut in 1994 with *A Million to Juan,* a modern-day adaptation of American writer Mark Twain's story "The Million-Pound Bank Note."

After his start in movies, Rodríguez was ready to learn more. He moved to New York and began taking acting classes and working in theater. There he met actor Russell Crowe. Crowe got him a part in *The Price of Glory,* which was released in 2000. Since then, Rodríguez has been in demand, with four movies in 2001 alone: *Crocodile Dundee in Los Angeles, Rat Race, Tortilla Soup,* and *Ali.* For the part of Ferdie Pacheco, Muhammad Ali's ringside physician in *Ali,* Rodríguez was chosen over **Benicio Del Toro,** John Leguizamo, and **Rubén Blades**

(see entries) for the part. "It's funny," he told Kathy Cano-Murillo of the *Arizona Republic.* "I've been in show business for 20 years. Now it's like all of a sudden Hollywood turned the lights on over my head."

Rodríguez did not give up on stand-up comedy with his success in the movies. He continued doing tours with his comedy show, and quipped that his big name from the movies helped him to fill seats at his stand-up shows.

## Performs Benefits for the Disadvantaged

Rodríguez is the head of his own company, Paul Rodríguez Productions. In 1991 his company produced the one-hour special "Paul Rodríguez Behind Bars," which aired nationally on the Fox Network. The show highlighted Rodríguez performing for prison inmates. Throughout his career, he has performed for the poor and disadvantaged. In 1992 he helped singer **Gloria Estefan** raise money to help the Florida victims of Hurricane Andrew. The benefit performance also included Whoopi Goldberg, Paul Simon, Rosie O'Donnell, and **Andy García** (see entries).

In addition to performing stand-up comedy in Las Vegas and Atlantic City, Rodríguez hosts and stars in the popular *El Show de Paul Rodríguez* on Univisión, the Spanish-language television network. He also appears as a Spanish-language spokesman for Miller Brewing Company, GTE Corporation, and Highland Superstores. Rodríguez is happy to reach out to his community, but he feels advertisers are allowing him to reach out only to a part of it. "I'm very proud of being Mexican American," he explained to Ruth Stroud in *Advertising Age,* "but I'm not just Mexican American—I'm American."

## For More Information

*Advertising Age,* October 16, 1989.

Cano-Murillo, Kathy, "Acting Role Helps Comic Fill Seats," *Arizona Republic,* June 7, 2001.

*Hispanic,* June 1994, p. 14.

*Hispanic American Almanac,* 2nd Edition, Gale, 1996.

*People,* June 27, 1983, p. 96.

*TV Guide,* July 1, 1989, p. 19.

Richard Rodríguez. *Reproduced by permission of the National Catholic Reporter.*

# Richard Rodríguez

Writer, journalist
Born July 31, 1944, Sacramento, California

*"We come from an expansive, an intimate, culture that has long been judged second-rate by the U.S. Out of pride as much as affection, we are reluctant to give up our past."*

Richard Rodríguez could not speak English when he began elementary school in California. As the son of Mexican American immigrants, he had grown up speaking nothing but Spanish at home. Still, he was quite successful in school, eventually earning degrees from several universities. Today he is a controversial social critic of bilingual education and affirmative action programs. He urges Hispanics in the nation not to think of themselves as foreigners but to consider themselves full Americans.

Rodríguez was born in 1944 in Sacramento, California, to parents who had immigrated to the United States from Mexico only a few years before. The Irish Catholic nuns at Rodríguez's school encouraged his parents to use English at home to help their children's performance in school. Rodríguez's parents agreed, wanting their children to blend into American society even though they could not. But Rodríguez regrets the loss of closeness that his family felt before they gave up that piece of their private culture. Throughout much of his adult life, he has struggled with the desire to recapture that private culture, while holding on to gains earned in the mainstream American culture.

Rodríguez reached the goals his parents wanted for him. He was an outstanding student throughout his academic career. After high school, he attended Stanford University, earning his bachelor of arts degree in English in 1967. Two years later he earned a master of arts degree in philosophy from Columbia University. He then worked toward a doctorate in English at the University of California at Berkeley for several years. During his doctoral work, he studied for a year in England.

## Frustration With Being Typed a "Minority"

Although Rodríguez achieved academic success, he eventually began to fight against the very policies that helped him achieve that success. Throughout his college years he received financial help partly because he was an ethnic minority. Later, he turned down teaching jobs that were offered to him as part of affirmative action programs (government policies designed to help minorities achieve equal status in the workplace). He found it ironic that the job offers were based on his identity as a "minority," when his achievements were based on his struggle to blend in with the "majority."

Instead, Rodríguez decided to become a journalist and writer. He began working with the Pacific News Service in San Francisco, eventually becoming an editor. His articles for the service have been picked up for publication by newspapers all over the country. Rodríguez has written for national newspapers such as the *Los Angeles Times* and for national magazines such as *Harper's*. He has also worked as a journalist and essayist for public television's *Mac-Neil/Lehrer NewsHour*.

Many of Rodríguez's articles have focused on what it means for Mexicans to come to America and to assimilate (become a part) to its culture. Many Mexicans, and their Mexican American children, fear that they will lose their identity—their culture—if they become a part of the American mainstream. "We come from an expansive, an intimate, culture that has long been judged second-rate by the U.S.," Rodríguez wrote in an essay in *Time*. "Out of pride as much as affection, we are reluctant to give up our past."

Rodríguez goes on to argue, however, that this type of thinking is wrong. He believes that what has made Mexican culture (and all Hispanic cultures) great is that it has grown through assimilation. The culture of Latin America, Rodríguez points out, clearly reflects the cultures of other nations—European and African—that have played a part in its history. The ability of Hispanics to interact and intermingle with other peoples is what defines them. "The remarkable legacy Hispanics carry from Latin America is not language—an inflatable skin—but breath itself, capacity of soul, an inclination to live," Rodríguez wrote in *Time*. "The genius of Latin America is the habit of synthesis. We assimilate."

## Three Essay Collections

Rodríguez's most intensely personal writings have been in three books—*Hunger of Memory: The Education of Richard Rodríguez, Days of Obligation: An Argument with My Mexican Father,* and *Brown: The Last Discovery of America.* Rodríguez spent six years writing *Hunger of Memory,* published in 1983. The autobiographical work—composed of five essays—offers an intense and thoughtful look at his humble beginnings, his education, and at how language has played a part in his life. In the book, Rodríguez argues against the idea that minorities should be hired for jobs simply because they are minorities. He also does not believe in bilingual education. Rodríguez feels that it simply widens the sense of separateness Hispanic students already feel from mainstream America.

In 1992 Rodríguez published *Days of Obligation.* In these essays, Rodríguez tries to understand the meaning of Mexico, his Mexican ancestors, the Mayans, and the Catholic religion from his father's viewpoint. In one essay, he explores the myth of **Joaquín Murieta** (see entry), the nineteenth-century California bandit. "In imaginatively exploring the life of such a myth," Ilan Stavans wrote in *Commonweal.* "Rodríguez comes to see the Rio Grande as a psychic injury dividing the idiosyncracies of Mexico and the United States."

In 2002 a third book of Rodríguez's essays hit the bookshelves: *Brown: The Last Discovery of America.* In this book, Rodríguez argues against the American habit of classifying everyone as either of the white race or the black race. He also argues that Hispanics are having a great impact on American culture even as they assimilate, changing it even as they are being changed by it. The color brown expresses his notion of a state of "in between," neither one thing or another. Rodríguez, who is homosexual, explores his own contradictory identity as a "queer Catholic Indian Spaniard at home in a tem-perate Chinese city [San Francisco] in a fading blond state in a post-Protestant nation."

Rodríguez's writings and ideas have earned him many awards. In November 1992 President George Bush presented him with a Charles Frankel humanitarian award. At the same time, his writings remain controversial among Mexican Americans. He is unfazed by the criticism and will no doubt continue his profound and highly articulate explorations of the concepts of ethnicity and identity.

## For More Information

"Brown: The Last Discovery of America," review, *Publisher's Weekly,* March 11, 2002, p. 66.
*Commonweal,* March 26, 1993, pp. 20–22.
Crowley, Paul, "An Ancient Catholic: An Interview with Richard Rodríguez," *America,* September 23, 1995, p. 8.
*Nation,* January 18, 1993, pp. 63–65.
*National Catholic Reporter,* November 20, 1992, p. 33.
*Time,* July 11, 1988, p. 84; January 25, 1993, pp. 69–70.

# Linda Ronstadt

Singer, actress
Born July 15, 1946, Tucson, Arizona

*"I loved the idea of doing a work particular to Mexico. La Pastorela is not found in Cuba or Venezuela. People tend to lump Hispanic cultures together."*

L inda Ronstadt is a singer who has made her mark in such varied styles as rock, country, operetta, old-fashioned ballads, and mariachi (Mexican street band) music. Almost every musical experiment Ronstadt has undertaken has met with success, fan approval, and hefty record sales.

Ronstadt was born in 1946 in Tucson, Arizona, to Mexican American parents Gilbert and Rosemary Ronstadt. Her father used to sing on local radio stations around Tucson and had also appeared with big bands in the area. During the Great Depression (a period in the 1930s when the nation suffered from an extremely slow economy and widespread unemployment), he gave up singing to run a hardware store.

Ronstadt and her brothers and sister were constantly exposed to the Mexican music their father loved while they were growing up (she would later make an album of his favorite songs). Ronstadt enjoyed harmonizing with her siblings, and decided by the age of six to become a singer. She promptly lost all interest in school. By her teen years, she was well-known at Tucson's Catalina High School for her outstanding voice.

Ronstadt says she developed a habit of rebellion early in life. She stuck to her ideas with singleminded determination. She attended the University of Arizona briefly, dropping out at eighteen to join her musician boyfriend in Los Angeles. With her boyfriend and another male musician, Ronstadt formed a folk-rock group called the Stone Poneys. The group's only hit was "Different Drum," a single from their second album, *Evergreen, Volume II,* released in 1967. An intense touring schedule, problems with drug abuse, and a series of disappointing concert appearances caused the Stone Poneys to break up after only a few years.

## Sad Solo Career

Ronstadt then began her solo career. By 1970 she had released two albums that fused country and rock styles: *Hand Sown … Home Grown* and *Silk Purse*. The latter album produced her first solo hit, the sorrowful "Long, Long Time." Today this song is considered a classic ballad. In fact, many actors listen to it to bring them to tears when they need to cry for sad scenes.

Ronstadt's voice seemed particularly suited to melancholy music. She has described her childhood as lonely and her early singing career as bleak. She was bothered by the stresses of constant touring, a difficult love life, and cocaine use. Music critics paid little attention to her work. To make matters worse, she suffered from stage fright.

In 1973 Ronstadt moved to a different recording company and hired a new producer and manager. The changes seemed to alter the direction of her life. The next year she recorded her first million-selling album, *Heart Like a Wheel*. By the mid-1970s, she had established herself as rock's most popular female star with hits such as "When Will I Be Loved?," "Desperado," "You're No Good," "Blue Bayou," and "Poor, Poor Pitiful Me."

## Makes the Leap to Opera

The musical leap from rock to opera is gigantic; few voices can make it successfully. In 1981 Ronstadt astonished critics and fans by making that leap gracefully. She sang a difficult soprano role in the Broadway operetta, *The Pirates of Penzance*. Three years later, she performed the part of Mimi in Giacomo Puccini's nineteenth-century opera *La Bohème*.

In the mid-1980s Ronstadt pushed her abilities in an entirely different direction. She recorded three albums of sentimental American love songs from the 1920s and 1930s: *What's New?, Lush Life,* and *For Sentimental Reasons.* For these songs she chose to be backed by the Nelson Riddle Orchestra. Her manager and friends tried to talk her out of the project, figuring that her fans would desert her and her record sales would plummet. Surprisingly, the albums were a great success. "Instead of trying to re-create another era's erotic climate," Stephen Holden wrote in *Vogue,* "[Ronstadt] pays homage to it with lovely even-handed line readings offered in a spirit of wistful nostalgia."

## Reaches Back to Mexican Roots

Ronstadt followed up these successes with a switch back to country. In 1986 she earned several awards for *Trio,* an album she recorded with country stars Dolly Parton and Emmylou Harris. In 1987 she went back to the songs of her childhood, releasing *Canciones de mi padre.* The album, her first in Spanish, featured mariachi songs that her father used to sing.

In 1989 Ronstadt returned to a mainstream sound with *Cry Like a Rainstorm— Howl Like a Wolf.* Several of the album's tracks featured Ronstadt singing with Aaron Neville. One of their duets, "Don't Know Much," went to the top of the charts.

In 1991 Ronstadt once again returned to her Mexican roots. She recorded *Mas canciones,* another album of traditional Mexican songs sung in Spanish. She also

Linda Ronstadt. *Reproduced by permission of Archive Photos, Inc.*

returned to the stage in *La Pastorela,* an updated version of the traditional Mexican folk play about the shepherds traveling to worship the infant Jesus. Directed by **Luis Valdez** (see entry), the play aired on public television. "I loved the idea of doing a work particular to Mexico," she told Edna Gunderson in *TV Guide.* "*La Pastorela* is not found in Cuba or Venezuela. People tend to lump Hispanic cultures together."

Ronstadt's next two projects focused on the Afro-Cuban music that invaded America during the 1940s and 1950s. She took part in the soundtrack recording of the 1992 movie *The Mambo Kings.* The film was based on the Pulitzer Prize-winning novel by **Oscar Hijuelos** (see entry). On the soundtrack, Ronstadt sings a classic torch song from the time, "Perfidia." She explored that music even further in 1993 when she recorded *Frenesí,* an album composed entirely of songs from the 1940s and 1950s.

## On to Other Genres and Collaborations

In 1994 Ronstadt continued to surprise the music world with her wide variety of talents. She offered *Winter Light,* her first pop album in four years. The record featured songs by such 1960s songwriters as Burt Bacharach, Carole King, and Brian Wilson of the Beach Boys. *People* magazine's Brian Carmody wrote that Ronstadt "is worth hearing, as always, and this new album only enhances her reputation as an accomplished interpreter of classic pop music."

In 1995 Ronstadt returned to a California folk rock style with her album *Feels Like Home,* which was well received by critics and fans. In 1996 she recorded an album of lullabies *Dedicated to the One I Love,* that included a duet with Aaron Neville on "Brahms Lullaby" that drew high praise. Nineteen ninety-eight's *We Ran* was a return to 1970s folk rock. In 1999 she teamed up for a second time with Dolly Parton and Emmylou Harris for the collection of traditional songs in *Trio II*. Richard Corliss wrote of the album for *Time:* "Harris, Ronstadt and Parton harmonize like a true trio in 10 rapturous airs spanning six decades. They could've been swapping these parts since girlhood. And the voices! Still pure—purer than on their solo CDs." Later in 1999 Ronstadt joined with Harris again for a country album, *Western Wall: The Tucson Sessions,* and a tour. Both were highly acclaimed.

Ronstadt had children relatively late in life and has done what she can to keep her personal life out of the public eye.

## For More Information

Amdur, Melissa, *Linda Ronstadt,* Chelsea House, 1993.

Corliss, Richard, *Trio II: Emmylou Harris, Linda Ronstadt, Dolly Parton,* review, *Time,* March 8, 1999, p. 82.

*Hispanic,* October 1988, pp. 10–14.

*People,* January 17, 1994, p. 23.

*Vogue,* November 1984.

*TV Guide,* December 21, 1991.

# Loretta Sanchez

U.S. Congresswoman
Born January 7, 1960, in Lynwood, California

In a stunning upset in 1996, Loretta Sanchez defeated a nine-time incumbent (someone who already holds a position) for a House of Representatives seat from her district in Orange County, California. With no political experience, this financial analyst received backing from major national educational and abortion rights groups as well as Hispanics, who all wanted to oust her opponent, Robert K. Dornan, due to his conservative views (viewpoints that favor the traditional approach and preserving established ways, generally supporting economic policies that favor business and political policies that maintain existing social structures). After the election, she was thrown into the spotlight when Dornan alleged that her slim victory was due to voter fraud (cheating). However, Sanchez prevailed and went on to win re-election in 1998 and 2000 by ever-widening margins. Though Sanchez holds many liberal views (viewpoints that favor policies that protect individual freedoms and civil rights and reform of existing social structures), including supporting abortion rights and gay rights, she is a fiscal (financial) conservative who tries to find common ground with the Republican party. Upon invitation from President Bill Clinton and Vice President Al Gore, she became co-chair of the Democratic National Committee in March 1999 during her second term in office.

## Growing Up in Orange County

Sanchez, one of seven children of Mexican immigrants, was born on January 7, 1960, in Lynwood, California. Her father, Ignacio Sandoval Sanchez, a machinist, and her mother, Maria Socorro (Macias) Sanchez, a secretary, met each other while working in a manufacturing plant in Los Angeles. Her mother helped organize a union at the plant. Since they spoke only Spanish in the home, Sanchez learned English in a Head Start program for disadvantaged children. The family moved to Anaheim in 1965. Sanchez remembers that some of the neighbors in Anaheim sold their homes and left rather than live near a Hispanic family.

Along with her siblings, who are now all professionals, Sanchez was an excellent student. She gives credit to her parents for her success. Her mother volunteered at her children's school, and her father demanded that

Loretta Sanchez. *Reproduced by permission of the Gamma Liaison Network.*

the children study hard and adhere to strict codes of behavior so that they would not face the same discrimination (being treated poorly because of a different ethnic background than others in the community) he had when he arrived in the United States. Still, Sanchez noted that racism persisted, telling Jim Lewis in *Harper's Bazaar,* "When I was growing up, Mexicans could only swim in the pool on Friday nights, because Saturday morning they changed the water. Since then, the city's gone from being mostly white to being half Latino. And yet the power structure hasn't changed: In 1988, they dressed people up to look like INS [Immigration and Naturalization Service] agents and sent them to the polls to discourage new immigrants from voting."

## The Successful Business Exec

In 1982 Sanchez graduated from Chapman University in Orange, California, with a bachelor of science in economics. She did well at Chapman and was voted student of the year. She went on to obtain a master's degree in business administration, specializing in finance, from American University in Washington, D.C. Afterward, she worked from 1984 to 1987 for the Orange County Transportation Authority as a special projects manager, where her first major success was in raising money to install emergency call boxes on the highways. Subsequently, she held a career as a financial analyst, mainly in areas of municipal and public finance. From 1987 to 1990 she was employed with Fieldman, Rolapp & Associates, in Irvine, California, as an assistant vice president, then with Booz, Allen, and Hamilton in Los Angeles from 1990 to 1993 as an associate. She was president of Amiga Advisors, Inc., in Los Angeles from 1993 to 1996.

Meanwhile, throughout the 1980s and 1990s Sanchez was active in community affairs, though mainly behind the scenes. She got involved with planning and financing for schools, libraries, and police stations, and helped raise funds for school programs and scholarships. She was not extremely political until the elections of 1992. Until then, she and her husband, Stephen Simmons Brixey, a securities trader, lived an upper-middle-class lifestyle and were members of the Republican party due to their fiscal conservatism. But she became disturbed by what she considered attacks on immigrants and women by Republicans, and felt that the party's social stances against issues like abortion and gay rights were out of step with hers.

## A Political Challenge

After switching to the Democratic party, Sanchez ran for a seat on the Anaheim City Council in 1994, campaigning under her married name, Loretta Sanchez Brixey. As a relative unknown, she came in eighth in a field of sixteen candidates. Later, in 1996, she decided to take on a much bigger challenge: opposing nine-term incumbent Robert Dornan for his seat in the U.S. House of Representatives from California's 46th District. Dornan not only endorsed right-wing (very conservative) social views, he was known for making outrageous statements to air his positions, earning him the nickname "The Mouth of the House." He frequently made negative comments about homosexuals, especially those with AIDS. Dornan was characterized as "B-1 Bob" for his relentless crusade for the California-made bomber and all things military, and he was a fervent supporter of gun rights. In addition, he was not known to be especially sympathetic to the needs of his Hispanic constituents, which made up about one-third of his district. However, since only about one-third of the eligible population cast votes, and because his largely Catholic constituency supported many of his conservative views, Dornan continued to win re-election.

When Sanchez decided to run against Dornan, the Democratic party initially backed a different candidate in the primary. After she won, local Democratic leaders "took their time getting behind her," according to Lewis in *Harper's Bazaar,* and he claimed that the National Organization for

Women (NOW) "was just about as reluctant." Dornan, who was $200,000 in debt after squandering funds on a failed 1996 presidential bid to begin with, did not think Sanchez was much of a threat to him, and he ended up putting less money into his House campaign than usual. However, Hispanic forces rallied behind Sanchez. She wound up outspending him $760,328 to $589,447.

Although Sanchez ran under her maiden name rather than her married name in this race, she concentrated on a platform of basic concerns like education, jobs, and Social Security, rather than controversial issues like immigration. Still, Dornan attacked her as a "Hispanic pretender" and "a carpetbagger" (an outsider who meddles in local politics). In November 1996, she won the seat in a surprise upset by a narrow margin of about a thousand votes.

The race was not exactly over. Dornan called for a recount, and alleged voter fraud. He maintained that Sanchez gained votes from Hispanic noncitizens signed up on voter rolls the previous year by a Hispanic community group; he alleged that some were even illegal immigrants. Investigations by the House of Representatives, the state of California, and the Orange County district attorney led to the dismissal of the election fraud charges. The House's investigation took over a year. It eventually concluded that although 784 of the votes were illegally cast, this was still 231 shy of Sanchez's victory. While the investigation was ongoing, Dornan, apparently optimistic that he would resume his seat, continued to show up on the House floor at times during votes. He also continued to make public appearances in which he verbally attacked Sanchez.

## The Hispanic Vote

Many political observers believe that Dornan's tactics seriously backfired within his district. There was growing frustration among Hispanic people after 1994, when California had passed Proposition 187. This measure, designed to keep undocumented immigrants from receiving state-funded social services, including welfare and medical care, would also have forced thousands of undocumented children out of California schools had the courts not eventually ruled against it. After Proposition 187 passed, Hispanic citizens of California across the state reported a rise in discrimination against them. While Sanchez had not had a high profile in the Hispanic community before the election, many angry voters saw the investigation of her victory in the election as an attack on Hispanics in general. Her popularity skyrocketed, while criticism of Dornan within the Hispanic community escalated. According to a *Los Angeles Times* poll conducted during the investigation, Dornan's favorability rating was only 27 percent among Hispanic voters. Vietnamese American voters were also being investigated, to their equal displeasure. And demographics continued to change in Orange County. In Sanchez's home base of Anaheim, for example, the Hispanic population grew from 30 percent to 47 percent of the city's population between 1990 and 2000. The non-Hispanic population dropped down to 36 percent.

## Taking Over

In the next election in November 1998, Dornan ran a bitter campaign against Sanchez in an attempt to reclaim his former seat, but she won with 57 percent of the vote. In 2000 she was re-elected with 60 percent of the vote.

In office, Sanchez focuses on education, crime reduction, economic development, and senior citizens' issues. Proud of the fact that she was the first member of Congress to have benefitted from the "Head Start" program, she is committed to continuing to provide opportunities for disadvantaged children. In her district, she has been involved in fourteen major federal grant projects that, by 2002, had reaped $300 million in federal monies to agencies in Orange County. She has served on several committees and subcommittees, including the House Committee on Education and the Workforce and the House Armed Services Committee.

During the 2000 presidential election campaign between Republican George W. Bush and Democrat Al Gore, Sanchez spoke out strongly to counter Bush's attempts to draw in the Latino vote. She pointed out that education for Hispanics and African Americans in the then-governor of Texas's home state had been dreadful, and warned that the Republican party would have to go further than speaking a few words of Spanish in its campaign to capture the Latino vote. She also had a small, but highly publicized, confrontation with her own party. In planning a $3 million fund-raising event for the Democrats, she booked the Playboy Mansion for the occasion. The Democrats did not want to be associated with the place and there was a showdown between the party and the determined congresswoman before she backed down on the issue. This did not seem to do any political harm.

For the Democratic primaries in 2002, Loretta Sanchez, strong in her district and in Congress, ran unopposed. Another California primary held her attention: her younger sister, Linda Sanchez, was running for the Democratic nomination for the 39th Congressional District of California at Los Angeles County. The uniqueness of the situation—two sisters running for Congress at the same time—was apparent when their mother taped a TV political advertisement for both of her daughters, praising them in Spanish. Linda Sanchez won in the primaries over five opponents then won the election of November 2002. Loretta and Linda Sanchez are the first sisters ever to serve together in Congress.

## For More Information

*Congressional Quarterly Weekly Report,* January 4, 1997, p. 52.

*Harper's Bazaar,* April 1997, p. 207.

*Hispanic,* October 1998, p. 48; November 1999, p. 35.

Loretta Sanchez Official Web site. Available at http://www.house.gov/sanchez (accessed June 21, 2002).

*New Republic,* October 27, 1997, p. 13.

*Roll Call,* February 5, 1998.

"Sister Duo Could Be a First in Congress," CNN.com, March 6, 2002. Available at http://www.cnn.com/2002/ALLPOLITICS/03/06/loretta.linda.sanchez.cnna/ (accessed June 21, 2002).

*Star Tribune* (Minneapolis, MN), December 19, 1996, p. 29A.

*Working Woman,* May 1999, p. 24.

# Carlos Santana

Musician
Born July 20, 1947, Autlán de Navarro, Mexico

*"I play music because I know it can elevate the spirit, because it has the power to build the bridge of love between people."*

In the late 1960s, when acid rock reigned and the British Invasion was still raging, Carlos Santana and his band introduced into the music scene a new Latin-based rock sound featuring an Afro-Cuban beat. This was what we now know as "world music," years before that name would catch up with the style. After soaring in popularity and becoming one of the biggest acts of the day, the group Santana went through various personnel changes. They continued to make music together even as Carlos Santana, finding new spiritual and musical paths, began to record jazz fusion on his own with many other top names. Though his rock records continued to sell vigorously, he would not have a radio hit after 1982.

Then, nearly two decades later in 1999, Santana became one of the most often-heard performers on the airwaves. He had teamed up with some of the hottest young acts of the day, including Lauryn Hill, Dave Matthews, and Everlast, along with the legendary Eric Clapton, to produce a work that harkened back to his early Latin sounds, but with a contemporary slant. With an irresistible hook and his trademark low, cool vocals, the single "Smooth" began racing up the charts, and the album, *Supernatural,* sold more than six million copies. The project overall won a phenomenal total of eight Grammy Awards, tying Michael Jackson's 1983 record for most Grammy Awards won on a single night. Some wondered if Santana's comeback could be attributed to the sudden boom in Latin music beginning in the late 1990s that spawned such names as Ricky Martin, Enrique Iglesias, and **Jennifer Lopez** (see entry). Santana, however,

credits his success to a higher force rather than a fad or marketing appeal. "It's not really chance or luck," he remarked to Jeff Gordinier in *Entertainment Weekly.* "My intention was to spread a spiritual virus."

Santana comes from a family with a long history of musicianship. He was born in 1947 in Autlán de Navarro, west-central Mexico, to José and Josephina Santana. Both his paternal grandfather and great-grandfather were musicians. His father, a *mariachi* (Mexican street band) violinist, taught him to play both the violin and the guitar.

While he was still young, Santana and his family moved to the city of Tijuana, just across the Mexican-American border from San Diego, California. It was there that he became influenced by American blues, listening to early recordings of guitarists B. B. King and T-Bone Walker. As he grew older, he began to play guitar in small nightclubs on the seamier side of Tijuana.

## Influenced by Jazz and Salsa

In the early 1960s, Santana's family moved again, this time to San Francisco, California. Jazz was a popular musical style in this cosmopolitan city, and it quickly influenced Santana's playing. He was especially drawn to the musical style of saxophonist John Coltrane, and his musical tastes were expanded even further after he began listening to salsa musicians such as **Tito Puente** (see entry). *Salsa* (Spanish for "sauce") is a fiery Latin American dance music of Afro-Cuban origin.

Santana founded the band Santana in 1966 with bass guitarist David Brown and keyboardist Gregg Rolie. The band's sound—a combination of blues, jazz, rock, and Afro-Latin American rhythms—caught on quickly in U.S. cities. A large audience developed among Mexican, Puerto Rican, and Latin American listeners. Soon, music-lovers of all colors and ethnicities were dancing to the band's rhythmic beat, a sound that came to be known as Latin rock.

The band Santana made its national debut to a mainstream audience at the three-day Woodstock festival in 1969. Although the band was still a local, San Francisco-area phenomenon and had not yet recorded an album, they played alongside such rock veterans as Jimi Hendrix, Janis Joplin, and the Who. A documentary of the festival, *Woodstock,* was released in 1970, and many critics consider Santana's rousing performance to be the highlight of the film. It brought the band to a worldwide audience. People who previously had not listened to jazz or Latin music now sought out the group's first albums.

## Spirituality Guides His Music

*Santana* (1969), *Abraxas* (1970), and *Santana III* (1972) all became best-selling albums with chart-topping singles like "Evil Ways," "Black Magic Woman" (recorded earlier by Fleetwood Mac), "Oye Como Va" (composed by Puente in the 1950s), and "Samba Pa Ti." In the early 1970s, Santana disbanded and reformed his group many times. He also sought out and performed with many other solo musicians, including John Coltrane and fellow guitarist John McLaughlin.

During this time Santana underwent a spiritual conversion to the teachings of Sri Chinmoy Ghose, an Indian mystic and poet. Sri Chinmoy emphasized the need to develop the heart over the mind and to celebrate God in all daily activities. Santana applied this teaching to his approach to music. As he told Jas Obrecht of *Guitar Player,* "Whether in a cry or in a party atmosphere, the music should exalt humanity and the spirit of humanity, which is the Lord." He also adopted the spiritual name "Devadip," which means "Eye of God."

Throughout the 1970s and 1980s, Santana switched between group and solo projects. The band continued to blend rock with salsa, and their 1981 release *Zebop!,* featuring the hit "Winning," was an especially big seller. Meanwhile, Santana used his solo work to express his deep religious feelings.

## Uses Music to Benefit Social Causes

Santana has also conveyed his message of spiritual awareness through a variety of political and social benefits. In 1981 he appeared in concert with yet another lineup of his band to benefit United Cerebral Palsy. In 1985 they reformed to participate in Live Aid, the worldwide benefit concert for famine victims in Ethiopia. The following year Santana joined with rap artists Run-D.M.C. at a Crack-Down concert to raise awareness about the dangers of crack cocaine. And in 1988 he helped organize the "Blues for Salvador" benefit concert that raised $100,000 for the children of El Salvador.

"Musicians can be healers, more so than politicians, senators, presidents, or generals," Santana told Ouellette in *Down Beat*. In 1991 he and his wife, Deborah, opened their home in Marin County, California, to local schoolchildren to show them what the life of a musician is like. The tour was part of a program sponsored by the Cities in Schools (CIS) organization, which accepts donations from businesses and individuals to help improve the lives of underprivileged students. Deborah Santana is a member of the board of directors of CIS.

## Ready to Come Back

In 1993 Santana toured with folk icon Bob Dylan, and in 1996 he toured with guitar great Jeff Beck. Though Santana still sold seats, he noticed that radio stations no longer played any of his music besides his early hits, and the media was not paying him much attention. He received a star on the Hollywood Rock Walk of Fame in 1996, but it would take him until 1998 to be inducted in to the Rock and Roll Hall of Fame.

By the late 1990s, Santana was looking for a comeback. He explained to Andy Ellis in *Guitar Player* that in his meditation and dreams, he had received instructions telling him: "We want you to hook up with people at junior high schools, high schools, and universities. We're going to get you back into radio airplay." He felt his music could have a positive effect on youth of the day. Along with producer Clive Davis, who had first signed him to his contract at Columbia in the 1960s, Santana devised a plan.

Working with his band, Santana managed to assemble a collection of some of the biggest talents in the industry, including Lauryn Hill, Wyclef Jean, Eagle Eye Cherry,

Carlos Santana. *Reproduced by permission of Ken Settle.*

Dave Matthews, Rob Thompson of matchbox twenty, Everlast, and the Dust Brothers, producers for Beck and the Beastie Boys. Even Eric Clapton made an appearance. The result was 1999's *Supernatural,* which reached number one on the *Billboard* album chart and generated a number-one single, "Smooth." *Supernatural* also became one of the most critically acclaimed CDs of the year and sold six million copies by the turn of 2000. The title, Santana told an *Entertainment Weekly* interviewer, "deals with the paranormal relationship between Lauryn Hill, Eric Clapton, and myself. Most of my collaborators said, 'I knew I was going to work with you because you were in my dreams.'" Surprisingly, *Supernatural* got nearly all of its airplay on pop and rock radio, with little support from

Latino stations, despite the fact that five of the tracks are in Spanish.

In February 2000 Santana won another eight Grammy Awards, including record of the year, for "Smooth," and album of the year and best rock album, for *Supernatural.* He also won an American Music Award that year for best album. For Santana, it is not about the recognition as much as it is touching people with his art.

## For More Information

*Detroit Free Press,* August 7, 1994, p. 4G.

*Down Beat,* August 1991, pp. 28–29; May 1992, p. 12.

*Encyclopedia of Rock,* edited by Phil Hardy and Dave Laing, Schirmer Books, 1988.

*Entertainment Weekly,* September 10, 1999, p. 151; December 24, 1999, p. 36.

*Guitar Player,* January 1988, pp. 46–54; January 1993, p. 58; January 1996, p. 61; August 1999, p. 74.

*Hispanic,* October 1992, p. 80.

*Rolling Stone,* August 19, 1999, p. 47.

*The Rolling Stone Encyclopedia of Rock & Roll,* edited by John Pareles and Patricia Romanowski, Rolling Stone Press/Summit Books, 1983.

Stambler, Irwin, *The Encyclopedia of Pop, Rock & Soul,* revised edition, St. Martin's, 1989.

# George Santayana

Philosopher, poet, novelist, critic
Born December 16, 1863, Madrid, Spain
Died September 26, 1952, Rome, Italy

*Although he was born in Spain and educated in the United States, George Santayana was a true citizen of the world.*

G eorge Santayana is recognized as one of the greatest philosophers of the twentieth century. He earned praise for his thoughtful, poetic writings and is credited with developing a universally appealing system of thought. While a young man, Santayana was a respected philosophy instructor at Harvard University. However, being a man of wide interests, he was not content to remain a teacher. Beyond thinking and writing, his main goal was to travel the world, and he spent the last forty years of his life realizing that goal. Although he was born in Spain and educated in the United States, Santayana was a true citizen of the world.

Santayana was born in 1863 in Madrid, Spain, to Augustín Ruiz de Santayana and Josephine Borras Sturgis. His parents had come from separate regions in Spain and the differences in their cultural upbringings were difficult to overcome. In an effort to ease their marital tensions, they decided to separate for a while in the late 1860s. When Santayana was about six years old, his mother and her children from her first marriage sailed to America to live in Boston, Massachusetts. Santayana and his father remained in Spain in the small town of Avila. Over the next few years, father and son grew close and forged a bond that would last for the rest of their lives.

Santayana was a gifted child who developed a love for language, literature, and the arts from his father. When they both finally sailed to United States in 1872, however, young Santayana was at a loss: he spoke no English. At the age of nine, he was placed in a kindergarten class with children who were half his age. But with the help of one of his half sisters, Susana, he quickly learned to speak almost fluent English, and by 1874 he was enrolled in the prestigious Boston Latin School. There he studied mathematics, public speaking, English, French, Greek, and Latin.

## Drawn to Architecture

Santayana's parents were not able to reconcile their differences, and in 1873 his father returned to Spain alone. Although Santayana loved his mother and half brothers and sisters, he was always closest to his father and was saddened by their separation. As a result, young Santayana withdrew socially, keeping mostly to himself and finding fulfillment in his studies. During this time, he became enchanted with architecture and read through all the books on the subject he could find. He made detailed drawings of buildings he saw around Boston and was soon creating original designs of palaces, cathedrals, and other buildings he imagined. Architecture remained one of his lifelong interests.

While growing up, Santayana's greatest love was literature, especially poetry. In his last years at the Boston Latin School, he served as editor of the school paper and won prizes for his poetry. After his graduation in 1882, he was accepted into Harvard University. During his time there, Santayana blossomed. He made many friends, was involved in several clubs, and took part in many social activities, including university theater productions. Santayana's academic major was philosophy, and he was greatly influenced in his studies by one of his Harvard instructors,

George Santayana. *Reproduced courtesy of the Library of Congress.*

renowned philosopher William James. James exposed Santayana to empiricism, the philosophical belief that all knowledge comes from experience and that people develop ideas after they have received information through their five senses.

Santayana longed for a life of travel and learning, so after graduating from Harvard with highest honors in 1886, he sailed back to Europe. He continued his studies in Germany and traveled throughout other countries, viewing the architecture of ancient cathedrals. While in Europe, he developed the foundation for his future philosophic views. His ideas stemmed from the scientifically based theory of naturalism, the belief that everything that happens in the world comes from natural, not supernatural, causes. For Santayana, the forces that controlled man were the same ones that controlled nature. He believed man was secondary to the natural world around him.

## Begins Teaching Philosophy

Santayana returned to Harvard in 1887 and completed his doctoral studies there two years later. He then planned to attend the Massachusetts Institute of Technology to study architecture, but William James convinced him to take over one of his classes at Harvard. Santayana agreed and his teaching career began. For the next twenty-three years, he lectured on philosophy to an increasing number of students, taking time off only to travel and to write. Among his students were future poets T. S. Eliot, Robert Frost, Wallace Stevens, and other bright young people who went on to make great contributions to the fields of journalism, history, and law.

Santayana maintained a keen interest in art, architecture, and poetry, and in 1894 he published his first book, *Sonnets and Other Verses*. More than anything he had wanted to be a poet, but most reviewers criticized his efforts. Two years later, however, Santayana won over the critics when he published a book on aesthetics (the study of the philosophy of art and beauty) called *The Sense of Beauty*.

Santayana's position in the field of philosophy was further strengthened by his multivolume work *The Life of Reason,* which was published in 1905 and 1906. This five-book series explores the ways in which common sense, society, religion, art, and science contribute to contentment in a life led by reason. Santayana was again praised for his work, and Harvard made him a full professor. Over the next few years, he published works in areas ranging from philosophy to literary criticism. Despite the success and recognition these books earned, however, Santayana was not satisfied. Instead of teaching, he wanted to see the world and to write about his experiences and ideas. In 1912 he was given the chance to pursue his dream.

## Pursues His Interest in Travel

That year Santayana's mother died, leaving him a small inheritance. He was a frugal man who managed his funds carefully; the money was more than enough to allow him to leave his position at Harvard and to spend the rest of his life traveling, studying, and writing.

For Santayana, travel meant a chance to experience new lands and new customs, which in turn increased his wide range of knowledge. Travel also fostered his sense of independence. Although he kept his Spanish citizenship and followed political events in his homeland, Santayana refused to settle down there. He did, however, frequently visit his father and his sister, who had moved back to Spain years earlier.

In 1927 Santayana published what many critics consider to be one of his most important philosophical works, *Skepticism and Animal Faith*. In this book, he departs from some of his earlier philosophical ideas. He sets out to show that people cannot always trust their senses to understand the natural world around them. Furthermore, he proposes that humans are able to function because of their natural "animal faith" (common sense), which allows them to interpret the world and lead meaningful lives.

Santayana believed that life can be divided into two realms—existence and essence. The realm of existence is made up of people, places, and other natural objects. The realm of essence is made up of ideas, colors, smells, and other things people come to know through their senses. Essences are thought to help people describe and understand existence. Santayana expanded on this idea in *The Realms of Being,* a four-volume work he published between 1927 and 1940.

## Writes a Bestselling Novel

Throughout the late 1920s and the 1930s, Santayana continued to write other works, both philosophical and literary. In 1936 he published a novel titled *The Last Puritan.* The book, which focuses on a man whose actions in life are determined by his sense of duty, became a bestseller and was translated into seven languages.

After finishing the last volume of *The Realms of Being,* Santayana ended his traveling days, settling down in Rome, Italy, in 1941. He retired to a convent called the Clinica della Piccola Compagna di Maria, which was better known as the Home of the Blue Nuns because of the color of the habits the nuns wore. While living at the convent, he completed work on his autobiography, *Persons and Places.*

Santayana spent his final years reading books from the convent's library, receiving admirers from around the world, and writing on subjects from politics to history. Shortly before his death, he began work on a book about the ancient Greek conqueror Alexander the Great. On September 26, 1952, Santayana died of stomach cancer. He was buried in Rome.

## For More Information

Arnett, W. E., *Santayana and the Sense of Beauty,* Peter Smith, 1984.

Carter, David, *George Santayana,* Chelsea House, 1992.

McCormick, John, *George Santayana: A Biography,* Paragon House, 1988.

Santayana, George, *The Last Puritan: A Memoir in the Form of a Novel,* Scribner's, 1936.

Santayana, George, *Persons and Places,* edited by William G. Holzberger and Herman J. Saatkamp, Jr., with an introduction by Richard C. Lyon, MIT Press, 1988.

# Cristina Saralegui

Television talk show host, journalist
Born January 29, 1948, Havana, Cuba

*"I'm going to continue trying to help Hispanics cope with the problems brought on by modern living. If that's wrong, then sue me."*

With her Spanish language talk show, Cristina Saralegui is Hispanic television's answer to Oprah Winfrey. The writer and talk show host is not afraid to face controversy and insists her only goal is to inform Hispanics. Some critics say her topics are immoral and her blonde appearance un-Latin, but thousands of fans continue to tune in, giving her show a top ranking.

Cristina Maria Saralegui was born in 1948 in Havana, Cuba, to Francisco and Cristina Saralegui. Her grandfather, Don Francisco Saralegui, was a successful magazine publisher in Cuba. He was also the dominant influence in her early life. When she was a child, he would often take her to see his company's huge printing presses and editorial offices.

In 1960, shortly after Fidel Castro had seized power in Cuba and had installed a Communist government, Saralegui and her family left their comfortable life in Havana. They began anew in Miami's Cuban exile community. After attending high school, Saralegui prepared to enter her family's traditional business by studying mass communications and creative writing at the University of Miami.

## Initial Career in Journalism

In 1967 Saralegui obtained her first job as an intern for *Vanidades Continentel,* Latin America's leading women's magazine. It was a huge challenge. Since she had attended high school and college in the United States, her English was better than her Spanish. She had to learn her original language all over again. She was successful enough to become features editor of the magazine by 1970. In 1976 she became the entertainment director for the *Miami Herald* newspaper. Three years later she was selected as the editor-in-chief of *Cosmopolitan-en-Español,* the Spanish-language version of *Cosmopolitan.* She held this position for ten years.

After twenty-three years as a journalist for Spanish language magazines and news-

papers, Saralegui moved into the television world in 1989. She became executive producer and host of *El show de Cristina* on Univision, the Spanish-language television network. The transition was not easy. She found that her personal appearance was an issue for the first time in her career. During her years as a writer, she spent most of her time behind a desk and never exercised. She had grown to a size eighteen.

Saralegui's good friends Emilio and **Gloria Estefan** (see entry) sent her their personal fitness trainer. Determined to improve her health and looks, she rearranged her routine to include jogging three miles a day. She began watching her diet, changed her hair, and shrank six dress sizes.

## Show Tackles Racy Issues

*El show de Cristina* became known for airing discussions on controversial topics, such as sex. Many of the topics were previously considered "taboo" in the Spanish-language media. At first, Saralegui was worried that she'd have a hard time finding Hispanic guests willing to talk about personal issues. Once again, her appearance also became an issue. "People would write me hate letters," she told a reporter for the *Chicago Tribune.* "How dare I try to represent Hispanics when I was so white? I tried to make them see it was racism."

Despite the initial harsh criticism, Saralegui's show has been a huge success. It has been rated the number one day-time television show and ranked among the top ten Spanish-language programs in the United States. *El show de Cristina* won an Emmy Award in 1991.

In 1991 the outspoken Saralegui also launched a three-minute daily radio show titled *Cristina opina* ("Cristina's Opinions"). The show gives her the chance to express her thoughts and concerns regarding Hispanic life. That same year she began another project, *Cristina la revista* ("Cristina the Magazine"). The monthly lifestyle magazine is an off-shoot of her television program.

## Emphasizes Hispanic Success Stories

By 1992 Saralegui had achieved another professional goal. She became producer and host of *Cristina,* the English-language version of her Spanish talk show. She was the first Hispanic to host daily television programs in two languages. She has also produced a series of TV specials celebrating the lives of leading Hispanic entertainers. The point behind the specials is motivational. Many of the Hispanic celebrities profiled came from very poor backgrounds. Through hard work and dedication, they achieved success.

*El show de Cristina* continued to tackle sensitive issues, such as AIDS (Acquired Immune Deficiency Syndrome), rape, and incest. The program, which aired in over fifteen countries, received its share of criticism. Through it all, Saralegui has remained firm in her convictions. "I'm going to continue trying to help Hispanics cope with the problems brought on by modern living," she explained to S. Lynne Walker of the *San Diego Union-Tribune.* "If that's wrong, then sue me."

Saralegui created her own foundation, Arriba la Vida (Up with Life) to increase

Cristina Saralegui. *Courtesy of Cristina Saralegui.*

AIDS awareness and education among Latinos. She has served as a jury member for various international beauty pageants, hosted a number of Latino special events, and worked as the Hispanic spokesperson for Crest toothpaste. In 1998, Saralegui wrote her self-help-laden autobiography, *Cristina! My Life as a Blonde,* and vowed that all proceeds from the book would directly benefit the foundation.

Saralegui and her husband, Marcos Avila, live in a mansion on the bay on Miami Beach's Palm Island. Her husband is also her manager and was one of the founders of the music group Miami Sound Machine. Saralegui has two daughters and a son. She has won numerous awards, including being listed as one of *Hispanic Business* magazine's "100 Most Influential Hispanics" in 1992. Saralegui has also been named one of the "Legendary Women of Miami" and has received the Corporate Leader Award from the National Network of Hispanic Women.

## For More Information

Anders, Gigi, "My Mother Has Always Been An Honest Friend," *Hispanic Magazine,* December 2001.
*Chicago Tribune,* May 31, 1992.
*Hispanic,* November 1991, pp. 18–24.
*Más,* July/August 1991, pp. 43–50.
*San Diego Union-Tribune,* April 27, 1993. p. E1.

# Junípero Serra

Franciscan missionary
Born November 24, 1713, Petra, Majorca
Died August 28, 1784, San Carlos de Carmel
    mission, California

*"For good or for bad, Junípero Serra's mark on the history of the American West is undeniable."*

The life of Junípero Serra, an eighteenth-century Spanish Franciscan missionary in North America, remains controversial to this day. Some view him as a pioneer who helped found settlements in California that grew into important cites such as San Diego and San Francisco and who brought Christianity to the native peoples of present-day California. Others claim he was a ruthless man who took over the natives' land and helped destroy their rich culture. For good or for bad, Junípero Serra's mark on the history of the American West is undeniable.

Serra was born Miguel José Serra in 1713 on Majorca, an island in the Mediterranean Sea off the eastern coast of Spain. His parents, Antonio and Margarita Serra, were peasant farmers, and Serra spent most of his childhood helping them in the fields around their village.

When not working in the fields, Serra spent his time in a Franciscan convent near his home. The Franciscans are a Roman Catholic order formed by Francis of Assisi in Italy early in the thirteenth century. They live under strict vows of poverty and prayer. The Franciscan friars at the convent quickly recognized the young Serra's intelligence and taught him reading, writing, Latin, mathematics, and theology. By the time he was sixteen, Serra had decided to become a Franciscan and entered the convent in the nearby capital of Palma. In 1731 Serra became a full member of the order and took the religious name of Junípero, who had been a companion of Francis of Assisi and who was known for his compassion.

## Feels Call to Missionary Work

Serra then studied for three more years to become an ordained priest and a professor of philosophy. Even after he was already admired as a distinguished preacher and teacher, Serra continued with his studies, earning his doctorate in theology in 1742. He then traveled around Majorca, lecturing and preaching to the islanders. By 1749, however, Serra began to feel that his life would have greater meaning if he were a missionary (a person who tries to convert others to different religious beliefs). He soon left his position in Majorca and sailed to Mexico to spread his religious teachings to the Mexicans.

Mexico had come under the domination of Spain in the early 1500s when Spanish soldiers led by conquistadors (conquerors) like Hernán Cortéz destroyed the Aztec and other native tribes. Over the years, Spanish missionaries traveled throughout the area known as New Spain, setting up missions to convert the native people to Christianity and to European ways. When Serra arrived in Mexico City in 1750, the missions there were already well established.

Serra spent a year in Mexico City learning the native languages, then went to the Sierra Gorda region about two hundred miles to the north to begin his mission work. Life at the missions was simple: in the morning, Serra conducted religious services for the Pame, the native inhabitants. Any Pame that missed services was given a lecture or even whipped. The Pame were forbidden to practice their own religious rituals and if they did, they were often whipped. During the day, the Pame tended the crops in the fields or helped build new stone churches or other structures. Serra stayed at the Sierra Gorda missions for eight years before returning to Mexico City to serve as a choirmaster and a supervisor of student priests.

## Practices Extreme Self-Denial

During this period, Serra developed a reputation for learning and for self-denial. Late at night, he would often whip his own

Junípero Serra. *Reproduced by permission of Corbis Corporation (Bellevue).*

body until his flesh split and bled. He rarely slept or ate, devoting most of his time to prayer. He believed that if he caused his body pain and overcame his physical passions, his spirit would become stronger. Those around him thought he was a saint.

Because of his religious enthusiasm, Serra was chosen in 1768 to be president of the missions in present-day Baja California, the long, thin peninsula extending south from the present-day state of California. These missions were previously run by Jesuits, members of the religious order the Society of Jesus. The king of Spain, Charles III, had ordered them removed from the area in 1767 because he believed they were becoming too strong and might take over his throne. At first, Serra was eager to begin his new work. He soon discovered the missions had been ransacked by Spanish soldiers looking for gold and most of the native people of the area had been killed off by European diseases like smallpox. Serra found he could change little in the area and became discouraged.

In 1769 José Gálvez, the visitor general of New Spain, asked Franciscan missionaries to colonize present-day California. This was done to prevent other explorers, such as the Englishman Francis Drake, from claiming the land that Spain believed it had already claimed. Serra believed he would be able to found a number of missions along the coast of California. In the spring of that year, Serra, a few other priests, and some Spanish soldiers began the march northward from Baja California.

## Founds First Mission

Serra officially established his first mission, San Diego de Acalá, on July 16, 1769. It was the first permanent European settlement in present-day California. He worked hard trying to convert the natives of the region to Christianity, but he was unsuccessful at first. Raids by the natives almost wiped out the mission. A ship finally arrived in the spring of 1770 to resupply the mission, and Serra led an party northward to a site near the present-day city of Monterey. There he founded his second mission, San Carlos de Carmel. By the end of the year, Serra had begun to baptize the natives of California.

Over the next twelve years, Serra founded seven more missions, including one on the site of present-day San Francisco in October 1776. He died at the San Carlos

mission on August 28, 1784, possibly from lung cancer. Missionary activity in California did not end with his death. His fellow Franciscans carried on his work, establishing another twelve missions by 1823 that helped to spur the growth of California. Many native people were baptized during the early days of these missions. Many more, however, were buried. In 1986 the Roman Catholic Church beatified Serra, which is last step in the process to officially declare a person a saint.

## For More Information

Ainsworth, Katherine and Edward C. Ainsworth, *In the Shade of the Juniper Tree,* Doubleday, 1970.

Dolan, Sean, *Junípero Serra,* Chelsea House, 1991.

Habig, Marion A., *Junípero Serra,* Franciscan Herald Press, 1987.

Moholy, Noel Francis, and Don DeNevi, *Junípero Serra: The Illustrated Story of the Franciscan Founder of California's Missions,* HarperCollins, 1985.

# Charlie Sheen

Actor
Born September 3, 1965, New York, New York

*"I didn't start out wanting to be an actor. I wanted to play baseball."*

T hough actor Charlie Screen's personal life has often attracted more press than his professional life, he has amassed an impressive number of screen credits in a variety of projects ranging from intense drama to silly comedy. His breakthrough came in 1986 with director Oliver Stone's *Platoon,* and he worked again with Stone on the gripping *Wall Street* the next year. Though at this point Sheen was quickly making a name for himself as one of the most promising actors of the so-called "Brat Pack," his career seemed to have peaked. He proved himself skilled at comedy in *Hot Shots* and its sequel, but never reached the critical success of his earlier work. Then, in the 1990s he racked up a string of bad publicity that included drug abuse and domestic violence. However, by 2000 Sheen's fortunes were on the rise again when he snagged a coveted lead role on the television series *Spin City* and won a Golden Globe Award for his performance two years later.

Charlie Sheen comes from a family of actors. His father, Martin Sheen, brothers, Ramón and **Emilio Estevez** (see entry), and sister, Renee Estevez, have all followed careers in Hollywood. But Sheen wanted to branch out from the family business. "I didn't start out wanting to be an actor," he admitted to Elvis Mitchell in *Interview.* "I wanted to play baseball and had been offered a scholarship to play at the University of Kansas." When his baseball career fell through, however, Sheen joined his father and siblings in front of the camera.

Sheen was born Carlos Irwin Estevez in New York City in 1965. (His father, Ramón Estevez, adopted "Martin Sheen" as his stage name in 1959). When Sheen was three years old, he moved with his family to Malibu, California. While growing up, he, his brother Emilio, and friends Christopher and Sean Penn spent their time acting in their own home movies. "When all the other kids were out surfing, smoking dope, and doing crazy things," he related to Todd Gold in *People,* "we were making super-8 movies."

Charlie Sheen. *Reproduced by permission of the Kobal Collection.*

Sheen often accompanied his father to movie sets. "I was always aware of what was going on technically [during film shoots]," he told Mitchell. When he was ten years old, Sheen spent eight months in the Philippines watching his father make *Apocalypse Now,* director Francis Ford Coppola's award-winning 1979 film about the Vietnam War. Sheen was present when his father suffered a near-fatal heart attack during the intense filming of the movie.

## Tries for a Career in Baseball

To stand out in his family, Sheen turned his attention in high school from acting to baseball. "I thought, If I can excel at this, they'll think I'm something," he explained in an interview with Tom Green for *Cosmopoli-*

tan. "*I'll* think I'm something." He went to a baseball camp in Missouri for four summers in a row. By the time he was a senior, Sheen was a star pitcher on his team and was given a chance to attend college on a baseball scholarship. His performance in the classroom, however, did not match that on the field. Having attended only about a third of his classes, he was not allowed to graduate and his scholarship was taken away.

After leaving high school without a diploma, Sheen decided to give acting a try. Since his brother Emilio had already begun his acting career under the family name Estevez, Sheen adopted his father's stage name. His first role was in the 1984 horror movie *Grizzly 2: The Predator.* His small part in the low-budget film gained little notice. "I played a camper," he told Mitchell. "I had a few scenes and I was eaten by a bear." Sheen quickly landed several other small roles, including parts in *Red Dawn* in 1984 and *Ferris Bueller's Day Off* in 1986.

Sheen's acting breakthrough came in 1986, when he played the lead character in Oliver Stone's Vietnam film, *Platoon.* Interestingly, when Sheen originally read for the part of the army recruit, Stone thought he was too young and chose his brother Emilio instead. Just before shooting was to begin, though, producers for the motion picture backed out. It took Stone a few years to gain the financial backing he needed to proceed with filming. This time, when Sheen reread for the part, Stone thought he was perfect.

## Platoon Brings Back Childhood Memories

Before filming on *Platoon* began, the cast had to participate in a two-week boot camp run by a retired Marine Corps captain. The camp and the filming, which took place in the Philippines, brought back a lot of memories for Sheen. Not all of them were pleasant. "I stepped off the plane and stopped," he recounted in the interview with Gold. "That smell hit me immediately: burning rubber, that poverty, that stench … that's always in the air."

Like his father in *Apocalypse Now,* Sheen got caught up in the intensity of making a war film. After he returned home, it took him a while to readjust, as he explained to Mitchell: "I was depressed for about a month after I got back. I was just walking around, lost in space. Because everything had been so exciting."

Sheen followed up *Platoon* with a role in another hit film directed by Stone, *Wall Street.* In this 1987 movie, Sheen portrayed a young stockbroker who is seduced into breaking the law by a greedy businessman, played by Michael Douglas. Martin Sheen also made an appearance in the film, playing Charlie's working-class father.

Sheen's performances in *Platoon* and *Wall Street* quickly led to other roles. In 1988 he starred in *Eight Men Out,* about members of the Chicago White Sox who plotted to fix the 1919 World Series. He also worked on *Young Guns,* a western that revolves around Billy the Kid and his gang. Among the other young actors in this film were Emilio Estevez, Kiefer Sutherland, and Lou Diamond Phillips.

## Stars in Film After Film

After that, Sheen became one of Hollywood's busiest actors, starring in one to three films a year. In 1989 he made the baseball comedy, *Major League,* in which he played a sorry major league team's ace pitcher, known as Wild Thing. (He reprised his role in *Major League II,* released in 1994.) In 1990 he appeared on screen in three different movies: the action/adventure *Navy SEALS,* a police drama titled *The Rookie,* and the comedy *Men at Work.* Emilio Estevez wrote, directed, and also starred in this last film, about garbage collectors who get caught up in a murder.

In 1991 Sheen played one of his most popular roles, ace fighter pilot Sean "Topper" Harley in *Hot Shots!* The comedy, which was produced by the makers of the *Naked Gun* series of films, pokes fun at Navy flier movies such as *Top Gun* and at other popular hits like *Dances with Wolves.* In the 1993 sequel, *Hot Shots! Part Deux,* Sheen's character, Harley, is sent by the president of the United States to take on Iraqi president Saddam Hussein. Later in 1993, Sheen played one of the swashbuckling swordsmen in *The Three Musketeers,* based on the classic adventure tale by nineteenth-century French novelist Alexandre Dumas.

## The Tide Turns

Quick success at a young age almost proved to be too much for Sheen. He told Laurence Gonzales that he remembers very little about filming *Eight Men Out:* "I was taking too many drugs and drinking too much at the time." Sheen received a star on the Hollywood Walk of Fame in September 1994. That same month, his newly released action movie *Terminal Velocity* reached the Top Five at the box office. But the tide

turned for him as he starred in a string of forgettable pictures such as *Major League II* (1994); *Terminal Velocity* (1994); *The Chase* (1994); *The Arrival* (1996); *Shadow Conspiracy* (1997); *Money Talks* (1997); *Postmortem* (1998); and *Five Aces* (1999).

Meanwhile, by 1995, Sheen's off-screen activities were making more headlines than his on-screen endeavors. He had run-ins with the law and problems with substance abuse. Two months after marrying model Donna Peele in 1995 he was sued by a college student who claimed he had hit her in 1994 when she refused to have sex with him. The case was settled out of court, but he and his wife filed for divorce in 1996. Then, in June 1997, Sheen pleaded no contest to throwing his girlfriend onto her face on the marble floor of his home in Agoura Hills, California. He was fined $2,800, given two years' probation, and ordered to perform three hundred hours of community service and attend counseling. "You will not see me back in this courtroom," Sheen told the judge, according to a *People* article.

However, in May 1998 Sheen entered a hospital for an overdose and then checked into a treatment center. He left the same day, though, and when his limousine was stopped by police, he was on medication and had been drinking. He later returned to the treatment center but left again within the week. His father, who attends Alcoholics Anonymous, then went to the Malibu municipal court house to tell authorities that his son might be violating probation by using illegal drugs. He reportedly took the step in order to get Sheen to change his destructive habits. In August of that year, a judge extended his probation for another year.

## Spin City

In 1999 Sheen had been sober for a year. He appeared in several movies, including a humorous cameo as himself in the acclaimed oddball picture *Being John Malkovich*. In July 2000, soon after his release from probation, Sheen was tapped to replace Michael J. Fox on the ABC prime-time comedy *Spin City*. (Fox quit the show after being diagnosed with Parkinson's disease.) It was the first time Sheen had worked regularly on a television series, and even more interesting, it pitted him against his father in the ratings. The elder Sheen had won two Emmy Awards for portraying the U.S. president on the highly rated political drama *The West Wing* on NBC in the same time slot on Wednesday nights. In 2002 the younger Sheen won a Golden Globe Award for his work on *Spin City*.

Playing New York Deputy Mayor Charlie Crawford, a character trying to shed his notorious past, the similarities between Sheen's on-screen and real-life personas did not go unnoticed by commentators. He basked in the publicity, telling reporters, according to Phil Rosenthal in the *Chicago Sun Times,* "To ignore the reality of the lifestyle I led at one time—for a long time—would be a disservice to the show. In a self-effacing way, to meet some of those elements head-on and deal with them comedically and to laugh at myself is a good way to dispel a lot of it and let everybody know that I'm moving toward a positive and productive future."

## For More Information

*Chicago Sun-Times,* July 18, 2000, sec. 2, p. 27.
*Cosmopolitan,* December 1987, pp. 102–08.
*Interview,* February 1987, pp. 35–40.
*People,* March 9, 1987, pp. 48–56; September 18, 1995, p. 208; June 23, 1997, p. 65; June 8, 1998, p. 68; June 15, 1998, p. 11; August 24, 1998, p. 89; October 16, 2000, p. 193.

# Sammy Sosa

Professional baseball player, philanthropist
Born November 12, 1968, San Pedro de
    Macoris, Dominican Republic

*"I have to continue to be the best player I can be."*

Outfielder Sammy Sosa of the Chicago Cubs entered the 1998 baseball season as a relatively unknown player to most Americans. His neck-and-neck battle that year with Mark McGwire of the St. Louis Cardinals for the major league single-season home run record made him a household name and a hero in the United States and in his native Dominican Republic. Sosa finished second to McGwire with 66 home runs—five more than the previous record—but he established himself as a legitimate star and will always be remembered in the baseball record books and in the hearts of baseball fans everywhere.

## Growing Up

Sammy Sosa was born November 12, 1968, in San Pedro de Macoris, Dominican Republic. (The Dominican Republic is located in the Caribbean Sea and shares an island with the country of Haiti.) His mother,

Lucrecia, raised him, his four brothers, and two sisters after her husband, Juan, a farmer, died. "We were poor," Sosa recalled. "We definitely were poor." Sosa sold oranges for ten cents, shined shoes for twenty-five cents, and worked as a janitor in a shoe factory to help with the family's finances. He, his mother, and his siblings lived in a two room residence that once was a public hospital.

San Pedro de Macoris is a town that has produced several major league players, including George Bell, Pedro Guererro, and Tony Fernandez. Boxing was Sosa's favorite sport until his brother Juan convinced him to try baseball. "I didn't play on a real team until I was 14, when my brother talked to me about being ready to play with them," Sosa related. "I played when I was little, but only in the streets. The streets were dirt. We didn't have gloves, we just used our hands. Instead of a ball, we'd take a sock and roll it up. We used sticks for the bats." Sosa played baseball in his bare feet and often used a milk carton for a mitt.

In 1985 professional scout Omar Minaya of the Texas Rangers invited the sixteen-year-old Sosa to a tryout in Puerto Plata, a five-hour bus ride for the young player. Sosa's raw potential impressed the scout. "He was 5–10, a frail kid with big hands and big feet," Minaya stated. "He worked out with some dirty baseball pants, old shoes with holes in them and a real thin baseball shirt with holes in it. I saw athletic talent, and I saw courage. I saw a guy who was not afraid to air it out and to play. I saw bat speed. I saw a good arm."

Minaya signed Sosa for $3,500. "I was offering $3000," Minaya said. "And he was at $4000. We negotiated for like half an

Sammy Sosa. *Reproduced by permission of Archive Photos, Inc.*

hour to get to that middle. I liked that about him. He had a great desire to play professional baseball, but he wasn't just going to go. He had some principles, and he felt he was worth a little more than I was offering him." Sosa bought himself a new bike and gave the rest of the money to his mother.

## Makes the Major League

In the spring of 1986 Sosa—who did not speak English—came to the United States for the first time. Within three years he was playing in the major leagues, appearing in 25 games for the Rangers in 1989, batting .238. Later that year Texas traded Sosa, along with second baseman Scott Fletcher and minor league pitcher Wilson Alvarez, to the Chicago White Sox for designated hitter Harold Baines and infielder Fred Manrique.

Sosa played his first full major league season in 1990. He had a solid start with 15 home runs, 70 runs batted in, and 32 stolen bases. The young right fielder was the only American Leaguer to reach double figures in doubles (26), triples (10), home runs, and stolen bases. "We knew he was very good," White Sox general manager Larry Himes said. "We didn't know it would come so quickly."

Early in his career Sosa felt the pressure of having a large family to support. He determined that the best way to succeed was to hit home runs and build his own personal statistics. "You've got to understand something about Latin players when they're young—or really any players from low economic backgrounds," Omar Minaya explained. "They know the only way to make money is by putting up offensive numbers."

Sosa struggled in 1991, batting only .203 with 10 home runs and 33 RBI in 116 games. The White Sox gave up on the young slugger and traded him before the 1992 season, along with pitcher Ken Patterson, to the crosstown Chicago Cubs for outfielder George Bell. The player the Cubs received was still learning to play the game. "When he first got here [to the Cubs], you could see he had great physical skills, but he was so raw," teammate Mark Grace recalled. "He didn't know how to play the game."

It was not until 1993 that Sosa arrived as an everyday player for the Cubs. He became the first player in Cubs history to both hit more than 30 home runs (33) and steal more than 30 bases (36). "People might have wanted so much from me before, and I might have

tried to do for them what I wasn't ready to do," Sosa explained. "But I work hard every day. I think I'm doing what a lot of people wanted me to do, though." Sosa marked his great year by purchasing a necklace with a medallion that said "30-30."

Over the next four years Sosa established himself as a solid but unspectacular major league player. A player's strike cut short the 1994 season and Sosa led his team in batting average (.300), home runs (25), RBI (70), runs (59), triples (6), and steals (22). The 1995 season was shortened to 144 games, but Sosa still hit 36 home runs (second in the National League), drove in 119 runs (second in the National League), stole 34 bases (seventh in the National League), and made his first All-Star Game appearance. "Our expectations are so high for him that there is no way he can live up to everybody's expectations on a daily basis," Chicago manager Jim Riggleman explained. "But he does put together those long stretches when he does some phenomenal things." Sosa won the Silver Slugger award as one of the three best-hitting outfielders in the National League.

## Slugger

Sosa challenged for the National League lead in home runs in 1996, but he suffered a broken right wrist when he was hit by a pitch in August. At the time of the injury he led the league with 40 home runs and had driven in 100 runs. The injury ended Sosa's consecutive game-playing streak at 304, the third longest current streak in the major leagues. "I have to take it like a man," he revealed. "This isn't an end to my career.

Sosa in action. *Reproduced by permission of Corbis Corporation (Bellevue).*

I'll come back." The injury forced Sosa to miss the final 38 games of the season.

In June 1997 the Cubs decided to lock up their slugger to a four-year, $42.5 million contract. "People always talk about the millions of dollars," Sosa said. "This is not my type of thing. Money doesn't mean anything to me. The only reason I'm here is because I play good." Sosa finished 1997 with a .251 average, 36 home runs (seventh in the National League), 119 RBI (sixth in the National League), and 22 stolen bases. The team, however, finished 68–94—tied for worst in the National League with the Philadelphia Phillies—after starting the season 0–14.

The Cubs entered the 1998 season full of confidence, despite the fact that the team had posted winning records in only four of their last twenty seasons and had last won the World Series in 1908. In the off-season the team made several big moves, picking up pitcher Rod Beck, formerly of the San Francisco Giants, outfielder Henry Rodriguez from the Montreal Expos, and shortstop Jeff Blauser from the Atlanta Braves. Hard-throwing rookie Kerry Wood also joined the roster and improved the pitching staff. The Cubs dedicated their season to long-time broadcaster, Harry Caray, who died before the campaign began.

Sosa welcomed his new teammates because they helped make the team better. "There was too much pressure last year," he confessed. "Pressure from the contract, pressure to do it all. I felt if I didn't hit a home run, we wouldn't win. I was trying to hit two home runs in one at bat. Now I don't feel that anymore."

Before the 1998 season Sosa dedicated himself to improving his own play. Despite being one of the leaders in home runs in the National League for several years, he had been chosen for only one All-Star Game. In 1997 Sosa led the league in strikeouts with 174, a new franchise (team) record, and his lifetime batting average was only .257. Chicago hitting coach Jeff Pentland convinced Sosa to slow down his swing, cut down on his strikeouts by taking more pitches, and hitting more to the opposite field. The right-fielder had one of the strongest arms in the league, but he had never worked to improve his defense. Many critics claimed that Sosa cared more about his personal statistics than doing the little things necessary to help the Cubs win.

During the off-season Sosa was determined to be more of a team player. "I went back home [to the Dominican Republic] and said to myself, 'I have to come back and be ready for 1998 and do what I have to do,'" he revealed. "I have to sacrifice myself and be a better contact guy. With the players we picked up, I said to myself I didn't have to go crazy, just be me."

## Race with McGwire

Armed with an improved swing and new attitude, Sosa put together one of the most remarkable months in major league history. From May 25 through June 21, he hit 21 home runs in 22 games. Then, in a game against the Detroit Tigers, Sosa broke the major league record for home runs in a month when he hit his nineteenth during June. Rudy York of the Tigers had set the record in 1937. "If I keep hitting home runs, maybe people will like me even more," Sosa said. "I feel like I'm just lucky to be in the right place at the right time. I was never thinking of setting the record. But I'm in pretty good shape right now and I'm a lot more disciplined at the plate." Sosa finished June with 20 home runs and reached the All-Star break with 33 for the season.

Sosa's hot streak suddenly propelled him into the race to break the single-season home run record of 61 set by Roger Maris of the New York Yankees in 1961. He joined Mark McGwire of the St. Louis Cardinals as the only two players in National League history to hit 30 home runs before July 1. Sosa laughed when compared to the big first baseman. "I'm not Mark McGwire," he explained. "Mark McGwire is the man. Mark McGwire is in a different world. He's my idol. He's the man."

Despite his hot streak, Sosa tried to keep his focus on helping the Cubs stay in contention for the National League playoffs. "I'm not going to go crazy," he said. "I'm not going to get over-anxious. I'm just going to keep the plan I have right now. I have to stay patient and thank God for giving me so much opportunity. I have to continue to be the best player I can be." Sosa was aided in his quest for the record by the fact that the media chose to focus its attention on McGwire. The St. Louis star faced crowds of reporters wherever he went while Sosa could concentrate on helping his team make the playoffs.

As the season progressed it became clear that Sosa and McGwire would compete to the wire for the National League home run title and also for the all-time single-season home run record. As the pressure built, Sosa decided to enjoy the ride. "Pressure is shining shoes and washing cars to support my family in the Dominican Republic," he

explained. "I go to bed happy every night. Some people don't have the character I have. I enjoy every day. I tell you true, I am having a good time. This is like a miracle for me. The person I was before I come to the United States, it's amazing. I just have to say, 'Thank you God for putting me in the situation I am in now.' It's amazing to me. When I was dreaming, I was dreaming just to make it to major leagues, not to be the person I am right now. This is a beautiful country. God bless America. I am the man in my country. Mark [McGwire] is the man in the United States."

The attention of baseball fans grew as both Sosa and McGwire approached Maris's record. McGwire was the first to reach 61 while his rival was stuck on 58. The Cubs and Cardinals met in St. Louis for their final match-up of the year. With Sosa watching from right field, McGwire made history when he hit number 62 into the left field stands. As the fans cheered and a national television audience looked on, Sosa came in from his position and gave his rival a hug, congratulating McGwire on his record-breaking moment.

Sosa did not quit after McGwire hit his historic round-tripper. With the Cubs still in contention for the National League wild-card playoff spot he went on another hot streak. Sosa hit four home runs in a three-game series against the Milwaukee Brewers lifting his season total to 62, once again breaking Maris's standard and tying McGwire. "It's unbelievable," Sosa stated. "It was something that even I can't believe I was doing. It can happen to two people, Mark and I. I have to say what I did is for the people or Chicago, for America, for my mother, for my wife, my kids and the people I have around me. My team. It was an emotional moment." The Cubs star became the first non-American born and first nonwhite player to hit 60 or more home runs in a season.

A week after his 62nd four-bagger, the Cubs and major league baseball held a Sammy Sosa Day in his honor. Sosa brought his family and friends to Wrigley Field for the ceremony, which was also attended by Commissioner Bud Selig, National League President Leonard Coleman, American League President Gene Budig, and members of the family of Roger Maris. Selig presented Sosa with the Commissioner's Historic Achievement Award, given for the first time to McGwire when he hit his 62nd home run. "Your achievements are legendary, but more importantly you've handled yourself with a class and dignity that has been unparalleled," Selig said. Unfortunately, Chicago lost the game 7-3 to the Cincinnati Reds.

McGwire retook the home run lead with 63, but Sosa once again tied up the race with a grand slam that helped Chicago defeat the San Diego Padres, 6-3. The Cubs right fielder then suffered through a 0-21 slump while the St. Louis star hit two more round-trippers to move ahead 65 to 63. Once again Sosa was up to the challenge, hitting two long balls in one game against the Milwaukee Brewers to once again pull even.

The great home run chase of 1998 went down to the final three games of the season. Sosa took the lead over McGwire for only the second time all year when he hit his 66th round-tripper against the Houston Astros. Forty-five minutes later, however, McGwire tied the race up again with a long ball against the Montreal Expos. "I guess McGwire and I were just meant to tie," Sosa explained.

McGwire finally took firm control of the record when he hit two home runs, numbers 67 and 68, in the second to last game of the season. He followed up that performance with two more round-trippers in the Cardinals' last game to finish the season with 70 home runs, 9 more than the previous record. "Fifty years from now, I hope people will remember me, too," Sosa related. "When they mention Mark McGwire, I hope they will also mention me. All year long, I've been saying he's the man. Nobody thought he would hit 70. That's something unbelievable."

Chicago entered the last game of the season tied with the San Francisco Giants for the National League wild-card playoff spot. "I've always said I'm more interested in the wild card than home runs," Sosa explained. "We've got a chance to make the playoffs. That's the only thing I'm thinking about."

Both teams lost their final games—the Cubs dropping a 4-3 eleven-inning decision to the Houston Astros—forcing a one-game playoff at Wrigley Field in Chicago. Though he did not hit a home run, Sosa chipped in two singles and scored two runs as the Cubs earned a playoff berth for the first time since 1989 with a 5-3 win over the Giants. "It felt great," Sosa exclaimed after earning his first-ever trip to the playoffs. "It's been unbelievable. Tonight, I forgot about the home run. I just wanted to win."

Despite the fact that Sosa finished second to McGwire with 66 home runs, his final statistics made the Chicago slugger the favorite to win the National League Most Valuable Player award. He finished the year with career bests in batting average (.308), RBI (158, first in the major leagues), runs scored (132, first in the major leagues), and hits

(198, tied for fifth in the National League). Sosa also led his team to the playoffs while McGwire's Cardinals stayed home. For their good-natured home run contest, *Sporting News* named Sosa and McGwire co-Sportsmen of the Year in 1998.

## Slimming Down and Rounding Out

In November 1999 Don Baylor took over as Cubs manager. Sosa, thrilled with another season of home runs (63 of them), was probably not prepared to hear what the new manager had to say. Baylor believed Sosa needed to work to become a more complete player, and he believed he needed to get into better shape. During the first half of the 2000 season, Sosa was frustrated with Baylor and not happy with the Cubs. He had a sore elbow that was effecting his game, but he didn't want to tell anyone for fear he would not be allowed to play. His agents began to negotiate a trade to the Yankees, but Sosa, in a sudden change of heart, decided to postpone that. He got to work. He finished the 2000 season with 50 home runs and decided to stick with the Cubs, signing a four-year, $72 million extension. He went to work to improve all aspects of his game and he slimmed down by about fifteen pounds, making him faster in the outfield.

In May 2001, Sosa hit his four hundredth home run. In his 2001 season Sosa might have captured another National League MVP award if Barry Bonds hadn't had his own greatest season of all time. Sosa went over 60 home runs and led the majors in RBI while hitting for the best average of his career.

In 2002 Sosa was considered one of baseball's greatest offensive players. At the age of thirty-three and playing in his fourteenth big league season, his swing was mature and he had a brilliant season as a true team player. Cubs hitting coach Jeff Pentland said of one of Sosa's 2002 swings in *Baseball Digest:* "I don't think I have ever seen him swing this good. His swing is so short and his knowledge is so improved, it's incredible. He's getting better with age, like a fine wine. As long as he stays healthy, I don't see him having any downside." He remains a superstar with fans, who may not have noticed all the work that had rounded out his playing. The public still knows him for his always-smiling face and endearing manner. "People will remember me because I have peace and love in my heart and because I have God and because I have a great, great smile on my face," Sosa said in a *Sporting News* article.

## Family Man

Sosa and his wife, Sonia, live in the Chicago area during the season with their four children, Keysha, Kenia, Sammy Jr., and Michael. His mother lives in a home in the Dominican Republic purchased by her son. Sosa owns many cars and bought a 60-foot yacht he named Sammy Jr. when he signed his last contract. In December 1998 then-First Lady Hillary Rodham Clinton invited Sosa to light the national Christmas tree in Washington, D.C.

Sosa wants to become a U.S. citizen someday. "You've got to go step by step and it takes about five to seven years after you get your green card [to become a citizen]," he said. "I'm a U.S. resident now. But when

I become a U.S. citizen, that will be a very happy day." Sosa sponsors Sammy Claus, a program that distributes gifts around the world to underprivileged children.

After hitting a home run Sosa taps his heart and kisses his index and middle fingers. Some people felt that this was showing off or a gang-related gesture, but Sosa explained that it was neither. "When I tap my heart, it means peace and love," he explained. "The other [kissing his index and middle fingers] is to send a kiss to my wife and mother."

Sosa is a favorite of the right-field fans at Wrigley Field in Chicago, a group he salutes at the beginning of every game. "He loves to play," former teammate Brian McRae said. "And guys that love to play—people take that the wrong way sometimes because they're flashy. That's their demeanor. Sammy has fun with the fans; he has a little boyish enthusiasm that maybe a lot more guys should have. Sammy wants the attention. He wants to be the most popular athlete in Chicago. He wants to be The Man and wants to play every day to prove that he is worth what he's making."

Throughout his career Sosa benefited from the advice of other players from his home town. "The players from San Pedro de Macoris helped me a lot," he stated. "They helped me feel more comfortable because they told me what I had to do." Sosa wears number 21 in honor of **Roberto Clemente** (see entry), the great Latin American player.

In September 1998 Hurricane Georges hit the Dominican Republic, causing major damage. "We have a lot of poor families in my country and I have to say this isn't a good time for a hurricane like that," Sosa explained. "Right now, the news that I've been hearing is it's a disaster down there. A lot of people are dying. Most people have no homes. I want to do everything I can to help those people in my country." Sosa supports schools and medical facilities in his homeland and helped organize a relief effort through the Red Cross for the victims of Hurricane Georges.

Sosa helps others—the unfortunate in the United States as well as the folks in the Dominican Republic—in a wide variety of efforts. He gives generously to the schools in his native country on an annual basis and he built a shopping mall that provides much-needed employment in his home town. He opened a medical center in the Dominican Republic in order to ensure health care for underprivileged kids. He gives his time to Wryler Children's Hospital P.I.P. Program in Chicago and he donates tickets to Cubs games to kids who can't afford them.

Sosa signed a contract with Warner Brothers in the spring of 2002 to do a film about his life.

## For More Information

*Atlanta Journal and Constitution,* September 15, 1998.
*Baseball Weekly,* August 31, 1994; November 8, 1995; February 21, 1996; July 24, 1996; August 28, 1996; January 15, 1997; July 2, 1997; January 7, 1998; March 25, 1998; September 23, 1998.
*Business Wire,* March 3, 1998.
*Dallas Morning News,* June 28, 1997; June 21, 1998; June 23, 1998; June 28, 1998; August 29, 1998; August 30, 1998; September 14, 1998.
Greenstein, Teddy, "Sammy Sosa: Evolution of a Big League Hitter: Cubs Slugger Continues to Improve as a Hitter—Establishing Season High Marks in Batting Average, Runs, RBI, Walks, and On-base Percentage in 2001," *Baseball Digest,* June 2002, p. 36.
*Los Angeles Times,* May 17, 1996; June 28, 1998; September 13, 1998; September 21, 1998; Sep-

tember 26, 1998; September 27, 1998; September 28, 1998.

*Newsday,* September 17, 1998; September 26, 1998; September 27, 1998; September 28, 1998.

*People,* September 9, 1998.

*Rocky Mountain News,* August 16, 1998; August 28, 1998; September 14, 1998; September 16, 1998.

Rosenthal, Ken, "Touching 'Em All; Two Years Ago, Sammy Sosa Groused at Criticism That His Game Was Lacking in Several Aspects. Then He Took It to Heart," *The Sporting News,* April 1, 2002, p. 48.

*St. Louis Post-Dispatch,* August 8, 1993; May 25, 1996; September 17, 1998; September 24, 1998; September 26, 1998.

*Sports Illustrated,* August 7, 1989; May 14, 1990; May 28, 1990; September 13, 1993; June 5, 1995; June 29, 1998; September 21, 1998; September 28, 1998.

*Star Tribune,* September 5, 1995; April 4, 1997; June 28, 1997; September 14, 1998; September 15, 1998.

*Time,* September 28, 1998.

*Toronto Star,* June 26, 1998; August 30, 1998.

*USA Today,* May 2, 1994; March 8, 1996; August 22, 1996; July 31, 1996; February 23, 1998; June 23, 1998; June 26, 1998; August 28, 1998; September 21, 1998; September 25, 1998; September 28, 1998.

*Washington Times,* September 24, 1998; September 26, 1998; September 27, 1998; September 28, 1998.

# Gary Soto

Poet, writer
Born April 12, 1952, Fresno, California

*"We—Mexican Americans—need to have our stories told by books and movies—to see ourselves doing something."*

**G**ary Soto began his career as an award-winning poet in the mid-1970s. By the early 1990s he had become a highly acclaimed writer of short stories and novels for young adults. In his entire collection of work, he has brought the sights and sounds of his barrio—the Spanish-speaking neighborhood where he was raised—vividly to life for all readers.

Soto was born in 1952 in Fresno, California, the center of the agricultural San Joaquin Valley. His parents, Manuel Soto and Angie Trevino, worked with his grandparents in the surrounding fields, picking grapes, oranges, and cotton. During the winter, or when field work could not be found, they worked in factories or warehouses. When Soto was five, his family moved to a Mexican American community on the outskirts of Fresno. A short time later, his father died in a factory accident. Soto's mother and grandparents had to struggle to raise young Gary, his brother, and his sister.

"I don't think I had any literary aspirations when I was a kid," Soto told Jean W. Ross in an interview for *Contemporary Authors*. "In fact, we were pretty much an illiterate family. We didn't have books, and no one encouraged us to read." While growing up, Soto had to help support his family by working in car washes or in the fields. Even though he graduated from high school with poor grades, he decided it was better to attend college than to work in a factory for the rest of his life.

## Changes Focus After Reading Book of Poems

Soto enrolled at Fresno City College and chose to major in geography simply because he liked maps. He then discovered *The New American Poetry,* a collection of poems edited by Donald Allen. After reading the poems in the book, he was eager to begin writing his own poetry. He transferred to California State University at Fresno and signed up for creative writing classes. One of his instructors there was noted poet Philip Levine.

In 1974 Soto graduated magna cum laude (the second-highest academic ranking available). The following year he married Carolyn Oda, the daughter of Japanese American farmers. By 1976 he had received his master's degree in creative writing from the University of California, Irvine. He then began teaching at the University of California, Berkeley, first as an associate professor and later as a senior lecturer in the English department.

Soto's career as a poet began while he was still in graduate school. His poems earned him the American Academy of Poets Prize and the *Discovery-Nation* Award in 1975. Within two more years, he had written enough poems to publish his first collection, *The Elements of San Joaquin.* The simply crafted poems in the book paint a grim picture of Mexican American people living in the barrios of Soto's youth and working in the fields of the San Joaquin Valley. Poverty and violence resound throughout. Despite its depressing tone, though, the collection has an underlying sense of hope, and many critics praised its realistic depiction of life for the region's Mexican American laborers. *The Elements of San Joaquin* won several literary awards, including the Bess Hokin Prize from *Poetry* magazine.

Soto's second book of poems, *The Tale of Sunlight,* was published in 1978 by the University of Pittsburgh Press. It, too, presents images of impoverished Mexican Americans as they struggle to survive under diffi-

cult living and working conditions. Whereas the poems in the first book are mainly autobiographical, many of the poems in this second collection offer impressions through the eyes of two characters: Molina, a young boy, and Manuel Zaragosa, a tavern owner. Soto continued to write poetry in the early 1980s, publishing three more collections by 1985.

That year, however, the writer changed his focus by penning *Living up the Street: Narrative Recollections,* a collection of twenty-one autobiographical short stories or vignettes. "I wanted to do something different," he explained to Ross, "and I'm glad I did. It was a testing ground to see if I could write prose. I didn't tire of poetry, but I wanted to move into a thicker forest." Critics noted Soto's skill in writing about the poverty and racism that surrounded the day-to-day life of his childhood. *Living up the Street* won the American Book Award for 1985. Soto followed up this book with two other prose works, *Small Faces* in 1986 and *Lesser Evils: Ten Quartets* in 1988.

## Writes for Young Readers

In the early 1990s Soto began writing short stories and novels aimed specifically at younger readers. "Literature can make a difference to the marginal kid," he explained to Nancy Needham in *NEA Today,* remembering his own awakening when he first read poetry. *Baseball in April, and Other Stories,* published in 1990, is a collection of eleven short stories about everyday events in a modern-day Mexican American neighborhood. Each story focuses on a different young person as its subject. For example, Alfonso wants to transform himself from an awkward young man into an Aztec warrior in "Broken Chain," and in "La Bamba," Manuel impresses his classmates with his lip-sync/dance performance at a school talent show until a scratch in the record ruins his act.

Even though almost all of Soto's stories for young readers take place in ethnic neighborhoods, his characters face conflicts that are universal. One example is his 1991 novel, *Taking Sides*. It follows Lincoln Mendoza, an eighth-grade Mexican American student, as he moves to a new neighborhood. One of the best basketball players for his old junior high school, he decides to join the basketball team at his new school. When his new team has to play a game against his old team, Mendoza must decide where his loyalties lie.

Soto has also used poetry and film to reach a younger audience. Two poetry collections, *A Fox in My Hands* (1991) and *Neighborhood Odes* (1992), present everyday aspects of Mexican American life through vivid descriptions—selling oranges door to door, running through a sprinkler on a hot summer afternoon, reading about the ancient civilizations of the Inca and the Aztec in a local library. Soto has also produced 16-millimeter films based on two of his short stories: "The Pool Party" is a ten-minute short for young viewers, while "The Bike" is a half-hour family feature.

After a successful start in writing for a younger audience, Soto wrote a series of novels for middle school and young adult readers in the early 1990s, including *Pacific Crossing, The Skirt,* and *The Pool Party.* Many of these novels have characters in common. The series continued in 1994 with the humorous novels *Crazy Weekend* and

Gary Soto. *Reproduced courtesy of Gary Soto.*

*Summer on Wheels.* These comic novels for young readers both feature the blood brothers Hector and Mando, two youngsters from East Los Angeles. "Readers will quickly become caught up in the boys' many schemes and escapades which occur with humorous regularity," remarked Maura Bresnahan in a *Voice of Youth Advocates* review of the novel. Bresnahan further noted that "Soto has created two wonderfully believable friends in Hector and Mando. They are typical boys on the cusp of adolescence."

## From Picture Books to Hard-Hitting YA Novels

Additionally, Soto has ventured into the arena of children's picture books. *Too Many Tamales* depicts the story of Maria, a young girl who misplaces her mother's wedding ring in tamale dough while helping to prepare a Christmastime feast. *Chato's Kitchen* introduces a cat whose efforts to entice the local "ratoncitos"—little mice—lead him to prepare abundant portions of fajitas, frijoles, enchiladas, and other foods. A critic for *School Library Journal* dubbed this picture book "really cool," further noting that "Soto adeptly captures the flavor of life in el barrio in this amusing tale." Chato makes a return appearance in the 2000 work *Chato and the Party Animals*. Further picture books from Soto include *The Old Man and His Door, Big Bushy Moustache,* and *Snapshots from the Wedding*.

Soto has stated that his 1994 young adult novel, *Jesse,* is a personal favorite and one in which the protagonist comes close to being autobiographical. Set in the late 1960s with the Vietnam War protests, United Farm Workers movement, and the promise of a better world, the novel tells the story of sixteen-year-old Jesse who has left home and school, escaping boredom and the abuse of his drunken stepfather. He goes to live with his older brother, struggles with poverty, and learns firsthand about discrimination.

In Soto's 1997 hard-hitting novel *Buried Onions,* his protagonist Eddie is trying to escape the poverty and gang violence of the Fresno, California barrio by taking vocational classes. When his cousin is killed, he is urged by his aunt to find the killer and avenge the death of his relative, but Eddie just wants to find a way out of this harsh world. A job in an affluent suburb goes awry when his boss's truck is stolen while in his care. Finally, with a gang member looking for him and with his money gone,

Eddie opts to join the military in hopes that he can find a better life.

In 1998 Soto published a well received collection of short stories for young adult readers, *Petty Crimes*.

## Other Projects

In 1993 Soto edited *Places of the Heart: New Chicano Fiction,* a collection of short stories by fifteen Mexican American writers. Through these writings—and through his own contributions to Hispanic literature—Soto hopes all Americans can share in the voices and experiences of Mexican Americans. His main goal, though, is to give Mexican American children an understanding of their heritage and their place in society. As he told Needham, "We—Mexican Americans—need to have our stories told by books and movies—to see ourselves doing something.

Meanwhile, Soto has continued with his output for adult readers, including poetry collections such as *Junior College* (1997) and *A Natural Man* (1999) as well as his *New and Selected Poems,* a volume selected as a finalist for the National Book Award. He has also written his first adult novels, *Nickel and Dime* (2000) and *Poetry Lover* (2001). Yet amazingly, this writer who first won over readers for his adult volumes of poetry, increasingly is becoming known as a author of books for younger readers.

Soto left his teaching career at Berkeley to become a full-time writer. "This poet has gassed up his car and gone forth to meet his readers," he remarked in an essay posted on his Internet home page, by way of explaining his success. "Over a nine-year period I have spoken to three hundred thousand teachers and students, possibly more.... In my garage sit boxes of fan letters and hand-drawn banners proclaiming me the best writer in the world. And why such a reception? Unlike most other contemporary poets and writers, I've taken the show on the road and built a name among la gente, the people. I have ventured into schools where I have played baseball and basketball with young people, sung songs, acted in skits, delivered commencement speeches, learned three chords on a Mexican guitar to serenade teachers.... I have gone to prisons and mingle with people who have done time.... My readership is strung from large cities, such as Los Angeles, to dinky Del Rey where peach trees outnumber the population by many thousands.... My business is to make readers from non-readers."

Among his many awards, Soto received the Literature Award from the Hispanic Heritage Foundation (1999), the Author-Illustrator Civil Rights Award from the National Education Association, and the PEN Center West Book Award for *Petty Crimes*. Soto was named Young People's Ambassador for the California Rural Legal Assistance (CRLA) and the United Farm Workers of America (UFW).

## For More Information

*America,* July 25, 1992, pp. 39–40+.

Bresnahan, Maura, review of *Summer on Wheels, Voice of Youth Advocates,* April, 1995, pp. 27–28.

*Contemporary Authors,* Volume 125, Gale, 1989, pp. 424–27.

Gary Soto Web site. Available at http://garysoto.com/ (accessed June 21, 2002).

*NEA Today,* November 1992, p. 9.

Review of *Chato's Kitchen, School Library Journal,* July, 1995, p. 69.

# Hernando de Soto

Spanish explorer
Born c. 1500, Jerez de los Caballeros, Spain
Died May 21, 1542, near present-day Ferriday, Louisiana

*"Although the de Soto expedition was a failure for Spain, it nevertheless was one of the most remarkable in the history of North America."*

Hernando de Soto was a Spanish explorer whose life was shaped by his relentless quest for gold in the New World. He helped the Spanish general Francisco Pizzaro bring about the fall of the great Inca empire in South America. Hoping to find treasure, he and his army traveled throughout the southeastern United States, becoming the first Europeans to explore that part of the country. In the process, he befriended and then betrayed many Native American tribes. He and his fellow Spaniards were probably the first white men to cross the Mississippi River.

De Soto was born around 1500 in the village of Jerez de los Caballeros in the Spanish province of Estremadura. He was a descendant of a noble family, but grew up with very little money. By the time he was nineteen years old, he had become a soldier and was sent to America to become the lieutenant of Pedro Arias de Avila, the governor of Spanish-controlled Darien (part of present-day Panama). During the 1520s, de Soto's job was to explore areas northward, conquer the native peoples, and claim the countryside for Spain. He was very successful.

In 1532 de Soto was sent to South America to help Pizarro lead the conquest of the area ruled by the Inca empire in present-day Peru. Together the two men traveled to the city of Cajamarca in the Andes Mountains to meet the Inca ruler Atahualpa. The day after the Spaniards arrived, Pizarro invited Atahualpa to dinner and then took him prisoner. The Inca revolted and Pizarro eventually killed Atahualpa. The following year, Pizarro, de Soto, and the Spanish army marched southeast to the Inca capital of Cuzco and quickly captured it, destroying the Inca empire forever.

## Longs for Adventure

After staying in present-day Peru for a few years, de Soto returned to Spain. His share of the Incan treasures had made him a rich and famous man. He married Arias de Avila's daughter Isabel. Quickly bored with life at home, he longed to return to the adventure and the riches of the New World. King Charles V of Spain obligingly made him governor of Cuba and *adelantado* (captain-general) of Florida. As the *adelantado,* de Soto was to explore the entire region of the present-day southeastern United States, start settlements, and conquer and convert the native peoples in that area to Christianity. A more important task for de Soto, however, was to find gold.

Before he had left Spain, de Soto had heard stories of gold and vast riches in the wild, uncharted territory he now controlled. He left Spain in 1538 chasing the promise of these untold riches. After dropping off

his wife in Cuba and gathering more supplies for his army of six hundred men and two hundred horses, de Soto sailed to the site of present-day Tampa Bay, Florida. He and his men landed on May 30, 1539.

When they found no gold in the area where they landed, de Soto and his men headed northward along the western coast. The explorers were pleased to find Florida had no mountains, knowing it would be easier to march on flat land. They were not pleased, though, to find swamps, mosquitos, insects, alligators, and snakes. They decided to set up winter camp in the area of present-day Tallahassee, Florida.

In the spring of 1540, the Spaniards headed northeast to look for gold and other valuables. Most of their searching proved worthless. In present-day Georgia, they gathered about 350 pounds of freshwater pearls, but nothing else. They continued to explore.

## Enslaves Native Americans

At first, the Native Americans welcomed and befriended the Spanish visitors. The queen of one tribe even directed de Soto to the spot where he gathered the pearls. However, this trust extended by the Native Americans was not returned by the Spaniards. De Soto conquered, destroyed, and enslaved those he met. A favorite trick of his was similar to that of Pizarro: de Soto would invite a chief to visit, then hold him for ransom. After the ransom was paid by the tribe, the chief was often killed and his people were captured. The Spanish forced the Native Americans to provide them with supplies. They were more concerned with finding gold than spreading the teachings of Christianity.

Word soon spread from one tribe to another that the Spanish were not to be trusted. The Native Americans became less friendly, making travel more dangerous for de Soto's men. The different tribes tried to fight the Spanish soldiers, but their weapons and methods usually proved ineffective against the more advanced arms and strategies of the Spanish army. To rid themselves of the invaders, the Native Americans began to direct de Soto and his men farther north to find gold.

The Spaniards traveled through the present-day states of Georgia, South Carolina, and North Carolina, then crossed the Appalachian Mountains into Tennessee before heading south into Alabama. In the fall of 1540, near Mobil Bay in present-day Alabama, de Soto and his men engaged in a fierce battle with a group of Native Americans led by Chief Tuscaloosa. Three thousand Native American warriors were killed while twenty-two Spanish soldiers lost their lives. After the battle, the Spaniards were forced to head to the northwest. They spent that winter in present-day northern Mississippi.

## Follows Visions of Gold

On March 4, 1541, as they prepared to break their winter camp, de Soto and his men were attacked by native warriors. In the fight, twelve Spaniards perished. Running low on supplies and horses, the remaining Spaniards pushed on, heading northwest. In May they came upon the wide Mississippi River just south of present-day Memphis, Tennessee. They camped along its banks for a month, building barges in order to cross it. Once they reached the other side of the river, they continued their quest for treasure.

Hernando de Soto. *Reproduced by permission of Corbis Corporation (Bellevue).*

The Native Americans in that area told de Soto stories of gold and silver, and he pushed his men westward through present-day Arkansas. The only treasures they found were buffalo hides.

Along the way, many soldiers were killed in fighting with Native Americans or died of hunger and illness. After spending the winter near present-day Camden, Arkansas, de Soto and his men worked their way south along the Mississippi River. Discouraged by his failure to find riches, de Soto fell ill, probably of malaria (a fever spread by mosquitos). On May 21, 1542, he died at the age of forty-two. So the Native Americans would not find de Soto's body, his soldiers weighted it with sand and cast it into the Mississippi River.

The riches de Soto had so desperately sought were never found. The remaining soldiers (about half of de Soto's original army) eventually made their way to Mexico and to Spain. The information they took back about the present-day southeastern United States later proved valuable to Europeans who colonized the area.

## For More Information

*Hispanic American Almanac: A Reference Work on Hispanics in the United States,* 2nd Edition, Gale, 1996.

Hudson, Joyce Rockwood, *Looking for De Soto: A Search through the South for the Spaniard's Trail,* University of Georgia Press, 1993.

Milanich, Jerald T., *Hernando De Soto and the Indians of Florida,* University Press of Florida, 1993.

Whitman, Sylvia, *Hernando De Soto and the Explorers of the American South,* Chelsea House, 1991.

Zadra, Dan, *De Soto: Explorer of the Southeast (1500–1542),* Creative Education, 1988.

# Reies López Tijerina

Social activist
Born September 21, 1926, near Falls City, Texas

*Reies López Tijerina thought that present-day Hispanics would not be so poor if the land claimed by the original Spanish explorers had been passed down to them through the generations.*

Reies López Tijerina is a fiery Mexican American activist who has urged Hispanics to stand up for their rights—even if it means fighting the United States government. His special cause was the recovery of land that he believed the United States had stolen from early Spanish settlers. He awakened many people to the plight of poor Mexican Americans. A controversial figure, Tijerina's methods were sometimes illegal.

Tijerina was born in 1926 in Texas, one of ten children of Antonio and Herlinda Tijerina. His father was a sharecropper (tenant farmer who gives a part of his crops to his landlord in place of rent). He grew up during the Great Depression, the period in the 1930s when the nation suffered from an extremely slow economy and widespread unemployment, and worked in his family's fields for most of his young life. When his family could not survive on the farm, they were forced into becoming migrant farm workers. Because of his family's frequent moves, Tijerina attended about twenty different country schools.

## Starts Out as a Preacher

As a child, Tijerina was influenced by his mother's strong Christian beliefs. As he grew older, he became interested in Bible study. At the age of eighteen, he entered the Assembly of God Bible Institute in Ysleta, Texas. He left the school after three years, married Maria Escobar, then set off to become an itinerant preacher (one who travels from place to place).

In the mid-1950s, Tijerina and a group of migrant families bought some land in Arizona. They started a cooperative settlement named Valle de la Paz, which means Valley of Peace. They built houses and a church, and tried living together in harmony. The local white people were not pleased with the community, which they considered a gypsy camp. They called Tijerina and the others communists. They harassed the group until the families were forced to leave.

## Fights for La Tierra

Tijerina looked around and saw other Hispanics suffering. He began to believe that his people's troubles were directly related to having *la tierra* ("the land") stolen from them. Tijerina thought that present-day Hispanics would not be so poor if the land claimed by the original Spanish explorers had been passed down to them through the generations. He traveled to Mexico to study old documents about land rights. He discovered an old treaty that had been signed after the Mexican War. The war had broken out in 1846 between Mexico and the United States over land claims in present-day southwestern United States. The Treaty of Guadalupe Hidalgo had promised protection for the land rights of Mexicans in that area of the United States.

In 1963 Tijerina helped to form an organization called the Alianza Federal de Mercedes (Federated Alliance of Land Grants). Its purpose was to represent the interests of Mexican Americans who wanted the U.S. government to return land they believed belonged to them. The group focused its efforts on land held by the U.S. Forest Service in New Mexico. In 1966 they staged a march on the state's capital where they presented their demands to the governor. They then tried to occupy and claim as their own an area of the Kit Carson National Forest.

Reies López Tijerina. *Reproduced by permission of AP/Wide World Photos.*

The government reacted by accusing Tijerina and the Alianza of vandalism. Fearing arrest, Tijerina disbanded the group. A few days later, however, he re-formed it as the Alianza Federal de Pueblos Libres (Federal Alliance of Free Towns).

## Arrested and Jailed

In 1967 the Alianza had a violent confrontation with authorities at a New Mexico courthouse. A policeman and a jailer were wounded, and Tijerina was arrested. After many court trials and appeals, Tijerina was finally convicted for his part in the courthouse incident and sentenced to jail for one to ten years. In 1971, after spending more than a year in prison, he was released under the condition that he not hold office in the Alianza for five years.

For a time, Tijerina took a nonviolent, peace-making stance in relations between Mexican Americans and the U.S. government. In 1976 he resumed presidency of the Alianza and continued his peaceful approach. He attempted, without success, to interest Mexican presidents in the Treaty of Guadalupe Hidalgo and the land rights issue of Mexican Americans.

During the 1980s Tijerina lost much support for his cause when he grew confrontational once again. He began a campaign against Jewish people. He blamed them for the loss of land grants and for the present-day problems of Mexican Americans.

## For More Information

Bernard, Jacqueline, *Voices From the Southwest: Antonio José Martínez, Elfego Baca, Reies López Tijerina,* Scholastic Book Services, 1972.

Blawis, Patricia Bell, *Tijerina and the Land Grants: Mexican Americans in Struggle for Their Heritage,* International Publishers, 1971.

Cummings, Richard, *Grito! Reies Tijerina and the New Mexico Land Grant War of 1967,* Bobbs-Merrill, 1970.

Jenkinson, Michael, *Tijerina,* Paisano Press, 1968.

# Lee Treviño

Professional golfer
Born December 1, 1939, Dallas, Texas

*"If I proved anything, it's that you don't have to be born into the country club set."*

W hen he was a young boy, Lee Treviño lived in a farmhouse located behind a golf course. Enchanted by the game but too poor to play it, he studied the forms of the golfers from his back yard. His studying paid off. Treviño went on to become a professional golfer, dominating the game in the early 1970s. When he retired from the Professional Golf Association (PGA) Tour in 1985, he had won thirty tournaments and had earned over three million dollars (third highest in PGA history). As a member of the Senior PGA Tour, he continues to win tournaments and to delight fans with his easy charm.

Lee Buck Treviño was born in 1939 on the outskirts of Dallas, Texas. Fatherless, he was raised by his mother Juanita, a cleaning woman, and her Mexican father, a gravedigger. Their four-room farmhouse was located on the back the Glen Lakes Country Club fairways. To help with the family finances, Treviño dropped out of school when he was fourteen years old. He found work on the golf course as a greenskeeper and caddy.

When he was seventeen, Treviño enlisted in the U.S. Marine Corps. While stationed on the island of Okinawa in the Pacific Ocean south of Japan, he played golf for the Marine Corps. After his discharge in 1961, Treviño returned to Texas and found a job as golf pro at a small Dallas club. After practicing for five years, he entered professional tournaments in 1966. In 1968 he achieved his first major victory at the U.S. Open, where he also became the first player in history to shoot all four rounds of the event under par (accepted average score). Treviño was on his way to the top of the PGA Tour.

## Best Player on the Tour

In 1970 Treviño was the leading money winner on the tour. The following year was his best as a professional. He became the only golfer in history to win the U.S., British, and Canadian Opens all in one year. Between April and July 1971, he won five tournaments. For these achievements, he was named PGA Player of the Year, Associated Press Male Athlete of the Year, and *Sports Illustrated* Sportsman of the Year.

With his extraordinary talents on the golf course, Treviño attracted a huge following of fans. They were also drawn to his light-hearted manner and his witty jokes on the course. In the middle of tournaments, Treviño has been known to stop to buy hot dogs and pop for the children in the surrounding galleries. Throughout his career, he has participated in benefit tournaments and has donated much of his earning to charities such as the March of Dimes and Multiple Sclerosis.

## Struck by Lightning

After his superb play in 1971, Treviño went on to win the British Open in 1972 and the PGA Championship in 1974, among other tournaments. In 1975, however, Treviño and two other golfers were struck by lightning during a tournament near Chicago. Even though he underwent surgery to correct a herniated disc in his back, the injury seriously affected his game (he still suffers from back problems due to the accident). He went winless in 1976 and 1978.

In 1980 Treviño made a comeback by winning the Texas Open and the Memphis Classic. He was also awarded the Vardon Trophy for the fewest strokes per round (69.73 for 82

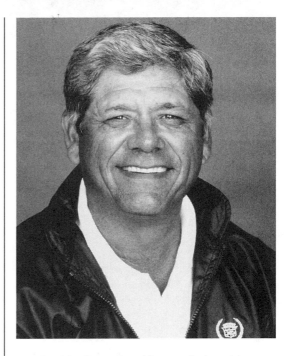

Lee Treviño. *Reproduced by permission of the PGA Tour, Inc.*

rounds), the lowest since golf great Sam Snead set the record in 1958. In 1981 he was elected to the World Golf Hall of Fame.

Treviño retired from the PGA tour in 1985. He became a golf commentator for NBC television, and conducted "Learn with Lee" golf clinics. His many product endorsements in commercials made him one of the most recognizable Hispanic faces in the United States, Mexico, Japan, and Latin America through Univision, the Spanish-language television network.

## Dominates the Senior Tour

However, Treviño could not stay idle for long. In December 1989, when he turned fifty, Treviño joined the Senior PGA Tour.

In his rookie season on the tour, he won seven tournaments and earned over one million dollars, a Senior tour record. Over the next two years, he continued his winning ways.

An injury in June 1992 quickly put an end to Treviño's streak. He had already won five tournaments that year and was on his was to being named the Senior Tour's Player of the Year (he eventually won the award). While hitting practice balls, Treviño tore a ligament in his left thumb. That December he underwent surgery.

By early 1994 Treviño had regained his winning form. In April he won the PGA Seniors Championship. It was his fourth major championship and his twentieth win in just four years on the Senior tour. By 1999 Treviño ranked second among all-time Senior Tour career money winners with twenty-eight Senior Tour victories. In 2002 Treviño, still going strong, was slated to play with Tiger Woods, Jack Nicklaus, and Sergio Garcia for the third annual "Lincoln Financial Group Battle at Bighorn," a one-round, two-player best-ball duel. The game was set to be televised on ABC Sports's Monday Night in July.

Treviño continues to be an inspiration to those who watch the game from the galleries and from behind the fences. "If I proved anything," he was quoted as having said by Larry Cardenas in *Hispanic,* "it's that you don't have to be born into the country club set."

## For More Information

Gilbert, Thomas W., *Lee Treviño,* Chelsea House, 1992.

*Hispanic,* May 1988, pp. 34–39.

"Lee Trevino to Headline Pro Line-Up At 1999 J. P. McCarthy Memorial Pal Invitational," *PR Newswire,* June 4, 1999, p. 3,203.

"Legends Young and Old, Tiger Woods, Jack Nicklaus, Sergio Garcia And Lee Trevino to Compete in the 'Lincoln Financial Group Battle at BIGHORN' on ABC Sports, Prime Time Live, Monday, July 29, 2002, 8 P.M.," *PR Newswire,* November 8, 2001, p. 4,613.

May, Julian, *Lee Treviño: The Golf Explosion,* Crestwood House, 1974.

*Sports Illustrated,* April 13, 1992, pp. 42–44; June 7, 1993, pp. 52–53; April 25, 1994, pp. 46–47.

# Luis Valdez

Playwright, screenwriter, director, producer
Born June 26, 1940, Delano, California

*"I have something to give. I can unlock some things about the American landscape."*

**P**laywright and director Luis Valdez is considered the father of Mexican American theater. In 1965 he founded El Teatro Campesino, a theater of farm workers in California. This project inspired young Mexican American activists across the country to use the stage to give voice to the history, the myths, and the present-day political concerns of Mexican Americans. In later years, Valdez has tried to portray Mexican American life for a mainstream audience, and his popular 1987 film *La Bamba* helped him do that.

Valdez was born in 1940 in Delano, California, into a family of migrant farm workers. At the age of six he began to work in the fields with his parents and nine brothers and sisters. Because his family had to travel around California's San Fernando Valley following the ripening of the crops, his education was continuously interrupted. Despite this, Valdez managed to finish high school and to attend San Jose State College. He majored in English and explored his interest in theater. While in college he won a writing contest for his play, *The Theft*. Later, the college's drama department produced *The Shrunken Head of Pancho Villa,* his play about the problems facing a Mexican couple in America.

After graduating from college in 1964, Valdez joined the San Francisco Mime Troupe, but he couldn't give up telling stories and writing plays. During this time he learned the techniques of agitprop (agitation and propaganda) theater, in which a play puts forth political views and tries to spur the audience to act on those views.

For years migrant farm workers had to endure unhealthy working conditions. They worked long hours for extremely low wages and received no benefits. Finally, in 1965, migrant grape pickers in Delano decided to go on strike. These workers were backed by the labor leader **César Chávez** (see entry) and the migrant worker union he helped found, the National Farm Workers Association.

## Brings Theater to Farm Workers

Two months after the strike began, Valdez joined Chávez in his efforts to organize the farm workers of Delano. It was there that Valdez brought together farm workers and students to found El Teatro Campesino (the Workers' Theater). The

Luis Valdez. *Reproduced by permission of Archive Photos, Inc.*

original function of this group of actor-laborers was to raise funds and to publicize the farm-worker strike and the grape boycott. Their efforts soon turned into a full-blown theatrical movement that spread across the country capturing the imagination of artists and activists.

By 1967 Valdez and El Teatro Campesino left the vineyards and lettuce fields to create a theater for the Mexican American nation. The movement evolved into *teatro chicano,* an agitprop theater that blended traditional theatrical styles with Mexican humor, character types, folklore, and popular culture. All across America, Mexican American theatrical groups sprang up to stage Valdez's one-act plays, called actos. The actos explored modern issues facing

Mexican Americans: the farm workers' struggle for unionization, the Vietnam War, the drive for bilingual education, the war against drug addiction and crime, and community control of parks and schools.

## Hands Down Rules for Mexican American Theater

In 1971 Valdez published a collection of actos to be used by Mexican American community and student theater groups. He also supplied the groups with several theatrical and political principles. Included among these were the ideas that Mexican Americans must be seen as a nation with roots spreading back to the ancient Aztecs and that the focus of all theater groups should be the Mexican American people. Valdez's vision of a national theater that created art out of the folklore and social concerns of Mexican Americans was successful. The Mexican American theater movement reached its peak in 1976.

Valdez and others in the movement then tried to expand the Mexican American experience into areas that would reach all Americans. In 1978 Valdez broke into mainstream theater with a Los Angeles production of his popular play *Zoot Suit,* about Mexican American gang members during the Los Angeles race riots of 1942–43. The following year the play moved to the Broadway stage in New York. It was then made into a film in 1982, but failed to please both critics and audiences. Valdez was hurt by the experience. "It's painful to make a passionate statement about something and then have people ignore it," he explained to Susan Linfield in *American Film.*

## La Bamba Brings Attention

Valdez remained determined to reach a national audience. His next play, *Corridos,* the dramatization of a series of Mexican folk ballads, was praised by theater critics. It was then made into a television production that aired on PBS in the fall of 1987. Valdez's breakthrough into mainstream American, however, came earlier that summer. He wrote and directed *La Bamba,* the screen biography of **Ritchie Valens** (see entry), the 1950s Mexican American rock-and-roll singer. Audiences across America learned not only about the tragically short life of Valens but also about the lifestyle and other elements of the Mexican American community. The movie was an overwhelming box office success.

In 1994 El Teatro Campesino and Mark Taper Forum co-produced Valdez's play *Bandido,* about the real life California outlaw Tiburcio Vasquez. Valdez portrays Vasquez (played by actor A Martinez in this production) as a man who turned to banditry to resist the domination of Anglos pouring into California in days of the Gold Rush of the mid-nineteenth century. "We have seen heroes made of Billy the Kid, Jesse James, Bonnie and Clyde," Valdez told Nina Siegal of *American Theatre.* "All I'm doing is raising Tiburcio Vasquez to his appropriate mythic status in the mythology of the Old West." He added, "Vasquez's situation is still relevant to Chicanos today and we are working to set a new way of looking at the creation of the West, to destroy the stereotypes and rework them to bring back our own heroes—even if they are tragic heroes."

In 1996 Valdez took on a new role as educator when he joined a group of progressive college professors who converted Fort Ord, a military base near Monterey, California, into a school of performing arts. The new California State University at Monterey Bay, which opened in September 1996, has a revolutionary curriculum in which students learn to use various forms of creative expressions to promote social change. The mid-1990s were a strange time for a progressive university to be funded in California, which had undergone a series of reactions against the changing population and the influx of immigrants. Valdez explained this. "Sometimes in the heart of a reaction, there are seeds of real change," he told Patti Hartigan of *American Theatre.* He has since divided his time between teaching at the university and directing El Teatro Campesino.

"My work comes from the border," Valdez told Gerald C. Lubenow of *Newsweek.* "It is neither Mexican nor American. It's part of America, like Cajun music." Valdez has continued to write for the theater, for television, and for motion pictures, focusing on the lives and histories of Mexican Americans. In 1994 he began work on the script for a film about the life of César Chávez, who died in 1993. He has also remained artistic director for El Teatro Campesino. In the process creating plays, he believes he is simply exposing America to another part of itself. "I have something to give," he explained to Lubenow. "I can unlock some things about the American landscape."

## For More Information

*American Film,* July/August, 1987, p. 15.

Hartigan, Patti, "The Morphing of Fort Ord," *American Theatre,* January 1996, p. 30.
*Newsweek,* May 4, 1987, p. 79.
*New York,* February 7, 1994, pp. 60–61.
*New Yorker,* August 10, 1987, pp. 70–73.
Siegal, Nina, "Reclaiming Vasquez's West," *American Theatre,* July-August 1994, p. 10.

# Ritchie Valens

Singer, guitarist, songwriter
Born May 13, 1941, Pacoima, California
Died February 3, 1959, Mason City, Iowa

*Ritchie Valens's story provided an opportunity for Americans to understand some of the problems and characteristics of the Chicano experience in America.*

Ritchie Valens was one of the first Chicano (Mexican American) rock musicians to have a song reach the top 10 on the music charts in America. He moved ethnic music into the popular mainstream. He might have gone on to even greater achievements, but his life was cut short when he was killed in a tragic plane crash. He was seventeen years old.

Valens was born Richard Valenzuela in 1941 in Pacoima, California. His heritage was Mexican Indian. He learned to play guitar at the age of nine and soon began to write his own songs. While a student at Pacoima High School, he formed a rock group called the Silhouettes. The band played at high school functions and at local dances.

When Valens was seventeen, he and his band were spotted by Bob Keene of Del-Fi

Ritchie Valens. *Reproduced by permission of AP/Wide World Photos.*

Records in Los Angeles. Impressed with its sound, Keene offered the band a recording contract. In 1958 one of the group's first singles, "Come On, Let's Go," became a hit on radio stations in the western states. Valens and the Silhouettes were off to a good start.

Late in 1958 Valens made his motion picture debut, singing "Ooh My Head" in the teenage rock-and-roll film *Go, Johnny Go!* By December of that year Valens had another hit with a sweet, slow love song called "Donna," which he had written for his girlfriend. The flip side, "La Bamba," was an upbeat adaptation of a Latino folk dance. Both songs rocketed onto the record charts, and Valens's teenage fans multiplied rapidly.

## Goes on Tour With Buddy Holly and the Big Bopper

Valens's face soon became known across America when he appeared on the popular Perry Como television show. He followed up with a tour of Hawaii. He then went on the road in the United States as part of a packaged rock tour featuring young stars Buddy Holly and the Big Bopper (J. P. Richardson).

The tour usually traveled by bus between concerts in different cities. Buddy Holly soon grew tired of the slow, cold, bumpy drives. He chartered a small plane to speed his group from Clear Lake, Iowa, to the next concert in Fargo, North Dakota. Richardson talked Holly's bassist (future country star Waylon Jennings) into giving up his seat.

Valens had never flown on a plane before and was eager to try. He flipped a coin with Tommy Allsup, Holly's guitarist, for the remaining seat on the plane. Valens won. Almost immediately after takeoff on the snowy February night, the plane crashed. Everyone aboard—Holly, Richardson, Valens, and the crew—were killed. Years later, singer Don McLean called it "the day the music died" in his classic song "American Pie."

## La Bamba Retells Life

Valens's brief career might have faded from memory if not for the popularity of his few hit songs. Rhino Records reissued his recordings and a three-disc set, *The History of Ritchie Valens.* Then in 1987, Columbia Pictures produced a successful film biography about Valens, *La Bamba.* The picture, written and directed by **Luis Valdez** (see entry) was enormously popular. It starred Lou Diamond Philips as Valens, and the soundtrack featured Hispanic musicians **Los Lobos** and **Carlos Santana** (see entries).

*La Bamba* introduced Valens to another generation of teens. Hispanic viewers approved of its authentic language and setting. The film also touched on the problem of forming a Chicano identity in America, and on family rivalry and cooperation in the Chicano community. Years after his short life ended, Ritchie Valens's story provided an opportunity for Americans to understand some of the problems and characteristics of the Chicano experience in America.

## For More Information

Goldrosen, John, and John Beecher, *Remembering Buddy,* Penguin, 1987.

Mendheim, Beverly, *Ritchie Valens: The First Latino Rocker,* Bilingual Press, 1987.

*U.S. News and World Report,* August 10, 1987, pp. 48–49.

# Francisco "Pancho" Villa

Mexican revolutionary and bandit
Born June 5, 1878, Río Grande, Durango, Mexico
Died July 20, 1923, Parral, Chihuahua, Mexico

*Francisco "Pancho" Villa carried with him the desires of the people of northern Mexico: to rule themselves freely and to improve their lives.*

**D**uring the Mexican Revolution, fought between 1910 and 1920, Pancho Villa commanded the large Army of the North. He played a part in some of the most important events of that time. To some Mexicans, he was nothing more than a bandit who robbed and killed. But to others, he was a legend who represented hope in the fight for the good of the common people. Villa carried with him the desires of the people of northern Mexico: to rule themselves freely and to improve their lives. Even after the revolt ended, his legend grew and people honored his name in *corridos* (songs). Nearly fifty years later, Villa's name was placed on the walls of the Mexican Congress alongside the other heroes of the Revolution.

Villa was born Doroteo Arango on June 5, 1878, in the village of Río Grande in the northern Mexican state of Durango. His parents, Agustín Arango and Micaéla Arámbula, were sharecroppers (poor farmers who work land owned by someone else). Like his two brothers and two sisters, Doroteo probably received little formal schooling as a child. He spent much of his time doing odd jobs for his parents on the farm.

In 1893 Agustín Arango died and Doroteo, as the oldest son, became the man of the house. The following year, while he was working in the fields, Doroteo saw the owner of the estate harassing one of his sisters. He quickly ran to a cousin's house, picked up a pistol, then returned home and shot the owner three times, wounding him seriously. Immediately afterward, Doroteo escaped on a horse, a fugitive at the age of sixteen.

## Becomes a Young Bandit

It was during his first year as a fugitive that he changed his name to Francisco Villa.

He stayed in the mountains near his home for the first few months, living off the land. Early in 1895 he was captured, but escaped after spending only a short time in jail. The local police made many attempts to capture Villa, but he constantly slipped out of their grasp. He did well as a bandit, robbing money and shipments from the mines in northern Mexico. With the money he stole, he helped his family and friends. At various times, he worked regular jobs—butcher, stonemason, miner. However, he had to leave these jobs and flee to the mountains when the police discovered his whereabouts.

During this period, Mexico was governed by an unjust president, Porfirio Diaz. Under his leadership, Mexico's social conditions worsened. Diaz favored the owners of the large farming estates, or *haciendas*. The common people had no voice in government; their land was taken from them and they sank deeper into poverty. By the early 1900s, even some wealthy landowners were unhappy with Diaz's strict and prejudiced government. In 1910 Francisco Madero, the son of a wealthy rancher from northern Mexico, called for a revolution to overthrow Diaz. Seeing his chance to fight for a fairer government, Villa joined the Mexican Revolution.

Over three hundred men of all social ranks joined Villa: poor peasants, middle-class farmers, rich hacienda owners. In the beginning, Villa's army lacked horses and supplies. After taking what they could from wealthy Mexicans who supported Diaz, the Villistas (Villa's soldiers) began to win battles. In May 1911, Villa and his men captured Cuidad Juárez, a city on the Mexican-American border opposite El Paso, Texas. Since Cuidad Juárez was then the main

entry point into Mexico from America, the Villistas controlled all the supplies coming into the country. Feeling helpless, Diaz resigned the presidency and sailed to Europe.

## Arrested and Almost Executed

Madero then took over the presidency, and Villa continued to battle forces loyal to Diaz. General Victoriano Huerta, commander of Madero's government forces, did not like the fact that Villa did not follow orders and acted on his own. Late in May, Huerta had Villa arrested for disobedience and for robbing civilians. Villa would have been executed if Madero had not intervened to save him. Sent to a prison in the capital of Mexico City, Villa remained there until he escaped in late December. He made his way north to El Paso where he began to reorganize the Villistas.

In February 1913 Huerta betrayed Madero, had him assassinated, and then assumed the presidency. Villa immediately returned to Mexico to avenge Madero's death. He soon joined forces with those under Venustiano Carranza, the governor of the state of Coahuila. Over the next few months, Villa's band grew larger and larger, and its victories began to mount. On November 15 the Villistas intercepted a coal train headed into Cuidad Juárez and snuck aboard. When the train arrived in the city, Villa and his men jumped off, surprised Huerta's troops there, and captured the city in only a few hours.

By the beginning of 1914, Villa had an army totaling some nine thousand men. He continued to rob the villages and the areas he conquered, but used the money collected to pay his men and to support the Revolu-

Francisco "Pancho" Villa. *Reproduced by permission of the Granger Collection, New York.*

tion. In June of that year he made his final attack against Huerta, capturing Zacatecas, the capital of Coahuila. Huerta's forces were wiped out and he abandoned the presidency less than a month later.

## Meets With Emiliano Zapata

After Carranza became the new Mexican president, his relationship with Villa began to fall apart. The two men disagreed over who should have control over certain areas in the country. By the autumn of that year, Villa had broken with Carranza and gathered the Villistas to fight against him. On December 4 Villa met with fellow revolu-

tionary leader **Emiliano Zapata** (see entry) to coordinate their attack against Carranza.

The alliance between Villa and Zapata never worked. Both men had different ideas for the Revolution and they could not unite against the strong forces of Carranza. In the spring of 1915, Alvaro Obregón, Carranza's leading general, began to destroy Villa's army. Within a three-month period, Villa lost over fifteen thousand men. By the end of summer, he no longer controlled a large army but a small group of bandit revolutionaries.

## Turns Against America

The American government, under President Woodrow Wilson, formally recognized the Carranza government in October 1915. This all but finished Villa as he could no longer obtain guns and supplies from across the border. In response, the Villistas became anti-American. In January 1916 they attacked a train near the city of Santa Isabel in the state of Chihuahua, killing fifteen Americans aboard. In the early morning of March 9, Villa sent the Villistas to raid Columbus, New Mexico. Buildings were burned to the ground, and soldiers and civilians were slaughtered. General John J. Pershing then led an American force into Mexico in pursuit of Villa, but gave up a year later when he realized he could not capture the Mexican revolutionary.

Villa's escape from Pershing earned him the respect of many Mexicans. Many more, however, no longer supported his cause. They were tired of the constant fighting and only wished for an end to the revolution. From 1917 to 1919, Villa led only minor, banditlike raids. On May 20, 1920, Carranza was assassinated and his successor, Adolfo de la Huerta, quickly signed an agreement with Villa to end the revolt. The government gave a large hacienda to Villa and paid benefits to the widows and orphans of the Villistas. The Mexican Revolution came to an end.

Villa had made many enemies during his years as a revolutionary, and they sought their revenge in 1923. In the early morning of July 20, while driving his car through Parral, Chihuahua, Villa was shot and killed by eight assassins. Three years later, robbers dug up his grave and stole his skull. Those criminals were never found.

## For More Information

Guzman, Martin Luis, *Memoirs of Pancho Villa,* University of Texas Press, 1965.

Machado, Manuel A., *Centaur of the North: Francisco Villa, the Mexican Revolution, and Northern Mexico,* Eakin Press, 1988.

O'Brien, Steven, *Pancho Villa: Mexican Revolutionary,* Chelsea House, 1994.

Rouverol, Jean, *Pancho Villa: A Biography,* Doubleday, 1972.

# Raquel Welch

Actress, singer
Born September 5, 1940, Chicago, Illinois

*"I've always thought the older I get the more people would see that I have more to me than just my good looks."*

The striking beauty that earned Raquel Welch international fame and fortune has sometimes been her enemy. She has won beauty contests and has been on countless magazine covers. She has starred on stage and in television specials, feature films, and fitness videos. After being repeatedly cast as a sexpot, Welch strove to earn respect and recognition as a serious actress. She tackled many acting challenges in a wide variety of roles in order to overcome the stereotype. One role she had not played, however, was that of a Latina. Oddly, when she was starting out in acting, she was warned not to emphasize her Hispanic heritage for fear of getting typecast. But it was playing Latina parts that brought about the remarkable comeback of the sixty-one-year-old actress. After the media had all but written Welch off during the 1990s, she suddenly reappeared in the early 2000s, starring in the film *Tortilla Soup* and in the popular PBS drama series *American Family,* as Dora, a Mexican American aunt.

Welch was born Raquel Tejada in 1940 in Chicago, Illinois. She was the daughter of Armand Tejada, a Bolivian immigrant of Spanish heritage, and Josephine Hall, an American. When Welch was two, her family moved to La Jolla, a beach town in southern California. In high school, Welch (known as "Rocky" to her friends) was very active. She was a cheerleader, a member of the drama club, and the vice president of her senior class. She also took ballet lessons. By the time she was fifteen, she had begun to enter and win beauty contests.

Welch graduated from high school in 1958, then took a job as weather girl with a local television station in San Diego, California. She also spent a year studying acting at San Diego State College. She married her high school sweetheart, James Westley Welch, in 1959. They had two children, Damon and Tahnee. After the couple divorced in 1964, Welch took her children to Hollywood, where she looked for work as an actress.

## Achieves International Stardom

For a time, Welch's career went nowhere. Then she met and married Patrick Curtis, a public relations man. He started his own firm and spent most of his time managing her career. As a result, she finally became a star. Two movie roles were significant in vaulting Welch to stardom. In 1966 she played a seri-

Raquel Welch. *Reproduced by permission of AP/Wide World Photos.*

ous scientist in a form-fitting skin-diving suit in the award-winning film *Fantastic Voyage.* The following year, in *One Million Years B.C.,* she was cast as Loana Sthell, a mostly silent cavewoman who cavorts around in a fur bikini. This film was a tremendous success in Europe, and Welch appeared on ninety-two European magazine covers. Her status as a sex symbol was established.

Welch's sexy image was further enhanced in 1967 when she wore a daring outfit to the Academy Awards ceremony. In the British comedy *Bedazzled,* she played the role of a deadly sin, Lillian Lust. Welch finished up the year by touring South Vietnam with comedian Bob Hope to entertain American soldiers stationed there during the Vietnam War.

Between 1968 and 1970, Welch was cast in many films that played up her sexy image. By the early 1970s, however, she began to chose roles that were viewed as controversial. In *Myra Breckenridge,* Welch played the manlike personality of the trans-sexual character Myron. Critics blasted the movie, which had been based on the novel by Gore Vidal.

## Fired for Being "Difficult"

Rumors circulated through Hollywood that Welch was becoming a difficult actress to work with. She denied this. "All I ever fought for was quality in my films," she explained years later to Carlos Briceno in *Hispanic.* "I really felt I was being penalized for being the sex symbol they had created, and that made my Spanish blood boil." Despite the rumors, Welch continued to work in films. In 1974 she finally achieved success when she received a Golden Globe Award for best actress for her part in *The Three Musketeers.*

In 1971 Welch divorced Curtis. Six years later she met French screenwriter/producer Andre Weinfeld. After they were married in 1980, Weinfeld helped manage her career. Her 1981 television special, *From Raquel with Love,* which he helped produce, received high ratings. But that same year Welch was humiliated when she was replaced by Debra Winger after she had already begun work on the film *Cannery Row.* The company producing the movie claimed Welch had behaved unprofessionally on the set. She believed she had been fired to cut the costs of production. She sued the company for $20 million, but eventually lost the case.

## Displays Wide Range of Talents

Welch was bitter over her firing and left Hollywood in 1981. Deciding she needed to take chances in her career, she accepted a role in a stage musical, *Woman of the Year.* Her singing and dancing performance was lauded by critics, and her reputation was beginning to transform. Her next role as a tough Native American woman in the 1982 television movie *The Legend of Walks Far Woman* showed she was capable of serious acting.

In 1984 Welch wrote a book, *The Raquel Welch Total Beauty and Fitness Program.* The book focused on preserving physical and mental health through yoga, diet, and exercise. Its success led the actress to release several home exercise videos that sold well.

During the late 1980s Welch took on a number of nonglamorous roles in television movies. In the 1987 film *Right to Die,* she portrayed a woman dying of amyotrophic lateral sclerosis, better known as Lou Gehrig's Disease. Critics praised her emotionally demanding performance, and many began to treat her as a serious actress. Welch was pleased. "I've always thought the older I get the more people would see that I have more to me than just my good looks," she explained to Briceno.

## Famine to Feast

Welch returned to film in 1994 with an appearance in the popular comedy sequel *The Naked Gun 33 1/2: The Final Insult.* But after that most of her appearances were in nightclubs or on infomercials and exercise videos. The media seemed content to leave her behind in the slot of an aging sex symbol.

During all of her career, Welch had only played a Hispanic part twice, and most of her audience had no notion of her Hispanic heritage. In 2001 she landed a starring role in the comedy film *Tortilla Soup* playing Hortensia, a flamboyant and somewhat delusional Latina grandmother with a crush on a widower played by Hector Elizondo. When she was asked about playing a Latina in an interview with FeatsPress of Cinema.com, she reflected: "Although I'm half Latin, I never learned how to speak Spanish. I can speak a little bit, and my accent's not bad, but it's only stuff I picked up along the way. My father never spoke Spanish at home, because it was the era when people tried to hide their ethnic roots rather than celebrate them. Everyone had to be part of the mainstream American pop culture. So I never got the sense from him that my Latin heritage was anything to be proud of. It was only much later that I realized what I was missing out on and this role is one of the few times I've had the opportunity to embrace my Latin heritage."

When the PBS series *American Family* aired in January 2002, Welch, at age sixty-one, was firmly back in the public eye and thoroughly immersed in the part of a Latina. The show, filmed around Los Angeles, is the first series on network television produced, written, and directed by Latinos. Welch explained how she became involved in this endeavor to a PBS interviewer: "Well, I basically got involved in being part of *American Family* because of [creator and director] Gregory Nava and my respect for him and his talent, and also because I am of Latin heritage on my father's side, and yet I am sort of Midwestern-American Anglo-Saxon on my mother's side. I've had this kind of a split personality most of my life and my career, so this gave me an opportunity to really be in an all Latin cast with a Latin creator, director, writer, and sort of feel like finally I can embrace that part of my own history."

Celebrating her heritage has changed Welch's life in other areas. She is learning to speak Spanish and planning a trip to her father's native land of Bolivia. She has appeared in the American Latino Media Arts Awards (ALMA) ceremony. She told Mireya Navarro of the *New York Times,* that she is finally able to embrace the Latina identity that the filmmakers who originally cast her had urged her to reject: "It was told to me that if I wanted to be typecast, I would play into that [Hispanic background]. You just couldn't be too different. My first big breakthrough part in *One Million Years B.C.* they died my hair blond. It's a marketing thing. And now I'm sure there are a lot of people who are marketing specialists just for the Latino community. They want those 35 million people to buy their products and to vote for them."

## For More Information

"American Family, An Interview with Raquel Welch," PBS Web site. Available at http://www.pbs.org/americanfamily/behind9.html (accessed June 21, 2002).

*Cosmopolitan,* May 1990, pp. 320–24.

Haining, Peter, *Raquel Welch: Sex Symbol to Super Star,* St. Martin's Press, 1984.

*Hispanic,* April 1988, pp. 20–24.

*Interview,* September 1993, pp. 130+.

"Interview with Raquel Welch," Article by Feats-Press, Cinema.com. Available at http://www.cinema.com/article/item.phtml?ID=602&Page=1 (accessed June 21, 2002).

Navarro, Mireya, "Raquel Welch Is Reinvented as a Latina," *New York Times,* June 11, 2002.

# Emiliano Zapata

Mexican revolutionary
Born August 8, 1883, Anenecuilco, Morelos, Mexico
Died April 10, 1919, Morelos, Mexico

*"Seek justice from tyrannical governments not with your hat in your hands but with a rifle in your fist."*

**E**miliano Zapata was a leader of the *campesinos* ("peasants") during the Mexican Revolution in the early 1900s. The Mexican dictator Porfirio Diaz, who gained control of the government in 1876, supported rich landowners who had seized the farming lands of the *campesinos* over the years. Without any say in the government, the powerless peasants sank deeper into poverty. When they finally rose in revolt, Zapata led the fight for the return of their stolen land. His many followers proudly called themselves Zapatistas. Although he died before the fighting ended, his memory lingers and is honored in stories, legends, and songs.

Zapata was born in the village of Anenecuilco in the Mexican state of Morelos. His family owned a small piece of land and some livestock. Even though a little better off economically than most *campesinos,* Zapata's family suffered many of the same problems. Portions of their land were unexpectedly taken over by the owners of neighboring haciendas, or huge plantations.

Zapata attended elementary school for only a short time and spent much of his youth learning to be a mule and horse trainer. After he was orphaned at sixteen, Zapata supported himself and his sisters in Anenecuilco by trading horses and working on the haciendas. Throughout Diaz's reign, called the *Porfiriato,* rich landowners continued to enlarge their haciendas by taking the lands of the *campesinos*. Any peasants who protested were jailed or killed.

By 1910, thirty hacienda owners controlled more than half the land in Morelos. Angered by their worsening situation, the peasants began to act. Because Zapata did not bow down to the rich landowners, the villagers of Anenecuilco trusted him and elected him president of the village council. His job was to safeguard the papers that showed the peasants' rightful ownership of the land that had been unjustly taken.

## The Revolution Begins

In November 1910, Francisco Madero, the son of a wealthy rancher from northern Mexico, led the call for a rebellion to overthrow the Diaz government. At first, Zapata did not join the revolt. When Madero promised land reforms if he were elected to office, Zapata quickly gathered his men for the fight and the Revolution was on. Zapata proved to be a skillful fighter and leader. He often outwitted the government soldiers and became a hero to the Zapatistas. By May 1911, rebel victories across Mexico forced Diaz to resign the presidency and to flee to

Europe. In the new elections in October of that year, Madero won the presidency.

Madero did not live up to his promises. He had no plans to break up the haciendas and return land to the *campesinos*. Instead, he demanded the Zapatistas lay down their arms. Zapata and his men refused to do so until their demands for land reform were met. When they continued their revolt, Madero called them bandits.

In response, Zapata issued his own revolutionary platform in November 1911. Named the *Plan de Ayala,* it called for all illegally seized land to be returned to its rightful owners. The plan also demanded that the government take one-third of the land from each hacienda and give it to the *campesinos*. To prove he was not a bandit, Zapata organized committees to help distribute fairly any returned land. He also set up a bank to give loans to the *campesinos* who obtained land.

## Zapata Fights for Land Reform

When the Madero government refused to listen to Zapata's demands, Zapata and his men began a new revolt. Since the Zapatistas had little food, clothing, and weapons, they fought by ambushing enemy villages and haciendas. After they looted what they needed, they gave the lands and anything else that remained to the *campesinos*.

In February 1913, Madero was suddenly murdered by his top general, Victoriano Huerta. Forces loyal to Madero quickly turned on Huerta and forced him from office in August 1914. A politician named Venustiano Carranza then took over the presidency.

While the government was rapidly changing hands, Zapata continued to press

Emiliano Zapata. *Reproduced by permission of Corbis Corporation (Bellevue).*

for land reforms. He submitted his plan to Carranza, but the new president rejected it and war seemed likely. Zapata then met with **Francisco "Pancho" Villa** (see entry), a bandit turned revolutionary. Villa controlled a large army in the northern part of Mexico. Carranza tried to keep the two revolutionaries from meeting, but he was unsuccessful. On December 4, 1914, Zapata and Villa met in the village of Xochimilco just outside of Mexico City. Together they planned to carry on the Revolution against Carranza and his government.

The alliance between Zapata and Villa proved to be worthless. Villa and his Army of the North had promised to send weapons and other materials to the Zapatistas, but they never did. Lacking the needed supplies, Zapata and his men could not in turn support Villa. The Army of the North suffered crushing defeats, and government troops soon tur0ned their attacks against the Zapatistas.

By the end of 1916, fighting was fierce all over the country, but the state of Morelos seemed to suffer the most. The state capital of Cuernavaca and hundreds of villages were destroyed, the sugar industry was ruined, and nearly half the people were killed. Those villagers not murdered were forced to settle in other regions of the country. The Zapatistas lost many men—they shrank from twenty thousand to only five thousand. Even so, they remained a threat, attacking areas around Mexico City. Their methods were often as brutal as those of the government troops. At one point, the Zapatistas blew up a train, killing many civilians aboard.

Zapata regained control of Morelos in 1917, but the Zapatistas were falling apart. They were hungry and tired of fighting. Many wanted to sign a peace treaty with the government even if the *Plan de Ayala* were not accepted. Zapata, however, refused to give in. He vowed to fight until the government guaranteed land reform for the *campesinos*. Even though the peasants continued to back Zapata, many northern rebels did not. Without national support for their cause, the Zapatistas were doomed.

Zapata finally met his end in 1919. Jesus Guajardo, a colonel in the government army, tricked Zapata into believing he wanted to join the Zapatistas. At first, Zapata was suspicious of Guajardo's offer, but he finally agreed to meet Guajardo at the Hacienda de Chinameca. It was a trap. When Zapata and a few of his men rode into the walled estate, government soldiers were waiting. A bugle sounded and the soldiers fired. Zapata fell dead from his horse.

Guajardo delivered Zapata's body to the Municipal Palace to prove his death and to discourage the peasants. The Zapatistas were not convinced. Many believed Zapata was still alive, and claimed he had escaped on his beautiful white horse, *As de Oro*. Some even stated they saw him riding in the dead of night. Although the Zapatistas continued the fight, Zapata's original goals for land reform were never fully met. A peace settlement that did not include his *Plan de Ayala* was eventually reached between the Zapatistas and the government. Despite this setback, many people in Mexico have not forgotten Zapata's dedication to the fight for their rights. For them, he has remained a hero.

## For More Information

Parkinson, Roger, *Zapata: A Biography,* Stein and Day, 1980.

Ruiz, Ramon Eduardo, *The Great Rebellion: Mexico, 1905–1924,* Norton, 1980.

*Travel Holiday,* October 1990, pp. 46–54+.

Womack, John, *Zapata and the Mexican Revolution,* Knopf, 1968.

# INDEX

*Discovery-Nation* Award
278
*Do the Right Thing* 214
Doctors. *See* Physicians
Domincan Republic
fiction 8
**Domingo, Placido 81–83,**
81 (ill.)
D'Onofrio, Vincent 78
*Don Rodrigo* 81
"Don't Know Much" 247
Dorantes, Andres 36
Dornan, Robert K. 248, 250
Douglas, Michael 105, 266
*Down and Out in Beverly Hills* 207
"Dr. Beat" 90
Dr. Gonzo (fictional character) 74
Dreyfuss, Richard 95, 207
Drug abuse 27
Garcia, Jerry 109
Sheen, Charlie 267
Drug Wars
Colombia 113
*Drug Wars: The Camarena Story* 74, 208
Dry Tortugas, discovery of 221
Dumas, Alexandre 267
Dunas, Jeff 77
Dust Brothers 255
Duvall, Robert 29
Dylan, Bob 107, 109, 255

# E

**E., Sheila 84–86,** 85 (ill.)
E Train 86
East Los Angeles Center for Law and Justice 126
*Echoes of an Era* 93
Editors
Saralegui, Cristina 259–62
Education
multiculturalism 100
parenting 237

Educational reforms
New York City public school system 100
school-based management program 100
Educators
Alvarez, Julia 3–9
Anaya, Rudolfo 9–12
Baca, Judith 18–21
Cavazos, Lauro 50–53
Escalante, Jaime 86–89
Fernandez, Joseph A. 98–101
Molina, Mario 181–85
Mora, Pat 185–88
Rodríguez, Gloria 235–38
*Eight Men Out* 266
*8 Million Ways to Die* 105
*El amor en los tiempos del cólera* 113
*El arroyo de la llorona y otros cuentos* 66
*El Bronx Remembered* 179
*El Cancionero/Mas y mas* 162
*El coronel no tiene quien le escriba* 111
*El general en su labertino* 113
"El Plan Espiritual de Aztlán" 124
*El show de Cristina* 260
*El Show de Paul Rodríguez* 242
El Teatro Campesino 288, 289, 290
El Teatro Puerto Rico 96
*Electric Company* 190
*Elegy on the Death of César Chávez* 12
*The Elements of San Joaquin* 278
*1100 Bel Air Place* 142
Elías Sourasky Prize in the Arts 174
Elite Modeling Agency 77
Elizondo, Hector 106, 299

Emmy Awards
Domingo, Placido 83
Manzano, Sonia 170
Moreno, Rita 189, 190
nomination 42
Olmos, Edward James 201
Rivera, Geraldo 234
Saralegui, Cristina 260
*Empress of the Splendid Season* 136
Endangered Species Act 167
*Enough* 155
Entrepreneurs. *See* Businessmen/ Businesswomen
Environment, effect of chlorofluorocarbons (CFCs) on 181
Environmental policies, U.S. 167
**Escalante, Jaime 86–89,** (87 ill.), 202
*The Escape Artist* 18
Escovedo, Pete 84
Escovedo, Shelia. *See* Shelia E.
Estefan, Emilio 90, 98
**Estefan, Gloria** 86, **89–92,** 91 (ill.), 225, 242
Estevanico 36
Estevez, Antonio 174
Estevez, Carlos Irwin. *See* Sheen, Charlie
**Estevez, Emilio 93–95,** 93 (ill.), 265, 266
Estevez, Ramon 93, 265
Estevez, Renee 93, 265
Everlast 253, 255
"Evil Ways" 254
Explorers
Cabeza de Vaca, Alvar Núñez 33–37
Coronado, Francisco Vásquez de 69–72
Ponce de León, Juan 220–22